EUCOTAX Series on European Taxation

Direct Taxation in Relation to the Freedom of Establishment and the Free Movement of Capital

EUCOTAX Series on European Taxation

VOLUME 9

Series Editors

Professor Peter HJ Essers
Professor Eric CCM Kemmeren
Dr. Gerard TK Meussen

Fiscal Institute of Tilburg/Centre for Company Law, Tilburg University

The titles in this series are listed at the back of this volume.

EUCOTAX Series on European Taxation

Direct Taxation in Relation to the Freedom of Establishment and the Free Movement of Capital

Mattias Dahlberg

Faculty of Law, Uppsala University

KLUWER LAW INTERNATIONAL

A C.I.P Catalogue record for this book is available from the Library of Congress.

ISBN 90-411-2363-6

Published by Kluwer Law International,
P.O. Box 85889, 2508 CN The Hague, The Netherlands
sales@kluwerlaw.com
http://www.kluwerlaw.com

Sold and distributed in North, Central and South America
by Aspen Publishers, Inc.
7201 McKinney Circle, Frederick, MD 21704, USA

Sold and distributed in all other countries
by Extenza-Turpin, Stratton Business Park,
Pegasus Drive, Biggleswade, Bedfordshire,
SG18 8TQ, United Kingdom

Printed on acid-free paper

Printed and bound by Antony Rowe Ltd, Eastbourne

Contents

Acknowledgements

My research for this book has primarily been made possible by a generous post-doctoral scholarship granted by the Swedish Research Council (*Vetenskapsrådet*). I have conducted my work at the Department of Tax Law, the Stockholm School of Economics. Professor Bertil Wiman has provided good working conditions, and he has supported the work in several concrete ways. Professor Emeritus Leif Mutén has shown a genuine interest in my research and has supported it in several ways, not least by providing valuable comments on the manuscript.

Professor Nils Mattsson of the Faculty of Law, Uppsala University, generously accepted to read large parts of the manuscript and gave valuable comments.

I have conducted research at the International Bureau of Fiscal Documentation (Amsterdam) and the Max-Planck-Institute for Intellectual Property Law, Competition Law and Tax Law in Munich. The period at the Max-Planck-Institute was partly made possible by grants from the Institute and KPMG (Stockholm). The Nordic Council for Tax Research provided a grant for the purchase of literature.

I am grateful to these individuals and institutions.

Sources available until September 2004 have been considered.

Mattias Dahlberg
Uppsala, September 2004

Abbreviations

ACT	Advance Corporation Tax (United Kingdom)
AG	Advocate General
ATS	Austrian schilling
BEF	Belgian franc
BEPG	Broad Economic Policy Guidelines
BFH	Bundesfinanzhof (Germany)
BV	besloten vennootschap (the Netherlands)
CBE	Commander of the British Empire
CFC	Controlled Foreign Company (Corporation)
CGI	Code Générale des Impôts (France)
CML Rev.	Common Market Law Review
Coreper	the Permanent Representatives Committee
DEM	German mark
DKK	Danish crown
EATLP	European Association of Tax Law Professors
EC	European Communities
EC MC	Model Tax Convention for the European Community
EBOR	European Business Organization Law Review
ECB	European Central Bank
ECJ	European Court of Justice
ECOFIN	Council of Economics and Finance Ministers
ECR	European Court Reports
ECSC	European Coal and Steel Community
EEA	European Economic Area
EGV	Vertrag zur Gründung der Europäischen Gemeinschaft
EFTA	European Free Trade Organisation

EL Rev.	European Law Review
EMU	European Monetary Union
ESP	Spanish peseta
EU	European Union
EuGH	Europäischer Gerichtshof
EUV	Vertrag über die Europäische Union
GATT	General Agreement on Tariffs and Trade
GebG	Gebührengesetz (Austria)
GmbH	Gesellschaft mit beschränkter Haftung
GBP	British pound
IBFD	International Bureau of Fiscal Documentation
ICTA	Income and Corporation Taxes Act (United Kingdom)
IFA	International Fiscal Association
KStG	Körperschaftsteuergesetz (Germany)
LUF	Luxembourg franc
marg.no.	marginal number
MC	Model (Tax) Convention
MCT	Mainstream Corporation Tax (United Kingdom)
NLG	Netherlands guilder
n.y.r.	not yet reported
OECD	Organisation for Economic Cooperation and Development
plc	public limited company
prop.	proposition
QC	Queen's Chambers
SA	Société Anonyme
RÅ	Regeringsrättens årsbok (Sweden)
SIEPS	Svenska institutet för europapolitiska studier
SJFU	Skrifter från Juridiska fakulteten i Uppsala
TEU	Treaty on European Union
TP	Tarifpost

1 Introduction

1.1 Background

For some time direct taxation was considered as an area with the almost exclusive competence of the individual Member States of the European Union. An important reason for this perception is the fact that to reach a decision in the Council on matters of direct taxation, unanimity is required. Unquestionably, taxation has been, and still is, an important issue for the Member States. By means of taxation, Member States, among other objectives, finance their welfare systems. Some politicians believe that if the European Union "intervenes" in the tax system of the Member States, the financing of the public sector of the Member States could be at risk. So far, in comparison to other areas of law, comparatively little has been achieved by the European Union regarding substantive law in the area of direct taxation on income.

Even against this background, the European Union has exercised considerable influence in the area of direct taxation of Member States. To begin with, tax measures by Member States may constitute obstacles to the fundamental freedoms provided for in the EC Treaty. In an increasing number of cases, the European Court of Justice has decided that specific elements of national tax legislation are in breach of fundamental freedoms provided for in the EC Treaty.

A specific piece of tax legislation that differs from the "normal" tax system of a Member State may, according to EC law, be considered to constitute unlawful state aid or harmful tax competition. For example, several Member States have applied tax measures that constituted harmful tax competition according to criteria decided upon by the Council in the Code of Conduct for business taxation.

Moreover, there have been a few legislative acts actually adopted in the field of direct taxation. For more than a decade only two directives had been accomplished with the objective of facilitating cross-border movements in this field of law: the Parent/Subsidiary Directive on cross-border dividends,[1] and the Merger Directive.[2] In

---

1 Council Directive 90/435/EEC of 23 July 1990 on the common system of taxation applicable in the case of parent companies and subsidiaries of different Member States.

2 Council Directive 90/434/EEC of 23 July 1990 on the common system of taxation applicable to mergers, divisions, transfers of assets and exchanges of shares concerning companies of different Member States.

2003 the Interest/Royalty Directive[3] and the Savings Directive[4] were finally adopted. In addition there is also a Code of Conduct on business taxation.[5]

Moreover, the Arbitration Convention, with the purpose of avoiding double taxation arising from the simultaneous use of arm's length legislation in different states, has been concluded by the Member States. A number of directives have, however, been proposed by the Council without having been adopted.

One should in this respect also mention that the related area of exchange of information on matters of taxation between Member States and their tax authorities has also been the subject of a measure at Community level. Already in 1977 a directive was adopted, Council Directive 77/799/EEC of 19 December 1977.

1.2 Framework Issues

1.2.1 Objective

The general objective of this study is to provide an analysis of the case-law of the European Court of Justice on the freedom of establishment and the free movement of capital in matters of direct taxation, primarily on income. There are several part-objectives. The *first part-objective* is to describe and analyse the Court's interpretation of "discrimination" and "restriction", both in general, and in particular regarding the freedom of establishment and the free movement of capital. In relation to the Court's case-law in matters of direct taxation, I analyse recent cases where the Court has applied a "barrier approach" rather than a "classic" discrimination analysis.

The *second part-objective* is to analyse grounds of justification advanced according to the rule-of-reason doctrine: some of which are accepted in principle by the Court, and some which are rejected by the Court. The grounds of justification accepted in principle which I discuss are: the prevention of tax abuse, the preservation of fiscal coherence, the effectiveness of fiscal supervision and the fiscal principle of territoriality. The rejected grounds which I discuss are, among others, the lack of harmonisation in the field of direct taxation, counterbalancing advantages, a new form of establishment being seen as subject to equal treatment, lack of Community competence in the field of tax treaty law and the protection of tax revenue.

3 Council Directive 2003/49/EC of 3 June 2003 on a common system of taxation applicable to interest and royalty payments made between associated companies of different Member States.

4 Council Directive 2003/48/EC of 3 June 2003 on taxation of savings income in the form of interest payments.

5 Conclusions of the ECOFIN Council meeting on 1 December 1997 concerning taxation policy, 6.1.98, OJ C 2/1.

The *third part-objective* is to analyse the characteristics of such national legislation on direct taxation that the Court has found to be in breach of the freedom of establishment and the free movement of capital. Strongly connected with that objective is the *fourth part-objective* which concerns the neutrality between different forms of establishment, in the form of either a branch or a subsidiary. For some time it has been clear that the Court strongly upholds equal treatment in the host state between branches and subsidiaries of non-resident companies. To what degree there is a requirement for such equal treatment in the home state is still uncertain. I elaborate on the neutrality between different forms of establishment from the perspective of both the host state and the home state. The pending *Marks & Spencer* case is subject to a thorough analysis in this respect.

The *fifth part-objective* is to study the degree of convergence between the freedom of establishment and the free movement of capital, especially in cases on direct taxation. In my view there is a high degree of convergence, even after considering Article 58 of the EC Treaty, and I find support for this in for example the cases C-35/98 *Verkooijen* and C-478/98 *Commission v. Belgium*. The *sixth and final part-objective* is to discuss the territorial extension of the free movement of capital: to what degree does it apply also in relation to third countries?

1.2.2 Perspective

Although the perspective of this study will follow from the subsequent analysis, it may be useful to address this issue separately at this initial stage. This study is intended as a scholarly work in the area of Community law and mainly two of the fundamental freedoms, the freedom of establishment and the free movement of capital, and, furthermore, their relation to the national tax legislation in the Member States of the European Union. The inquiry is made from a Community law perspective. Although I have an academic background in Swedish fiscal law, the discussion is intended to be free from the perspective of a specific Member State.

In this respect something should also be said on how the national law of the Member States will be dealt with. In general, I will follow how the European Court of Justice interprets the meaning of the national legislation at issue in the specific cases dealt with. It is of course possible that the European Court of Justice has misinterpreted the exact meaning of national tax law of a specific Member State. However, in the hopefully unlikely event of a misinterpretation of national legislation, the Court's interpretation of Community law is still valid.

1.2.3 Delimitations

This study is mainly limited to the case-law of the European Court of Justice in matters of direct taxation (primarily on income) in relation to the freedom of establishment and the free movement of capital. There are a growing number of cases from the Court in matters of direct taxation in relation to all fundamental freedoms. I have found it almost impossible, however, to provide a reasonably thorough analysis of all cases dealing with direct taxation in relation to all fundamental freedoms within the frames of one book. Of course, there are important cases on direct taxation in respect of the other fundamental freedoms. Where specific issues in those cases are vital for the understanding of the cases on the freedom of establishment and the free movement of capital, I have naturally tried to consider and refer to those cases to the extent possible. For example, case C-204/90 *Bachmann* deals with the free movement of workers. In that case the European Court of Justice developed "the preservation of fiscal coherence" as a ground of justification in the public interest. Even if the *Bachmann* case deals with another fundamental freedom than the ones primarily considered in this study, the case is important also for the freedom of establishment and the free movement of capital and therefore I discuss it quite thoroughly.

In general I have decided to discuss cases concerning both individuals and companies. The reason is that that the basic questions dealt with in those cases are sufficiently similar to be dealt with together in the same study. However, as regards the taxation of individuals and primarily the freedom of establishment, one important delimitation is made for this study. One field, which I will only briefly deal with in Chapter 3, concerns the correlation between, on the one hand, taxation, and on the other hand, social benefits. This correlation was put into the focus of Community law with case C-279/93 *Schumacker*, and it is still a field where the Court is continuously providing important case-law. The reason for not dealing with this interesting and important issue is that it both requires and deserves a separate study.

This study contains analyses of a large number of cases from the European Court of Justice on the two fundamental freedoms in relation to direct taxation. Even so, I do not deal with all cases decided by the European Court of Justice in this field of law. However, with the cases dealt with it is my intention to be able to provide answers to the questions asked. Moreover, there is a large number of cases pending at the European Court of Justice, some where an opinion from the Advocate General has been presented, and some where not even an opinion is available. Within the scope of this study, it has only been possible to deal with a few of them. An important exception is case C-446/03 *Marks & Spencer*, which is thoroughly dealt with even though there is as yet no opinion from the Advocate General. The reason for dealing with the *Marks & Spencer* case requires an explanation at this stage. The decision by the Special Commissioners on the national law in the United Kingdom is, in my view, so well-reasoned and elaborate that it is necessary to consider it also in this study, which is focused on the case-law of the European Court of Justice. The Special Commissioners make an analysis of that case-law that I find necessary to discuss.

Furthermore, it should be noted that the general questions of Community law which I cover in Chapter 1 are only intended to serve as a starting point for the following case-law analysis. In Chapter 1 it is not my objective to add anything considerably new to the current discussion. However, in the following case-law analysis, mainly Chapters 3 to 6, I return to these general matters, and in relation to the cases on direct taxation analysed my objective is, of course, to go beyond mere reference.

Here something should also be said about Chapter 2. It is only intended to provide a general background to the study. In this chapter I deal partly with how matters of direct taxation are covered by the EC Treaty, and partly with the work within the European Union to legislate in the field of direct taxation. The reason for this overview is to provide a background to the significance of the case-law of the European Court of Justice in the field of direct taxation. Of course, the study in Chapter 2 could be enlarged on each of the topics discussed, but with the growing bulk of tax law cases from the European Court of Justice, that would also be difficult to provide in one volume.

Finally, it should be noted that there is an almost overwhelming amount of articles dealing with the cases subject to this study. I have decided to focus my analysis on the decisions the European Court of Justice and where I have found it appropriate refer to relevant books and articles, without any claim to full coverage.

1.2.4 Outline

The study has the following outline. *Chapter 1* is an introduction to the study. The initial part of Chapter 1 (sections 1.1 to 1.4) contains a background as well as a declaration of purpose and perspective. Furthermore, the initial part of Chapter 1 contains an analytical framework. In this framework the methods for the forthcoming analysis is presented. The final part of Chapter 1 (sections 1.5 to 1.8) discusses the role of the European Court of Justice (section 1.5), legal and interpretative theory in Community law (section 1.6), general principles in Community law (section 1.7), and the relationship between Community law and the national laws of the Member States (section 1.8).

Chapter 2 deals with direct taxation in relation to the EC Treaty and the general Community policy. Section 2.2 tries to target the present policy of the European Union, and the Commission in particular, on matters of direct taxation and company taxation. To what extent the EC Treaty deals with matters of direct taxation is discussed in section 2.3. Since the creation of the European Communities, direct taxation including company taxation has been the subject of numerous inquiries and reports. Two of the most important reports are the 1992 Ruding Report and the 2001 Staff Report, which are discussed in sections 2.4 and 2.5 respectively. The results achieved on harmonising direct taxation, and more particularly, company taxation, are presented in section 2.6. It should be underlined that it is not my intention to give a thorough analysis of such measures. The intention is rather to identify in which general areas it has been possible for the European Union to reach the unanimous decision required in the area of direct taxation. The package to tackle harmful tax competition is the subject of section 2.7. In section 2.8 there is an overview of the 1990 proposal on a directive on cross-border offsetting of losses. Concluding remarks are given in section 2.9.

The principle of non-discrimination and grounds for justifying discriminatory and otherwise restrictive measures is the subject of *Chapter 3*. The chapter begins in section 3.2 with an analysis of the meaning of discrimination and restrictions according to the EC Treaty as interpreted by the European Court of Justice. There is an overview of the four fundamental freedoms in section 3.3. The right to invoke the EC Treaty and its fundamental freedoms is the subject of section 3.4: the right to invoke the EC Treaty has also been labelled "the treaty access test". The meaning of direct and indirect discrimination is further developed in section 3.5. A closely connected phenomenon is what constitutes objectively comparable situations, which is discussed in section 3.6. In its recent case-law the Court has moved away from the concept of discrimination to the concept of "non-discriminatory restrictions" and the vaguer notion of "barriers" and similar expressions. These concepts are discussed in section 3.7. According to the case-law of the European Court of Justice, restrictions can be justified even if there is no immediate support of that in the EC Treaty. In this study I have labelled this practice of the Court "the rule-of-reason doctrine". In section 3.8 there is an account of the rule-of-reason doctrine. To generalise, the Court in some cases on direct taxation and fundamental freedoms has accepted three or four different grounds of justification in the rule-of-reason doctrine: the effectiveness of fiscal supervision, the coherence of the fiscal system and the prevention of abuse and possibly also the preservation of the fiscal principle of territoriality. The first three grounds of justification are further developed in section 3.9. Potentially, there can be other grounds of justification that the Court has accepted, which is something I will deal with in Chapter 5.

Chapter 4 deals with the freedom of establishment and is, together with Chapters 3, 5 and 6, one of the core chapters of this study. The analysis begins with the wording of the Articles of the Treaty dealing with the freedom of establishment. The focus is, however, on the practice of the European Court of Justice. Instead of dealing with the cases in strict chronological order, I have classified the cases on the basis of, among other factors, where the restriction takes place, the home or host state, and which form of entity is at issue. Of course, one case may relate to several questions. In that event, the major presentation of the case, and the facts constituting it, will be made in relation to that question which I believe to be the most important. The question of who is covered by the freedom of establishment is analysed in section 4.2. Moreover, in that section I discuss the meaning of the term "establishment". Section 4.3 contains an analytical framework for the subsequent case-law analysis in Chapter 4. In this framework I present the major questions that will be asked in relation to the cases on the freedom of establishment in matters of direct taxation. A separate question is the neutrality between different forms of establishment, such as branches and subsidiaries. Another question is whether the home state and the host state treat subsidiaries of foreign and domestic parent companies neutrally. I have categorised the cases in the following way. In principle, my analysis contains three categories of cases, depending on in which state the (assumed) restriction takes place: (i) home state restrictions, (ii) host state restrictions and (iii) borderline cases between the home state and host state perspectives. The home state and host state perspectives are divided into three sub-categories: first, companies establishing branches; secondly, companies establishing subsidiaries and individuals establishing branches; and thirdly, individuals establishing branches (host state perspective) or other cases (home state perspective). Host state restrictions are covered in section 4.4 and home state restrictions in section 4.5. The *Marks & Spencer* case is so important that I have decided to cover it in a special section, section 4.6. One reason for its importance is that it targets the Court's recent vague explanations of why a specific measure is in breach of a fundamental freedom. Another reason, connected with the first one, is what constitutes objectively comparable situations. On this matter, the Special Commisioners elaborated thoroughly. Borderline cases between home and host state restrictions – primarily case C-307/97 *Saint-Gobain* – are discussed in section 4.7.

Chapter 5 deals with grounds of justification that have been advocated in cases on the freedom of establishment and direct taxation. In section 5.2 I deal with such grounds that have in principle been accepted by the Court. Those grounds have been introduced in Chapter 3, but in this chapter there is a wider analysis covering several cases on each ground. Grounds that the Court has rejected as valid grounds of justification are discussed in section 5.3. This includes, for example, counterbalancing advantages, lack of Community competence and loss of tax revenue.

The free movement of capital and payments is the subject of *Chapter 6*. An overview of Articles 56 to 60 of the EC Treaty on the free movement of capital is given in section 6.2. Section 6.3 deals, among other things, more closely with Article 56 (1) of the EC Treaty. The relationship between the free movement of capital and other fundamental freedoms is the subject of section 6.4. The emphasis in that section is, of course, on the relationship between the free movement of capital and the freedom of establishment, which is the other fundamental freedom in the focus of this study. The significance of the statutory grounds of justification contained in Article 58 of the EC Treaty is covered in section 6.5. An important aspect is the relation between Article 58 and the rule-of-reason doctrine, which is dealt with in the light of, for example, case C-35/98 *Verkooijen*. Accepted and rejected grounds of justification according to the rule-of-reason doctrine, are discussed in section 6.7. In comparison to the corresponding discussion in relation to the freedom of establishment, this part is short. One reason is that I come to the conclusion that there is a high degree of "convergence" between the rule-of-reason doctrine applied on the freedom of establishment and on the free movement of capital: the analysis regarding the freedom of establishment has in this respect a strong bearing also on the free movement of capital. According to the wording of Article 56 of the EC Treaty, the free movement of capital also applies in relation to third countries. To what extent this is practiced in fact is discussed in section 6.8. General conclusions are presented in *Chapter 7*.

1.2.5 On Terminology and Similar Matters

In the present study, the term "the EC Treaty" will be used when referring to the 1957 Treaty of Rome as amended from time to time. If otherwise not stated, the numbering of Articles in the EC Treaty will be used as it is presently (2004) numbered, albeit mentioning the number which the Article had at the time when, for example, a case was decided by the European Court of Justice.

I will alternately use the expressions "the European Court of Justice" and "the Court", always with an initial upper-case letter to distinguish it from national courts. Accordingly, I refer to national courts by using an initial lower-case letter.

"Coherence" has evolved as an important ground for justifying at least some forms of restrictions on the fundamental freedoms in the area of direct taxation. The European Court of Justice tends to use the expression "cohesion" in the English language versions of its decisions, but in the present study I considered the expression coherence more in keeping with other language versions, such as the French "*cohérence*" and the German "*Kohärenz*".

The term "Member State" is naturally reserved for states which are members of the European Union. Countries applying for membership are "candidate countries" and other non-Member States are called "third countries".

I will use the more generally accepted adjective "Dutch" rather than "Netherlands", even if the latter adjective is preferred by the European Court of Justice.

In my case-law analyses I will refer to "the facts of the underlying case". By this expression I mean the facts of the case at the level of the national court, where the national court has decided to stop the proceedings and refer a question of interpretation to the European Court of Justice. As will be discussed later in this chapter, the European Court of Justice in its preliminary rulings will, at least in principle, only deal with the interpretation of Community law; however, the facts are vital for understanding the cases also with respect to the judgment of the European Court of Justice. Moreover, it will become evident in the following case-law analyses that the Court may be influenced by the facts of the underlying cases. Vanistendael concludes that the role of the Court is most often limited to deciding questions of law and not those of questions of fact.

However, in his view, the distinction between questions of law and fact is often very difficult to draw; a view which I certainly share.[6]

Regarding national legislation at issue in cases before the European Court of Justice, I will use the past tense when referring to it. The focus of this study is on Community law, and it has not been possible for me to inquire whether different pieces of national legislation are in force or not. It should be noted that even when I use the past tense, the national legislation at issue may (partly) still be in force.

There are various techniques of referring to the case-law of the European Court of Justice. I will use the following method. There is a full reference to the cases in the list provided in the Bibliography at the end of the book, for example case C-324/00 *Lankhorst-Hohorst GmbH v. Finanzamt Steinfurt* [2002] ECR I-11779. When referring to the case in the separate chapters of the study, there is an abbreviated reference: case C-324/00 *Lankhorst-Hohorst* for a general reference to the case, and case C-324/00 *Lankhorst-Hohorst*, para. 36, when referring to a specific paragraph of the case.[7]

The reference applied to books and articles is also detailed in the footnotes. The reason is to make it easier to identify the different publications when reading the text, but without having to resort to the Bibliography for each book or article. The Bibliography, however, contains complete references to, for example, books and articles invoked.

When referring to previous numbering of the Articles of the EC Treaty, there is always an indication that the numbering has been changed and what the present number of the Article in question is.

Something should also be said about the reference to the freedom of establishment. I refer to it as the freedom of establishment, even if some authors and also the Court sometimes refer to it as "the right of establishment".[8]

1.3 Analytical Starting Points

For the European Union to reach a decision on matters of direct taxation, unanimity is required. Largely as a consequence hereof, little has been achieved in the area of direct taxation.

---

6 Vanistendael, "The Role of the European Court of Justice as the Supreme Judge in Tax Cases", *EC Tax Review*, 1996, pp. 114-122, p. 115.

7 When referring to the opinion of the Advocate General, I apply a method illustrated with the following example: Opinion of AG Mischo in case C-324/00 *Lankhorst-Hohorst*, para. 90.

8 The headline of Chapter 2 of Title III of the EC Treaty is "the right of establishment". Still, Article 43 of the EC Treaty refers to "the freedom of establishment".

The freedoms of the EC Treaty are, however, applicable also in the area of direct taxation.[9] The European Court of Justice has in a sharply increasing number of cases decided on the consistency of national legislation on direct taxation with the four freedoms provided for in the EC Treaty. The Commission has, however, for many years conducted much work within the area of direct taxation, and especially in the field of company taxation. Several major inquiries on company taxation have been delivered: most notably the 1992 Ruding Report and, more recently, the 2001 Staff Report.

A basic assumption of this study is that all proposals on unified corporate taxation of the European Union must consider the findings of the European Court of Justice on the compatibility of national tax legislation with Community law. Accordingly, the core of this study is an analysis of the decisions of the European Court of Justice on the compatibility of national tax legislation with the freedom of establishment and the free movement of capital.

This basic assumption is shared by the 2001 Staff Report, which states: "[T]oday the jurisprudence of the CJ [European Court of Justice] strongly influence almost all aspects of company tax law. There is good reason to believe that this influence will continue to increase."[10] The status of the European Court of Justice and the importance of the Court's case-law have two major implications for the 2001 Staff Report. First, any possible solution to the existing tax obstacles will have to take into account the existing judgments of the European Court of Justice. Secondly, it is necessary to analyse to what extent the European Court of Justice jurisprudence demands further coordination between Member States, i.e. beyond the mere correction of Treaty infringement.[11] It is evident that these two implications are important for this study.

Another basic assumption of this study is that the national legislator of the individual Member States must consider and follow the case-law of the European Court of Justice when revising old tax legislation and adopting new legislation in this area of law.

Basically, there are two questions which govern the analysis of the case-law:

(i) What characterises the national tax legislation which the European Court of Justice has declared to constitute discrimination?

(ii) Which grounds of justification have been accepted by the European Court of Justice?

---

9 The European Court of Justice declares for example in case C-307/97 *Saint-Gobain* (para. 57): "According to settled case-law of the Court, although direct taxation is a matter for the Member States, they must nevertheless exercise their taxation powers consistently with Community law …". Cf. also e.g. C-251/98 *Baars*, para. 17, and joined cases C-397/98 and C-410/98 *Metallgesellschaft and Others*, para. 37.

10 2001 Staff Report, p. 387.

11 *Ibid.*

To give a framework for this analysis, there are also two other areas that need to be discussed. First, the general discussion in the European Union on matters of direct taxation. As will follow, the objective of that discussion is to underline the relative importance of the case-law of the European Court of Justice. It is not the intention to present any analysis of the measures in the area of direct taxation actually adopted. This area will be discussed in Chapter 2. Secondly, a general analysis of the prohibition against discrimination according to Community law. This area will be subject to a comparatively thorough analysis because it is of immediate importance for the analysis of the freedom of establishment and the free movement of capital.

The analytical core of this study will be in Chapter 3 on the principle of non-discrimination, Chapter 4 on the freedom of establishment, Chapter 5 on grounds of justifications and finally Chapter 6, which deals with the free movement of capital. Case-law from the European Court of Justice is important for this study. There are two areas where cases from the European Court of Justice are especially important for this study: what constitutes discrimination and which circumstances may justify such discriminations.

In relation to this, two principal considerations have been made. First, not all cases relating to matters of direct taxation will be subject to the same comparably thorough analysis as other cases. In general, early cases will be covered less thoroughly than recent ones. Secondly, not all cases will be discussed in relation both to what feature of national tax law constituted discrimination, and the grounds of justification discussed by the European Court of Justice. The purpose of the case-law analysis is to uncover the present principal standpoints of the Court and, with a more modest ambition of completeness, how those standpoints have evolved.

1.4 Previous Research

The general theme of this study is direct taxation and Community law. That is a topic which has been subject to increasing scholarly interest. It is not possible to refer to all previous research. I have already mentioned two important studies from the Commission, the 1992 Ruding Report and the 2001 Staff Report. Both reports are general studies of systems for direct taxation in the Member State and the obstacles for cross-border transactions.

There are some scholarly studies in recent years that more or less deal with the questions covered by this study. To begin with Martín Jiménez's Ph.D. thesis *Towards Corporate Tax Harmonisation in the European Community* should be mentioned. It was published in 1999. Martín Jiménez covers the attempts by the Community to harmonise direct taxation, and also includes a comparison with the US federal tax system. Case-law from the European Court of Justice in direct tax matters on the freedom of establishment and the free movement of capital – the core of this study – is also discussed. That analysis is only one of many elements of European law examined by Martín Jiménez. Another difference is that the European Court of Justice has resolved a number of cases after the publication of that study.

An important study is Cordewener's doctoral dissertation *Europäische Grundfreiheiten und nationales Steuerrecht*, published in 2002. Cordewener's massive study covers many of the questions also dealt with in the present study. His objective goes beyond that of this study: Cordewener deals, for example, with all fundamental freedoms and all cases from the European Court of Justice on matters of direct taxation and, furthermore, also with German constitutional law. Cordewener's study is naturally of importance for the present one. Moreover, in 2002 Pistone's Ph.D. thesis was published – *The Impact of Community Law on Tax Treaties: Issues and Solutions*. The objective of Pistone's study is different from this one: his analysis of Community law and direct taxation has the objective of forming the fundament for a multilateral tax treaty within the European Union. The case-law analysis of Pistone is, however, of immediate interest to this study.

Van Thiel has published both a doctoral dissertation and a specific case-law analysis, which are of interest for this study. Van Thiel's dissertation, *Free Movement of Persons and Income Tax Law: the European Court in Search of Principles*, was published in 2002. The outline of Van Thiel's study is different from the present one: in general one could say that Van Thiel sorts the material in relation to specific (constitutional) principles. Moreover, it should be noted that Van Thiel does not specifically deal with the free movement of capital, and a case-law analysis of what the Court considers to be discriminatory or constitute a restriction and the grounds of justification that may apply. Moreover, it should be noted that in 2001 Van Thiel also published a book providing a case-law analysis of judgments by the European Court of Justice in the field of direct taxation: *EU Case-law on Income Tax (Part 1)*. Van Thiel's objective in that study is, however, different from that of this study. His objective is rather to analyse and comment on all cases from the European Court of Justice on matters of direct taxation. His study is focused on a wide range of questions and is more of a handbook, albeit on a scholarly basis.

In 2003 Pinto's Ph.D. dissertation was published – *Tax Competition and EU Law*. In Chapter 5 Pinto deals with the Court's practice in matters of direct taxation and the freedom of establishment and the free movement of capital. Pinto examines these freedoms in relation to national countermeasures against harmful tax competititon such as CFC legislation.

There are several Nordic doctoral dissertations that border this study. Helminen's doctoral thesis from 1999 on *The Dividend Concept in International Law* should be mentioned. That is also the case with Ståhl's *Aktiebeskattning och fria kapital-*

rörelser,[12] Winther-Sørensen's *Beskatning af international erhvervsindkomst*[13] and Brokelind's *Une interprétation de la directive sociétés mères et filiales du 23 juillet 1990*.[14]

1.5 On the European Court of Justice

1.5.1 Introduction

This study is to a major extent based on case-law from the European Court of Justice. Therefore I find it necessary to discuss the role of the European Court of Justice, its method of legal interpretation, and the legal value of its decisions. In particular, the legal method applied by the European Court of Justice is in many ways different from the legal methods applied by national courts. To understand the case-law that will be discussed later on, I find it worthwhile to discuss a few topical issues regarding the European Court of Justice. It would of course have been possible to give a more thorough analysis of each of the sub-topics dealt with in this part of Chapter 1. The reason why I still decided to discuss the selected topics is to formulate the basis upon which I have formed my opinion on the subsequently analysed cases.

It is well established that the legal method of the European Court of Justice emphasises the purpose and objective of different Community acts. One explanation for this could be the lack of clarity of these acts. In the area of direct taxation, the Court in a number of cases has interpreted the meaning of the fundamental freedoms contained in the EC Treaty. Perhaps by its nature as a frame-work treaty, the EC Treaty is a legal instrument containing broad and sometimes vague provisions: it is the objective of the European Court of Justice to fill those provisions with content when deciding specific cases. This is no marginal difference compared with the legal method used in matters on direct taxation decided by national courts, where legislation tends to be very detailed.

According to Article 220 of the EC Treaty, the European Court of Justice shall ensure that in the interpretation and application of the EC Treaty, law is observed. The Court consists of 25 Judges, one from each Member State, and the Court may sit in plenary sessions.[15] The Court is assisted by Advocates General.[16] Article 222 of the EC Treaty stipulates that the duty of the Advocates General is to make "… reasoned

[12] Uppsala, 1996 [The taxation of investment in shares and free capital movements].

[13] Copenhagen, 2000 [The taxation of international business income].

[14] Lund, 2000 [An interpretation of the Parent/Subsidiary Directive of the 23 July 1990].

[15] Article 221 of the EC Treaty.

[16] Article 222 of the EC Treaty.

submissions on cases brought before the Court of Justice, in order to assist the Court in the performance of the task assigned to it in Article 220". It is important to note that the Advocates General shall act with "complete impartiality and independence".[17] Moreover, an Advocate General shall make his opinion in "open court", also according to Article 222 of the EC Treaty.

1.5.2 The Purpose of the European Court of Justice

The purpose of the European Court of Justice is stipulated in Article 230 of the EC Treaty. The European Court of Justice shall review the legality of:

- acts adopted jointly by the European Parliament and the Council;
- acts of the Council, of the Commission and of the ECB, other than recommendations and opinions; and
- acts of the European Parliament intended to produce legal effects vis-à-vis third parties.

The European Court of Justice has jurisdiction in actions brought by a Member State, the Council or the Commission on the following grounds, according to Article 230, section 2 of the EC Treaty: lack of competence, infringement of an essential procedural requirement, infringement of the EC Treaty or any rule of law relating to its application, or misuse of powers.

If an action is well-founded, the European Court of Justice shall declare the act concerned to be void.[18]

National courts of the Member States are obliged to interpret national law as far as possible in conformity with Community law. Furthermore, if a national court finds that there is a conflict between Community law and a national provision, the court shall disregard the national provision – the doctrine of direct effect. I will return to that aspect of Community law in section 1.8.

Basically, judgments by the European Court of Justice can be divided into two separate categories.[19] On the one hand, there are actions which have their beginning in the European Court of Justice. If a case begins in the Court, it will also end in the Court. On the other hand, there are actions which have their beginning in a national court. In

---

17 *Ibid.*

18 Article 231 of the EC Treaty.

19 Hartley, *The Foundations of European Community Law*, 5th ed., Oxford University Press, Oxford, 2003, p. 63.

such cases the decision of the European Court of Justice will form part of the decision of the national court, when it finally decides the case.

The cases decided by the European Court of Justice that will be dealt with in this study primarily belong to the second category. Those cases have originally been referred to the European Court of Justice by national courts asking for "preliminary rulings" on matters of law: the correct interpretation of Community law. I will more specifically deal with the institute of "preliminary rulings" in section 1.5.5.

1.5.3 The Procedure of the European Court of Justice

There are a few issues on the procedure of the European Court of Justice that I find important to address in this section. The Court consists of 25 Judges: one Judge for each Member State, according to Article 221 of the EC Treaty.

The division of the work of the European Court of Justice is stipulated in the protocol on the statute of the Court. Article 16 of the protocol deals with the chambers of the Court. It is provided that the Court shall form chambers of three and five Judges. There is also a Grand chamber consisting of eleven Judges. In exceptional circumstances it shall sit as a full Court.

Article 17 of the statute of the Court stipulates when decisions of the Court shall be valid. Decisions shall only be valid if an uneven number of Judges are sitting in the deliberations. When chambers of three or five Judges are deciding, the decisions are only valid if they are taken by three Judges. Decisions of the Grand chamber shall be valid only if nine Judges are sitting, and the requirement for the full Court is eleven Judges sitting in the deliberations.

The procedure before the Court can largely be divided into two parts: one written and one oral. The written procedure consists of the exchange of written documents between the parties, institutions and others that are involved in the case.[20] The oral procedure consists of the reading of the report presented by the Judge acting as rapporteur, the hearing by the Court of agents, advisers and lawyers and of the submissions of the Advocate General.[21] If there are witnesses and experts, they are also heard by the Court.[22]

The Judge acting as rapporteur of a specific case prepares a report on the case in which are summarised the facts of the case and the arguments presented by the parties.

20 Article 20 of the Protocol on the Statute of the Court of Justice.

21 *Ibid.*

22 *Ibid.*

Moreover, the Court has made it a practice to put questions to the legal representatives that are present at the oral hearing.[23]

1.5.4 The Advocates General

The Advocates General could be said to have the same status as the Judges of the Court, albeit with different duties.[24] Article 222 (2) of the EC Treaty stipulates:

> "It shall be the duty of the Advocate-General, acting with complete impartiality and independence, to make, in open court, reasoned submissions on cases which, in accordance with the Statute of the Court of Justice, require his involvement."

The Advocate General takes part in the oral hearing before the Court. The most important contribution is, however, the written opinion of the case submitted by the Advocate General.[25]

The opinion of the Advocate General differs considerably in form from the decision of the Court. Generally an opinion consists of the following parts. First, there is an analysis of the facts of the underlying case before the national court. Secondly, there is a reference to relevant legislation both at the national and the Community level, including previous case-law from the European Court of Justice. Thirdly, the reasons put forward by the parties and those who have responded to the remittance of the Court, for example Member States, are presented. Fourthly, the Advocate General will deliver his opinion. It should be underlined that the Advocate General is not restricted to the reasons advanced by the parties.[26]

The opinion of the Advocate General is an independent analysis of the case where he considers, for example, the legislation at issue and the previous case-law of the Court. The opinions are generally of high quality, and they frequently serve to give a better understanding of the Court's reasoning in its decision. It should be underlined that the Court is not bound by the opinion of the Advocate General, even if it is well

23 Craig and de Búrca, *EU Law*, 3rd ed., Oxford University Press, Oxford, 2003, p. 94.

24 Hartley, *The Foundations of European Community Law*, 5th ed., Oxford University Press, Oxford, 2003, p. 57.

25 However, there is under exceptional circumstances no need for an opinion ("submission") by the Advocate General. According to Article 20 of the Protocol on the Statute of the Court of Justice, where the Court considers that the case raises no new point of law, it may decide, after hearing the Advocate General, that the case shall be determined without an opinion from the Advocate General.

26 Hartley, *The Foundations of European Community Law*, 5th ed., Oxford University Press, Oxford, 2003, pp. 58-59.

known that the Court in most cases follows this recommendation, even if not always in the same elaborate manner.[27]

1.5.5 Preliminary Rulings and the Significance of Previous Cases

The national legal system of the Member States is to a large extent the vehicle by which Community law is made effective in the Member States. However, national courts may find it difficult to interpret Community law such as the EC Treaty. Rulings on the interpretation of Community law acts may be required by a national court to establish whether national law is compatible with Community law. An instrument to solve this problem is provided for in the EC Treaty: the right to ask the European Court of Justice for a *preliminary ruling*.

More precisely, Article 234 (ex Article 177) of the EC Treaty stipulates that the European Court of Justice has the jurisdiction to give preliminary rulings on (a) the interpretation of the EC Treaty, (b) the validity and interpretation of acts of the institutions of the Community and of the ECB, and (c) the interpretation of the statutes of bodies by an act of the Council, where those statutes so provide. This study will almost entirely focus on rulings on the interpretation of the EC Treaty.

It is for a national court or tribunal to request a preliminary ruling from the European Court of Justice. According to Article 234 (2) of the EC Treaty, such a request can be made if it is considered that a decision on the question is necessary to enable the national court to give a judgment.

Thus the objective of the European Court of Justice regarding the institute of preliminary rulings is to assist national courts with the interpretation of Community law. It should be emphasised that the relationship between national courts and the European Court of Justice is reference-based: the Court is not an appellate body in this area of law.

As regards preliminary rulings on the interpretation of the EC Treaty, the following is of special importance. The Court only *interprets* the EC Treaty: it does not consider whether the actual national legislation is valid or not in relation to the EC Treaty. As a result of the interpretation provided by the Court, the national court may, however, have to apply national law in a way it would otherwise not have done. In other words, the national court may, on the basis of the interpretation provided by the Court, come to the conclusion that a provision of national law is incompatible with the EC Treaty.

Article 234 of the EC Treaty declares that only "courts and tribunals" of a Member State may ask for a preliminary ruling. In the area of tax law, this was a question which

---

27 Cf. Craig and de Búrca, *EU Law*, 3rd ed., Oxford University Press, Oxford, 2003, p. 94.

the Court had to specially consider in case C-134/97 *Victoria Film A/S*.[28] In that case the Court decided that the Swedish Revenue Law Commission (*Skatterättsnämnden*) was not a court or tribunal in the sense of Article 234 of the Treaty.[29] Moreover, if the European Court of Justice considers that it has already provided an answer to the question of interpretation referred to it, then thc Court does not have to answer.[30] In the view of Tridimas the system of preliminary rulings in combination with the principles of primacy of Community law and direct effect, has redefined constitutionalism at the European level and facilitated a re-allocation of powers at different levels.[31]

It has become obvious that the European Court of Justice considers that national courts should rely on previous case-law from the Court; in other words, the Court accepts and even advocates a theory of precedence regarding its own case-law. This theory of precedence works both in relation to the Court itself, and in relation to national courts. To put it more straightforwardly: the Court should as a general rule follow its own precedents, and national courts should also follow the precedents of the Court. It is apparent that the Court in its case-law on direct taxation and fundamental freedoms frequently refers to other decisions by the Court itself in this particular field of law. On the question of precedence, Arnull concludes that the general position is that the Court is not *bound* by its previous decisions, but in practice it does not often depart from them.[32]

There is no obligation for a court or tribunal to make a reference for a preliminary ruling. In brief the so-called *acte clair* doctrine means that if Community law is so

28 Case C-134/97 *Victoria Films A/S*.

29 In its decision in case C-234/97 *Victoria Film A/S*, the Court emphasised that at the time when an application for a preliminary decision was lodged with the Swedish Revenue Law Commission the taxpayer's situation had not been the subject of any decision by the tax authorities (para. 16). In the view of the Court it was only where the taxpayer and the Swedish National Tax Board brought an action challenging a preliminary decision (by the Revenue Law Commission) that the court or tribunal, before which the matter was brought, performs "… a judicial function with the object of reviewing the legality of an act determining a taxpayer's assessment to tax" (para. 18). Which forms of national courts and tribunals can ask for a preliminary ruling according to Article 234 of the EC Treaty is discussed e.g. in Lang, "Die Bedeutung des Vorabentscheidungsverfahrens für das Abgabenverfahren", in *Das EuGH-Verfahren in Steuersachen*, Holoubek and Lang (ed.), Linde Verlag, Vienna, 2000, pp. 99-118.

30 Cf. e.g. cases C 28-30/62 *Da Costa en Schaake NV, Jacob Meijer NV and Hoechst-Holland NV v. Nederlandse Belastingadministratie*.

31 Tridimas, "Knocking on Heaven's Door: Fragmentation, Efficiency and Defiance in the Preliminary Reference Procedure", *CML Rev.*, 2003, pp. 9-50, at p. 10. The three levels where a re-allocation of powers have taken place are, according to Tridimas, (a) at supranational level, from the governments of the Member States to the institutions of the Community, (b) at national level, from the executive and the legislative branches of government to the judiciary, and (c) within the national judiciary itself, from the national courts of last instance to lower national courts (*ibid.*).

32 Arnull, *The European Union and its Court of Justice*, Oxford University Press, Oxford, 1999, p. 529. Arnull even identifies a tendency in the ECJ's case-law from the beginning of the 1990s to "confront the implications of earlier case-law" (*ibid.*).

clear that there is no need for a preliminary ruling, the national court will not ask for one. In addition, the *acte éclairé* doctrine means that if there is a clear precedent from the European Court of Justice, there is no obligation to ask for a preliminary ruling.[33] As previously noted, it is for the national court to decide whether it wants to ask for a preliminary ruling or not. In Case 283/81 *CILFIT* the European Court of Justice declared: "... paragraph (3) of Article 177 [present Article 234] is to be interpreted as meaning that a court or tribunal against whose decision there is no judicial remedy under national law is required, where a question of Community law is raised before it, to comply with its obligation to bring the matter before the Court of Justice, unless it has established that the question raised is irrelevant or that the Community provision in question has already been interpreted by the Court or that the correct application of Community law is so obvious as to leave no scope for any reasonable doubt. The existence of such a possibility must be assessed in the light of the specific characteristics of Community law, the particular difficulties to which its interpretation gives rise and the risk of divergences in judicial decision within the Community."[34] In case C-99/00 *Kenny Roland Lyckeskog* the European Court of Justice provided further interpretation of the meaning of Article 234 (3) of the EC Treaty, and what constitutes a court or tribunal against whose decisions there is no judicial remedy under national law: a court which "shall bring the matter before the [European] Court of Justice". A national court whose decisions can only be appealed to the national supreme court if that court decides the case to be admissible, is not a court of last resort in the meaning of Article 234 (3).[35]

The exact meaning of the *CILFIT* case has been interpreted differently by different scholars, and I refrain from entering a discussion on that vast topic here.[36] In July 2000 there was an amendment to Article 104 (3) of the Court's Rules of Procedure. According to this provision the Court can reject a reference for a preliminary ruling: (i) where the question referred is identical to a question which the Court has previously decided, (ii) where the answer can clearly be deduced from existing case-law, and (iii) where the answer admits no reasonable doubt.[37]

---

33 See e.g. De la Mare, "Article 177 in social and political context", in *The Evolution of EU Law*, ed. Craig and de Búrca, Oxford University Press, Oxford, 1999, pp. 215-260, at pp. 223-224; and Hettne and Öberg, "Domstolarna i Europeiska unionens konstitution", *SIEPS*, 2003:15, Stockholm, 2003, p. 32.

34 Case 283/81 *Srl CILFIT and Lanificio di Gravardo SpA v. Ministry of Health*, para. 21.

35 Cf. Tridimas, "Knocking on Heaven's Door: Fragmentation, Efficiency and Defiance in the Preliminary Reference Procedure", *CML Rev.*, 2003, pp. 9-50, at p. 41.

36 Cf. e.g. Arnull, *The European Union and its Court of Justice*, Oxford University Press, Oxford, 1999, pp. 515-517.

37 Cf. Tridimas, "Knocking on Heaven's Door: Fragmentation, Efficiency and Defiance in the Preliminary Reference Procedure", *CML Rev.*, 2003, pp. 9-50, at p. 18. Tridimas considers the provision in question to be the procedural expression of the precedent value of the Court's rulings (*ibid.*).

When a reference for a preliminary ruling is made, the European Court of Justice transmits copies of the reference to (i) the parties in the national proceedings, (ii) the Member States, and (iii) the Commission.[38] If a measure of the Council is at issue, the reference will also be transmitted to that body.

All those who have received a transmittal of the reference for a preliminary ruling may give a written observation to the Court and may, furthermore, attend the oral hearing. They who attend the hearing present their submissions. At the hearing the Advocate General gives his opinion, and, finally, the Court delivers its decision. The national court may request a second reference on a new issue or a clarification of the previous ruling.

There has been a strong increase in the number of references from national courts to the European Court of Justice for preliminary rulings, especially in recent years.[39]

1.6 On Legal and Interpretative Theory in Community Law

1.6.1 Approaches to Interpretation

The objective of this section is to introduce certain important aspects of legal theory in relation to Community law. The section is merely intended as a stepping-stone for the forthcoming analysis of cases on direct taxation from the European Court of Justice. Even so I consider it important to outline some general positions on the interpretation of Community law, before entering the analysis of specific case-law from the European Court of Justice.

An initial question is of course if there is a *special* interpretative theory or method that applies for Community law. More precisely, it may be asked if there is a special interpretative method of the European Court of Justice. It has even been questioned whether the European Court of Justice in reality deals with matters of strict "interpretation": it has been argued that the Court rather exercises "invention", behind the curtain of "interpretation".[40]

---

[38] Cf. Hartley, *The Foundations of European Community Law*, 5th ed., Oxford University Press, Oxford, 2003, pp. 69-70.

[39] Cf. Tridimas, "Knocking on Heaven's Door: Fragmentation, Efficiency and Defiance in the Preliminary Reference Procedure", *CML Rev.*, 2003, pp. 9-50, at p. 16. For a preliminary ruling to be decided by the ECJ, it takes about two years from the date when the case is lodged. Cf. Jann, "Das Vorabentscheidungsverfahren: Grundfragen, Verfahrensablauf und aktuelle Entwicklungen", in *Das EuGH-Verfahren in Steuersachen*, Holoubek and Lang (ed.), Linde Verlag, Vienna, 2000, pp. 13-24, at p. 21 (Jann refers to the situation in 1997 and 1998, which largely remains unchanged).

[40] Cf. Rasmussen, *On Law and Policy in the European Court of Justice: A Comparative Study in Judicial Policy-making*, Dordrecht, Nijhoff, 1986.

In my view, the European Court of Justice does deal with legal interpretation in a sense similar to the method of interpretation exercised by courts in many countries. However, there are factors which make the interpretation different from the interpretation *normally* exercised in national courts when interpreting national legislation. This study is focused on two fundamental freedoms provided for in the EC Treaty. The main question dealt with in the core chapters of this study concerns the compatibility of national tax legislation with those freedoms. It will become evident that it is very difficult from the mere wording of those fundamental freedoms, as manifested in the EC Treaty, to establish whether the national provision is in conflict with the freedoms or not. Other interpretative measures than the mere analysis of the Treaty wording will be necessary.

Bengoetxea and others outline six arguments of legal reasoning that are especially important in Community law.[41] I consider their outline both clear and well-founded, and here I will recapitulate the arguments as a basis for the forthcoming case-law analysis.

(1) *The argument from contextual harmonisation.* Because a singular provision of Community law belongs to a larger legislative system, such as the EC Treaty or a specific Directive, it should be interpreted in the light of the whole statute to which it forms a part.

(2) *The argument from precedent.* If a text has previously been subject to judicial interpretation it ought *prima facie* to be interpreted in conformity with the previous interpretation. It should, however, be observed that there is no strict doctrine of binding precedent in Community law. Still, according to Bengoetxea and others, the European Court of Justice "... must clearly pay strong regard to the over-time coherence of the decisions they hand down in individual cases".[42]

(3) *The argument from analogy.* If a legal provision is significantly analogous with similar provisions, especially those in the same field of law, an interpretation of the first-mentioned provision will be justified even if it goes beyond the ordinary meaning of the provision as long as it creates a like treatment of like cases.

(4) *The logical-conceptual argument.* If a recognised legal concept is used in a legal provision, the concept should be interpreted in such a way that it maintains the generally accepted meaning through the whole system, or through a distinct branch of that system.

---

41 Bengoetxea, MacCormick and Moral Soriano, "Integration and Integrity in the Legal Reasoning of the European Court of Justice", in *The European Court of Justice*, de Búrca and Weiler (ed.), Oxford University Press, 2001, pp. 43-85, at pp. 46-47.

42 Bengoetxea, MacCormick and Moral Soriano, *op. cit.*, p. 46.

(5) *The argument from general principles of law*. Suppose that a general principle of law applies to the specific area of law that is the subject of interpretation. In that case one should favour that interpretation of the legal provision which is most in conformity with that principle. If there are several principles that apply one should favour that principle which both in general and in the particular field of law has the greatest importance. This applies in general to principles of law contained in both Community law and such principles commonly recognised in the Member States.

(6) *Legal systems in general recognise an argument from history*. That legal systems in general recognise an argument from history means that "… a statute or a group of statutes have over time come to be interpreted in accordance with a historically evolved understanding of the point and purpose of the statute or group of statutes taken as a whole, or historically evolved understanding of the conception of rightness it embodies".[43] The consequence of this approach is that a provision should be interpreted in a way that it is compatible with the "historically evolved understanding of point and purpose or of rightness".[44]

Bengoetxea, MacCormick and Moral Soriano state, and I agree in full, that this approach has had "spectacular relevance" for Community law by the doctrines of supremacy and direct effect of Community norms.

The previously referred to arguments for interpretation have for a long time been well known and accepted in the legal tradition of the Member States, but also in many other countries. Accordingly, a subsequent question is whether there are specific characteristics for the interpretation, or legal method, applied by the European Court of Justice? I will elaborate on that question in the following section.

1.6.2 Characteristics of Legal Reasoning at the Level of the European Court of Justice

1.6.2.1 Introduction

The purpose of this section is to give a general picture of the legal method applied and developed by the European Court of Justice. Perhaps the most correct position is that the Court does not apply one distinct method, but a variety of methods. I share the provisional answer of Bengoetxea, MacCormick and Moral Soriano, that there is

43 *Ibid.*

44 *Ibid.*

no specific theory for the legal reasoning of the European Court of Justice,[45] and that applies also for its case-law on matters of direct taxation.

However, there are specific circumstances relating to, for example, the status of the European Union as a supranational organisation and the general design of Community acts, and those circumstances are important for the legal method developed and applied by the European Court of Justice. I will here mention a few such circumstances which I consider important for the forthcoming case-law analysis.

The traditional starting point when interpreting an act is the wording, and the European Court of Justice also applies this approach. However, if a term in a Community act is the same as a term used in the national law of a Member State, one should not necessarily assume that the same meaning of the term would also apply for the term in Community law.[46]

Moreover, the Court attaches great importance to the context of an individual provision of Community law. In my view one could very well argue that the actual wording of a provision is less important than the overall context of that provision.

Objectives of a Community act are important for its interpretation. General objectives of the Community are contained in, for example, the EC Treaty and the Treaty on The European Union. In its teleological method of interpretation, the European Court of Justice uses these objectives.

If the wording does not lead to a clear result, the context and the objectives at a specific time of Community law development apply as means for interpretation. As regards the specific area of tax law, there is hardly one particular method applied by the Court. Vanistendael explains as a characteristic of the legal framework within which the Court operates "… the absence of any specific provision or tradition with respect to the interpretation of tax law".[47]

1.6.2.2 Consequences following from the Design of Community Acts

The focus of this study will be on the interpretation of the EC Treaty. The EC Treaty has a special position in Community law since it is an act decided upon by the Member States and not through particular Community bodies, such as the Parliament, the Council and the Commission. There are, of course, other Community acts. Article

[45] Bengoetxea, MacCormick and Moral Soriano, *op. cit.*, p. 48.

[46] Nielsen, *EU ret*, 2nd ed., Thomson/Gadjura, Copenhagen, 1999, p. 138.

[47] Vanistendael, "The Role of the European Court of Justice as the Supreme Judge in Tax Cases", *EC Tax Review*, 1996, pp. 114-122, at p. 115.

249 of the EC Treaty stipulates that in order to carry out their task and in accordance with the provisions of the EC Treaty, the Parliament, acting jointly with the Council, and the Commission, shall make regulations and issue directives, take decisions, make recommendations or deliver opinions.

An important characteristic of the EC Treaty is that it manifests a variety of general objectives and principles. This is of course appropriate for the act constituting the Community. However, there is not much guidance when a particular national court wishes to decide whether a national provision is in accordance with a fundamental freedom laid down in the EC Treaty. Furthermore, there are normally no available preparatory works to the different legal acts, which, had they been available, would have provided for assistance in the process of interpretation.

The Community law situation with an absence of detailed legislation and preparatory works is different from the situation in the Member States. In general I would say that tax law constitutes one of the most detailed fields of legislation of the Member States. Moreover, preparatory works may serve as important instruments of interpreting the legislation which they have prepared.

As a consequence of this lack in detail of the EC Treaty, the interpretation of the Treaty by the European Court of Justice is of crucial importance.

1.6.2.3 The Different Languages of the European Union

For several years there have been twelve official languages of the European Union: Danish, Dutch, English, Finnish, French, German, Greek, Irish, Italian, Portuguese, Spanish and Swedish. With the ten new Member States joining in 2004, there are even more official languages of the Union. All languages have equal status in Community law. As regards the EC Treaty, Article 314 of that Treaty declares that all language versions are equally authentic.

The fact that Community acts, such as the EC Treaty, exist in different language versions gives rise to questions of interpretation. How should one interpret an act which has different meanings in different language versions? The Vienna Convention on the Law of Treaties deals with that question. According to Article 33 (3) of the Vienna Convention, the terms of the Treaty to be interpreted are presumed to have the same meaning in each authentic text. However, it is still possible that the meaning is different in different language versions. Article 33 (4) deals with this problem: "Except where a particular text prevails in accordance with paragraph 1, when a comparison of the authentic texts discloses a difference of meaning which the application of Articles 31 and 32 does not remove, the meaning which best reconciles the texts, having regard to the object and purpose of the Treaty, shall be adopted." Accordingly, when there is a difference in meaning between different language versions, that meaning shall be applied which best reconciles the different texts. When deciding this meaning of reconciliation, the object and purpose of the Treaty as a whole shall be taken into account.

In my view the approach contained in the Vienna Convention is similar to the one adopted by the European Court of Justice, but perhaps from another starting point than the one contained in the Vienna Convention. Article 31 of the Vienna Convention contains the general rule for interpreting treaties, and it emphasises an "objective" approach where the wording of the Treaty text has particular importance. The "ordinary meaning" of the disputed meaning of a term is the very starting point. The approach of the European Court of Justice is somewhat different in this respect.

It may even be said that the European Court of Justice is less bound by the wording of Community acts than national courts are bound by the wording of national legislation in the field of taxation.[48] Instead, the purpose of the act and general policy objectives are more important when the Court interprets Community acts. The meaning which best reconciles such general objectives will be adopted by the Court.

1.6.2.4 Other Characteristics

Another explanation for the manner of legal reasoning applied by the European Court of Justice is that the Judges come from different national legal traditions, even if they all, more or less, have common denominators. Hence, it has been necessary for the Judges to develop for themselves common strategies and methods in order to reach decisions.

The decisions of the Court are taken with a majority of the votes. If there is a minority opinion, that opinion will not be contained in the judgment.[49] The fact that the minority view is unknown may be a factor which influences the composition of the judgment of the Court: as a measure of "compensation" to the minority, the judgment is less clear than it otherwise would have been. Normally, chambers of the Court consisting of three and five Judges take the decisions.[50] It is also possible for a Grand chamber to take a decision, and that chamber will consist of thirteen Judges.[51]

It is a common feature for national courts to make use of *travaux préparatoires* when interpreting national legislation. The situation as regards such means of assistance is,

---

48 Hartley even considers that when there are no linguistic problems the ECJ does not give any decisive weight to the literal wording. Hartley, *The Foundations of European Community Law*, 5th ed., Oxford University Press, Oxford, 2003, p. 72.

49 Cf. Craig and de Búrca, *EU Law*, 3rd ed., Oxford University Press, Oxford, 2003, p. 95.

50 Article 16 of the protocol on the statute of the Court of Justice.

51 *Ibid.*

however, much different in Community law, as previously noted. The *travaux préparatoires* to the Treaties have never been made public. As regards secondary legislation, the discussions at the Council and Commission meetings are not published. However, it has occurred that the Court has relied on the minutes from such meetings.[52]

In contrast, objectives of acts of legislation contained in, for example, preambles are of importance in the method of interpretation applied by the European Court of Justice.[53]

1.6.3 Steps in the Reasoning of the European Court of Justice

Regarding the judgments of the European Court of Justice, Article 36 of the protocol on the statute of the Court somewhat laconically states: judgments shall state the reasons on which they are based. They shall contain the names of the Judges who took part in the deliberations.

Over time specific steps of the design of the judgments of the Court have evolved. Those steps are interesting to consider separately in this chapter as an introduction to the forthcoming case-law analysis. Bengoetxea, MacCormick and Moral Soriano present a scheme of ten steps, which I consider most interesting.[54] Therefore I will here refer those steps as modelled and described by them, but I will only consider these steps in relation to cases brought before the Court by national courts and tribunals requesting a preliminary ruling. Bengoetxea, MacCormick and Moral Soriano categorise the different steps as either aspects of discovery (D), aspects of procedure (P), and aspects of justification (J).

Step 0. The legal problem (P).[55] The case begins when a dispute is lodged before the Court by a national court or tribunal. At the Registrar's office of the Court the case is processed, and the first measure will be to translate the reference into the other official languages. The Member States and the EU institutions will be informed of the case and asked whether they wish to make any observations and intervene. The public is also made aware of the case because the summary of the preliminary question is published in the Official Journal.

---

52 Craig and de Búrca, *EU Law*, 3rd ed., Oxford University Press, Oxford, 2003, p. 98.

53 Cf. e.g. Sevón, "Rättskällor och lagtolkning i EG-domstolen", in *Festskrift tillägnad Edward Andersson*, Sevón, Frände, Olsson, Ryynänen and Tikka (ed.), 2003, pp. 335-341, at p. 338.

54 Bengoetxea, MacCormick and Moral Soriano, "Integration and Integrity in the Legal Reasoning of the European Court of Justice", in *The European Court of Justice*, ed. de Búrca and Weiler, Oxford University Press, 2001, pp. 43-85, at pp. 51-60.

55 Bengoetxea, MacCormick and Moral Soriano start with "Step 0", which I accordingly do too.

Step 1. Categorising the legal problem (P, D). The Registrar and the Research and Documentation Division make an initial analysis of the case and search for (i) precedents, (ii) related cases pending before the Court, (iii) pieces of national legislation that need clarification, (iv) further factual information from the national court.

Step 2. Identifying the applicable rules (D). At this step the Court identifies all relevant legislation. It is common that the parties have invoked legal provisions that they consider applying to the case. However, the Court is not bound to apply the provisions invoked by the parties.

Step 3. Introducing the major premise (J). When the provisionally applicable provision or set of provisions has been selected, the major premise will also be identified. Usually, this is unproblematic because the parties, the referring national court and intervening parties, such as the Commission, all have identified the same provisions. In some cases, however, the legal issue is which relevant provisions apply.

Step 4. Deciding on the validity of the chosen provision (J). The provision that applies to the case must, of course, be valid. There are questions of validity that are "dressed up" as questions of interpretation for reasons of legal procedure. In particular, Bengoetxea, MacCormick and Moral Soriano state that the European Court of Justice has no jurisdiction, under preliminary references, to decide on the compatibility of domestic law with Community law. Therefore, the references enquiring into the validity of provisions of the law of a Member State will be reformulated as questions on the interpretation of Community law.[56] As we shall see, this is not an uncommon way of formulating questions to the Court in cases dealing with the compatibility of provisions of direct taxation with, for example, the freedom of establishment and the free movement of capital.

Step 5. Deciding on the need to interpret (D). The Court has now reached the step where the relevant provision of Community law has been chosen. This step includes the question of whether it is necessary to interpret the provision at issue. Here one should note that the Court may have previously dealt with the same interpretative question, and consequently there may be applicable precedents. In the *Da Costa*[57] and *CILFIT*[58] cases the Court developed the *acte clair* doctrine, previously discussed in this chapter, which in brief means that where a norm is clear there is no need for interpretation.

---

[56] Bengoetxea, MacCormick and Moral Soriano, "Integration and Integrity in the Legal Reasoning of the European Court of Justice", in *The European Court of Justice*, ed. de Búrca and Weiler, Oxford University Press, 2001, pp. 43-85, at p. 54.

[57] Joined cases 28-30/62 *Da Costa en Schaake NV v. Nederlandse Belastingadministratie.*

[58] Case 283/81 *CILFIT Srl v. Ministero della Sanità.*

Step 6. Interpreting the chosen provision (J). If the provision at issue needs interpretation the Court will of course interpret it. Here, I will not specifically deal with different methods of interpretation that the Court may apply, however, the topic has been briefly covered in section 1.6.1.

Step 7. Stating the law (J). The major premise of the case is formulated by the Court in a way that covers the facts of the case. This means that the Court must take into account the facts of the underlying case, as settled and established by the referring court, which the Court cannot question. Furthermore, the Court has to select the facts which are relevant and also to qualify and classify those facts, so that the major premise is formulated against the background of the correct facts.

Step 8. Establishing the facts (P, J). Even if the facts are in principle not at issue for the European Court of Justice, it will anyway put much effort into presenting the facts in such a way that the case may eventually serve as a precedent.

Step 9. The syllogism (P, J). The final step is the conclusion from the syllogism consisting of the previous steps. Bengoetxea, MacCormick and Moral Soriano point out that deduction does not solve the whole justification process, but it works as a negative test: if the decision does not follow from the premises, then the decision cannot be said to be justified.[59]

1.7 On General Principles in Community Law

General principles of law are an important part of Community law. Bernitz stresses that Community law is still not a "complete" legal system, but a system with considerable gaps in different areas of law.[60] Several of these general principles are contained in different acts of Community Law. For example, the EC Treaty contains several such principles, of which some will be discussed further in this section. According to Tridimas, the European Court of Justice has, among others, recognised the following principles of Community law: the principle of equal treatment or non-discrimination, the principle of proportionality, the principle of legal certainty, the principle of the protection of legitimate expectations, the protection of the fundamental rights, and the rights of defence.[61]

---

59 Bengoetxea, MacCormick and Moral Soriano, "Integration and Integrity in the Legal Reasoning of the European Court of Justice", in *The European Court of Justice*, ed. de Búrca and Weiler, Oxford University Press, 2001, pp. 43-85, at p. 60.

60 Bernitz, *Sverige och europarätten*, Norstedts Juridik, Stockholm, 2002, p. 38.

61 Tridimas, *The General Principles of EC Law*, Oxford University Press, Oxford, 1999, p. 4.

Article 6 (1) of the EC Treaty declares that the European Union is based on "the principles of liberty, democracy, respect for human rights and fundamental freedoms, and the rule of law, principles which are common to the Member States". Furthermore, Article 6 (2) states that the European Union shall respect fundamental rights, as laid down in the European Convention for the Protection of Human Rights and Fundamental Freedoms of 1950.

The European Court of Justice has independently created and manifested the general principles of law that it applies.[62] The Court applies a wide range of sources of law, not only Community law. Furthermore, it should be noted that according to Article 7 of the EC Treaty, the Council[63] acting in unanimity[64] may determine the existence of a serious and persistent breach by a Member State of principles mentioned in Article 6 (1), after inviting the government of the Member State in question to submit its observations.[65]

These general principles of law are binding not only on the Community and its institutions, but also on Member States and individuals in areas where the Community has legal competence.[66]

Article 10 of the EC Treaty contains the general principle of loyalty. It stipulates that Member States shall take all appropriate measures to ensure fulfilment of the obligations arising out of the EC Treaty or resulting from action taken by the institutions of the Community. The measures may be either general or particular. Member States shall also facilitate the achievement of the Community's tasks. Furthermore, Member States

---

62 Bernitz, *Sverige och europarätten*, Norstedts Juridik, Stockholm, 2002, p. 39.

63 That is, the Council meeting in the composition of the Heads of State or Government, according to Article 7, paragraph 1 of the Treaty on the European Union.

64 The proposal should be made either by at least one third of the Member States or by the Commission and after obtaining the assent of the European Parliament, according to Article 7, paragraph 1 of the Treaty on the European Union.

65 The relationship between national constitutional law of the Member States and Community law is a vast subject, which will not be dealt with any further in this part. It should however be mentioned that Sweden dealt with the question when entering the European Union, 1 January 1995, in a special provision of the Statute of Government (*regeringsformen*), Chapter 10, section 5. It could be said that Sweden constitutionally has adopted the German Solange doctrine (on the Solange doctrine, see for example Nielsen, *EU ret*, 2nd ed., Thomson/Gadjura, Copenhagen, 1999, p. 106). Chapter 10, section 5 of the Statute of Government states that the Parliament (*Riksdagen*) may delegate decision-making powers to the European Communities as long (*så länge*) as they have a protection of fundamental rights and freedoms that is equivalent to those contained in the Statute of Government and in the European Convention for the Protection of Human Rights and Fundamental Freedoms (signed in Rome on 4 November 1950).

66 It has been asked whether the principle of proportionality was part of Swedish legal tradition before membership of the European Union, but today the principle has been referred to in several cases by, among others, the Supreme Administrative Court (*Regeringsrätten*). Bernitz, *Sverige och europarätten*, Norstedts Juridik, Stockholm, p. 39.

shall abstain from any measure that could jeopardise the attainment of the objectives of the EC Treaty.

The principle of proportionality[67] is nowadays expressed in the EC Treaty. Article 5 stipulates that any action by the Community shall not go beyond what is necessary to achieve the objectives of the Treaty. The principle of proportionality means that public interference may not go beyond what is necessary in order to achieve the underlying aims of the interference.[68] The European Court of Justice has referred to the principle by applying the phrase "appropriate and necessary".[69] It could be said that there are three questions that should be posed when applying the principle of proportionality. First, is the interference aimed at achieving the objective in question? Secondly, is the interference *necessary* to achieve the objective or is there a less far-reaching alternative at hand? Thirdly, is the public benefit from the interference reasonable in proportion to the damage that the interference causes for the individual? This last question is more of a general consideration of the interference.

I also deal with the principle of proportionality in Chapter 3 in relation to the rule-of-reason doctrine.[70]

The principle of subsidiarity is stipulated in Article 5 of the EC Treaty. Article 5 (1) states that the Community shall act within the limits of the powers conferred upon it by the EC Treaty and of the objectives assigned to it in that Treaty. There are, however, limits also to those powers of the European Union. Article 5 (2) of the EC Treaty deals specifically with the principle of subsidiarity. The principle of subsidiarity means, according to this provision, that under certain conditions Member States and not the European Union shall take legislative action. The conditions for the principle to apply – and for the Community to take legislative action – are first, that the objectives of the proposed action cannot be sufficiently achieved by the Member States. Secondly, by reason of the scale or effects of the proposed action, the Community can better achieve the objectives.

It should be mentioned that the principle of subsidiarity is also stipulated in Article 2 of the Treaty on the European Union. This provision states that the objectives of the European Union shall be achieved while respecting the principle of subsidiarity as defined in Article 5 of the EC Treaty.

---

67 Reference to in the Swedish cases RÅ 1996 ref. 40, RÅ 1996 ref. 44 and RÅ 2000 ref. 49.

68 Bernitz, *Sverige och europarätten*, Norstedts Juridik, Stockholm, 2002, p. 41.

69 *Ibid.*

70 General studies on the principle of proportionality include, for example, Emliou, *The Principle of Proportionality in European Law*, London, 1996; and Moëll, *Proportionalitetsprincipen i skatterätten*, Acta Societatis Juridicae Lundensis, No 147, Juristförlaget i Lund, 2003 (where the latter is particularly concentrated on the proportionality principle and tax law).

1.8 On the Relationship between Community Law and National Law

1.8.1 Introduction

One important characteristic of the relationship between Community law and national law is the doctrine of "direct effect". This doctrine, although questioned by some, has had a vital impact on the development of Community law. That Community law may have direct effect, and accordingly will have to be considered by national courts has meant that the system of preliminary rulings by the European Court of Justice has been vitalised. In this section I will briefly deal with the supremacy of Community law and the doctrine of direct effect.

1.8.2 The Supremacy of Community Law and Claims of Reparation

In a large number of cases, the European Court of Justice has declared the supremacy of Community law over national law. A renowned example is Case 106/77 *Simmenthal*[71] where the Court, among other things, had to decide what consequences flow from the direct applicability of a provision of Community law in the event of incompatibility with a subsequent legislative provision of a Member State.[72] The European Court of Justice declared that according to "… the principle of precedence of Community law, the relationship between provisions of the treaty and *directly applicable measures of the institutions* on the one hand and the national law of the Member States on the other is such that those provisions and measures not only by their entry into force *render automatically inapplicable any conflicting provision of current national law* but – in so far as they are an integral part of, and take precedence in, the legal order applicable in the territory of each of the Member States – *also preclude the valid adoption of new national legislative measures to the extent to which they would be incompatible with Community provisions*".[73] This statement by the Court leaves little doubt on the supremacy of directly applicable Community law over conflicting national law. But even if a provision of Community law is not directly applicable, there are occasions where Community law still has precedence over national law.[74]

The relationship between national constitutional law and Community law has been the subject of decisions by supreme courts of several Member States, most notably the German *Bundesverfassungsgericht* in two cases commonly referred to as Solange

---

[71] Case 106/77 *Administrazione delle Finanze dello Stato v. Simmenthal SpA.*

[72] Case 106/77 *Simmenthal*, para. 13.

[73] Case 106/77 *Simmenthal*, para. 17 (emphasis added).

[74] Kapteyn and VerLoren van Themaat, *Introduction to the Law of the European Communities*, 3rd ed., Kluwer Law International, London/The Hague/Boston, 1998, p. 551.

I from 1974 and Solange II from 1986. In Solange I the *Bundesverfassungsgericht* declared that it had the right to review Community regulations against the fundamental rights of the German constitution as long as (*solange*) the process of integration in the Community had developed to the stage where the Community itself had a codified catalogue of fundamental rights adopted by a democratically and elected parliament. Furthermore, the *Bundesverfassungsgericht* required that such a Community catalogue would have to include the same rights and guarantees as the German constitution. The *Bundesverfassungsgericht* altered its approach in Solange II. The *Bundesverfassungsgericht* concluded that Community law had reached a stage where it fulfilled the requirements declared in Solange I. The German constitutional court stated that as long as (*solange*) this guarantee was at hand, the court would not consider cases that challenged Community law with the German constitution.

As regards directives, Member States have failed on a number of occasions to implement them correctly, be it either in time or even at all. In the important decision in the joined cases C-6 and 9/90 *Francovich et al. v. Italy* the European Court of Justice declared that Member States that do not implement Community law correctly are liable for damages suffered by individuals through the breach of Community law. In the *Francovich* case the European Court of Justice stipulated three conditions for individuals to claim reparations:[75]

(i) The result prescribed by the directive must entail the grant of rights to individuals.

(ii) It must be possible to identify the content of those rights on the basis of the provisions of the directive.

(iii) There must be a causal link between the breach of the state's obligations and the loss and damage suffered by the injured parties.

According to the Court in the *Francovich* case, reparations had to be made relying on the national system of the Member States. The practice of the European Court of Justice has continued to develop in this area. The *Francovich* case did leave questions unanswered. Considering later case-law, Kapteyn and VerLoren van Themaat deduce three conditions for a right of reparation if three cumulative conditions were satisfied:[76]

(i) The rule of law infringed was intended to confer rights on individuals.

(ii) The breach was sufficiently serious.

[75] Kapteyn and VerLoren van Themaat, *op. cit.*, p. 565.

[76] Kapteyn and VerLoren van Themaat, *op. cit.*, pp. 567-568.

(iii) There was a direct causal link between the breach of the state's obligations and the damage sustained by the injured parties.[77]

1.8.3 The Doctrine of Direct Effect

The relationship between Community law and national law has been subject to a broad scholarly discussion. In principle the prevailing view is that Community law forms an integral part of the national legislation of the Member States which their courts are bound to apply. However, Community law contains elements of both legislative reasoning and technique that is different from the traditional national legislation of Member States. Consequently, Community law may be *perceived* as a separate system, even if it is not. If there is a conflict between national law and Community law, the latter has precedence. The European Court of Justice declared this already in 1964 in Case 6/64 *Costa v. ENEL.*[78]

Prechal defines "direct effect" in the following way: "[d]irect effect is the obligation of a court or another authority to apply the relevant provisions of Community law, either as a norm which governs the case or as a standard for legal review."[79]

Up to 1970 the doctrine of direct effect emerged from questions put forward by national courts to the European Court of Justice as to whether private parties could rely on different provisions of the EEC Treaty in cases against the national authorities – labelled "vertical direct effect".[80] After 1970 the European Court of Justice was also asked whether provisions of Community law could be relied upon by private parties against other private parties – labelled "horizontal direct effect".[81]

---

[77] In the joined cases C-46/93 and C-48/93 *Brasserie du Pêcheur SA v. Bundesrepublik Deutschland and The Queen v. Secretary of State for Transport, ex parte: Factortame Ltd and others*, para. 74, the European Court of Justice declared: "...where a breach of Community law by a Member State is attributable to the national legislature acting in a field in which it has a wide discretion to make legislative choices, individuals suffering loss or injury thereby are entitled to reparation where the rule of Community law breached is intended to confer rights upon them, the breach is sufficiently serious and there is a direct causal link between the breach and the damage sustained by the individuals".

[78] Case 6/64 *Flaminio Costa v. ENEL.*

[79] Prechal, "Does Direct Effect Still Matter?", *CML Rev.* 2000 p. 1048 (with further references). Prechal concludes that in recent years there are very few cases of the ECJ where the question of direct effect was a "real issue". Prechal, "Direct Effect Reconsidered, Redefined and Rejected", in *Direct Effect: Rethinking a Classic EC Legal Doctrine*, Prinssen and Schrauven (ed.), Europa Law Publishing, Groningen, 2002, pp. 17-41, at p. 17.

[80] Kapteyn and VerLoren van Themaat, *Introduction to the Law of the European Communities*, 3rd ed., Kluwer Law International, London/The Hague/Boston, 1998, p. 529. A well-known example of "vertical direct effect" is Case 26/62, *Van Gend en Loos v. Nederlandse Administratie der Belastingen.*

[81] Kapteyn and VerLoren van Themaat, *op. cit.*, p. 529. An early example of "horizontal direct effect" is Case 43/75 *Defrenne v. Sabena.*

It can be deduced from the case-law of the European Court of Justice that three conditions have to be fulfilled if a provision of Community law has direct effect:

(i) *The content of the obligation must be clear and precise.* This condition does not require, however, that the provision in question is free from interpretative difficulties or from complex wording.[82]

(ii) *The wording of the provision must make the obligation unconditional and unqualified.* According to Kapteyn and VerLoren van Themaat a provision is conditional as long as it is inapplicable for a certain period. When that period has come to an end the provision is accordingly applicable.[83] The Member States shall not be left with any discretion regarding the date when the obligation must be fulfilled.

(iii) *The absence of discretion in the implementation of obligations.* Kapteyn and VerLoren van Themaat consider this condition to be the most important. They note that the absence of discretion could also be said to be part of the other two criteria.[84]

However, in recent years the doctrine of direct effect has come under criticism for being hollow. It has been argued that this doctrine has been stretched so far that the scope for Community law not having direct effect has been severely minimised. Prechal argues that the concept of direct effect has become so wide and diluted that it has lost its explanatory value.[85] It is not my intention to enter into this discussion here, but the question of whether the subsequently analysed provisions on the freedom of establishment and the free movement of capital have direct effect will be noted. Bernitz explains the consequences of direct effect of Community law in the area of direct taxation in the following way:[86] Community law with direct effect is superior to national law. National courts and tax authorities are obliged not to apply national tax law that is in conflict with Community law. That can be achieved either by explicitly setting aside national law or by interpreting national law in a way that makes it consistent with Community law.

---

82 Kapteyn and VerLoren van Themaat, *op. cit.*, p. 530.

83 *Ibid.*

84 Kapteyn and VerLoren van Themaat, *op. cit.*, p. 533.

85 Prechal, "Does Direct Effect Still Matter?", *CML Rev.* 2000 p. 1068.

86 Bernitz, "EG-rättens likabehandlingsprincip som instrument för skatteharmonisering", in *Festskrift till Gustaf Lindencrona*, Arvidsson, Melz and Silfverberg (ed.), Norstedts Juridik, Stockholm, 2003, pp. 93-108, at p. 106.

1.8.4 Consequences of a Breach of the EC Treaty by a Member State

Article 228 of the EC Treaty deals with the situation where the European Court of Justice has decided that a Member State has failed to fulfil an obligation under the EC Treaty. In that situation the Member State shall be required to take the necessary measures to comply with the judgment of the Court.[87] It is for the Commission to supervise that the Member State in question fulfils its obligation of compliance. If the Member State does not comply, the Commission is obliged to act.[88] It shall first hear the Member State in question by permitting it to submit an observation. Furthermore, the Commission shall issue a reasoned opinion where it specifies the points on which the Member State has not complied with the Court's judgment.

The Commission shall stipulate a time limit within which the Member State will have to take the necessary steps to comply with the judgment of the Court. If the Member State fails to do this, the Commission may bring a case before the Court. When filing the case to the Court, the Commission is obliged to specify the amount of the lump sum or penalty payment to be paid by the Member State which it finds appropriate.[89]

1.8.5 Consequences of the Court's Case-law in the Field of Direct Taxation

This study is focused on the case-law of the European Court of Justice in the field of direct taxation. All cases subject to analysis deal with the interpretation of fundamental freedoms and the question of whether national measures are in breach of those freedoms. The Court has exclusive competence of interpreting the EC Treaty. National courts are bound by the decisions of the European Court of Justice.

Moreover, the fundamental freedoms of the EC Treaty discussed in this study all have direct effect. That means that there is no need for any legislative act implementing the fundamental freedoms, and, for example, national courts and parliaments have to abide by the fundamental freedoms as interpreted by the Court.

In Chapter 2 there will be an overview of the provisions of the EC Treaty which deal with matters of direct taxation. Already at this stage it should be noted that today it is clear that the European Union has competence in the field of direct taxation. The adoption of directives in this field is clear evidence of that. However, to reach a Community decision in the field of direct taxation, unanimity among the Member States is required.

87 Article 228 (1) of the EC Treaty.

88 Article 228 (2) of the EC Treaty.

89 Article 228 of the EC Treaty.

2 Direct Taxation: the EC Treaty and Community Policy

2.1 Introduction

This chapter is intended to present the policy and the EC Treaty framework for the work of the European Union in the field of direct taxation. The core of the general study is, however, only one element of Community policy in this field of law: the case-law of the European Court of Justice on the freedom of establishment and free capital movements in relation to direct taxation. Even so, I consider it essential to provide a wider picture to understand the significance of that case-law.

This chapter contains the following parts. *Section 2.2* gives a general presentation of the tax policy of the European Union. The main source is two policy documents from the Commission published in 2001. The EC Treaty and direct taxation is the subject of *section 2.3*. Provisions of the EC Treaty which expressly refer to matters of direct taxation are discussed. Furthermore, the Commission has published several major studies on European company taxation. *Section 2.4* deals with the 1992 Ruding Report. The 2001 Staff Report is discussed in *section 2.5*. Finally, *section 2.6* deals with results achieved on harmonisation of company taxation within the European Union. That section is only intended as a brief survey of these results. One recent result, the package to tackle harmful tax competition, is discussed separately in *section 2.7*. The 1990 proposal on a directive on the cross-border offsetting of losses is presented in *section 2.8*. Concluding remarks are made in *section 2.9*.

2.2 General Presentation of the Present European Union Tax Policy

2.2.1 Introduction

It is no understatement that direct taxation in recent years has been the focus of the policy debate of the European Union. Generally, there are two main issues that have been addressed. First, there is the question of "harmful tax competition". A majority of the Member States wish to abolish certain preferential tax regimes harboured by some of the Member States. The *Primarolo Report*[1] identified a number of such regimes. It

---

1 Report of the Code of Conduct group on business taxation as submitted to the ECOFIN Council on 29 November 1999 (the group was chaired by Mrs Primarolo and thus known as "the Primarolo Report").

has been difficult to reach unanimity among the Member States for adopting measures countering harmful tax practices. Secondly, there is the question of substituting a qualified majority requirement for the unanimity requirement now applicable to Council decisions on matters of direct taxation. This is a question that has gained increasing interest by the fact that the European Union in 2004 has been expanded with ten new Member States. If the unanimity requirement is maintained, the expanded number of Member States will inevitably mean an increased risk of not reaching unanimity on Community measures in the field of direct taxation.

2.2.2 The Commission's 2001 Tax Policy Document

2.2.2.1 General Policy Objectives

An important tax policy document is the 2001 communication from the Commission: Tax policy in the European Union – Priorities for the years ahead.[2] As a starting-point for the discussion, the Commission quotes the strategic goal for the European Union declared by the European Council in Lisbon 2001: "... to become the most competitive and dynamic knowledge-based economy in the world, capable of sustainable economic growth with more and better jobs and greater social cohesion".

The Commission notes that the third stage of the European Monetary Union (EMU) has put budgetary developments into focus, and the Broad Economic Policy Guidelines (BEPG) have forced Member States to examine their tax policies. Budgetary balance has developed as an important objective of the fiscal policy of the Member States, also for those Members that are not part of the EMU.

Three general objectives of the tax policy of the European Union are declared. First, it should focus on the removal of tax obstacles to the exercise of the four freedoms. Furthermore, tax consequences must be clear to the tax subjects. Both the removal of tax obstacles and the demand for clarity require that tax systems are made simpler and more transparent. The Commission notes that the work against harmful tax competition by the European Union and the OECD serves increased transparency. However, it is interesting to note that the Commission recognises that "... some degree of tax competition within the EU may be inevitable and may contribute to lower tax pressure".[3]

Secondly, tax measures by the European Union have to contribute to a higher efficiency in the goods, services and capital markets as well as a properly functioning labour market. As regards tax policy these also include the removal of tax obstacles and

2 Tax policy in the European Union – Priorities for the years ahead. COM(2001) 260 final.

3 Tax policy in the European Union – Priorities for the years ahead. COM(2001) 260 final, p. 8.

distortions, a simplification of the national tax systems and a more efficient system for tax collection in order to offset any possible losses of revenue from the co-ordinated elimination of tax obstacles.

Thirdly, the European Union should continue to facilitate efforts to cut nominal rates and broaden the tax base that are considered to reduce the economic distortions associated with Member States' tax systems. In my view, these three objectives can hardly be seen as separate; they are linked and functions of each other.

It should be underlined that it is not the objective of the Commission to establish a single unified tax system for the European Union. As long as national tax systems are in line with Community law, there is no need for harmonisation. The Commission even states, "... in many tax fields harmonisation is neither necessary nor desirable in view of the widely differing characteristics of Member States' tax systems and different national preferences".[4]

The Commission is furthermore of the view that a move to qualified majority decisions on certain tax issues is indispensable, but it is common knowledge that some Member States such as the United Kingdom, Ireland and Sweden, at present at least, are strong opponents.

2.2.2.2 Specific Objectives for Company Taxation

More specifically, as regards company taxation, an important objective of the Commission is to ensure that EU company tax systems facilitate increased cross-border activity and modern organisational structures of companies.[5] Concerning the present situation of company taxation, it is, according to the Commission, characterised by numerous cases of discrimination, double taxation, excessive administrative costs due to complicated administrative procedures and delays in tax refunds.

The Commission is critical of the decision process so far in the field of direct taxation. The Commission favours decisions being made after the proposal of directives and regulations, because these are adopted after full discussion in the Council, the Parliament and the Economic and Social Committee. Furthermore, the European Court of Justice may enforce such legislative acts.[6] However, few acts have finally been adopted, even if a number of them have been proposed. "Soft legislation" is also considered as a possible measure. The Code of Conduct for business taxation is such a measure.

4 Tax policy in the European Union – Priorities for the years ahead. COM(2001) 260 final, p. 9.

5 Tax policy in the European Union – Priorities for the years ahead. COM(2001) 260 final, p. 16 *et seq.*

6 Tax policy in the European Union – Priorities for the years ahead. COM(2001) 260 final, p. 21.

"Soft legislation" is characterised by the fact that it is not legally binding, but it exerts a "peer pressure" on the Member States to make them comply.

2.2.3 The Commission's View on Company Taxation as of 2001

In 2001 the Commission also published a report where it presented its views on company taxation – Towards an Internal Market without Tax Obstacles.[7] This report is based on a wider and more thorough report, the 2001 Staff Report,[8] which will be discussed later on in this chapter. It should be underlined that it is not my purpose in the present study to give a detailed description and analysis of either the Commission report or the Staff Report.

The Commission predicts that the enlargement of the European Union will raise new and emphasise existing problems with European company taxation.[9]

It is worth noting that the Commission favours a two-track strategy for European company taxation. The first track includes targeted measures that will address the most urgent problems in the short- and mid-term. The second track is "a comprehensive solution" including a consolidated corporate tax base for the entire EU activities of the companies in question.[10]

2.2.4 The Commission's 2003 Tax Policy Report

In November 2003 the Commission published a follow-up report[11] ("Communication") to the one presented in 2001, which was discussed in the previous section. The report deals with the present situation regarding the two-track strategy against tax-related inefficiencies and obstacles to cross-border economic activity in the Internal Market. One track consists of targeted immediate solutions and the other track comprises steps to a common consolidated tax base for business within the European Union.

---

7 Towards an Internal Market without Tax Obstacles. A Strategy for Providing Companies with a Consolidated Corporate Tax Base for their EU-wide Activities. COM(2001) 582 final.

8 Company Taxation in the Internal Market. SEC(2001) 1681 (subsequently referred to as "the 2001 Staff Report").

9 The thirteen candidate countries were Bulgaria, the Czech Republic, Cyprus, Estonia, Hungary, Latvia, Lithuania, Malta, Poland, Romania, Slovakia, Slovenia and Turkey. From 1 May 2004 all but Bulgaria, Romania and Turkey joined the EU as full Member States.

10 Towards an Internal Market without Tax Obstacles, A Strategy for Providing Companies with a Consolidated Corporate Tax Base for their EU-wide Activities. COM(2001) 582 final, p. 11.

11 An Internal Market without Company Tax Obstacles Achievements, Ongoing Initiatives and Remaining Challenges. COM(2003) 726 final.

Here I will only relate those parts of the report which deal with the significance of the case-law of the European Court of Justice, and the implications on Member States' tax systems.

The Commission recognises that some areas, so far, have been successful. It is noted that "[t]he case law of the European Court of Justice is gaining in importance". The need for companies to deal with 25 or, in the future, even more tax systems clearly remains the primary problem, according to the Commission.

The Commission specifically recognises that the number of important corporate tax cases submitted to the European Court of Justice has increased significantly. In relation to this, the Commission declares: "However, a piecemeal approach to tax obstacles by way of litigation could lead to new problems in Member States' tax legislation and perhaps even – in the worst case – prove harmful for the completion of the Internal Market."[12]

It seems obvious that the Commission in general supports the negative integration process conducted by the European Court of Justice, but that it does not consider that process to be sufficient. Moreover, one could also notice a fear of the results of the "piecemeal approach" that the Court has to take in its case-law.

The decisions by the European Court of Justice sometimes have "assymetrical effects", according to the Commission.[13] The reason is, of course, that the consequences of decisions involving the tax legislation of one Member State are not always clear in relation to other Member States. In its 2001 report the Commission stated that it intended to co-ordinate the study of the consequences for all Member States on decisions by the European Court of Justice. The Commission has tested that approach in relation to the tax treatment of occupational pensions and investment funds. The readiness of some Member States to cooperate could have been better, in the view of the Commission.

The Commission notes that a tentative discussion at the working group level has taken place regarding the effect of the Court's decision in case C-324/00 *Lankhorst-Hohorst* on the permissibility of thin capitalisation rules.

The Commission concludes that the reluctance of some Member States to co-ordinate their tax systems can only lead to more and more decisions by the Court, an outcome that such Member States "might perceive as 'destructive'".[14] Therefore the Commission

---

12 An Internal Market without Company Tax Obstacles Achievements, Ongoing Initiatives and Remaining Challenges. COM(2003) 726 final, p. 6.

13 An Internal Market without Company Tax Obstacles Achievements, Ongoing Initiatives and Remaining Challenges. COM(2003) 726 final, pp. 6-7.

14 An Internal Market without Company Tax Obstacles Achievements, Ongoing Initiatives and Remaining Challenges. COM(2003) 726 final, p. 7.

hopes for a better discussion among Member States on the Court decisions in the area of taxation.

Furthermore, the Commission recognises the importance of the case-law of the Court, in relation to the treatment of cross-border losses and the status of tax treaties vis-à-vis Community law.

2.2.5 Concluding Remarks

Today it is almost a truism that the Community's achievements in the field of direct taxation are rather modest. Some directives have been adopted that also have been subject to continuous revision. The package against harmful tax competition was finally adopted in June 2003.

Even if the Commission has undertaken considerable efforts to reach a decision on measures to remove barriers to intra-Community trade in the area of direct taxation, comparably little has been achieved so far. Is it the intention of the Commission to harmonise Member States legislation on direct taxation? The verb *to harmonise* in the field of direct taxation is hardly *le mot de ralliement* – the watchword – of today. In a speech held in Ostia, Italy, 5 December 2003, Frits Bolkestein[15] explained: "The notion that Brussels has a long-term agenda of wholesale tax harmonisation is just utter nonsense. The continuing tax barriers between our Member States often amount to legal discrimination in the terms of the EU Treaty. At the same time, they result in real substantial losses to the welfare of our economies and our citizens. It may be difficult to put a figure on the losses but businesses active 'in the field' know all too well that they occur. For *both* these reasons the tax barriers must be removed, in the short term by targeted measures and in the longer term by a systematic solution such as a common EU tax base."[16]

Even if the policy of the Commission is not to harmonise in the field of direct taxation, it surely is active in the work on removing tax barriers to cross-border transactions within the Community.

15 At the time, Mr Frits Bolkestein was member of the European Commission in charge of the Internal Market and Customs as well as EU Corporate Tax Reform.

16 Bolkestein, "EU Corporate Tax Reform: Progress and New Challenges, Opening Address at the European Commission Conference on Company Taxation", *EC Tax Review*, 2004, pp. 5-6, at p. 6.

2.3 The EC Treaty and Direct Taxation

2.3.1 Introduction

There is little explicit reference in the EC Treaty to matters of direct taxation. There are, however, a few such provisions. Article 58 was included with the Maastricht Treaty in 1992 and added to the part of the EC Treaty dealing with the free movement of capital and payments. Article 58 (1) (a) provides that Article 56, which is the basic provision of this freedom, shall be without prejudice to the right of the Member States to apply the relevant provisions of their tax law which distinguish between taxpayers who are not in the same situation with regard to their place of residence or with regard to the place where the capital is situated. The actual meaning of this provision has been the subject of much discussion, which I will deal with in Chapter 6.

Articles 90 to 93 deal with indirect taxation, which is outside the scope of this study. Of more peripheral interest here is Article 163 on research and technological development. The Article states that the Community shall have as an objective to strengthen the scientific and technological basis of the Community. For this purpose the Community shall support "the removal of legal and fiscal obstacles to that cooperation".[17]

Furthermore, the part of the EC Treaty which deals with environmental issues also makes brief mention of fiscal provisions of the Member States. Article 174 of the EC Treaty stipulates the objectives of the Community policy on the environment. Those measures include, for example, preserving, protecting and improving the quality of the environment as well as protecting human health. The Council shall decide what action is to be taken by the Community in order to achieve the Community objectives as stated in Article 174 of the EC Treaty.[18] "[P]rovisions primarily of a fiscal nature", are stipulated in Article 175 of the EC Treaty as a means of reaching the environmental objectives of the Community. A special decision-making procedure is also provided for in Article 175 of the EC Treaty, however, unanimity by the Council is still required.

Article 293 of the EC Treaty explicitly deals with matters of direct taxation. It is provided in Article 293 in the field of tax law that Member States shall, so far as is necessary, enter into negotiations with each other with a view to securing for the benefit of their nationals "the abolition of double taxation within the Community".

---

[17] That is, cooperation between "undertakings", including small and medium-sized undertakings, research centres and universities in their research and technological development activities of high quality (Article 163 (2) of the EC Treaty).

[18] Article 175 of the EC Treaty.

2.3.2 Articles 94 and 95 of the EC Treaty

It is undisputable that the European Union has normative competence in the area of direct taxation. Title VI of the EC Treaty deals with the "approximation of laws".[19] Article 94 stipulates that the Council shall issue directives for the approximation of such laws, regulations or administrative provisions of the Member States "as directly affect the establishment or functioning of the common market". The Council shall act unanimously. A proposal from the Commission on the directive shall be presented before the European Parliament and the Economic and Social Committee.

The fact that the Council has to act unanimously unquestionably limits the prospects for an "approximation" of legislation on direct taxation within the Community.

Article 95 of the EC Treaty does clear the way for decisions by the Council acting by a qualified majority.[20] However, Article 95 (2) explicitly excludes "fiscal provisions" from the scope of such decisions. Article 95 (1) was introduced by the Single European Act in 1986 with the aim of strengthening the decision making-power of the Council. The Member States were, however, not ready to surrender their *de facto* veto power in matters of taxation.

The Commission is of the opinion that it is important that decisions on mutual assistance and administrative cooperation are taken in the Council by a qualified majority, as provided under Article 95 of the EC Treaty.[21] Today such decisions would need unanimity in accordance with Article 93 of the EC Treaty.

2.3.3 Article 293 of the EC Treaty

As previously noted, Article 293 (ex Article 220) of the EC Treaty also refers to matters of direct taxation and stipulates:

> "Member States shall, so far as is necessary, enter into negotiations with each other with a view to securing for the benefit of their nationals:
>
> …
>
> – the abolition of double taxation within the Community".

---

19 More precisely, Title VI of the EC Treaty deals with common rules on competition, taxation and approximation of laws.

20 Cf. Article 251 of the EC Treaty.

21 Tax Policy in the European Union – Priorities for the Years Ahead, COM(2001) 260 final, p. 7.

In case C-336/96 *Gilly*, the European Court of Justice declared that this provision does not have direct effect. The Court stated that the provision merely defines a number of matters on which the Member States are to enter into negotiations with each other, but only "as far as necessary".[22] Thus the abolition of double taxation is such a matter. According to the Court it is clear from the wording that the provision "cannot itself confer on individuals any rights on which they might be able to rely before their national courts".[23]

In my view Article 293 leaves one question unanswered: What is meant by "double taxation"? Is it economic double taxation or international juridical double taxation, or, perhaps, both? I would say that it is reasonably clear that the Article at least refers to international juridical double taxation, and the extent to which it might refer to economic double taxation is limited.[24]

Tax treaties on income and capital serve to avoid international juridical double taxation. The treaty network between the Member States is today, however, still incomplete, even if the remaining gaps are few. After Sweden and Portugal signed a tax treaty in August 2002, 18 years after entering treaty negotiations, the only missing link between the 15 Member States (before the 10 new Member States in 2004) is that between Greece and Ireland.[25]

2.3.4 The "Competence Declaration" in Matters of Direct Taxation

The question of whether the European Court of Justice was competent in matters of direct taxation was for some time in doubt.[26] However, for the past two decades it has been clear that the Court has this competence. The way in which the Court

---

22 Case C-336/96 *Gilly*, para. 15. On Article 293 (ex Article 220) of the EC Treaty, see e.g. Rädler, Tax treaties and the internal market, Annex 6 to the 1992 Ruding Report, pp. 371 – 379.

23 Case C-336/96 *Gilly*, para. 16.

24 Avery Jones interprets the reference in Article 293 (ex Article 220) of the EC Treaty to "double taxation" in the following way: "Double taxation can mean a number of things but here probably means no more than the type of double taxation that tax treaties normally solves, which is far from eliminating all cases of economic double taxation." Avery Jones, "Flows of Capital between the EU and Third Countries and the Consequences of Disharmony in European International Tax Law", *EC Tax Review*, 1998, pp. 95-106, at p. 96. On Article 220 of the EEC Treaty (present Article 293 of the EC Treaty) see also Lindencrona, *Skatter och kapitalflykt*, Jurist- och samhällsvetareförbundets Förlags AB, Stockholm, 1972, p. 27.

25 Eicker, *EC Tax Scene*, Intertax 2002, p. 521.

26 An example of the diverging views on the competence of the Community (and thereby also of the ECJ) is the opinion of AG Darmon in case C-175/88 *Biehl*. In his opinion in this case AG Darmon explained (para. 10): "It is of course quite clearly for the Member States alone to lay down the rules governing income tax; as Community law stands at present, direct taxation is outside the scope of the EEC Treaty." Today, we know for certain that this is not true.

formulates this competence is somewhat ambiguous. For example in case C-311/97 *Royal Bank of Scotland* the Court declared: "The first point to be made is that, although direct taxation falls within their competence, the Member States must none the less exercise that competence consistently with Community law and avoid discrimination on grounds of nationality ...".[27] This declaration by the Court means that it considers itself to have competence also to decide on the compatibility of national legislation on direct taxation with fundamental freedoms. I refer to it as the "competence declaration". The first time the Court expressed this "competence declaration" in matters of direct taxation (in relation to individuals) was in case C-279/93 *Schumacker*.[28] The declaration in the *Schumacker* case was a bit different from the previously quoted declaration in the *Royal Bank of Scotland* case. In the *Schumacker* case the Court declared: "Although, as Community law stands at present, direct taxation does not as such fall within the purview of the Community, the powers retained by the Member States must nevertheless be exercised consistently with Community law ...".[29] But already in 1995 when the *Schumacker* case was decided by the European Court of Justice, measures on direct taxation had been adopted by the Community, most notably the 1990 Parent/Subsidiary Directive and the Merger Directive. Direct taxation did fall within the purview of the Community, even if the unanimity requirement made such acts of legislation rare.

Still, there is another aspect which makes both versions of the "competence declaration" ambiguous. On the one hand Member States are sovereign in the area of taxation – of which the unanimity requirement in the Council on such matters is an expression. On the other hand, that competence must be exercised consistently with Community law.[30] Yet, the effect of the Court's decisions in the area of direct taxation is clear: for example, national courts are bound by the preliminary rulings of the Court. Member States retain their sovereignty in the field of taxation, but only to the extent that it is consistent with Community law.[31]

---

27 Case C-311/97 *Royal Bank of Scotland*, para. 19. See similar declarations by the ECJ in e.g. case C-279/93 *Schumacker*, para. 21, and case C-294/97, *Eurowings*, para. 32.

28 Cf. Wathelet, "Direct Taxation and EU Law: Integration or Disintegration?", *EC Tax Review*, 2004, pp. 2-4, at p. 2.

29 Case C-279/93 *Schumacker*, para. 21.

30 Mutén strongly questions whether it is possible to keep the veto power of individual Member States in a Community with 25 Member States. Mutén, "Skattesuveräniteten och det internationella samarbetet – några funderingar", in *Festskrift tillägnad Edward Andersson*, Sevón, Frände, Olsson, Ryynänen and Tikka (ed.), 2003, pp. 211-223.

31 Van Thiel similarly concludes that the idea of an exclusive national competence for income taxes must be rejected. Van Thiel, *EU Case Law on Income Tax, Part 1*, IBFD, Amsterdam, 2001, p. 16.

2.4 The 1992 Ruding Report on European Company Taxation

2.4.1 Background

Matters of direct taxation have been subject to inquiries and official reports by the Community practically from its beginning. An early report was the 1962 Neumark Report, which dealt with general principles which should govern tax harmonisation and also included recommendations.[32] In the following I will present two of the more recent reports: the 1992 Ruding Report (section 2.4) and the 2001 Staff Report (section 2.5).

2.4.2 General Objectives

In 1990 the Commission formed a special Committee on the subject of European company taxation.[33] The chairman of the Committee was Professor Onno Ruding, and it is accordingly known as the Ruding Committee. The results were presented in 1992.

It was the objective of the Committee to consider three general questions:[34]

(1) Do differences in taxation among Member States cause major distortions in the internal market, particularly with respect to investment decisions and competition? Special attention was given to those distortions considered to be discriminatory.

(2) In so far as distortions arise, are they likely to be eliminated simply through the interplay of market forces and tax competition between Member States, or is action at the Community level required?

(3) What specific measures are required at the Community level to remove or mitigate these distortions?

In addition, the Ruding Committee examined to what extent tax measures should be used to enforce social and economic objectives, such as the fair treatment of small and medium-sized business, as well as regional development. The Committee did, hardly surprisingly, find distortions in the internal market due to differences in taxation. Several

---

32 Martín Jiménez, *Towards Corporate Tax Harmonisation in the European Community*, Kluwer Law International, London/The Hague/Boston, 1999, p. 107.

33 Report of the Committee of independent experts on company taxation. Delivered by the Commission of the European Communities, March 1992 (here referred to as the 1992 Ruding Report). The 1992 Ruding Report was preceded by other reports, such as the Neumark Report of 1962 and the van den Tempel Report of 1970. On these reports see e.g. Martín Jiménez, *Towards Corporate Tax Harmonisation in the European Community*, pp. 106-115.

34 The 1992 Ruding Report, p. 24.

different forms of distortion were identified. One concerned investment decisions. Of particular concern for the Committee in that respect was the way in which Member States discriminated against foreign investment. Another form of distortion dealt with certain cross-border transactions, such as transfer pricing. The final category of distortions constituted the lack of transparency of national tax systems.

Consequently, taxpayers were considered to have considerable costs of complying with the demands of foreign tax systems within the Community. In order to deal with the identified problems, the Ruding Committee proposed a number of actions at Community level, actions which will be referred to later on in section 2.4.

2.4.3 Identified Problem Areas and Potential Countermeasures

A general conclusion of the Committee was that there were differences between the company tax systems of the Member States. Those differences included for example such basic elements as the statutory company tax rate and the company tax base. There were also differences regarding the tax treatment of cross-border income flows, such as dividends, interest and royalty payments.

Both through a simulation study and an empirical study, the Committee tried to identify whether differences in company taxation were the cause of major distortions and whether they were discriminatory. The Committee concluded that there had in fact been some convergence in the area of company taxation of Member States, for example reducing both company and personal statutory tax rates and reducing tax concessions.

The Committee identified three areas where the Community should concentrate its priorities:[35]

(a) removing those discriminatory and distortionary features of countries' tax arrangements that impede cross-border business investment and shareholding;

(b) setting a minimum level for statutory company tax rates and also common rules for a minimum tax base, so as to limit excessive tax competition between Member States intended to attract mobile investment or taxable profits of multinational firms, both of which tend to erode the tax base in the Community as a whole;

(c) encouraging maximum transparency of any tax incentives granted by Member States to promote investment with a preference for incentives, if any, of a non-fiscal character.

[35] The 1992 Ruding Report, p. 13.

The Committee also delivered specific recommendations, which were divided into three categories. The recommendations also fell into specific phases in time for implementing them.

The measures were divided into the following categories: (a) elimination of the double taxation of cross-border income flows, (b) company taxes, and (c) other issues. The time phases for the measures to be taken were, for phase I, the end of 1994, for phase II, immediately with a view to implementation during the second phase of economic and monetary union, and for phase III (1 January 1999) it was "envisaged" as being concurrent with full economic and monetary union.

2.4.4 Elimination of Double Taxation of Cross-border Income Flows

The elimination of double taxation of cross-border income flows was the general objective of category (a). This general objective included six different part-objectives with recommendations on how to achieve those part-objectives.

The first part-objective was to eliminate withholding taxes levied by source countries on dividends paid by subsidiaries to parent companies. The Committee had two recommendations for achieving this part-objective. The first recommendation was to extend the scope of the Parent/Subsidiary Directive to include all enterprises subject to corporate income tax irrespective of their legal form (phase I). Subsequently, the directive should be extended to include all other enterprises subject to income tax. The second recommendation was to introduce a substantial reduction in the participation threshold as prescribed in the Parent/Subsidiary Directive (phase I).

The second part-objective was to ensure a sufficient level of taxation at source in order to combat tax evasion. The Committee recommended that the Commission through a directive prescribe a uniform withholding tax of 30 per cent on dividends paid by EC-resident companies. There should be a waiver where appropriate tax identification was provided (phase II).

The third part-objective was to eliminate other withholding taxes levied by source countries on payments between enterprises in different Member States. In relation to this part-objective, the Committee recommended that the proposed interest and royalty directive be adopted. Furthermore, the interest and royalty directive should be extended to cover all such payments between enterprises (phase II).

Eliminating double taxation arising from transfer-pricing disputes was the fourth part-objective. The Committee first recommended that the Commission urge all Member States to ratify the Arbitration Convention as soon as possible (phase I). Furthermore, it recommended that the Commission act together with Member States to establish appropriate rules or procedures on transfer-pricing adjustments (phase I).

The fifth part-objective was to reduce impediments (obstacles) to cross-border investments that were likely to create losses in the early years of business. To reach this part-objective, the Committee proposed three measures. First, that Member States adopt the draft directive on losses of permanent establishments and subsidiaries in other Member States (phase I). Secondly, that all Member States introduce full vertical and horizontal offsetting of losses within groups of enterprises at national level (phase II). Thirdly, the extension of the draft directive to allow full Community-wide loss offset within groups of enterprises (phase III).

The sixth part-objective was to ensure that bilateral agreements for minimising double taxation were on a "proper footing". Accordingly, the Committee urged Member States to conclude bilateral tax treaties, where no such treaties existed. Member States should also extend their tax treaties with other Member States if the treaties had a limited coverage (phase I). The Committee also recommended action to be taken by the Commission in cooperation with Member States to define a common tax treaty policy, both between Member States and with third states (phase I).

2.4.5 Company Taxes

Company taxes were the subject of the measures of category (b). The first part-objective was to reduce discrimination between the tax treatment of domestic source income and foreign source income. In order to reach this part-objective the Committee issued three recommendations. The first recommendation was that the existing discrimination regarding the taxation of dividends from profits earned in another Member State be removed. In relation to that recommendation, Member States which applied imputation taxes on the distribution of profits earned in another Member State, should be obliged, on a reciprocal basis, to allow such taxes to be reduced by corporate income tax paid in another Member State in respect of dividends remitted by a subsidiary or profits earned by a permanent establishment (phase I). The final recommendation was that Member States with different forms of tax relief for dividends received by domestic shareholders from domestic companies, be obliged, on a reciprocal basis, to provide equivalent relief for dividends received by domestic shareholders from companies in other Member States (phase I).

The second part-objective was to achieve a more fully harmonised corporation tax system within the Community. To achieve this, the Committee recommended that the Commission and the Member States examine alternative approaches to determine the most appropriate common corporate tax system for the Community. This part-objective was to be achieved within phase III.

The third part-objective was to reduce the risks of serious erosion of corporate tax revenue. In order to achieve this part-objective, the committee issued three recommendations. First, it was recommended that the Commission prepare a draft directive.

Such a directive should prescribe a minimum statutory corporate tax of 30 per cent for all companies within the Community. The minimum tax rate would apply regardless of whether profits were retained or distributed as dividends (phase I). Secondly, it was recommended that all Member States adopt a maximum corporate tax rate of 40 per cent (phase II). Thirdly, it was recommended that there only be one company income tax within the Community. If that would prove impossible, local taxes should be added when fixing the company tax rate in the interval of 30 to 40 per cent (phase II).

The fourth part-objective dealt with a range of different measures. There should be a set of minimum standards for the tax base covering phases I and II:

- depreciation practices (to include intangibles such as goodwill),
- leasing,
- stock valuation,
- provisions,
- business expenses,
- headquarter costs of enterprises,
- pension contributions by or for expatriate workers,
- carry-over of losses, and
- capital gains.

The fifth part-objective concerned rules on the time when taxes were payable, because those varied between Member States. The Committee recommended the Commission to try to establish common rules through harmonising the time when taxes were payable (phase II).

The sixth part-objective was to improve neutrality between different forms of business organisation. In this respect, the Committee recommended the Commission to try to establish common rules with the purpose of permitting unincorporated enterprises to be taxed in the same way as companies, and that such taxation apply for a minimum period of time (phase II).

2.4.6 Other Issues

The third category, labelled (c), dealt with other issues, including the removal of different burdens arising from additional mixed-based taxes. The Committee recommended that Member States with a multibase local tax replace them with an on-profits tax levied on the same base as the central government company tax (phase II).[36]

2.5 The 2001 Staff Report

2.5.1 Introduction

The 2001 Staff Report[37] can be seen as a follow-up report to the 1992 Ruding Report, and it was also prepared with the support of the Commission. Both the Ecofin Council and the Coreper had asked the Commission to produce the inquiries presented in the 2001 Staff Report. The preparation of the 2001 Staff Report was made by two panels. One panel consisted of academics and experts, mainly in the field of economics. The other panel consisted of experts from the business community and social partners at Community level.

The 2001 report identified a range of tax obstacles to cross-border economic activities. The underlying fact for the existence of such obstacles is, of course, the existence of the then 15 different tax jurisdictions within the Community. This fact raises a number of consequences, among them, according to the Report:[38]

(i) companies are obliged to allocate profits to each jurisdiction on an arm's length basis by separate accounting, i.e. on a transaction-by-transaction basis;

(ii) Member States are reluctant to allow relief for losses incurred by associated companies whose profits fall outside the scope of their taxing rights;

(iii) cross-border reorganisations entailing a loss of taxing rights for a Member State are liable to capital gains taxation and other charges;

(iv) double taxation may occur as a result of conflicting taxing rights.

Another considerable obstacle with tax law consequences is that legislation and conventions on financial accounting differ between Member States.[39]

---

[36] It is interesting to note that Professor Ruding in recent years has been sceptical on the question of whether "real progress on company taxation can be achieved in the European Union". The reason is the lack of political support and the veto power of the Member States. Ruding, "The Long Way to Removing Obstacles in Company Taxation in Europe", *European Taxation*, 2002, pp. 3-6, esp. pp. 5-6.

[37] The 2001 Staff Report, p. 7. For an analysis of the 2001 Staff Report, see e.g. Schön, "The European Commission's Report on Company Taxation: A Magic Formula for European Taxation?", *European Taxation*, 2002, pp. 276-286.

[38] The 2001 Staff Report, p. 16.

[39] The 2001 Staff Report, p. 16. Other obstacles are different rules between Member States on determining taxable profit, arrangements for collection and administration of tax, and varying tax treaty networks.

2.5.2 Problems with Achieved Results on Harmonising European Company Taxation

At the time of publication of the 2001 Staff Report, in effect only three acts of legislation had been achieved within the specific area of European company taxation: the Merger Directive, the Parent/Subsidiary Directive and the Arbitration Convention.[40]

The 2001 Staff Report identified a range of problems with the measures achieved thus far. The purpose of the Parent/Subsidiary Directive is to abolish withholding taxes on dividends paid within the Community between associated companies. According to the report, the effectiveness of the Directive was, however, limited. The reasons were that it did not cover all companies subject to company tax and that it only applied to direct holdings of more than 25 per cent. Furthermore, some national company tax legislations had, according to the report, a built-in bias in favour of domestic investment. The imputation system of some Member States were said to have such effects. The report presents an example. Some imputation systems provide for a tax credit to resident (individual or corporate) shareholders for the tax paid on the company level. The credit is usually not available to non-resident shareholders and is furthermore not normally granted in respect of foreign dividends.[41]

Likewise, the Merger Directive posed problems, according to the Report. One objective of this Directive is to provide for deferral of capital gains charges in a variety of corporate reorganisations. Remaining problems include:[42]

(1) Not all situations are covered. The Merger Directive does not include all companies subject to company tax. A situation such as the centralisation of production is not covered by the scope of the Directive.

(2) The applicability of the Directive is limited because there is no unified EU company legislation for cross-border mergers. The remaining alternative forms of cross-border mergers are share-for-share exchanges and transfers of assets.

(3) The implementation of the Directive differs significantly between Member States. According to the Staff Report, Member States have chosen different conditions for the tax deferral that the Directive provides for. The reason for the varying conditions is the prevention of tax avoidance. According to the Staff Report, this significantly limits the scope of the Merger Directive and leaves situations of double taxation unrelieved.

[40] Presented in section 2.6.

[41] The 2001 Staff Report, p. 17.

[42] The 2001 Staff Report, p. 18.

The 2001 Staff Report also deals with cross-border loss compensation. The Commission has proposed a directive on the treatment of cross-border losses, but the directive has not been adopted. Furthermore, transfer pricing and tax treaty issues are discussed in the Staff Report.

2.5.3 Solutions to Tax Obstacles within the Community

The 2001 Staff Report discusses two approaches to deal with tax obstacles within the Community. Those approaches are:[43]

(1) Targeted solutions that seek to remedy individual obstacles.

(2) More comprehensive solutions that seek to address the underlying causes of the obstacles.

Regarding targeted solutions, problems with both the Merger Directive and the Parent/Subsidiary Directive have to be dealt with. The proposed directive on the cross-border loss offset is analysed. A number of amendments are proposed. One alternative that is discussed is the Danish system of "joint taxation". Moreover, both transfer pricing and tax treaties issues are discussed.

Four different comprehensive approaches are discussed in the 2001 Staff Report.

(1) Home state taxation.[44] This approach is based on mutual recognition. The tax base is calculated according to the tax legislation of the company's home state. The home state would be the state where the company has its headquarters. The home state approach is considered as an optional method for companies in Member States with a sufficiently similar tax base.

(2) Completely new and harmonised EU rules for the determination of a single tax base at European level, which would create a parallel European tax system. This approach has been labelled "common (consolidated) base taxation".

(3) A "European corporate income tax". This system would mean that tax could be levied at the European level and all or a part of the tax revenue would go to the European Union.

(4) A "traditional" approach, which would mean the harmonisation of national rules on company taxation to form a single EU company tax base, which would replace existing national systems.

---

[43] The 2001 Staff Report, p. 20 *et seq.*

[44] Cf. Lodin and Gammie, *Home State Taxation: Tax Treaty Aspects*, IBFD, Amsterdam, 2001.

2.6 An Overview of Harmonised European Company Taxation

In this section there will be a presentation of the results of the attempts on harmonising company taxation in the European Union. As previously noted, until recently only three main acts of legislation have been adopted: the Merger Directive, the Parent/Subsidiary Directive and the Arbitration Convention.

The main purpose of this presentation is to provide a context for the comparative importance in the field of direct taxation of decisions by the European Court of Justice, which form the core of this study. A subordinate purpose is to target the issues on which the required unanimity has been reached in matters of direct taxation.

Directive 90/434/EEC on the common system of taxation applicable to mergers, transfers of assets and exchanges of shares concerning companies of different Member States (the Merger Directive) was adopted on 23 July 1990. The general purpose of the Directive is to facilitate the reorganisation of companies located in different Member States.

A common characteristic of Member States' tax systems has been to facilitate corporate reorganisations within national boundaries, by allowing for the deferral of tax on what is conceived of as unrealised capital gains. But as soon as a cross-border transfer of the tax base has occurred, tax on capital gains might be levied. The Merger Directive took more than 20 years to adopt.[45]

There are four types of transactions that are covered by the Directive: (i) legal merger, (ii) legal division, (iii) transfer of asset, and (iv) exchange of shares.

Council Directive 90/434/EEC on the common system of taxation applicable in the case of parent companies and subsidiaries of different Member States, in short the Parent/Subsidiary Directive, was decided on 23 July 1990. The objectives of the Directive are outlined in the preamble. The Directive intends to create conditions within the Community that are "analogous" to those of an internal market in order to ensure the establishment and effective functioning of the common market. Moreover, operations as "the grouping together of companies of different Member States" within the common market, should not be hampered by restrictions, disadvantages or distortions that arise from Member States' tax systems. The preamble furthermore states that it is necessary to introduce in regard of groups of companies tax rules that are "neutral from the point of view of competition". Finally, a general purpose of the Directive was to create a system where enterprises increase their productivity and improve their competitive strength at the international level.

45 Terra and Wattel, *European Tax Law*, 3rd ed., Kluwer Law International, London/The Hague/New York, 2001, p. 374.

There are two typical tax consequences that the Directive seeks to mitigate. First, the state where the subsidiary is resident may levy a withholding tax on outbound dividends. Secondly, the state where the parent company is resident may tax the inbound dividends. The result of this taxation may be economic double taxation, or even multiple taxation. The Directive was proposed in 1969, but German and Dutch opposition delayed the adoption for 20 years.[46]

The purpose of the Arbitration Convention is also to contribute to the abolishment of double taxation within the European Union. It could be said to be a task of the international tax law to ensure that transactions within a multinational group of companies are priced at arm's length. Pricing on transactions within the group shall be made as if the companies were not associated. States have national legislation aimed at achieving this arm's length pricing. Transactions between companies of the same group are of course not uncommon. Real losses or profits of the group, however, do not occur until transactions are made with companies outside of the group.

The exchange of information between tax authorities is of course essential for both the assessment and recovery of taxes. Tax treaties based on the OECD Model normally include an exchange of information provision. As previously noted, there still remains one bilateral relation with no tax treaty applicable: there is no tax treaty between Greece and Ireland, moreover some treaties are missing with and among the new Member States. The exchange of information has also been the subject of measures at Community level. Already in 1977 a directive was adopted, Council Directive 77/799/EEC of 19 December 1977.

The Directive only applies to the exchange of information for tax assessment, and not the recovery of taxes, according to Article 1 (1) of the Directive. Taxes covered by the exchange of information are noted in Article 1 (1) and (2) of the Directive, and include for example: taxes on total income or on total capital, taxes on elements of income or capital, taxes on capital gains, and payroll taxes and wage withholding taxes. As regards the personal scope of the Directive, information on both residents and non-residents may be exchanged. In principle one could say that all the information necessary for national tax authorities to make a tax assessment may be exchanged. Article 2 (2) of the Directive requires Member States, if necessary, to carry out special inquiries to be able to deliver the required information. The information is to be exchanged through the competent authorities of the Member States, for example the Ministry of Finance. Information may be exchanged in three different ways: (i) on request, (ii) automatically and (iii) spontaneously.

---

46 Terra and Wattel, *European Tax Law*, 3rd ed., Kluwer Law International, London/The Hague/New York, 2001, p. 336.

2.7 The Package to Tackle Harmful Tax Competition

2.7.1 Introduction

The Commission has for several years tried to convince the Council to adopt a package to tackle harmful tax competition. The package contains three parts: (i) a non-binding Code of Conduct for business taxation, (ii) a directive on the taxation of income from savings and (iii) a directive on the elimination of withholding taxes on cross-border payments of interest and royalties between companies.

The Council already endorsed a Code of Conduct on 1 December 1997, but as regards the two proposed directives, a decision could not be reached. It is no secret that the Member States especially have had difficulty in agreeing on the proposed Savings Directive. However, on 3 June 2003 the Council finally adopted the package including all three parts, but at the time of writing it is still uncertain whether the Directive will come into force. In the following section I will present these three acts of legislation.

2.7.2 The Code of Conduct for Business Taxation

The Code of Conduct for business taxation is annexed to the conclusions of the Ecofin council meeting on 1 December 1997 concerning tax policy.[47] It should be observed that the Code of Conduct is not legally binding on the Member States, and is rather intended to exercise "peer pressure" on them. In section B of the Code of Conduct are listed six examples of factors to be taken into account when assessing whether a measure constitutes harmful tax competition. Among these criteria can be mentioned:

- whether advantages are ring fenced from the domestic market, so that they do not affect the national tax base,
- whether advantages are granted even without any real economic activity and substantial economic presence within the Member State offering such tax advantages, or
- whether the tax measures lack transparency, including where legal provisions are relaxed at administrative level in a non-transparent way.

In the Code of Conduct, Member States commit themselves not to introduce new tax measures which are considered harmful according to the Code. This commitment is labelled "standstill". Furthermore, Member States commit themselves to re-examine the existing legislation and established practices, with regard to the underlying principles

[47] OJ C 2 of 6 January 1998, p. 1.

of the Code, with a view to amending legislation where it is harmful. This commitment is called “rollback”.

2.7.3 The Savings Directive

It took considerable efforts to reach unanimity on the Savings Directive, but on 3 June 2003 it was finally adopted.[48] The main component of the Savings Directive is the automatic exchange of information on interest payments from savings.[49] The Directive also contains an alternative method applied for by Austria, Belgium and Luxembourg: to levy withholding taxes, albeit for a transitional period, instead of exchanging information.

A central term of the Directive is “paying agent”. A paying agent established in a Member State will have to provide information in respect of an interest payment to, or for the benefit of, the beneficial owner of the payment if he is an individual resident in another Member State. There are four categories of interest payments, which I will not discuss here. Information will be exchanged when the beneficial owner of an interest payment is an individual who is resident in another Member State than the Member State in which the paying agent is established. That information will be exchanged automatically by the state of the paying agent to the tax authority, or equivalent, in the other Member State. The exchange will take place at least once a year.

If the Directive is implemented from 1 July 2005, the withholding tax rates of Austria, Belgium and Luxembourg will be 15 per cent from the beginning, rising to 20 per cent from 1 January 2008, and finally rising to 35 per cent from 1 January 2011. These Member States will, as a general rule, retain 25 per cent of the charged tax and pay 75 per cent of that tax to the Member State of residence of the beneficial owner of the interest payment.

2.7.4 The Directive on Cross-border Payments of Interest and Royalties

The Directive on the taxation of cross-border payments of interest and royalties was also adopted on 3 June 2003.[50] The main objective behind the Directive is to eliminate double taxation of cross-border flows of interest and royalties. Even if there is an

[48] Council Directive 2003/48/EC of 3 June 2003 on taxation of savings income in the form of interest payments.

[49] On the Savings Directive see e.g. Scoon and Carter, “EU Savings Directive Saved at Last?”, *Tax Notes International*, 23 June 2003, pp. 1179-1184.

[50] Council Directive 2003/49/EC on a common system of taxation applicable to interest and royalty payments made between associated companies of different Member States.

extensive network of tax treaties between Member States, there is still a risk for double taxation of these types of income. For example, tax treaties as a general rule do not cover triangular situations, which the Directive in effect does cover.[51]

2.8 The 1990 Proposal on a Directive on Cross-border Offsetting of Losses

There have been several proposals on directives, "draft directives", in the area of direct taxation. One important proposal that so far has not been adopted is the 1990 proposal for a directive on the cross-border offsetting of losses.[52] This directive was intended to remove obstacles to cross-border business. Within the jurisdiction of a Member State it is normally possible under national law to take into account losses by both a branch and a subsidiary, albeit with certain limitations. In a cross-border situation, however, it is rarely permitted to take foreign losses into account. It was the objective of the directive to neutralise these different situations by extending the right to consider foreign losses. The directive would apply between companies within a corporate group and between a headquarter and its branch. It has proved impossible to decide on the adoption of the directive. Terra and Wattel suggest that the reason behind this reluctance is the inclusion of losses of foreign subsidiaries and the principle of mutual recognition of loss determination, a suggestion which in my view seems plausible.[53]

Even if the directive on cross-border losses has not been adopted, the EC Treaty and the freedom of establishment have had an impact on Member States' legislation. Cases such as C-141/99 *AMID*, C-250/95 *Futura Participations* and C-264/96 *ICI* and the pending case C-446/03 *Marks & Spencer* deal with the national treatment of corporate losses, and those cases will be further discussed in Chapter 4.

2.9 Concluding Remarks

In this chapter there has been a presentation of both the treatment of matters of direct taxation in the EC Treaty and Community policy in such matters.

---

[51] A critical analysis of the interest and royalties directive is given in Distaso and Russo, "The EC Interest and Royalties Directive – A Comment", *European Taxation* 2004, pp. 143-154.

[52] Proposal for a Council Directive concerning arrangements for the taking into account by enterprises of the losses of their permanent establishments and subsidiaries situated in other Member States, COM(90) 595 final of 6 December, OJ C 53 of 28 February 1991, p. 30.

[53] Terra and Wattel, *European Tax Law*, 3rd ed., Kluwer Law International, London/The Hague/New York, 2001, p. 441.

Regarding the EC Treaty one should note that unanimity is required in the Council for Community legislation on the approximation of laws in, for example, the area of tax law. Member States retain a veto power in tax matters. Obviously this is a strong impediment for Community measures being taken.[54]

In several reports and inquiries the Commission has emphasised the need for Community measures to remove obstacles for cross-border transactions and to realise an internal market. The growing number of cases from the European Court of Justice where measures of national tax legislation have been found to be in breach of fundamental freedoms bear evidence of a need for measures to be taken at Community level. So far, little has been achieved, beyond the adoption of a few directives.

The piecemeal decisions by the European Court of Justice removing isolated obstacles to the fundamental freedoms must be considered second best compared to measures at Community level where more general solutions can be adopted. Lodin identifies the problem in the following way.[55] The European Court of Justice can only react to questions which are put to it by Member States, national courts and the Commission. In addition, the Court is bound to the questions of the specific cases, and consequently the Court's decisions are strongly casuistic. Community legislation in the area of direct taxation is an expression of "positive integration", whereas the case-law of the European Court of Justice in this area expresses "negative integration".

At present, the replacement of the unanimity requirement in cases on direct taxation seems the only plausible way for comprehensive Community measures in this field of law. The steady flow of cases from the European Court of Justice declaring national tax legislation to be in breach of fundamental freedoms is evidence that there is a need for such unified measures. Decisions taken by the Council with a qualified majority might be the required solution for the Community lawmakers to keep equal pace with the European Court of Justice.[56] The proposal for a Constitution for Europe is a step in the direction of qualified majority decisions in the area of direct taxation, but only

[54] Vanistendael advocates that Member States should retain fiscal autonomy because full fiscal sovereignty is not possible within the internal market. Vanistendael explains: "[T]he union should acquire the power to set minimal standards for rates and rules on the tax basis. Within these limits the member states should be free to compete with each other and to do as they like. That is the difference between fiscal sovereignty and fiscal autonomy." Vanistendael, "No European Taxation without European Representation", *EC Tax Review*, 2000, pp. 142-143, at p. 143. In my view, such a solution seems reasonable, at least when taking account of the case-law of the ECJ, which means that Member States' fiscal sovereignty already today is limited by rules on the fundamental freedoms of the EC Treaty.

[55] Lodin, "EU och inkomstbeskattningen – varför händer så litet?", in *Festskrift tillägnad Edward Andersson*, Sevón, Frände, Olsson, Ryynänen and Tikka (ed.), 2003, pp. 135-150, at pp. 148-149.

[56] Draft treaty establishing a Constitution for Europe. Adopted by the European Convention on 13 June and 10 July 2003. Submitted to the President of the European Council in Rome. 18 July 2003. 2003/C 169/01.

regarding measures on company taxation relating to administrative cooperation or combating tax fraud and tax evasion.[57]

This study is an attempt to analyse the Court's decisions on matters of direct taxation in relation to the freedom of establishment and the free movement of capital. Perhaps it can in some way shed some light on the position of the EC Treaty as interpreted by the European Court of Justice, and on the requirements for tax legislation not to be in breach of those fundamental freedoms.

[57] Article III-63 of the proposal for a Constitution for Europe stipulates: "Where the Council of Ministers, acting unanimously on a proposal from the Commission, finds that measures on company taxation relate to administrative cooperation or combating tax fraud and tax evasion, it shall adopt, by a qualified majority, a European law or framework law laying down these measures, provided that they are necessary for the functioning of the internal market and to avoid distortion of competition. That law or framework shall be adopted after consultation of the European Parliament and the Economic and Social Committee."

3 The Prohibition against Discrimination and Non-discriminatory Restrictions in Relation to the Rule-of-reason Doctrine

3.1 Introduction

This chapter deals with the principle of non-discrimination and grounds for justifying discriminatory and otherwise restrictive measures. This account is intended as a foundation for the analysis in Chapters 4, 5 and 6 on the freedom of establishment and free movement of capital. Both the principle of non-discrimination and grounds for justifying discriminatory and restrictive measures have evolved in relation to all fundamental freedoms, and, of course, not only in cases on direct taxation. Accordingly, this chapter contains a general analysis of these two aspects of Community law.

The general objective of this chapter is to discuss the prohibition of restrictions, including discriminatory measures, as stipulated in the EC Treaty and interpreted by the European Court of Justice. More specifically, there are three part-objectives with this chapter. First, to give a broad description of the prohibition against restrictions on the fundamental freedoms. Secondly, to exemplify measures in the field of direct taxation which constitute a restriction. Thirdly, to introduce and describe the rule-of-reason doctrine that the European Court of Justice has developed to justify certain measures that otherwise would have been prohibited on the ground that they restrict a fundamental freedom and where no statutory limitation or exception in the EC Treaty applies.

The chapter has the following outline. The prohibition against discrimination is generally discussed in *section 3.2*. An overview of the fundamental freedoms is presented in *section 3.3*. It is my purpose in this section to describe the freedoms as they are defined in the EC Treaty, and furthermore to identify statutory limitations and exceptions applying to these freedoms. The freedom of establishment and the free movement of capital will, of course, be dealt with in a more thorough way in subsequent chapters. *Section 3.4* deals with the "treaty access test": to be able to invoke the EC Treaty freedoms it is necessary to be covered by the Treaty.

The prohibition against direct and indirect discrimination is the subject of *section 3.5*. The meaning of objectively comparable situations is discussed in *section 3.6*. The notion of non-discriminatory restrictions is dealt with in *section 3.7*.

The rule-of-reason doctrine, developed by the European Court of Justice, containing non-statutory grounds for justifying restrictions accepted in principle is introduced in *section 3.8*. A more thorough analysis of the grounds of justification in the public interest is given in *section 3.9*. Important cases from the European Court of Justice are used to illustrate the different grounds. The discussion of different grounds of justification – accepted in principle by the Court – is merely intended as an introduction. I will return to them in a more thorough analysis in Chapters 5 and 6.

3.2 The Prohibition in the EC Treaty against Discrimination and Non-discriminatory Restrictions

3.2.1 Introduction

It can hardly be said that one particular provision in the EC Treaty constitutes a general prohibition against discrimination. Rather, there are a number of provisions, with varying degree of concreteness, that manifest the principle of non-discrimination and prohibit discrimination in different areas.[1] It may very well be argued that the entire EC Treaty is permeated by the principle of non-discrimination.

Closely linked with the principle of non-discrimination is the principle of equal treatment. In the 2001 Staff Report it is pointed out that the principle of equal treatment "… is of particular importance to, and forms a fundamental element of, the provisions of the Treaty which establish the internal market."[2] It is furthermore stated that "… violations of the equal treatment principle generate tax obstacles to cross-border economic activity in the internal market."[3]

Presently the EC Treaty could be said to consist of four different areas dealing with non-discrimination.[4] First, there is Article 13 of the EC Treaty, which was amended with the Nice Treaty. Article 13 provides that the Council may take appropriate action to combat discrimination based on sex, racial or ethnic origin, religion or belief, disability, age or sexual orientation. Secondly, there is a prohibition against such discrimination. Article 12 of the EC Treaty contains a general prohibition against discrimination based on nationality. Furthermore, there is a prohibition against discrimination based on

---

1 Cf. Wouters, "The Principle of Non-discrimination in European Community Law", *EC Tax Review*, 1999, pp. 98-106, at p. 98. Moreover, Wouters argues convincingly that Community law may indirectly contain a general provision stating the prohibition of discrimination, because Article 6 of the TEU refers to the fundamental rights guaranteed by the European Human Rights Convention (*ibid.*).

2 The 2001 Staff Report, p. 389.

3 *Ibid.*

4 Cf. Craig and de Búrca, *EU Law*, 3rd ed., Oxford University Press, Oxford, 2003, p. 389-390.

nationality regarding the free movements: Article 28 and 29 (on the free movement of goods), Article 39 (on the free movement of workers), Article 43 (the freedom of establishment), Articles 49 and 50 (on the freedom to provide services) and Articles 56 and 58 (the free movement of capital).[5] Thirdly, the EC Treaty stipulates equal treatment between men and women according to, for example, Articles 137 and 141. Fourthly, non-discrimination between consumers and producers in the field of agriculture is prescribed in Article 34. Regarding discrimination, this study will only deal with the second area of prohibition against discrimination in the EC Treaty, namely discrimination on the basis of nationality, and, as will become clear, criteria similar to, but with the same effect as nationality.

Furthermore, in its case-law the European Court of Justice has made it clear that the prohibition against discrimination according to the fundamental freedoms of the EC Treaty also extends beyond mere discrimination, and thus also includes a prohibition against non-discriminatory restrictions.

3.2.2 On the Meaning of Discrimination

An initial question is, of course, what is meant by discrimination. Generally speaking, it means treating similar situations differently, but also treating different situations in the same manner.[6] The meaning of discrimination developed early in the case-law of the European Court of Justice, but in relation to the ECSC Treaty.[7] An early example of a case where the meaning of discrimination evolved is Case 13/63 *Italy v. the Commission* (known as the "Italian refrigerators" case).[8] In that case the European Court of Justice declared that the different treatment of non-comparable situations did not automatically lead to the conclusion that there was a case of discrimination; an appearance of discrimination in form may correspond to an absence of discrimination in substance. In broad terms discrimination can be defined as treating similar situations differently, or different situations alike.

Article 12 of the EC Treaty stipulates that within the scope of the EC Treaty any discrimination on grounds of nationality shall be prohibited. This prohibition shall

---

5 It should be observed that the free movements of goods, services and capital literally refer to "restrictions" instead of "discrimination". The free movement of persons (i.e. the free movement of workers and the freedom of establishment), however, refers to discrimination. I will return to this dichotomy in section 3.3.

6 Kapteyn and VerLoren van Themaat, *Introduction to the Law of the European Communities*, 3rd ed., Kluwer Law International, London/The Hague/Boston, 1998, pp. 168-169.

7 Wouters, "The Principle of Non-discrimination in the European Community Law", *EC Tax Review*, 1999, pp. 98-106, at p. 102.

8 Case 13/63 *Italy v. the Commission*. See also Wouters, *ibid*.

be upheld without prejudice to any special provisions contained in the EC Treaty. Furthermore, Article 12 stipulates that the Council may adopt rules to prohibit such discrimination as previously mentioned in the Article. In that case, the Council must follow the procedure laid down in Article 251 of the EC Treaty.[9] There is no explicit addressee of the rule contained in Article 12 of the EC Treaty. It is unquestionable, however, that it addresses Member States, as well as Community institutions. Whether or not private parties are addressed is a matter for discussion.[10]

The meaning of Article 12 was explained in an illuminating way by the AG Jacobs in the joined cases C-92/92 and C-326/92 *Phil Collins*:[11]

> "10. ... The fundamental purpose of the Treaty is to achieve an integrated economy in which the factors of production, as well as the fruits of production, may move freely and without distortion, thus bringing about a more efficient allocation of resources and a more perfect division of labour. The greatest obstacle to the realization of that objective was the host of discriminatory rules and practices whereby the national governments traditionally protected their own producers and workers from foreign competition. Although the abolition of discriminatory rules and practices may not be sufficient in itself to achieve the high level of economic integration envisaged by the Treaty, it is clearly an essential prerequisite.
>
> 11. The prohibition of discrimination on grounds of nationality is also of great symbolic importance, inasmuch as it demonstrates that the Community is not just a commercial arrangement between the governments of the Member States but is a common enterprise in which all the citizens of Europe are able to participate as individuals. /.../ No other aspect of Community law touches the individual more directly or does more to foster that sense of common identity and shared destiny without which the 'ever closer union among the peoples of Europe', proclaimed by the preamble to the Treaty, would be an empty slogan."

As regards the four fundamental freedoms, there are specific non-discrimination provisions. On several occasions the European Court of Justice has dealt with the relationship between the general prohibition against discrimination, contained in Article 12 of the EC Treaty, and the more specific prohibitions regarding the separate fundamental freedoms.

---

9 Article 251 of the EC Treaty deals with the comprehensive procedure of adopting a Community *act*.

10 Kapteyn and VerLoren van Themaat, *op. cit.*, p. 172.

11 Joined cases C-92/92 and C-326/92 *Phil Collins*.

A characteristic example is the decision in the joined cases of C-397/98 and C-410/98 *Metallgesellschaft and Others*, where the European Court of Justice declared:

> "38. It follows from the Court's case-law that the general prohibition of all discrimination on grounds of nationality laid down by Article 6 of the Treaty[12] applies independently only to situations governed by Community law for which the Treaty lays down no specific non-discrimination rules ...".[13]

It should be noted that there is case-law from the European Court of Justice also on the interpretation of the general prohibition against discrimination on the basis of nationality in Article 12 of the EC Treaty, which, however, is beyond the scope of this study.[14]

3.2.3 Terminological Issues on "Discrimination" and "Restrictions" and the Host State and Home State Perspectives

It may at this stage be appropriate to deal with a few terminological issues important for the subsequent discussion.[15] Discrimination can be divided into two different forms – direct and indirect discrimination. They are also often referred to as overt and covert discrimination.

Direct discrimination means discrimination on the basis of nationality. Suppose that a piece of legislation of a Member State stipulates that only nationals of that state may hold a specific office. That could constitute direct discrimination.

Indirect discrimination is not based on nationality, but on another criterion which has the same effect as if nationality had been the criterion applied. Suppose, for example, that the legislation of a Member State stipulates that to hold a specific office, an individual has to have an exam from a university located in that state. Clearly, that legislation does not at first glance discriminate against nationals of other states. However, it is likely that the majority of people having exams from universities in the Member State at issue also will be nationals of that state. In the view of the European Court of Justice, such a distinction could constitute indirect discrimination.

---

[12] The present Article 12 of the EC Treaty.

[13] The ECJ refers to Case 305/87 *Commission v. Greece*, para. 12 and 13; case C-1/93 *Halliburton Services*, para. 12; case C-311/97 *Royal Bank of Scotland*, para. 20; and case C-251/98 *Baars*, para. 23.

[14] Kapteyn and VerLoren van Themaat state that the old case-law on Article 7 of the EEC Treaty is also of relevance to the interpretation of Article 6 (presently Article 12) of the EC Treaty, Kapteyn and VerLoren van Themaat, *Introduction to the Law of the European Communities*, 3rd ed., Kluwer Law International, London/The Hague/Boston, 1998, p. 163.

[15] It should be noted that all these terms will be subject to further discussion in sections 3.5 and 3.6.

There is a third category of measures prohibited according to the fundamental freedoms of the EC Treaty: *non-discriminatory restrictions*. As will be discussed in the following, the language of the Court has become vaguer on what form of impediment a national measure constitutes in relation to a fundamental freedom. In recent years the Court has chosen only to express that a measure is a "barrier" or "hindrance". In my view such terms are not necessarily equivalent to a "non-discriminatory restriction" which is a measure that applies without distinction to nationality or a similar criterion.

Both discrimination and non-discriminatory restrictions can in principle be viewed from two different perspectives, the "*home state perspective*", by some also referred to as the "state of origin", and the "*host state perspective*". The *host state* is, to simplify it somewhat, the Member State to or in which, for example, goods are delivered, work is performed, business is established, services are performed and capital is distributed. It could be said that the fundamental freedoms traditionally have been considered primarily to protect against discrimination in the host state. However, the problem of discrimination may also be regarded from the *home state*. The home state may also have measures that constitute impediments to cross-border movements secured by the fundamental freedoms of the EC Treaty.

In this study, I will use the terms discrimination and non-discriminatory restrictions in the meaning that they can occur both in the host state and the home state. However, it is perhaps most common, at least traditionally, that a case of discrimination will occur in the host state. In the field of direct taxation there has in recent years been an increase in the cases concerning home state restrictions. Still, discrimination may also take place in the home state, and a non-discriminatory restriction can also occur in the host state.

A final note should be made regarding the term "restriction". All the fundamental freedoms provided for in the EC Treaty prohibit "restrictions", with two literal exceptions, albeit no substantial exceptions regarding connotation.[16] When the term "restrictions" is used in the EC Treaty in relation to the fundamental freedoms, the term is used in a wide sense including both discrimination and non-discriminatory restrictions. Subsequently, I will refer to this notion of restriction as "restrictions in a wide sense".

In *section 3.3*, there will be an overview of how the fundamental freedoms are formulated in the EC Treaty.

16 Section 3.3.6.

3.2.4 Other Forms of Discrimination

Reverse discrimination refers to a situation where a state imposes a more burdensome taxation on its own nationals or residents than on foreigners or non-residents.[17] For example in the *Asscher* case, dating from 1996, the European Court of Justice declared that "… Article [43] nevertheless cannot be interpreted in such a way as to exclude a given Member State's own nationals from the benefit of Community law where by reason of their conduct they are, with regard to their Member State of origin, in a situation which may be regarded as equivalent to that of any other person enjoying the rights and liberties guaranteed by the Treaty".[18] The European Court of Justice made the same conclusion in the *Halliburton* case from 1994.[19] According to Dutch tax law a special tax exemption applied on transfers of immovable property owned by companies incorporated in the Netherlands. The Dutch government maintained that there was no discrimination because the situation was completely internal. The European Court of Justice was of another opinion because the tax exemption was not granted if the transferor of the immovable property was foreign. In this case there was no discrimination against a foreigner in the Netherlands; instead there was a "reverse" discrimination against Dutch companies in situations containing a link to foreign matters.

The question of *horizontal discrimination* has been accentuated in relation to bilateral treaties between Member States. An example may illustrate the question. EU Member States A and B are parties to a tax treaty. EU national X is a resident of EU Member State C and conducts business in state B. There is no tax treaty between Member States C and B. Can X invoke the beneficial tax treatment of the tax treaty between state A and state B on the basis of the principle of non-discrimination, as manifested in the EC Treaty? It could be argued that X, as a national of state C, is discriminated against in this situation when compared with residents of states A and B, which benefit from the tax treaty between state A and B; there is horizontal discrimination when comparing the tax situation of a resident of state C doing business in states A and B with that of nationals of those states doing business in states A and B.

---

[17] Cf. Hinnekens, "The Search for the Framework Conditions of the Fundamental EC Treaty Principles as Applied by the European Court to Member States' Direct Taxation", *EC Tax Review*, 2002, pp. 112-119, at p. 114.

[18] Case C-107/94 *Asscher*, para. 32.

[19] Case C-1/93 *Halliburton Services*.

3.2.5 Limitations, Exceptions and the Rule-of-reason doctrine

Even if there is an infringement of a fundamental freedom, there are situations where such an infringement can be accepted under Community law. The first situation is where there is an explicit limitation or exception provided for in the EC Treaty. There are such limitations to all fundamental freedoms, but they apply only in extraordinary cases. In the following *section 3.3* there will be an overview of all fundamental freedoms and there I will relate the limitations and exceptions provided for.

The second situation concerns the rule-of-reason doctrine developed by the European Court of Justice in its case-law. According to this doctrine, an infringement of a fundamental freedom will under specific conditions be accepted if it meets a ground of justification in the public interest. The rule-of-reason doctrine has been considered by the Court in all of the cases on direct taxation subject to analysis in this study. A thorough introduction to the rule-of-reason doctrine is given in *sections 3.3 and 3.8 to 3.9.*

3.3 An Overview of the Fundamental Freedoms and the Prohibition against Non-discriminatory Restrictions

3.3.1 Introduction

Article 3 of the EC Treaty stipulates activities of the Community to achieve the Community objectives set out in Article 2 of that Treaty. One of the activities is the creation of an internal market, Article 3 (1) (c). According to that provision an internal market is characterised by the abolition, between Member States, of obstacles to the free movement of goods, persons, services and capital. In a number of cases the European Court of Justice has declared that provisions of Member States' legislation on direct taxation are obstacles to fundamental freedoms of the EC Treaty.

One objective of this study is, as previously mentioned, to discuss tax measures that the European Court of Justice has considered with a view to whether they constitute restrictions to the freedom of establishment and the free movement of capital.

An important feature of Community law is that even if a breach of a fundamental freedom is established, such a breach may still be justified. Restrictions to the fundamental freedoms can be accepted both according to explicit limitations and exceptions in the EC Treaty, and according to grounds of justification in the public interest specially developed by the European Court of Justice, known as the rule-of-reason doctrine.

For the fundamental freedoms to apply there must be a cross-border element involved. Bergström and Bruzelius conclude that the fundamental freedoms contain two basic principles. First, there is a prohibition of discrimination on grounds of nationality or origin. Secondly, there is a right to cross the borders of the Member States without any disproportionate restrictions.[20]

It is the European Court of Justice that has developed the notion of discrimination and non-discriminatory restrictions. It is especially regarding the free movement of goods that some of the most important cases have evolved, such as the *Cassis de Dijon* and *Dassonville* cases subsequently discussed. Moreover, it is also in relation to the free movement of goods that the rule-of-reason doctrine was developed.

A central question of the debate on the fundamental freedoms is to what extent the jurisprudence of the European Court of Justice on one fundamental freedom – originally the more elaborate case-law on the free movement of goods – also applies to the other fundamental freedoms. The view that one should regard the case-law on all fundamental freedoms homogeneously has been called "convergence" or a "global approach". In the following an overview will be given of some of the vital cases on these issues in relation to all freedoms. It should be noted that the rule-of-reason doctrine will also be separately discussed in section 3.8.

In this overview of the fundamental freedoms there will be a description of and an introduction to the four fundamental freedoms of the EC Treaty. I will concentrate on how these freedoms are defined and relate some of the statutory limitations and exceptions that are provided. Moreover, there will also be a survey of some of the most important cases regarding each fundamental freedom where the Court has developed the meaning of discrimination and non-discriminatory restrictions, as well as the rule-of-reason doctrine.

3.3.2 The Free Movement of Goods

3.3.2.1 The EC Treaty

The EC Treaty prohibits different forms of obstacles to the free movement of goods. First, according to Article 23 of the EC Treaty there is a prohibition of customs duties and charges levied with the result that foreign goods are more expensive than their domestic equivalent. According to the same provision the Community shall be based on a customs union. The customs union shall cover all trade in goods with the effect that customs duties on imports and exports are prohibited. Furthermore, there shall be a common customs tariff with third countries.

---

[20] Bergström and Bruzelius, "Home-state Restrictions on the Freedom of Establishment in a Swedish Income Tax Law Perspective", *Intertax*, 2001, pp. 233-241, p. 234.

Article 24 of the EC Treaty provides that products coming from a third country shall be considered to be in free circulation in a Member State if specific conditions are fulfilled. To begin with, it is required that the import formalities have been complied with. Moreover, it is necessary that any customs duties or charges having equivalent effect which are payable have been levied in that Member State. Finally, it is stipulated that the products must not have benefited from a total or partial drawback of such duties or charges.

Secondly, there are *quantitative trade barriers* and, thirdly, there are *fiscal trade barriers*. Quantitative trade barriers comprise trade quotas and import restrictions, among other things.[21] Fiscal trade barriers consist of, for example, taxes and excise duties, as well as other forms of monetary barriers. More precisely, Article 25 of the EC Treaty stipulates that customs duties on imports and exports, and charges having equivalent effect, shall be prohibited between Member States.

In addition, quantitative restrictions and all measures having an equivalent effect on imports and exports between Member States are prohibited between Member States according to Articles 28 and 29 of the EC Treaty. There are, however, exceptions and limitations to the prohibition of quantitative restrictions between Member States. Article 30 of the EC Treaty stipulates the following exceptions and limitations for quantitative restrictions:

- public morality, public policy or public security;
- protection of health and life of humans, animals or plants;
- protection of national treasures possessing artistic, historic or archaeological value;
- protection of industrial and commercial property.

Prohibitions and restrictions that are accepted according to one or more of the above-mentioned grounds may "… not constitute a means of arbitrary discrimination or a disguised restriction on trade between Member States".[22]

The prohibition against fiscal trade barriers of one Member State on products of other Member States is stipulated in Article 90 of the EC Treaty. According to Article 90 (1) no Member State shall impose, directly or indirectly, on the products of other Member States any internal taxation of any kind that exceeds the taxation imposed directly or indirectly on similar domestic products. In addition to this, Article 90 (2) provides that no Member State shall impose any "internal taxation" on the products of other

[21] Cf. Bernitz and Kjellgren, *Europarättens grunder*, 2nd ed., Norstedts Juridik, Stockholm, 2002, p. 189.

[22] Article 30 of the EC Treaty.

Member States, which means indirect protection of other products. Harmonisation of indirect taxes is the subject of Articles 92 and 93.

The relationship between, on the one hand, Articles 23 to 25 and, on the other hand, Articles 90 to 93, is noteworthy. They are to be considered as mutually exclusive,[23] even if they both concern fiscal charges. Articles 23 to 25 deal with duties or charges levied due to the cross-border transfer of goods. Articles 90 to 93 deal with the internal fiscal policy of a state and prevent discrimination of goods when they have entered a state.

In the subsequent case-law discussion of section 3.3.2.2, I will entirely focus on cases dealing with the interpretation of the term discrimination with regard to the prohibition against quantitative restrictions contained in Articles 28 to 31 of the EC Treaty. The reason for that is that I consider those cases to be especially important in relation to the evolvement of the concept of discrimination and non-discriminatory restrictions, as well as the rule-of-reason doctrine.

3.3.2.2 The Case-law of the European Court of Justice

In a large number of cases the Court has declared that the rules on equal treatment and the prohibition of discrimination forbid not only direct discrimination by reason of nationality, but also all indirect forms of discrimination which, by means of other criteria of differentiation, in fact lead to the same result.[24] In the ground-breaking Case 152/73 *Sotgiu* the Court declared: "The rules regarding unequal treatment ... forbid not only overt discrimination by reason of nationality but also all covert forms of discrimination which, by the application of other criteria of differentiation, lead in fact to the same result ... criteria such as place of origin or residence of a worker may, according to circumstances, be tantamount, as regards their practical effect, to discrimination on grounds of nationality ...".

Another early case where the Court further developed the notion of discrimination is Case 8/74 *Dassonville*.[25] The Court declared that not only discriminatory national measures were prohibited according to Article 36 (now Article 30) of the EC Treaty, but also other forms of measures restricting the free movement of goods. Furthermore, in the *Dassonville* case the Court indicated that some restrictions may be justified, and thereby provided an embryo for the rule-of-reason doctrine.

---

23 Craig and de Búrca, *EU Law*, 3rd ed., Oxford University Press, Oxford, 2003, p. 607.

24 Cf. e.g. Case 152/73 *Sotgiu*, para. 11; and case C-279/93 *Schumacker*, para. 26.

25 Case 8/74 *Procureur du Roi v. Dassonville*.

More precisely, the *Dassonville* case dealt with Belgian law, which required that goods that had a designation of origin could be imported only if they carried a certificate from the government of the exporting country which certified the right to such a designation. Dassonville imported Scotch whiskey into Belgium from France, however, without having the required certificate from the relevant British authorities. It would have been difficult to acquire such a certificate because the goods were already circulating in another Member State, namely France. The Court declared that national measures must not constitute a means of arbitrary discrimination or a disguised restriction on trade between Member States.[26] The national measure was considered by the Court as a measure equivalent to a quantitative restriction as prohibited by the Treaty. Moreover, the seeds of the rule-of-reason test as a means of justification were sown by the Court in this case. The Court explained that if a Member State takes measures to prevent unfair practices in this connection, it is however subject to the condition that these measures should be reasonable and that the means of proof required should not act as a hindrance to trade between Member States and should, in consequence, be accessible to all Community nationals.

The Court's judgment in the *Dassonville* case was further developed in the seminal Case 120/78 known as *Cassis de Dijon*.[27] Even if it is a well-known case it is inevitable to discuss it also in this study, at least as a benchmark for the subsequent cases in the field of direct taxation. The case concerned Article 30 (now Article 28) of the EC Treaty on the free movement of goods. The applicant wanted to import a liqueur of the brand *Cassis de Dijon* from France to Germany. German legislation stipulated a minimum alcoholic strength of 25 per cent for the marketing of liqueurs in Germany. But the *Cassis de Dijon* liqueur had an alcoholic level of only 15 to 20 per cent. The applicant argued that this German provision had the equivalent effect of a quantitative restriction according to Article 30 (now Article 28) of the EC Treaty.

The Court came to the conclusion that this piece of national legislation had the principal effect of promoting alcoholic beverages which had a high alcoholic content by excluding from the national market products of other Member States that did not meet those national requirements.

In conclusion the Court in the *Cassis de Dijon* case confirmed what it had already put forward in Case 8/74 *Dassonville*: Article 30 (now Article 28) could also apply to national rules that did not discriminate against imported products, but where the national rules inhibited trade anyway because they were different from the trade rules that applied in the country of origin.[28] If goods were lawfully marketed in one Member

[26] *Ibid.*

[27] Case 120/78 *Rewe-Zentrale AG v. Bundesmonopolverwaltung für Branntwein.*

[28] Cf. Craig and de Búrca, *EU Law*, 3rd ed., Oxford University Press, Oxford, 2003, p. 638.

State, they should also be lawfully marketed in other Member States. This could be said to constitute the principle of mutual recognition.[29]

Moreover, in the *Cassis de Dijon* case the Court further developed the rule-of-reason doctrine from the *Dassonville* case. In the *Cassis de Dijon* case the Court declared that obstacles arising from disparities between national legislation to movements within the Community must be tolerated as long as those provisions satisfy mandatory requirements such as the effectiveness of fiscal supervision, the protection of public health, the fairness of commercial transactions and the defence of the consumer.[30]

The scope of the *Dassonville* and *Cassis de Dijon* cases was, however, somewhat limited by the Court's judgment in the *Keck and Mithourd* case.[31] Keck and Mithourd were selling goods in France at a price below their own purchase price, a procedure that was contrary to a provision of French law from 1963 as amended in 1986. It should be noted that the law did not ban sales at a loss. Keck and Mithourd claimed that this French rule was in conflict with, among others, the free movement of goods. In its response the Court declared that Article 30 (present Article 28) of the EC Treaty prohibits obstacles to the free movement of goods when national law imposes requirements to be met when disposing of such goods. As examples of such requirements the Court mentioned designation, form, size, weight, composition, presentation, labelling, and packaging.[32] The Court continued:

> "[C]ontrary to what has previously been decided, the application to products from other Member States of national provisions restricting or prohibiting *certain selling arrangements* is not such as to hinder directly or indirectly, actually or potentially, trade between Member States within the meaning of the *Dassonville* judgment … so long as those provisions apply to all relevant traders operating within the national territory and so long as they affect in the same manner, in law and in fact, the marketing of domestic products and of those from other Member States."[33]

If those conditions were fulfilled there would be no restriction, such as would prevent market access or impede access any more than it impedes the access of domestic products. Accordingly, the Court considered such rules to fall outside of the scope of Article 30 (present Article 28) of the EC Treaty. The French legislation at issue

---

29 *Ibid.*

30 Case 120/78 *Cassis de Dijon*, para. 8.

31 Joined cases C-267/91 and C-268/91 *Criminal proceedings against Keck and Mithourd*, [1993] ECR I-6097.

32 Joined cases C-267/91 and C-268/91 *Keck and Mithourd*, para. 15.

33 Joined cases C-267/91 and C-268/91 *Keck and Mithourd,* para. 16 (emphasis added).

did not impose a general prohibition on resale at a loss. Consequently, such selling arrangements were not covered by Article 30 (present Article 28) of the EC Treaty.

The *Keck and Mithourd* case has been regarded as an answer by the Court to the rising number of cases following from its previous judgments on the free movement of goods where restrictions on that freedom were prohibited.[34]

In conclusion, the Court's case-law on the free movement of goods has made it clear that as regards this freedom there is a prohibition not only in relation to direct discrimination but also in relation to indirect discrimination and non-discriminatory restrictions. However, the *Keck and Mithourd* case was a step by the Court to limit the number of cases where national measures were found to be in conflict with the fundamental freedom at issue. Moreover, the case-law recognises that there are more reasons that may justify an infringement of the fundamental freedom than the statutory limitations and exceptions provided for in the EC Treaty. In this study I refer to this method of justification as the rule-of-reason doctrine.[35]

3.3.3 The Free Movement of Workers and the Freedom of Establishment

3.3.3.1 The EC Treaty

The free movement of persons is divided into two freedoms: the freedom of movement for workers and the freedom of establishment. The freedom of movement for workers is manifested in Articles 39 to 42 of the EC Treaty. Article 39 (1) stipulates the basic rule that the freedom of movement for workers shall be secured within the Community. This freedom entails the abolition of any discrimination based on nationality between workers of the Member States as regards employment, remuneration and other conditions of work and employment.

The content of the freedom of movement for workers is clarified in Article 39 (3) of the EC Treaty. It covers, for example, the right to accept offers of employment and to stay in a Member State for the purpose of employment. Article 39 (3) specifies acceptable limitations to the free movement of workers, which are limitations justified on grounds of public policy, public security or public health.[36]

---

34 The Court has confirmed its judgment in the *Keck and Mithourd* case on the scope of the free movement of goods in case C-405/98 *Gourmet International Products*. See also Farmer, "The Court's Case Law on Taxation: a Castle Built on Shifting Sands?", *EC Tax Review*, 2003, pp. 75-81, at p. 80.

35 On the rule-of-reason doctrine and its historical development see Cordewener, *Europäische Grundfreiheiten und nationales Steuerrecht*, Verlag Dr. Otto Schmidt, Cologne, 2002, pp. 60-67 (with further references).

36 It should be noted that the provisions of Article 39 of the EC Treaty do not apply to employment in the public service, according to Article 39 (4) of the same Treaty.

Articles 43 to 48 of the EC Treaty cover the freedom of establishment. The freedom of establishment will be more thoroughly dealt with in Chapter 4. In general, an establishment can be divided into two separate forms: primary establishment and secondary establishment. Primary establishment means the establishment of, for example, a new company or other *undertaking* in another Member State. Secondary establishment means the establishment in another Member State of, for example, an agency, a branch or a subsidiary. The general difference between primary establishment and secondary establishment is that the secondary establishment has a stronger tie with activities conducted in the home state.

The freedom of establishment shall according to Article 43 (2) include the right to take up and pursue activities as self-employed persons and to set up and manage "undertakings" (business activities). This freedom is, according to Article 43, particularly aimed at companies or firms within the meaning of Article 48 (2), under the conditions laid down for the nationals of the country where such establishment is made. It is also stipulated that the freedom of establishment in this respect is subject to the provisions of the Chapter relating to capital, Article 48 (2) of the EC Treaty. According to Article 48 (1) the prohibition also applies to restrictions on the setting up of agencies, branches or subsidiaries by nationals of any Member State established in the territory of any Member State.

There are also statutory limitations and exceptions in the EC Treaty to the freedom of establishment. Article 45 (1) of the EC Treaty stipulates that the provisions on the freedom of establishment "... shall not apply, so far as any given Member State is concerned, to activities which in that State are connected, even occasionally, with the exercise of official authority". Furthermore, Article 45 (2) provides that the Council may, acting by a qualified proposal from the Commission, rule that the provisions on the freedom of establishment shall not apply to certain activities.

The European Court of Justice has interpreted Article 45 (1) in a strict manner, which seems correct because of the infringement of a fundamental freedom it permits. Further limitations and exceptions contained in Article 46 of the EC Treaty are:

> "1. The provisions of this Chapter and measures taken in pursuance thereof shall not prejudice the applicability of provisions laid down by law, regulation or administrative action providing for special treatment of foreign nationals on grounds of public policy, public security or public health.
>
> 2. The Council shall, acting in accordance with the procedure referred to in Article 251, issue directives for the coordination of the abovementioned provisions."

In other words, Article 46 provides that Member States may take measures that hinder the freedom of establishment if those measures fulfil specific objectives. Accordingly, it is stipulated that provisions laid down by law, regulation or administrative action are accepted even if they are in conflict with the freedom of establishment, if they provide for *special treatment for foreign nationals* on grounds of:

- public policy,
- public security, or
- public health.

Regarding direct discrimination, the European Court of Justice declared in case C-311/97 *Royal Bank of Scotland* concerning the freedom of establishment: "According to settled case-law, only an express derogating provision, such as Article [46] of the EC Treaty, could render such discrimination compatible with Community law ...".[37] The freedom of establishment is more thoroughly covered in Chapters 4 and 5.

3.3.3.2 The Case-law of the European Court of Justice

For national measures that constitute direct discrimination on the free movement of workers, only express limitations and exceptions provided for in the EC Treaty may serve as a legitimate "justification".[38] Indirect discrimination of the freedom is also prohibited but may be justified if there is either an express derogation in the EC Treaty, or an objective justification based on case-law, also referred to as mandatory requirement.[39]

The Court defined indirect discrimination in case C-237/94 *O'Flynn*, regarding the free movement of workers, in the following way:

> "[C]onditions imposed by national law must be regarded as indirectly discriminatory where, although applicable irrespective of nationality, they affect essentially migrant workers or the great majority of those affected are migrant

---

[37] C-311/97 *Royal Bank of Scotland*, para. 32. The case-law that the court refers to (*ibid.*) is Case 352/85 *Bond van Adverteerders and Others*, para. 32 and 33, and case C-288/89 *Stichting Collectieve Antennevoorziening Gouda and Others*, para. 11.

[38] Cf. e.g. case C-415/93 *Bosman.*

[39] Cf. Barnard, "Fitting the Remaining Pieces into the Goods and Person Jigsaw?", *EL Rev.* 2001, pp. 35-59, at p. 38. The question of whether a piece of national legislation which constitutes indirect discrimination may be justified according to the rule-of-reason doctrine is not undisputed. In my view indirect discrimination is also covered by that doctrine – case C-204/90 *Bachmann* is such an example. This issue is further developed in section 3.8.

> workers, where they are indistinctly applicable but can be more easily satisfied by national workers than by migrant workers or where there is a risk that they may operate to the particular detriment of migrant workers."[40]

As regards the rule-of-reason doctrine, the Court declared in case C-237/94 *O'Flynn*: "It is otherwise only if those provisions are justified by the objective considerations independent of the nationality of the workers concerned, and if they are proportionate to the legitimate aim pursued by national law."[41] Barnard concludes that as with the *Dassonville* formula, it is enough for a discrimination to be at stake if there is a potential effect on the free movement.[42]

Another well-known case on the free movement of workers is case C-415/93 *Bosman*. That case concerned rules laid down by sporting associations on transfer fees paid between football associations. If a football player's contract with one club had expired, the player could not join another club if the new club did not pay a transfer fee to the old club. This rule was not discriminatory because it applied in the same manner within the Member State in question as it applied in relation to a club in another Member State. However, according to the Court the rule on transfer fees did affect the transfer of players between Member States and was capable of impeding the freedom of movement of workers. Accordingly, it is now clear that the free movement of workers also includes a prohibition against non-discriminatory restrictions, in spite of the reference in Article 39 (2) to the mere prohibition against "any discrimination based on nationality".

An additional case where the Court seems to have established the boundaries of the free movement of workers in a similar way to the *Keck and Mithourd* case is case C-190/98 *Graf*.[43] The case concerned Austrian legislation which provided that a worker who had been employed for more than three years was entitled to a compensation when his work came to an end, however, with the exception of where the employment terminated on the initiative of the worker himself. The German national in question, Mr Graf, had worked for his Austrian employer for four years when he terminated his contract to take up employment in Germany. The German worker was accordingly not entitled to the compensation. Graf argued along the lines of the Bosman case, that the denial of the compensation was in breach of the free movement of workers. The Court did,

40 Case C-237/94 *O'Flynn*, para. 16.

41 Case C-237/94 *O'Flynn*, para. 17.

42 Barnard, Fitting the remaining pieces into the goods and persons jigsaw?, EL Rev. 2001, pp. 35-59, at p. 39.

43 Case C-190/98 *Graf v. Filzmozer Maschinenbau GmbH.*

however, not consider there to be any breach of that freedom. The condition at issue was according to the Court:

> "… not dependent on the worker's choosing whether or not to stay with his current employer but on a future and hypothetical event, namely the subsequent termination of his contract without such termination being at his own initiative or attributable to him. … Such an event is too uncertain and indirect a possibility for legislation to be capable of being regarded as liable to hinder free movement for workers where it does not attach to termination of a contract of employment by the worker himself the same consequence as it attaches to termination which was not at his initiative or is not attributable to him …"[44]

Also as regards the freedom of establishment, the European Court of Justice makes a distinction between direct discrimination, indirect discrimination and non-discriminatory restrictions. One case that generally is considered to encompass direct discrimination is Case 270/83 *Avoir fiscal* which dealt with the discrimination in France of foreign companies with French branches, which were not granted the benefits of the French imputation system.[45] An example of indirect discrimination is case C-330/91 *Commerzbank*, where the Court explicitly referred to Case 152/73 *Sotgiu* as a basis for treating the case as a case of indirect discrimination. Finally, an example of non-discriminatory restrictions is case C-250/95 *Futura Participations*.

3.3.4 The Freedom to Provide Services

3.3.4.1 The EC Treaty

The freedom to provide services is covered by Articles 49 to 55 of the EC Treaty. Restrictions on the freedom to provide services within the Community are prohibited according to Article 49 of the EC Treaty. Article 49 stipulates that restrictions on the freedom to provide services shall be prohibited in respect of nationals of Member States who are established in a state of the Community other than that of the person for whom the services are intended.

The term "services" is defined in Article 50 of the EC Treaty. "Services shall be considered to be 'services' [sic] within the meaning of the EC Treaty if they are normally provided for remuneration, insofar as they are not governed by the provisions relating

[44] Case C-190/98 *Graf*, para. 24-25.

[45] An important case on the treatment of branches is case C-307/97 *Saint-Gobain*, which is dealt with in section 4.7.

to freedom of movement for goods, capital and persons. In particular the term services shall include (a) activities of an industrial character, (b) activities of a commercial character, (c) activities of craftsmen, and (d) activities of the professions."

There are also limitations and exceptions to the freedom to provide services. Article 51 refers to Articles 45 to 48 of the EC Treaty, which, among other things, provide limitations and exceptions to the freedom of establishment. For an overview of those exceptions and limitations, cf. supra *section 3.3.3*.

If one compares the free movement of services with the free movement of workers and the freedom of establishment one should in my view note that distinct from those two other freedoms, the free movement of services refers to a more temporary activity. Conversely, the free movement of workers and the freedom of establishment are more stable and continuous in their nature.[46]

3.3.4.2 The Case-law of the European Court of Justice

The distinction between direct and indirect discrimination has also been made in relation to the freedom to provide services. An example of this is case C-288/89 *Gouda* where the Court declared that direct discrimination is discrimination based on nationality, which may only be justified according to an express derogation in the EC Treaty itself. In the Gouda case the Court also recognised that the freedom included a prohibition against indirect discrimination and non-discriminatory restrictions, where a reference to the public interest could serve as a ground of justification. Furthermore, the Court provided a list of overriding grounds of justification in the public interest.

Over the years it has become increasingly clear that the freedom to provide services also includes a prohibition against non-discriminatory restrictions.[47] An early example is case C-76/90 *Säger*.[48] Another well-known and important case is C-275/92 *Schindler*.[49] That case concerned United Kingdom legislation on a prohibition for foreigners to hold national lotteries. The German public body Schindler sent envelopes from the Netherlands to the United Kingdom with an invitation to participate in a lottery, including application forms. The German body did not comply with the United Kingdom legislation on the providing of such lottery services. According to the European Court of Justice, a law provision which prohibited large lotteries was an obstacle to providing services, even if the legislation did not specifically discriminate

[46] Cf. case C-55/94 *Gebhard.*

[47] Cf. Craig and de Búrca, *EU Law*, 3rd ed., Oxford University Press, Oxford, 2003, p. 819.

[48] C-76/90 *Säger v. Dennemeyer & Co. Ltd* (and also AG Jacobs' opinion in this case).

[49] Case C-275/94 *Schindler.*

against foreign lotteries. Consequently, the United Kingdom law at issue constituted a non-discriminatory restriction. Moreover, the Court recognised that such a rule, constituting a non-discriminatory restriction, could be justified by overriding reasons in the public interest: the rule-of-reason doctrine.

A final example is case C-384/93 *Alpine Investments* which concerned a piece of legislation prohibiting "cold calling" in the financial services business. The Court recognised that this form of marketing could be successful and that the prohibition against it was a non-discriminatory restriction on the freedom to provide services. The measure could, however, be justified by reasons in the public interest such as maintaining the good reputation of the national financial sector, albeit with the prerequisite that the national measure at issue was proportionate to its objectives.

3.3.5 The Free Movement of Capital and Payments

3.3.5.1 The EC Treaty

Articles 56 to 60 of the EC Treaty cover the free movement of capital and payments. Article 56 (1) stipulates that all restrictions on the movement of capital between Member States and between Member States and third countries shall be prohibited. Article 56 (2) stipulates the same prohibition of restrictions on payments between Member States and between Member States and third countries.

Articles 57 to 60 contain limitations and exceptions to the free movement of capital and payments. It is noteworthy that Article 58 specifically deals with tax law. It stipulates that the provisions of Article 56 shall be without prejudice to the right of Member States:

(a) to apply the relevant provisions of their tax law which distinguish between taxpayers who are not in the same situation with regard to their place of residence or with regard to the place where their capital is invested;

(b) to take all requisite measures to prevent infringements of national law and regulations, in particular in the field of taxation and the prudential supervision of financial institutions, or to lay down procedures for the declaration of capital movements for purposes of administrative or statistical information, or to take measures which are justified on grounds of public policy or public security.

The free movement of capital is more thoroughly covered in Chapter 6.

3.3.5.2 The Case-law of the European Court of Justice

The free movement of capital is according to the wording of Article 56 of the EC Treaty a freedom that prohibits restrictions, which in my view includes a prohibition against both discrimination and non-discriminatory restrictions. That is also the way in which the Court has interpreted the term "restrictions" contained in Article 56.[50] As in relation to the previously discussed freedoms, there are EC Treaty provisions also containing limitations and exceptions to this freedom. For example, Article 58 contains limitations to this freedom especially regarding the area of tax law.

In comparison to the other fundamental freedoms there are relatively few cases from the European Court of Justice on the interpretation of the free movement of capital. The major reason for this is that it was first with the 1992 Maastricht Treaty that the present Article 56 was given direct effect. Previously, the free movement of capital had in effect been granted according to Directive 88/361/EEC, where the provision on the free movement of capital had been declared to have direct effect.[51]

Furthermore, there are good grounds to consider the case-law based on grounds of justification contained in the rule-of-reason doctrine, also to the free movement of capital, a view which is supported by, for example, case C-35/98 *Verkooijen*, para. 39-46. The relationship between the exceptions provided for in Article 58 in the field of taxation, vis-à-vis the rule-of-reason doctrine, is thoroughly discussed in Chapter 6.

3.3.6 Concluding Remarks and the Question of Convergence

The provisions of the EC Treaty on the free movement of goods, persons, services and capital all prohibit *restrictions* on those freedoms. In my view the meaning of "restrictions" in a broad sense refers to both direct and indirect discrimination, as well as non-discriminatory restrictions. There are, according to their wording, two provisions that could speak in favour of a more limited scope of two fundamental freedoms. Article 39 (2) on the free movement of workers expressly prohibits *discrimination* based on nationality. Article 43 (2) on the freedom of establishment has also a limited wording of its prohibition because it only refers to national treatment in the host Member State: "… under the conditions laid down for its own nationals …". The European Court of Justice has, however, ruled that both Article 39 (2) and Article 43 (2) include a prohibition against restrictions, and accordingly also apply to unequal treatment in the

50 Cf. e.g. case C-439/97 *Sandoz*, and case C- 478/98 *Commission v. Belgium*.

51 Joined cases C-358/93 and C-416/93 *Bordessa and Others*, para. 33.

Member State of origin. In case C-415/93 *Bosman*, the Court generally declared that "… nationals of Member States have in particular the right, which they derive from the Treaty, to leave their country of origin to enter the territory in another Member State and reside there in order there to pursue an economic activity".[52] Furthermore, the Court declared in the Bosman case that "[p]rovisions which preclude or deter a national of a Member State from leaving his country of origin in order to exercise his right to freedom of movement therefore constitute an obstacle to that freedom *even if they apply without regard to the nationality of the workers …*".[53]

Regarding the freedom of establishment, the European Court of Justice made it clear in, for example, case C-264/96 *ICI*[54] that Article 43 (2) also contains a prohibition against restrictions in the home state. The Court stated: "… even though, according to their wording, the provisions concerning freedom of establishment are directed mainly to ensuring that foreign nationals of companies are treated in the host Member State in the same way as nationals of that State, *they also prohibit the Member State of origin from hindering the establishment in another Member State of one of its own nationals or of a company incorporated under its legislation which comes within the definition contained in Article [48]*".[55]

An important question is to what extent there is *convergence* between the different fundamental freedoms on how to define discrimination and non-discriminatory restrictions, as well as what is the meaning of the rule-of-reason doctrine. In my view there is a high degree of convergence, but the approach by the Court is not necessarily identical between the different freedoms. A problem for assuming full convergence between all fundamental freedoms is the difference in substance between them. The freedoms regarding workers and establishment deal with persons and to a large extent also individuals. That is not necessarily so regarding services and definitely not so regarding goods and capital. Barnard discusses a "global test" regarding the free movement of goods, services and persons. The conclusion is that it may not be feasible because of the different approaches previously taken regarding the separate freedoms.[56]

---

52 Case C-415/93 *Union royale belge des sociétés de football association ASBL v. Jean-Marc Bosman, Royal club liégeois SA v. Jean-Marc Bosman and others and Union des associations européennes de football (UEFA) v. Jean-Marc Bosman*, para. 95.

53 Case C-415/93 *Bosman*, para. 96 (emphasis added).

54 Case C-264/96 *Imperial Chemical Industries plc (ICI) v. Kenneth Hall Colmer (Her Majesty's Inspector of Taxes)*. See also Case 81/87 *The Queen v. H.M. Treasury and Commissioners of Inland Revenue, ex parte Daily Mail and General Trust plc*.

55 Case C-264/96 *ICI*, para. 21 (emphasis added).

56 Barnard, "Fitting the Remaining Pieces into the Goods and Persons Jigsaw?", *EL Rev*. 2001, pp. 35-59, at p. 59.

Cordewener advocates the following reasons why the basic structure of all fundamental freedoms should be identical ("convergence"). To begin with, Article 3 (1) (c)[57] and Article 14 (2)[58] of the EC Treaty do not make any distinction between the different freedoms.[59] One must agree with Cordewener, that these EC Treaty provisions do not make any distinction between the different freedoms. Still, the referred provisions are in my view too general to constitute the basis for any certain knowledge on the degree of convergence between the freedoms. However, Cordewener also refers[60] to objectives such as legal certainty and clarity which in my view speak strongly in favour of a high degree of convergence.

I would like to make the following conclusion. Even if at present there is no complete convergence between all fundamental freedoms, there are considerable similarities and an unquestionably strong influence between them all. In my view there is a strong resemblance between them in the way of identifying discrimination, non-discriminatory restrictions and acceptable grounds of justification, according to the rule-of-reason doctrine, between the different freedoms. The fact that there are differences between the freedoms, for example that some directly concern individuals and other legal entities and others only goods or capital may make it difficult for complete convergence. However, my final consideration in this section will anyway be that there is and should be, to a large extent at least, conformity in the interpretation and application of all fundamental freedoms. Important reasons for a high degree of convergence are the need for predictability and simplicity in the application and interpretation of Community law. Furthermore, there is case-law supporting a high degree of convergence. In case C-55/94 *Gebhard* the Court ruled that the basic conditions of the rule-of-reason doctrine[61] are identical between all fundamental freedoms. However, one cannot necessarily infer from the *Gebhard* case that a ground of justification that is accepted in principle regarding one freedom is also accepted regarding the other freedoms. That is in my view natural because the fundamental freedoms are different, for example regarding their material scope. Moreover, there is some diversity on how the Court has defined discrimination and non-discriminatory

---

[57] Article 3 (1) (c) of the EC Treaty stipulates that the activities of the Community shall include "... an internal market characterised by the abolition, as between the Member States, of obstacles to the free movement of goods, persons, services and capital".

[58] Article 14 (2) of the EC Treaty stipulates that "[t]he internal market shall comprise an area without internal frontiers in which the free movement of goods, persons, services and capital is ensured in accordance with the provisions of this Treaty".

[59] Cordewener, "The Prohibitions of Discrimination and Restriction Have Both Been Intended to Achieve a Fully Integrated Internal Market in the European Union", Report to the 2004 EATLP Conference in Paris, unpublished manuscript, 19 pp., at p. 17.

[60] *Ibid.*

[61] Section 3.8.

restrictions regarding the different freedoms. For example, in scholarly doctrine it has been advocated that the *Keck and Mithourd* case on the free movement of goods – and the limitation of the freedom that this case in effect meant – cannot be translated to the free movement of persons, and moreover with caution regarding the freedom to provide services.[62] However, the notion of direct and indirect discrimination, as well as non-discriminatory restrictions, applies for all fundamental freedoms.

3.4 Access to the EC Treaty

3.4.1 The EC Treaty and Remarks on the Citizenship of the European Union

To invoke the fundamental freedoms and the prohibition against discrimination it is of course necessary to be covered by the scope of the EC Treaty – to have "treaty access".

One starting point for dealing with this question is Article 12 of the EC Treaty, which contains the general prohibition against discrimination. As previously mentioned, Article 12 stipulates that "[w]ithin the scope of this Treaty, and without prejudice to any special provisions contained therein, any discrimination on grounds of nationality shall be prohibited". It has been discussed whether the clause "within the scope of this Treaty" would exclude all situations that lack a cross-border economic nexus.[63] That would mean that the EC Treaty and the prohibition against discrimination and the fundamental freedoms would not cover cross-border situations without any economic nexus to the Community.

At present, Terra and Wattel[64] submit, there is no requirement for an economic nexus, which is an opinion I agree with. To begin with, in the Treaty on European Union of 1992 (the "Maastricht Treaty"), the European Economic Community Treaty was renamed the European Community Treaty. This change is a clear indication that this basic treaty is no more exclusively focused on economic affairs. Furthermore, the Treaty on European Union meant the introduction of a citizenship of the European Union.[65] Article 17 of the EC Treaty stipulates that every person holding the nationality

---

[62] Scheuer declares: "Für den Bereich der Niederlassungsfreiheit ist ebenso wie für die anderen Gestaltungen der Personenfreizügigkeit anzunehmen, dass die Grundsätze der 'Keck- und Mithourd'-Rspr. ... nicht übertragen werden können ...". Scheuer, in Lenz and Borchardt (ed.), *EUV/EGV*, 3rd ed., Bundesanzeiger Verlagsgesellschaft mbH, Cologne, 2003, Article 43, marg. no. 10.

[63] Terra and Wattel, *European Tax Law*, 3rd ed., Kluwer Law International, London/The Hague/New York, 2001, pp. 23-24.

[64] Terra and Wattel, *op. cit.*, p. 24.

[65] Part two, Articles 17-22 of the EC Treaty.

of a Member State shall be a citizen of the Union, and that citizens of the Union shall enjoy the rights conferred by the EC Treaty, and shall furthermore be subject to the duties imposed thereby. In addition, Article 18 of the EC Treaty stipulates that every citizen of the European Union shall have the right to move and reside freely within the territory of the Member States. This right is, of course, subject to the limitations and conditions laid down in the EC Treaty and by measures adopted to give it effect.[66] For this study, the "treaty access test" is especially important as regards the free movement of persons (free movement of workers and the freedom of establishment).[67] The free movement of capital targets the capital at issue and not specifically in whose hands it is transferred, which is similar to the design of the free movement of goods.

The present treaty access test could be said to consist of two conditions: (i) a person needs to possess treaty status, for example worker or entrepreneur, and (ii) there must be some cross-border element.

It is interesting to note that the right for EU citizens to move within the Union does not require any economic nexus, according to Article 18. One could ask whether that also implies an extension of Article 12 and the more general prohibition against discrimination, and the answer might very well be yes.[68] A question relevant for this study is the relationship between the citizenship of the Union and the fundamental freedoms contained in Articles 39 (free movement of workers), 43 (freedom of establishment) and 49 (freedom to provide services). It has been argued that the two sets of provisions are to be treated separately.[69] Barnard concludes that the European Court of Justice tries as far as possible to decide cases on the basis of Articles 39, 43 and 49 of the EC Treaty, and only where that is not possible resorts to Articles 17 and 18. She puts forward two reasonable explanations for this: (i) the established Treaty provisions (with secondary legislation) contain a clearer and more developed catalogue of rights, and (ii) if the person is a legal entity it is unlikely that the citizenship provisions will apply to it.[70]

The question of treaty access or not has been subject to considerable discussion in several cases on direct taxation before the European Court of Justice. Subsequently,

---

66 Moreover, the Council Directive 90/436/EEC of 28 June 1990 on the right of residence provides (*inter alia*) that Member States shall grant the right of residence to nationals of Member States who do not enjoy this right under other provisions of Community law and to members of their families (Article 1).

67 Terra and Wattel, *European Tax Law*, 3rd ed., Kluwer Law International, London/The Hague/New York, 2001, p. 34.

68 Cf. Terra and Wattel, *op. cit.*, pp. 23-28.

69 Barnard, *The Substantive Law of the EU: the Four Freedoms*, Oxford University Press, Oxford, 2004, p. 420.

70 *Ibid.*

I will discuss three such cases. All three cases deal with individuals, and it could be said that it is regarding individuals that the question of treaty access has been most frequently discussed over the years. However, as regards companies an important question has been which factor should connect a company to a specific Member State, such as the seat of a company or where the company is registered. I will deal with that specific company law question in the case-law analysis of Chapter 4 on the freedom of establishment. Finally, I wish to note that in the subsequent case-law analysis of this section I will only focus on the treaty access issue, and other questions will largely be left out.

3.4.2 Case C-112/91 *Werner* (26 January 1993)

The *Werner*[71] case dealt with German tax legislation and tax benefits granted to persons resident in Germany. The European Court of Justice considered whether the tax law at issue was compatible with the freedom of establishment. The facts of the underlying case were the following. Mr Werner was a German national, but he had lived with his wife in the Netherlands since 1961. Mr Werner was a dentist, and until October 1981 he worked as an employed dentist in Aachen, Germany. From that date, however, he was self-employed with his own dental practice, also in Aachen.

The German tax authorities emphasised that Mr Werner was only subject to limited tax liability in Germany. According to German tax legislation, a person was subject to unlimited taxation – resident for tax purposes – in Germany if he was residing or had his usual abode in that state.[72] In contrast, individuals who had no residence in Germany or did not habitually reside there were only subject to limited taxation.[73] Mr Werner was not resident in Germany according to the tax law of that state, even if he still was a German national.

The core of the tax problem for Mr Werner was that individuals resident in Germany for tax purposes were entitled to certain tax benefits. There was a preferential tax scale, the "splitting tariff" for married couples and the right to deduct specific costs.[74] The Court considered whether this difference in treatment between residents and non-residents was in conflict with the freedom of establishment.[75] The Court concluded that the only

[71] Case C-112/91 *Hans Werner v. Finanzamt Aachen-Innenstadt*.

[72] Case C-112/91 *Werner*, para. 3.

[73] *Ibid.*

[74] *Ibid.* It should be noted that besides the rules on income taxation, there were corresponding rules in the wealth tax system (*Vermögensteuergesetz*).

[75] Case C-112/91 *Werner*, para. 11.

factor which took the case out of its "purely national context" was the fact that Mr Werner lived in a Member State other than that in which he practiced his profession.[76] According to the European Court of Justice, that was not enough for Mr Werner to be covered by the EC Treaty and the freedom of establishment. In conclusion, there was nothing preventing the Member State where Mr Werner was a national from imposing a more burdensome taxation on him.[77]

3.4.3 Case C-107/94 *Asscher* (27 June 1996)

Mr Asscher was a Dutch citizen working in the Netherlands, but resident for tax purposes in Belgium.[78] In the Netherlands, Mr Asscher was the director of a company of which he was the sole shareholder. He also worked in Belgium, where he was the manager of a company governed by Belgian law, which carried out its business entirely in Belgium.[79]

In 1986 Mr Asscher had emigrated from the Netherlands to Belgium, a transfer which, however, did not change his activities carried out in either of these states. As regards the remuneration that he earned in the Netherlands, it was taxed exclusively in the Netherlands according to the Dutch-Belgian tax treaty. In Belgium he was taxed on the remaining part of his income. Mr Asscher's income in the Netherlands was taxed at a rate of 25 per cent, which was the higher rate applicable for certain non-resident taxpayers.[80]

In the present context of "treaty access", the *Asscher* case is interesting in relation to the following question: Did Mr Asscher as a Dutch citizen have the right to invoke Community freedoms in relation to tax levied by the Netherlands?

First, the Court declared that the provisions of the EC Treaty that provide for the freedom of establishment cannot be applied to situations which are purely internal to a Member State.[81] Secondly, it declared that "... Article 52 [Article 43] nevertheless cannot be interpreted in such a way as to exclude a given Member State's own nationals from the benefit of Community law where by reason of their conduct they are, with regard

[76] Case C-112/91 *Werner*, para. 16.

[77] Case C-112/91 *Werner*, para. 17.

[78] Case C-107/94 *P.H. Asscher v. Staatssecretaris van Financiën*.

[79] Case C-107/94 *Asscher*, para. 12.

[80] Case C-107/94 *Asscher*, para. 26. The ECJ began by concluding that the question of whether the higher tax rate for non-residents was compatible with Community law was to be decided in relation to the freedom of establishment, and not in relation to the free movement of workers.

[81] Case C-107/94 *Asscher*, para. 32.

to their Member State of origin, in a situation which may be regarded as equivalent to that of any other person enjoying the rights and liberties guaranteed by the Treaty".[82] The Court specifically noted that Mr Asscher, after moving from the Netherlands, had pursued activities at the same time both in the Netherlands and in Belgium, and that those dual activities had had direct repercussions on the calculation of his income tax in the Netherlands for the taxable year in question. Consequently, the Court concluded that Mr Asscher had exercised the rights and liberties recognised by the EC Treaty, and that he was entitled to rely on the EC Treaty provisions in question.[83]

In the present case there was an undisputable cross-border nexus, even if it was the state where Mr Asscher was a national that imposed the tax in question. From the Court's decision it seems important that Mr Asscher performed his activities both in the Netherlands, where he was a national, and in Belgium where he was resident. There was a cross-border economic nexus, but it is in my view difficult to draw any general conclusion from this case.

3.4.4 Case C-336/96 *Gilly* (12 May 1998)

Even though the *Gilly*[84] case deals with the free movement of workers it is of importance when discussing access to the EC Treaty. The facts of the underlying case were the following. Mr and Mrs Gilly were resident in France, close to the border with Germany. Mr Gilly was of French nationality and worked as a teacher in France. Mrs Gilly was a German national, but had by marriage also acquired French nationality. She worked as a teacher in a state primary school in Germany, close to the French border.

The case concerned the compatibility of the taxation of the German public service remuneration, received by Mrs Gilly, with the free movement of workers. In focus was the 1959 French-German tax treaty. Article 13 (1) of the treaty stipulated as a main rule that income from dependent work should be taxed in the state where it was carried out, which in this case was Germany. An exception was provided in Article 13 (5): In the case of frontier workers, income was to be taxed in the recipient's state of residence.

Taxpayers that received remunerations and pensions from the public sector were, according to Article 14 (1) of the treaty, liable to tax for that income in the state in

[82] *Ibid.* In this instance the ECJ refers to Case 115/78 *Knoors v. Secretary of State for Economic Affairs*, para. 24; case C-61/89 *Bouchoucha,* para. 13; case C-19/92 *Kraus v. Land Baden-Würtemberg,* para. 15; and case C-419/92 *Scholz v. Opera Universitaria di Cagliari.*

[83] Case C-107/94 *Asscher*, para. 33.

[84] Case C-336/96 *Mr and Mrs Robert Gilly v. Directeur des services fiscaux du Bas-Rhin.*

which it was paid. Teachers resident in one treaty state, who temporarily worked in the other treaty state, were by a rule of exception in Article 16 of the Treaty, liable to tax on pensions and similar income in their state of origin (residence).

Article 20 (2) (a) (cc) of the tax treaty dealt with the elimination of double taxation. It provided that profits and other income arising in Germany and taxable there according to the treaty, should also be taxable in France if they accrued to a person resident in France. The German tax should not be deductible for the calculation of the taxable income in France. The recipient was, however, entitled to a tax credit to be set off against the French tax charged on the taxable amount which included that income. For all other income the tax credit should be equal to the amount of the French tax on the relevant income. Mrs Gilly was entitled to such a tax credit.

The application of the tax treaty between Germany and France meant that the taxation of "frontier workers" differed depending on whether they worked in the private sector or in the public sector. Furthermore, if they worked as teachers in the public sector a differentiation was made on the basis of whether or not they had the nationality of the state of the authority that employed them, and whether the time of employment was short or not.[85] According to the tax treaty, Germany had the full right to tax on Mrs Gilly's salary, but her salary was also subject to tax in France. For Mrs Gilly, the German tax on her income considerably exceeded the French tax on the same income. Mrs Gilly was not entitled to the German splitting tax rate regime. In the end Mrs Gilly paid more tax in Germany than she would have done if the income would have been taxed in France only and not at all in Germany.[86]

The question to be addressed here is whether Mrs Gilly's situation was covered by the EC Treaty and the free movement of workers. To begin with the answer, the European Court of Justice decided that the situation in fact was covered by the EC Treaty rules on the free movement of workers.[87]

The French government had contended that Mrs Gilly had not exercised in France the freedom provided by Article 48 of the Treaty, because she had worked in her state of origin, Germany.[88] As already mentioned the Court did not agree with this opinion. "It need merely be pointed out here", the Court declared, "that Mrs Gilly has acquired French nationality by her marriage and works in Germany whilst residing in France."[89]

[85] Case C-336/96 *Gilly*, para. 18.

[86] A more detailed study of the *Gilly* case is provided by Vanistendael, "Case Note on C-336/96", *CML Rev.*, 2000, pp. 168-179.

[87] Case C-336/96 *Gilly*, para. 19.

[88] Case C-336/96 *Gilly*, para. 20.

[89] Case C-336/96 *Gilly*, para. 21.

Therefore, in the view of the Court, she had to be considered as a worker in France exercising her right to freedom of movement, when working in Germany. The fact that she retained her German nationality did in no way affect that she was a French national working in another Member State.[90]

In conclusion, the fact that Mrs Gilly was both a French national and resident for tax purposes in France, and in addition worked in Germany, was decisive for the EC Treaty and the free movement of workers to apply.

3.4.5 Conclusion

In all three cases, C-112/91 *Werner*, C-107/94 *Asscher* and C-336/96 *Gilly*, the nationality requirement was indisputably fulfilled: the cases only concerned Community citizens.

Furthermore, in all three cases the economic substance requirement was fulfilled. When it comes to matters of taxation this requirement normally tends to be at hand: it is, of course, an income of some kind that is subject to taxation and the economic substance requirement normally tends to be fulfilled.

However, what really was at stake in these three cases was whether the cross-border nexus requirement was fulfilled. That requirement was not fulfilled in the *Werner* case, but in both the *Asscher* and the *Gilly* cases. Mr Werner was a German national and the matter dealt with German taxation. The only circumstance in that case which had a cross-border nexus was that Mr Werner was resident in the Netherlands. In the view of the Court, the nexus to the Netherlands was not enough.

In the light of the subsequent *Asscher* case and predominantly the *Gilly* case, I doubt if the Court today would have come to the same conclusion in the *Werner* case. In my view Mr Werner was "punished" with a more burdensome taxation in Germany just because he had chosen to reside for tax purposes in the Netherlands. Admittedly, it is a well-established principle that there is nothing restricting a Member State from taxing its own nationals in a more burdensome way than foreigners, because the taxation of the nationals of a state is considered a strictly internal affair subject to the tax sovereignty of that state. In the *Werner* case, however, there was a cross-border circumstance: Mr Werner's residence in the Netherlands.

The Court distinguished the *Werner* case also in the *Asscher* case. Mr Asscher was a Dutch citizen working in the Netherlands, but non-resident for tax purposes in that state. Mr Asscher was also working in Belgium where he was resident for tax purposes.

[90] Case C-336/96 *Gilly*, para. 21.

The Court considered that the more burdensome taxation in the Netherlands was a breach of the freedom of establishment. The major difference from the *Werner* case was that Mr Asscher in fact conducted business in *both* Belgium and the Netherlands. In contrast, Mr Werner worked only in Germany.

However, if one considers the latest case of the three, the *Gilly* case, I find it reasonably clear that the *Werner* case would have been decided differently today. Mrs Gilly worked in Germany only, but was a national and resident of France. In relation to the *Werner* case the only differing circumstance is that she was a national of France because she was married to the French national, Mr Gilly. Mr Werner was not a Dutch citizen, but in effect the two cases were similar, because Mr Werner was resident in the Netherlands. It is my opinion that Dutch citizenship should today not have been required of Mr Werner for fulfilling the cross-border requirement and being granted treaty access.

3.5 Direct and Indirect Discrimination

3.5.1 Introduction

The European Court of Justice has settled that "... discrimination arises through the application of different rules to comparable situations or the application of the same rule to different situations".[91] As regards direct taxation, it is the view of the European Court of Justice that the situation of residents and of non-residents in a given situation is generally not comparable.[92] The reason is that there are "... objective differences between them from the point of view of the source of the income and the possibility of taking account of their ability to pay tax or their personal and family circumstances".[93]

The EC Treaty prohibits discrimination on the basis of nationality irrespective of whether it is openly based on nationality or indirectly based on nationality.[94] The following terminology is used when making this distinction. *Direct discrimination* is based directly on nationality: there is an unequal treatment based on the nationality. *Indirect discrimination* is the form of discrimination which is not based directly on nationality but has the same effect as if the discrimination had been based on

91 For example case C-80/94 *Wielockx*, para. 17.

92 For example case C-80/94 *Wielockx*, para. 18.

93 *Ibid.*

94 Kapteyn andVerLoren van Themaat, *Introduction to the Law of the European Community*, 3rd ed., Kluwer Law International, London/The Hague/Boston, 1998, p. 168.

nationality. Cases on direct taxation before the European Court of Justice often deal with indirect discrimination. The reason is that liability to tax is based on other criteria than nationality: principally the residence and source criteria.

In case C-1/93 *Halliburton*, the European Court of Justice declared "that the rules regarding equality of treatment forbid not only overt discrimination by reason of nationality or, in the case of a company, its seat, but all covert forms of discrimination which, by the application of other criteria of differentiation, lead in fact to the same result".[95] Furthermore, it should be observed that there is somewhat of a terminological confusion regarding the terms overt and covert discrimination: from time to time the European Court of Justice, as well as others, alternatively use the terms direct and indirect discrimination. In this study I will regard the two sets of terms as synonymous, but will use the terms direct and indirect discrimination.[96]

There is no discrimination if the potentially discriminatory measures are justified according to the rule-of-reason doctrine. In case C-237/94 *O'Flynn*, the European Court of Justice stated that national provisions are not discriminating if "… those provisions are justified by objective considerations independent of the nationality of the workers concerned, and if they are proportionate to the legitimate aim pursued by the national law".[97]

One should be aware that it is not always easy to ascertain whether the European Court of Justice considers direct or indirect discrimination to be at issue.

3.5.2 Direct Discrimination

One of the earliest cases from the European Court of Justice in the area of direct taxation is generally considered to deal with direct discrimination. The case is C-270/83 *Avoir fiscal*, dating from 1986. French companies that received dividends were granted a special tax credit called "*avoir fiscal*". The tax credit was only granted to persons who had their habitual residence or registered office in France. This French law was considered to discriminate against companies (insurance companies in this case) whose registered offices were in another Member State but which had French branches. The

---

95 Case C-1/93 *Halliburton Services*, para. 15. An early case where the distinction between direct and indirect discrimination was manifested is Case 152/73 *Sotgiu v. Deutsche Bundespost*, and another example is case C-237/94 *John O'Flynn v. Adjudication Officer*. See also case C-250/95 *Futura Participations*, para. 22.

96 On this topic see Wouters, "The Principle of Non-discrimination in European Community Law", *EC Tax Review*, 1999, pp. 98-106, at p. 103.

97 Case C-237/94 *O'Flynn*, para. 19. The ECJ (*ibid.*, para. 19) referred to (among others) the following cases in support of this view: case C-204/90 *Bachmann*, para. 27; and case C-111/91 *Commission v. Luxembourg*, para. 12.

comparison establishing the discrimination was of course with companies which had their seat in France.

Another example of direct discrimination in the area of direct taxation is case C-311/97 *Royal Bank of Scotland*. The case concerned the compatibility of Greek taxation of Greek branches (permanent establishments) of foreign banks compared with the taxation of banks resident in Greece. The Court came to the conclusion that there was a case of discrimination and that it was direct: Greek legislation made a difference in treatment between residents and non-residents. Residence for companies such as banks was based on their seat. According to Article 48 of the EC Treaty the seat of a company is a differentiating criterion, like nationality for individuals.

The distinction between direct and indirect discrimination is important because, at least according to the traditional approach, because direct discrimination can only be justified on those grounds explicitly mentioned in the EC Treaty. Those grounds providing for exceptions and limitations to the fundamental freedoms, have been referred to in the previous sections on the fundamental freedoms.[98] In case C-311/97 *Royal Bank of Scotland*, the European Court of Justice declared: "According to settled case-law, only an express derogatory provision, such as Article [46] of the EC Treaty, could render such discrimination compatible with Community law ...".[99]

3.5.3 Indirect Discrimination

When defining indirect discrimination it is necessary to consider it in relation to direct discrimination. If, on the one hand, a provision of national law, or Community law for that matter, applies a criterion such as nationality, that may, as discussed previously, constitute a case of direct discrimination. If, on the other hand, national law uses other criteria for distinguishing between different categories of persons, indirect discrimination may be at issue. It should be stressed that when it comes to indirect discrimination there may at first glance seem to be no difference in treatment: the different criteria used seem neutral.[100] But if those criteria in fact lead to a result that is a difference in treatment, there may be a case of indirect discrimination.

---

98 In principle those justifications, or with another terminology, limitations and exceptions, are stated in Articles 30, 39 (3) and (4), 45 and 46 (1), 55 (with references) and 58 (1) (b).

99 Case C-311/97 *Royal Bank of Scotland*, para. 32. In that case the ECJ also referred following supporting cases: Case 352/85 *Bond van Adventeerders and Others*, para. 32 and 33, and case C-288/89 *Stichting Collective Antennevoorziening Gouda and Others*, para. 11.

100 Cf. Wouters, "The Principle of Non-discrimination in European Community Law", *EC Tax Review*, 1999, pp. 98-106, at p. 103.

Individuals are often subject to taxation in a state on other criteria than nationality, and because of that indirect discrimination might occur. Farmer[101] identifies the following examples of conditions for a national law to constitute indirect discrimination:

(1) the foreign national is treated differently from the national;

(2) more foreign nationals than nationals are likely to receive such treatment; and

(3) the foreign national and the national are in the same tax position or substantially the same position, i.e. the differences in the situations of the foreign national and the national do not justify the different treatment.

Nowadays, there are a number of cases from the European Court of Justice on indirect discrimination in matters of direct taxation. Case C-330/91 *Commerzbank*[102] can serve as an introductory example. The German bank Commerzbank had a permanent establishment in the United Kingdom. The permanent establishment of Commerzbank issued loans to companies in the United States on which it received interest. According to the tax treaty between the United Kingdom and the United States, that interest would have been tax exempt if it had been received by a resident of the United Kingdom. Commerzbank received a refund from the United Kingdom of the overpaid tax. Commerzbank, however, also claimed interest on the overpaid tax, which was denied by the tax authorities in the United Kingdom. The reason for the denial was that Commerzbank was not a resident of the United Kingdom. The European Court of Justice declared in the *Commerzbank* case that the Court's practice shows that the rules regarding equality of treatment do not only forbid direct discrimination by reason of nationality or, in the case of a company, its seat. It also forbids "all covert forms of discrimination which, by the application of other criteria of differentiation, lead in fact to the same result".[103]

Indirect discrimination, albeit justified, was at issue in case C-204/90 *Bachmann*, which is thoroughly dealt with in section 3.9.3. Mr Bachmann was a German national that was employed in Belgium. In Belgium Mr Bachmann was denied the benefit of deducting contributions paid in Germany on sickness, invalidity and life insurance contracts. The reason for the refusal was that Mr Bachmann would not be liable to tax in Belgium on the capital sums issuing from those contracts. The Court came to

[101] Farmer, "EC law and Direct Taxation – Some Thoughts on Recent Issues", *EC Tax Journal*, 1995/96, pp. 91-108, at p. 93.

[102] C-330/91 *The Queen v. Inland Revenue Commissioners, ex parte Commerzbank AG.*

[103] Case C-330/91 *Commerzbank*, para. 14. The European Court of Justice refers to Case 152/73 *Sotgiu v. Deutsche Bundespost*, para. 11.

the conclusion that the relevant national provisions of Belgian law did not make any distinction on behalf of the nationality of workers.[104] However, the Court also came to the conclusion that workers who had carried out an occupation in one Member State and who were subsequently employed in another Member State, would normally have concluded their pension and insurance contracts, and likewise with insurers, in their state of origin.[105] In effect, this provision of Belgian law constituted an indirect discrimination. Finally, however, the Court came to the conclusion that the ground of the coherence of the Belgian fiscal system justified this difference in treatment.

As already noted, perhaps the most important effect of the difference between direct and indirect discrimination is that different grounds of justification apply according to the rule-of-reason doctrine. As regards direct discrimination, only grounds of limitation explicitly recognised in the EC Treaty may be used. But as regards indirect discrimination, the European Court of Justice has developed separate grounds of justification not, at least not explicitly, mentioned in the EC Treaty.

It has also been questioned whether according to the rule-of-reason doctrine grounds of public interest may serve to justify national measures that are indirectly discriminatory. Wathelet provides a good picture of the uncertainty: "[W]ould the Court be ready to admit that the reasons of overriding general interest justify mere restrictions as well as discrimination, with perhaps the exclusion of direct discrimination? Up to now, this dilemma has never been presented to the Court in such clear terms, even though in all the cases which I have cited or cite below, there was never any question of justifications expressly mentioned in the Treaty; Member States never rely on the exercise of public authority, public policy, public health or public security to justify their tax measures. But it is also true that an overriding general interest has only rarely been admitted by the Court."[106] In my view, however, it is clear that measures of indirect discrimination may also be justified on grounds of public interest and that the Court's decision in the *Bachmann* case is evidence of that. Mr Bachmann was treated differently in Belgium because he was not resident there. That was a case of potential indirect discrimination by reason of (non-)residence, a criterion similar to nationality.

[104] Case C-204/90 *Bachmann*, para. 8.

[105] Case C-204/90 *Bachmann*, para. 9.

[106] Wathelet, "The Influence of Free Movement of Persons, Services and Capital on National Direct Taxation: Trends in the Case Law of the Court of Justice", *Yearbook of European Law*, Eeckhout and Tridimas (ed.), Volume 20, Oxford University Press, Oxford, 2001, pp. 1-33, at p. 16 (cf. also p. 6).

3.5.4 Discrimination in Matters of Direct Taxation

It is a common feature of tax legislation in many countries not to use nationality as the determining criterion for the differentiation between tax subjects, even though there are exceptions. Rather, a common distinction in national tax legislation and tax treaty law is made between residents and non-residents, and a general characteristic is that states will grant residents a more beneficial tax treatment than non-residents. The Court has frequently recognised that a distinction made between residents and non-residents may very well cause discrimination and a breach of fundamental freedoms contained in the EC Treaty. If special tax benefits are granted to residents, and if the persons resident mainly consist of nationals of that state, the tax legislation at issue operates mainly to the detriment of nationals of other Member States, according to the Court.[107] Under such circumstances, tax benefits granted only to residents of a Member State may constitute indirect discrimination by reason of nationality.[108] Both direct and indirect discrimination will typically take place in the host state, but may also occur in the home state regarding for example foreign-source income.[109]

In an increasing number of cases the European Court of Justice has declared that national measures that do not constitute discriminatory measures, either direct or indirect, may still be in breach of the fundamental freedoms of the EC Treaty. Such impediments can be called non-discriminatory restrictions.[110] Non-discriminatory restrictions may take place both in the host state and in the home state.

Besides direct and indirect discrimination, and non-discriminatory restrictions, one may also discern a fourth category constituting differences in taxation between Member States. Terra and Wattel have labelled this group "disparities".[111] The term disparities refers to fully acceptable differences between the tax systems of the Member States, such as differences in tax rates. In my view, one should, however, bear in mind that in specific circumstances these "disparities" between Member States may very well turn into unlawful situations such as discrimination or non-discriminatory restrictions.

Gammie describes in an elegant way the different forms of discrimination or non-discriminatory restrictions ("barriers", to use Gammie's terminology) that the Court

---

107 Cf. e.g. case C-279/93 *Schumacker*, para. 28.

108 Case C-279/93 *Schumacker*, para. 29.

109 Cf. Terra and Wattel, *European Tax Taw*, 3rd ed., Kluwer Law International, London/The Hague/New York, 2001, p. 43.

110 *Ibid.*

111 *Op. cit.*, p. 44.

may face and then have to consider whether any justifications may apply.[112] The following situations may arise:

(1) a host state tax rule that involves a directly discriminatory difference in treatment on grounds of nationality;

(2) a host state tax rule that involves an indirectly discriminatory difference in treatment by reference to a criterion other than nationality but of similar effect;

(3) a home state tax rule that involves a difference in treatment based on nationality and creates a barrier to the exercise by its taxpayers of their Treaty freedoms or makes the exercise of those freedoms less attractive;

(4) a home state tax rule involving a difference in treatment based on some other criterion with similar effect and creating a barrier to the exercise by its taxpayers of their Treaty freedoms or making the exercise of those freedoms less attractive; and

(5) a tax rule (whether in the host or home state) that involves no discrimination or discriminatory difference in treatment but nevertheless may operate as a barrier to the exercise of a Treaty freedom and make the exercise on a Treaty freedom less attractive.

As will be discussed in the case-law analysis of Chapters 4 to 6, the terminology of the European Court of Justice is not altogether consistent, and that is also the case regarding the different commentators on the Court's practice. In the Court's recent case-law one can discern an unwillingness to declare a national measure to be discriminatory, even if that seems to have been possible. Rather, the Court uses a more vague line of argument when it declares that the national measure at issue simply constitutes an impediment to the fundamental freedom in question. This line of argumentation is sometimes referred to as a "restriction approach". Farmer, however, states that all the tax cases which the Court has decided upon could be considered as cases of discrimination, albeit with the exception of one of the measures dealt with in case C-250/95 *Futura Participations*.[113]

[112] Gammie, "The Role of the European Court of Justice in the Development of Direct Taxation in the European Union", *Bulletin*, 2003, pp. 86-98, pp. 91-92.

[113] Farmer, "The Court's Case Law on Taxation: a Castle Built on Shifting Sands?", *EC Tax Review*, 2003, pp. 75-81, at p. 81. One could also note that Farmer categorises case C-81/87 *Daily Mail* as a case on discrimination. Farmer, "EC Law and Direct Taxation – Some Thoughts on Recent Issues", *EC Tax Journal*, 1995/96, pp. 91-108, at p. 93, footnote 6.

3.6 The Meaning of "Objectively Comparable Situations"

3.6.1 Introduction

An important step in deciding whether a discriminatory measure[114] is at issue is the comparison of the situation of a national – or "resident" – and a non-national – or "non-resident". It is only where the situation of a resident and a non-resident are "objectively comparable" that a case of discrimination may be at issue.

A comparison between different situations is necessary when applying a "classic" discrimination analysis. Predominantly in the case-law of the Court, such an analysis has been made in the host state between residents and non-residents. In the view of the Court, the situations of residents and non-residents are not as a general rule comparable, even if the case-law bring evidence that they very well might be. In my view, discrimination can also occur in the home state, which is something that will be addressed in Chapter 4.

In the following account there will be an analysis of the meaning of "objectively comparable situations" in that case-law of the European Court of Justice.

3.6.2 Individuals

3.6.2.1 Case C-279/93 Schumacker *(14 February 1995)*

To begin with discrimination and the perspective of the host state, the European Court of Justice has emphasised that, in relation to direct taxes, the situations of residents and of non-residents are not, as a general rule, comparable.[115] In case C-279/93 *Schumacker* the Court describes in an elaborate way the reason why.[116] Even if the *Schumacker* case deals with the taxation of individuals, the reasoning of the Court is interesting also with respect to how the comparison is made in relation to companies, dealt with in section 3.6.3 below.

Mr Schumacker was a Belgian national. He worked in Germany. The Schumacker family had no income in Belgium, but Mr Schumacker earned an income in Germany. According to the tax treaty between Belgium and Germany, Mr Schumacker's income was to be taxed in the state of his employment, which was Germany. German tax legislation had a so-called splitting tariff for married couples applied to residents only.

[114] "Discrimination" from the perspective of the host state.

[115] Case C-279/93 *Schumacker*, para. 31.

[116] Case C-279/93 *Schumacker*, para. 32-34.

According to this, residents were subject to a lower tax rate than non-residents. As Mr Schumacker was a non-resident, he was subject to the higher tax rate. The European Court of Justice had to decide whether this difference in treatment was in line with the free movement of workers according to Article 39 (ex Article 48) of the EC Treaty.

The Court correctly noted that in most cases the income of a non-resident derived from a Member State is only part of his total income. The total income is concentrated in his state of residence. The Court correctly referred to the OECD Model Convention, and the fact that according to that Model Convention the overall taxation of taxpayers is made by the state of residence. The income of a person is normally concentrated in his state of residence. Traditionally, the state of residence has been seen as having the best access to the information, such as personal and family circumstances, required to tax its own residents.[117]

One major conclusion of the Court was that the fact that a law provision of a Member State that does not grant a non-resident certain tax benefits that it grants to a resident, is not, as a rule, discriminatory because those two categories of taxpayers are not in comparable situations.[118] Increased mobility has, however, in some cases turned these traditional assumptions upside down, which the *Schumacker* case exemplifies.

One major conclusion of the Court was that where the non-resident in question received no significant income in his state of residence, but obtained the major part of his income in the other Member State where he was employed, the situations were comparable. Accordingly, the Court considered there to be no objective difference between the situation of a resident and that of a non-resident engaged in a comparable employment in the host state, at least that there was no difference justifying different treatment as regards taking into account for tax purposes the taxpayer's personal and family circumstances.[119]

In the view of Wathelet, the *Schumacker* decision means that as the state of employment refused to apply the "splitting" tax rate regime to the non-resident, who received no significant income in his state of residence, the German law at issue constituted an indirect discrimination.[120]

[117] Cf. case C-279/93 *Schumacker*, para. 33.

[118] Case C-279/93 *Schumacker*, para. 34.

[119] Case C-279/93 *Schumacker*, para. 36-37.

[120] Wathelet, "The Influence of Free Movement of Persons, Services and Capital on National Direct Taxation: Trends in the Case Law of the Court of Justice", *Yearbook of European Law*, Eeckhout and Tridimas (ed.), Volume 20, Oxford University Press, Oxford, 2001, pp. 1-33, at p. 7. The "Schumacker doctrine" has been confirmed by the ECJ in other cases such as C-80/94 *Wielockx* and C-391/97 *Gschwind*.

In summary the "Schumacker doctrine" means, in my view and for the purposes of this study, the following. The situations of residents and non-residents are not, as a general rule comparable. However, where a non-resident earns a major part[121] of his income in the host state, he may be in a situation comparable to that of a resident in that state. In addition, if the situations are found to be comparable, the host state shall permit personal allowances and deductions. In the following section I will deal with case C-80/94 *Wielockx*, which confirms the important *Schumacker* decision.[122]

3.6.2.2 Case C-80/94 **Wielockx** *(11 August 1995)*

In case C-80/94 *Wielockx* the European Court of Justice also elaborated on what constitutes objectively comparable situations. The underlying case before the national court dealt with Mr Wielockx, who was a Belgian national also living in Belgium. However, he worked in the Netherlands where he earned his total income. Because he was not resident in the Netherlands, he was denied the deduction for tax purposes of contributions to a pension reserve. The fundamental freedom at issue in this case was the freedom of establishment, and not, as in the *Schumacker* case, the free movement of workers, but that has little significance for the specific issue of what constitutes objectively comparable situations.

To begin with, the Court declared that in relation to direct taxes, the situations of residents and non-residents in a state are not generally comparable. The reason is that there are objective differences between them from the point of view of the source of the income and the possibility of taking account of their ability to pay tax or their personal and family circumstances.[123] A difference in treatment of those resident and non-resident taxpayers could accordingly not *in itself* be categorised as discrimination within the meaning of the EC Treaty.[124]

---

121 See also Van Raad who notes that the ECJ in the *Schumacker* case "mysteriously" added to the phrase "a major part" of his income, the phrase "and almost all his family income". Van Raad, "The Impact of the EC Treaty's Fundamental Freedom Provisions on EU Member States' Taxation in Border-crossing Situations – Current State of Affairs", *EC Tax Review*, 1995, pp. 190-201, at p. 195.

122 The general applicability of the ECJ's decision in the *Schumacker* case has been questioned by Avery Jones, "Carry on Discriminating", *European Taxation*, 1996, p. 46. One important question is whether the Schumacker doctrine applies also to credit countries and not only exempt countries. In the *Schumacker* case, Belgium, Mr Schumacker's state of residence, applied the exemption method. How would the ECJ have decided whether Mr Schumacker would have had the right in Belgium to make a credit for the "extra non-residential-tax" paid in Germany? Could the Schumacker doctrine still apply in relation to credit countries? The answer of Avery Jones is no. Farmer has advocated that the Schumacker doctrine also would apply in relation to credit countries. Farmer, "EC Law and National Rules on Direct Taxation: a Phoney War?", *EC Tax Review*, 1998, pp. 13-29.

123 Case C-80/94 *Wielockx*, para. 18.

124 Case C-80/94 *Wielockx*, para. 19.

The present situation was, however, different according to the Court. Mr Wielockx was a non-resident taxpayer in the Netherlands, but he received all his income there. In that situation he was objectively in the same situation, so far as concerns income tax, as a resident of that state who did the same work there: both were taxed in that state alone and their taxable incomes were the same.[125]

The Court concluded that if a non-resident taxpayer is not given the same tax treatment as a resident regarding deductions from his taxable income, his personal situation will not be taken into account in any of the involved Member States. The tax authorities of the state where he works will not take his personal situation into account because he is not resident there, and the state of resident will not take them into account because he receives no income there. The result would be that the overall tax burden was more burdensome in comparison with residents that were allowed the deduction.[126] Consequently, under these circumstances the situation of a non-resident was objectively comparable with the situation of a resident. In addition, the Court decided that the Dutch law was discriminatory.

3.6.2.3 Recent Case-law and the Schumacker Doctrine

There have been several cases since the 1995 *Schumacker* decision dealing with the conditions when residents and non-residents should be treated in the same way. I will not deal specifically with this issue, the reason being that it is too large to be covered in this study.[127] This issue has rightly been thoroughly discussed in recent literature.[128]

Still, there seems to be a tendency for the European Court of Justice to be moving to a position where residents and non-residents should be treated equally in the host state, even if, for example, the non-resident does not earn the major part of his income in the host state. Case C-234/01 *Gerritse* deals with a Dutch musician performing in Germany. Mr Gerritse performed as a drummer at a radio station in Berlin. He received a fee of about DEM 6,000 and had related direct business expenses of DEM 1,000. The German income tax rate was 25 per cent, which resulted in a tax of DEM 1,500

[125] Case C-80/94 *Wielockx*, para. 20.

[126] Case C-80/94 *Wielockx*, para. 21.

[127] See also section 1.2.3 Delimitations.

[128] See e.g. Wattel, "Progressive Taxation of Non-residents and Intra-EC Allocation of Personal Allowances: why Schumacker, Asscher, Gilly and Gschwind Do Not Suffice", *European Taxation*, 2000, pp. 210-223; Mattsson, "Does the European Court of Justice Understand the Policy behind Tax Benefits based on Personal and Family Circumstances", *European Taxation*, 2003, pp. 186-194; and Hinnekens, "European Court Challenges Flat Rate Withholding Taxation of Non-resident Artists: Comment on the Gerritse Decision", *EC Tax Review*, 2003, pp. 207-213.

and DEM 112 in solidarity tax. Mr Gerritse's worldwide income was DEM 62,000, and apparently the income from Germany was only a fraction of his total income. The major part of Mr Gerritse's income the year in question was earned in the Netherlands and in Belgium.

Mr Gerritse was taxed in Germany with 25 per cent of his gross income. He could neither benefit from the deduction of costs, nor from the progressive taxation, including a tax-free allowance, which residents enjoyed.[129]

In its decision, the Court repeated the basics of the Schumacker doctrine, and one could at a first instance believe that the situation of the non-resident Mr Gerritse would not be considered objectively comparable to that of a resident. However, that is the final outcome of the ruling. The Court concludes that according to the tax treaty between Germany and the Netherlands, the German income of Mr Gerritse was subject to the progressive income taxation in that state. Non-residents and residents were considered by the Court to be in comparable situations. A higher tax rate applicable to non-residents in Germany would constitute indirect discrimination, in the view of the Court.

Hinnekens makes this well-founded conclusion: "The *Gerritse* decision clearly means a further step in the progressive approximation in the tax treatment of resident and non-resident persons for purposes of Community tax law as distinct from traditional international tax law."[130]

3.6.3 Companies

3.6.3.1 Case C-311/97 **Royal Bank of Scotland** *(29 April 1999)*

In case C-311/97 *Royal Bank of Scotland* the European Court of Justice had to consider whether the compared situations were objectively comparable or not. The case concerned the taxation in Greece of resident banks and branches of non-resident banks. The Court began its reasoning by recapitulating the Court's practice regarding individuals and what constitutes comparable situations.[131] The Court made the conclusion that resident and non-resident individuals could not in general be considered to be in comparable situations: "... there are objective differences between them from

[129] Case C-234/01 *Gerritse*, para. 24.

[130] Hinnekens, "European Court Challenges Flat Rate Withholding Taxation of Non-resident Artists: Comment on the Gerritse Decision", *EC Tax Review*, 2003, pp. 207-213, at p. 211.

[131] Case C-311/97 *Royal Bank of Scotland*, para. 26.

the point of view of the source of income and the possibility of taking account of their ability to pay tax or their personal and family circumstances".[132]

More specifically, in the *Royal Bank of Scotland* case the Court came to the conclusion that there were no objective differences between resident banks and non-resident banks established in Greece through branches. There was no difference between resident and non-resident banks in Greece, neither regarding the method for calculating the taxable base, nor regarding the calculation of tax.[133]

It was true that companies with their seat in Greece were subject there to unlimited tax liability on their worldwide income in that state. In contrast, branches (permanent establishments) of foreign companies were subject to limited tax liability in Greece on the income attributable to the branch in Greece. However, the Court declared, that circumstance based on "the limited fiscal sovereignty of the State in which the income arises in relation to that of the State in which the company has its seat is not such as to prevent the two categories of companies from being considered, all other things being equal, as being in a comparable situation as regards the method of determining the taxable base".[134]

3.6.3.2 Case C-141/99 **AMID** *(14 December 2000)*

Case C-141/90 *AMID* (*Algemene Maatschappij voor Investering en Dienstverlening NV*) will serve as an example of how the Court identifies comparable situations when dealing with home state restrictions. AMID was a Belgian company with its seat and head office in Belgium. AMID also had a branch in Luxembourg. According to the tax treaty between Belgium and Luxembourg, the income of the Luxembourg branch was tax exempt in Belgium. In 1981 AMID made a loss in Belgium of about BEF 2,000,000, whereas the Luxembourg branch made a profit of about BEF 3,500,000. According to Belgian tax legislation, it was not possible to set off the Belgian loss against the Luxembourg profit. As a consequence, AMID sought to deduct its 1981 loss in Belgium from its Belgian profits of 1982. However, that deduction was denied by the Belgian tax authorities for the reason that according to Belgian legislation the loss of 1981 should have been set off against the profits made the same year in Luxembourg, all with the result that the deduction in 1982 could not be allowed.

[132] Case C-311/97 *Royal Bank of Scotland*, para. 27. The ECJ referred to the cases C-279/93 *Schumacker*, para. 31-32; C-80/94 *Wielockx*, para. 18; and C-107/94 *Asscher*, para. 41.

[133] Case C-311/97 *Royal Bank of Scotland*, para. 28.

[134] Case C-311/97 *Royal Bank of Scotland*, para. 29.

AMID lodged complaints against this treatment according to Belgian tax law and argued that the provisions at issue were in breach of the EC Treaty and the freedom of establishment. AMID claimed that the Belgian provisions placed companies with branches abroad at a disadvantage compared with companies with branches in Belgium only.[135] The Court concluded, as regards the comparison, that by setting off Belgian losses against profits exempted by a tax treaty, the legislation of Belgium established a differentiated tax treatment between companies incorporated under national law having establishments on national territory only and those having establishments in another Member State.[136] The Court continued: "... where such companies have a permanent establishment in a Member State other than that of origin and a convention to prevent double taxation binds the two States, those companies are likely to suffer a tax disadvantage which they would not have to suffer if all their establishments were situated in the Member State of origin".[137]

In this case the comparison was made with the home state as the starting point. The two situations which are compared are, on the one hand, the establishment of a branch in another Member State, and, on the other hand, the establishment of a branch in Belgium. When making this comparison the Court identified a difference in tax treatment, which was considered as a breach of the freedom of establishment.

3.6.3.3 Conclusion

Also regarding the discrimination analysis applied to companies, the European Court of Justice decides whether the different situations are objectively comparable or not. However, in my view there is a difference between the comparison made regarding individuals and the comparison made regarding companies, at least in the early case-law of the Court. When it comes to individuals more factors are considered: for example personal and family circumstances. That was at least true for cases such as *Schumacker* and *Wielockx*.

The comparison made regarding companies has historically been narrower than the one applied on individuals. The general situation of companies is not subject to comparison. Instead, the comparison is focused on whether, for example, a non-resident company is granted the same beneficial tax treatment as a resident company. The general statement by the Court that, as a general rule, the situations of residents and non-residents are not comparable, seems less valid regarding companies than regarding individuals,

135 Case C-141/99 *AMID*, para. 14.

136 Case C-141/99 *AMID*, para. 23.

137 *Ibid.*

at least concerning the treatment in the host state and from a historic perspective. Recent case-law from the Court, for example the *Gerritse* case, indicates that the more comprehensive comparison regarding individuals is, in fact, less comprehensive.

An additional example of this narrow approach regarding companies are the joined cases C-397/98 and C-410/98 *Metallgesellschaft and Others*, were subsidiaries in the United Kingdom of foreign parent companies were not granted the benefit of group income election, which they would have been if the parent companies had been resident in the United Kingdom. The comparison was made between United Kingdom subsidiaries with, on the one hand, resident parent companies, and, on the other hand, non-resident parent companies. The comparison was limited to whether the United Kingdom subsidiaries of the different parent companies could benefit from the system for group income election.[138]

3.7 Non-discriminatory Restrictions

3.7.1 The Meaning of Non-discriminatory Restrictions

In recent years it has become evident that the fundamental freedoms of the EC Treaty go even further than the mere prohibition of discrimination, be it either direct or indirect.

The European Court of Justice has developed a "doctrine" according to which national measures are prohibited even if they are not discriminatory, on the condition that they otherwise have a restrictive effect on cross-border movements within the Community. Such other measures are in this study referred to as *non-discriminatory restrictions.*[139]

When making the distinction between discriminatory measures and non-discriminatory restrictions it is important to emphasise the difference between the terms *"host state"* and *"home state"*. The host state would be the state where a national of another Member State is subject to discrimination, direct or indirect. However, according to the Court's view on restrictions the Member State where a person is a national may also impose obstacles to cross-border movements.

138 Cf. joined cases C-397/98 and C-410/98 *Metallgesellschaft and Others*, esp. para. 51-56.

139 On the development of fundamental freedoms into prohibitions of restrictions, see Lehner, "Limitation on the National Power Of Taxation by the Fundamental Freedoms and Non-discrimination Clauses of the EC Treaty", *EC Tax Review*, 2000, pp. 5-15.

The terminology of the EC Treaty is not completely in line with prohibition of restrictions as regards all four freedoms. An overview of the freedoms in this specific respect gives the following result.

As regards the free movement of goods, Article 28 of the EC Treaty prohibits "[q]uantitative *restrictions* on imports and all measures having equivalent effects" – accordingly, on the basis of the Treaty wording, the free movement of goods, not only prohibits discrimination, but also the even wider concept of "restrictions". The freedom of establishment provides, according to Article 43 of the EC Treaty, that "*restrictions* on the freedom of establishment of nationals of a Member State shall be prohibited".[140]

Regarding the freedom to provide services, Article 49 of the EC Treaty stipulates that "*restrictions* on freedom to provide services within the Community shall be prohibited in respect of nationals of Member States who are established in a State of the Community other than that of the person for whom the services are intended". Article 56 (1) of the EC Treaty stipulates that "... all *restrictions* on the movement of capital between Member States and between Member States and third countries shall be prohibited".[141] However, when it comes to the free movement of workers, Article 39 (2) of the EC Treaty provides that this freedom "... shall entail the *abolition of any discrimination* based on nationality...".[142] It may strongly be questioned whether this line of wording provides any substantial difference in relation to the other freedoms providing prohibitions on restrictions rather than discrimination.

Today, it is clear from the jurisprudence of the European Court of Justice that the fundamental freedoms also include a prohibition against restrictions in the home state (state of origin). An early example of this approach, albeit not in the area of direct taxation, is case C-19/92 *Kraus* from 1993.[143] The *Kraus* case dealt primarily with the free movement of workers. The Court declared that "... Article [43] of the Treaty may not be interpreted in such a way as to exclude from the benefit of Community law the nationals of a given Member State when, owing to the fact that they have lawfully resided on the territory of another Member State and have there acquired a vocational qualification which is recognised under Community law, they are, with regard to their

[140] Emphasis added. Article 43 (2) of the EC Treaty (on the freedom of establishment) refers to equal national treatment of non-nationals. This could be perceived as if this freedom did not cover restrictions, but only discrimination. This is, however, not the case according to the ECJ, cf. e.g. Case 81/87 *Daily Mail*.

[141] A similar prohibition is stipulated in Article 56 (2) of the EC Treaty on the free movement of payments between Member States and between Member States and third countries.

[142] Emphasis added.

[143] Case C-19/92 *Kraus v. Land Baden-Württemberg*. Cf. Martín Jiménez, *Towards Corporate Tax Harmonization in the European Community*, Kluwer Law International, London/The Hague/Boston, 1999, p. 219.

State of origin, in a situation which may be assimilated to that of any other persons enjoying the rights and liberties guaranteed by the Treaty".[144] Thus, Article 43 of the EC Treaty also includes a prohibition against restrictions by the state of origin.

For some time, it has been clear that the European Court of Justice has upheld a prohibition against restrictions in the state of origin as regards the free movement of goods. An early example of this is the *Dassonville* case from 1974.[145] Regarding the free movement of capital it is clear from both the wording of Article 56 of the EC Treaty and the case-law of the Court, that the free movement of capital also includes a prohibition against restrictions in the state of origin (or "home state", with the terminology I use in this study, which, however, may sound a bit peculiar regarding the free movement of capital).

A seminal case from the Court, the *Gebhard*[146] case, cast away all doubt on the question of whether all fundamental freedoms contain a prohibition against restrictions. In this case the Court declared that "… national measures *liable to hinder or make less attractive* the exercise of the fundamental freedoms guaranteed must fulfil four conditions …".[147] The following two factors should be observed. First, the Court addresses all freedoms, including the free movement of workers. Secondly, the words "liable to hinder or make less attractive" are wide enough to cover both discrimination and restrictions that are non-discriminatory.

The European Court of Justice has in several cases manifested that restrictive measures taken by the home state are also prohibited. In, for example, the case *X AB and Y AB v. Riksskatteverket*[148] the European Court of Justice declared:

> "As far as the provisions concerning freedom of establishment are concerned, it must be pointed out that, even though, according to their wording, those provisions are mainly aimed at ensuring that foreign nationals and companies are treated in the host Member State in the same way as nationals of that State, they also prohibit the Member State of origin from hindering the establishment in another Member State of one of its nationals or of a company incorporated under its legislation which comes within the definition contained in Article 58 of the Treaty …".

---

144 Case C-19/92 *Kraus*, para. 15. The Court also declared that the same approach applies for the free movement of workers, Case C-19/92, *Kraus*, para. 16.

145 Case 8/74 *Procureur du Roi v. Benoît and Gustave Dassonville.*

146 Case C-55/94 *Gebhard.*

147 Case C-55/94 *Gebhard*, para. 37 (emphasis added). The four conditions mentioned will be developed in a later subsection.

148 Case C-200/98 *X AB and Y AB*, para. 26.

Other cases where the European Court of Justice has manifested this view are, for example, *Daily Mail*,[149] *ICI*[150] and *Baars*.[151]

3.7.2 Illustration of Restrictions in the Area of Direct Taxation

It may be appropriate to begin the discussion of the case-law of the European Court of Justice with an example of a national measure constituting a restriction. Because the following discussion will focus on breaches of the freedom of establishment and the free movement of capital, I will discuss a case regarding another fundamental freedom. My intention here is rather to emphasise what characterises a restrictive national measure. For this discussion the *Jessica Safir*[152] case has been chosen.

The *Jessica Safir* case concerned Swedish legislation on savings in the form of capital life insurance (K-insurance). There was a difference in the taxation between insurances taken out with Swedish companies and with companies established abroad. Jessica Safir had taken out a life insurance with a foreign insurance company.

The Swedish legislation on the taxation of life insurances taken out with Swedish insurers had the following general characteristics. Insurance companies established in Sweden were liable to tax in Sweden according to Law (1990:661) on Yield Tax on Pension Funds. The tax was levied on the insurer (that is the company providing the insurance) and based on the yield from the capital insurance. The yield from the insurance was calculated according to a standard method. The method of calculation was based on the capital of the insurer at the end of the year preceding the assessment to tax, with a deduction for the insurer's financial liabilities at that time. The capital basis was multiplied with the average government bond yield in the year before the tax year. The resulting standard yield was taxed at 27 per cent.[153]

There was no right for persons who had taken out life insurance policies with companies established in Sweden to deduct premiums from their taxable income. Proceeds from such life insurance policies were, however, not taxable. The same applied for persons that had taken out life insurances with companies established abroad.

---

149 Case C-81/87 *The Queen v. H.M. Treasury and Commissioners of Inland Revenue, ex parte Daily Mail and General Trust plc.*

150 Case C-264/96 *Imperial Chemical Industries plc (ICI) v. Kenneth Hall Colmer (Her Majesty's Inspector of Taxes).*

151 Case C-251/98 *C. Baars v. Inspecteur der Belastingdienst Particulieren/Ondernemingen Gorinchem.*

152 Case C-118/96 *Jessica Safir v. Skattemyndigheten i Dalarnas Län, formerly Skattemyndigheten i Kopparbergs Län.*

153 Case C-118/96 *Jessica Safir*, para. 4.

The Swedish legislation on the taxation of life insurances taken out with insurers established abroad had the following general characteristics. Premiums paid for such foreign insurers were taxed according to the Premium Tax Law (1990:660). The purpose of the Premium Tax Law was to secure neutrality between life insurances taken out with Swedish insurers and foreign insurers. The Premium Tax Law stipulated that individuals or legal entities, domiciled or permanently resident in Sweden, who had taken out life insurances, were liable to a state tax on the premiums paid. The tax paid was 15 per cent of the amount of the premium. These taxpayers had to register themselves and declare the payment of premiums to the tax authorities (*Skattemyndigheten*).

According to the Premium Tax Law, the Swedish tax authorities had, at the request of the taxpayer, the right to grant an exemption from payment of tax, or to reduce the tax by half. Exemption or reduction was to be granted if the company with which the insurance was taken out, was subject, in the state where it was established, to a revenue tax that was comparable to that payable by insurance companies established in Sweden.[154] It was put forward that the rule on exemption or reduction was intended to prevent the saver who had taken out a capital life insurance with a company established abroad from being subject to a higher taxation than if the insurance had been taken out with an insurer established in Sweden.[155] The Court found that the Swedish tax legislation established different tax regimes for capital life insurance policies depending on whether they were taken out with Swedish or foreign life insurance companies.[156]

A Swedish tax court (*Länsrätten i Kopparbergs län*) asked the European Court of Justice for a preliminary ruling on whether Articles 6, 59, 60 or 73b and 73d of the EC Treaty "… preclude the application of national legislation on taxation of capital life assurance such as the legislation in question in the main proceedings".[157]

The European Court of Justice therefore had to determine whether the Swedish legislation "creates obstacles to the freedom to provide services", and if such obstacles were justified.[158] The main points were the following.[159] First, the Court noted that persons having insurances with foreign insurance companies must register themselves and declare premium payments to a central body, *Skattemyndigheten*. Secondly, the surrender of an insurance was more costly if the insurance was taken out with a foreign life insurance company. Thirdly, if a person with an insurance in a foreign company

[154] Case C-118/96 *Jessica Safir*, para. 11.

[155] Case C-118/96 *Jessica Safir*, para. 12.

[156] Case C-118/96 *Jessica Safir*, para. 24.

[157] Case C-118/96 *Jessica Safir*, para. 20.

[158] Case C-118/96 *Jessica Safir*, para. 25.

[159] Case C-118/96 *Jessica Safir*, para. 26-29.

applied for an exemption or reduction of the premiums the Swedish tax authorities (*Skattemyndigheten*) required precise information concerning the income tax to which the foreign company was subject, unless the tax authorities were already in possession of that information. Fourthly, the Court found that there were differences in the tax assessment as regards insurers not established in Sweden. This difference could create uncertainty for those who wanted to take out insurances with foreign companies.

The Court concluded that the Swedish legislation in question contained "*a number of elements liable to dissuade*" individuals from taking out capital life insurance with companies not established in Sweden and "*liable to dissuade*" insurance companies from offering their services on the Swedish market.[160]

The *ratio decidendi* of the European Court of Justice did not focus on whether the Swedish legislation was discriminatory or not, but rather that it had the effect of dissuading on the one hand nationals from choosing foreign life insurances, and on the other hand of dissuading foreign life insurance companies from offering their services on the Swedish market. The European Court of Justice seems not to rule out that the Swedish legislation might be discriminatory, but rather emphasises that the complexity of the Swedish legislation makes it difficult to decide whether it is discriminatory or not.[161]

3.7.3 Concluding Remarks

It has often been held that the prohibition against discrimination is an expression of equal treatment. In addition, the prohibition against non-discriminatory restrictions is rather an expression of the freedom of cross-border movements. Ehlers considers the fundamental freedoms primarily to fulfil the objective of equal treatment. Moreover, Ehlers recognises that the fundamental freedoms also encompass the freedom to cross-border movements, but that is secondary to the objective of equal treatment.[162] In general I agree with this view. However, one could ask whether there is any difference between the two ways of interpreting the material scope of the fundamental freedoms.

Lang argues convincingly for the position that in those cases where the European Court of Justice has applied the vaguer "barrier" or "restriction" approach in tax law cases, it has in fact made a stop in the analysis where the next step ultimately would

---

160 Case C-118/96 *Jessica Safir*, para. 30.

161 Cf. case C-118/96 *Jessica Safir*, para. 32.

162 Ehlers, "§ 7 Allgemeine Lehren", in *Europäische Grundrechte und Grundfreiheiten*, Ehlers (ed.), de Gruyter Recht, Berlin, 2003, pp. 154-157.

have been the conclusion that the measure also is discriminatory. Lang advances: "Untersucht man die bisher vom EuGH im Bereich des Steuerrechts aufgrund der Grundfreiheiten entschiedenen Fälle, zeigt sich, dass auch in jenen Fallkonstellationen, die vom Schrifttum als Beispiele für ein Beschränkungsverbot gesehen werden, die Bildung von Vergleichspaaren möglich ist. Daher drängt sich der Verdacht auf, dass auch bei den Grundfreiheiten die Deutung als Beschränkungsverbot keine eigenständige Rechtsprechungslinie darstellt, sondern lediglich eine verkürzte Argumentation. Daher ist auch in den als Beschränkungsverbot gedeuteten Fallkonstellationen eine Vergleichbarkeitsprüfung möglich, wobei – ebenso wie beim Gleichheitsgrundsatz – der Vergleich auch zur gesamten Rechtsordnung oder zur Nicht-Regelung vorgenommen werden kann."[163] Von Bahr also expresses difficulties in making a difference between direct discrimination and other forms of restrictions.[164]

In the forthcoming case-law analysis, it will be my aim to consider whether the Court in fact applies such a shortened analysis in cases concerning non-discriminatory restrictions. If the Court in fact applies a shortened analysis stopping before a case of discrimination has been discerned, there may be special objectives behind such an approach. I am here thinking of the rule-of-reason doctrine, which, according to how the Court itself has elaborated the basic steps of it, only applies to measures that are non-discriminatory. A reason for the Court's purported way of shortening the analysis could be that it wishes to leave the door open for applying the rule-of-reason doctrine. I will return to this issue in section 3.8 which deals with the rule-of-reason doctrine.

In the case-law analysis of Chapters 4 and 6 the following should be borne in mind when the Court in a specific case has decided the disputed measure constitutes a non-discriminatory restriction. Is there not always a comparison made when the disputed measure in question is identified, and if no comparison can be identified, could it have been made by the Court? As discussed previously, the comparison between different situations is the core of identifying whether a measure is discriminatory or not.

---

163 "An examination of cases which to date have been decided by the European Court of Justice in the area of the tax law in respect of fundamental freedoms shows that, even in those cases given in the literature as examples of non-discriminatory restriction, the formation of comparable situations is possible. Therefore there is a suspicion that even with respect to the fundamental freedoms, the interpretation as non-discriminatory restriction does not represent an independent basis for the decisions, but merely a shortened analysis. Therefore it is possible that, as with those cases interpreted as non-discriminatory restriction, a test for comparison is permitted, whereby – as with the principle of equality – a comparison can be carried out with the total legal system or with an unregulated system." Lang, "Kapitalverkehrsfreiheit und Doppelbesteuerungsabkommen", in *Kapitalverkehrsfreihet und Steuerrecht*, Lechner, Staringer and Tumpel (ed.), Linde Verlag, Wien, 2000, pp. 181-196, at p. 189 (references omitted).

164 Von Bahr, "Något om EG-domstolens praxis på skatteområdet", in *Festskrift till Gustaf Lindencrona*, Arvidsson, Melz and Silfverberg (ed.), Norstedts Juridik, Stockholm, 2003, pp. 67-82, at p. 73.

3.8 The Rule-of-reason Doctrine

3.8.1 Introduction

As previously mentioned, the EC Treaty stipulates four fundamental freedoms: the free movement of goods, services, persons and capital. There are, however, limitations and exceptions to those freedoms. Such limitations and exceptions are provided in the EC Treaty in relation to the specific freedoms, and have been briefly addressed in the previous presentation of the fundamental freedoms. A more thorough analysis of the limitations and exceptions to the freedom of establishment and the free movement of capital will be presented in the subsequent chapters on those freedoms.

Besides the limitations and exceptions granted by the EC Treaty, the European Court of Justice has developed specific grounds for "justifying" obstacles to the fundamental freedoms. These grounds of justification are to be kept separate from the limitations and exceptions granted according to the EC Treaty. The emergence of the rule-of-reason doctrine has previously been discussed in relation to, for example, the cases *Dassonville*, *Cassis de Dijon*, and *Keck and Mithourd*. The Court has accepted a wide range of grounds of justification that constitute grounds in the public interest according to the rule-of-reason doctrine regarding the different fundamental freedoms of the EC Treaty, albeit rarely in the field of direct taxation.

The traditional view is that if a national measure constitutes direct discrimination, only explicitly mentioned grounds stipulated in the EC Treaty may serve as a ground of justification.

If the measure constitutes indirect discrimination or another form of obstacle not constituting direct discrimination, then the case-law-based grounds of justification in the public interest may apply. For example, in respect of the freedom to provide services the Court has accepted the protection of the person to whom a service is provided, the protection of intellectual property, the protection of workers and consumers (including, in the case of insurance services, the protection of policy holders and of insured persons), the preservation of national historic and artistic treasures, the maintenance of order in society, and the protection of investor confidence in the national financial market.[165]

[165] Wouters, "The European Court of Justice and Fiscal Barriers to Companies' Cross-border Establishments", in *Current Issues of Cross-Border Establishment of Companies in the European Union*, Wouters and Schneider (ed.), Maklu, Nomos, Juridik & Samhälle, Antwerpen, 1995, pp. 101-141, at pp. 119-120 (with further case-law references).

3.8.2 The Different Conditions of the Rule-of-reason Doctrine

There are several ways in which one can list the different steps of the rule-of-reason doctrine. Hinnekens provides a thorough "EC-compatibility tree", including the following basic components.[166] It should be noted that I have made some minor amendments to the steps modelled by Hinnekens and reduced them somewhat.

(i) Does the tax measure fall within the scope of Community law and the fundamental freedoms contained in the EC Treaty? If the answer is yes, the following step should be examined.

(ii) Does the tax measure belong to a category of national or bilateral tax measures that the European Court of Justice has deemed to be in conformity with Community law principles?[167] If the answer is yes, the measure is *per se* acceptable and no further steps of the rule-of-reason test needs to be examined. However, if the answer is no, the following step has to be examined.

(iii) Is the tax measure at issue compatible with the EC Treaty principle of non-discrimination as interpreted by the ECJ? If the measure is not discriminatory, and not even constituting a non-discriminatory restriction (an acceptable "disparity"), the measure is accepted under Community law. Thus it is only if the answer is no that the following question will have to be addressed.

(iv) Is the tax measure accepted according to an explicit limitation or exception contained in the EC Treaty, such as Article 46 of the EC Treaty referring to grounds of public policy, public security or public health? In my view those situations should be rare when a tax measure would fall within the material scope of such limitations to the fundamental freedoms of the EC Treaty. Accordingly,

[166] Hinnekens, "Justifications – EC Perspectives for Justifications of Discriminatory and Restrictive Tax Measures of Member States", Report to the 2004 EATLP Conference in Paris, unpublished manuscript, 10 pp., at p. 7.

[167] As measures accepted by the ECJ as in line with Community law principles, Hinnekens refers to the "Gilly case law" (*ibid.*). In case C-336/96 *Gilly* (para. 24) the ECJ declared that the Member States are "... competent to determine the criteria for taxation on income and wealth with a view to eliminating double taxation – by means, *inter alia*, of international agreements". The ECJ correctly referred to the OECD MC as a model on which Member States' tax treaties are based (*ibid.*). The number of tax measures which *per se* are in line with Community law principles seems in my view to be rather limited. From the *Gilly* case one could perhaps infer support for the view that tax treaties is an area which Community law does not inflict upon. Moreover, the ECJ in the *Gilly* case declared (para. 30) that the criterion of nationality as applied in the French-German tax treaty was a criterion for allocating fiscal jurisdiction, and such a differentiation could not be discriminatory according to Article [39] of the EC Treaty and the free movement of workers. In the view of the ECJ the second indent of Article [293] gave the contracting parties (France and Germany in this case) the competence to define the criteria for allocating their powers of taxation between them, with a view to eliminating double taxation (*ibid.*, para. 30).

a negative answer to this question means that the next question will have to be considered.

(v) If the measure constitutes an indirect discrimination or a non-discriminatory restriction, is it justified by an imperative reason in the public interest? Hinnekens' approach is here somewhat different from mine, because he considers only restrictive measures to be justified by these grounds of justification. In practice, one should not over-emphasise this difference. As will be discussed in subsequent chapters, the Court has rarely decided that grounds of justification in the public interest apply in cases on direct taxation. If such a ground of justification is considered to apply, the next step has to be considered.

(vi) Is the measure necessary and proportionate? A measure is considered necessary if it is suitable and if there is a casual link between the measure and the aim which it seeks to achieve. Likewise, a measure is proportionate if the objective of the measure cannot be achieved by less restrictive (or, in my view also less discriminatory) means. It is not always easy to distinguish between the test of necessity and the test of proportionality: they may be blurred. If the answer is yes, and the measure is both necessary and proportionate, the next step applies.

(vii) Is the non-discriminatory or non-restrictive or excusable tax measure in conformity with the principles of the EC Treaty (other than those on the fundamental freedoms)? If the measure is not, it is not "EC-compatible".

There are other ways of formulating the rule-of-reason doctrine. Terra and Wattel apply the following model. The rule-of-reason doctrine as developed by the European Court of Justice could be summarised into six different steps or conditions.[168]

(i) Is the protection of the public interest already subject to harmonisation at EU level? If that is the case, Member States are not entitled to adopt measures of their own.

(ii) Does the national measure that constitutes a restriction distinguish between domestic and foreign goods, services, persons or capital? If that is the case, the national measure cannot as a general rule be accepted. However, the Treaty does contain statutory limitations and exceptions to this general rule.

(iii) Does the legislation of the home Member State, even if it deviates from the domestic measure, provide equivalent protection of the objective of public interest that it intends to serve?

[168] Cf. Terra and Wattel, *European Tax Law*, 3rd ed., Kluwer Law International, London/The Hague/New York, 2001, pp. 32-33.

(iv) Is the restrictive measure justified by public interest of a non-economic nature, which *in abstracto* can outweigh a Treaty freedom? As regards matters of direct taxation, the following reasons have been considered to justify restrictive national measures:

- the effectiveness of fiscal supervision (cf. *Cassis de Dijon* and *Futura Participation*),
- the coherence of the fiscal system (most notably the *Bachmann* case),
- the prevention of abuse,
- the fiscal principle of territoriality (cf. *Futura Participations*).

(v) Is the specific restrictive measure appropriate for the protection of the public interest involved?

(vi) Is the specific measure proportionate in its restrictive effects in relation to the legitimate aim pursued? A related question is whether there are no equally effective measures that could be taken and that would be less restrictive on cross-border movements within the Community.

Van Thiel also lists six different steps or conditions for determining what constitutes discrimination.[169] To a large extent those six conditions coincide with the ones listed by Terra and Wattel.

3.8.3 Case C-55/94 *Gebhard* (30 November 1995)

The European Court of Justice has for some time developed grounds for justifying obstacles to the four freedoms into what has become the rule-of-reason doctrine. In the *Gebhard* case,[170] the Court concluded, in a clear and distinct way, the basic steps of the rule-of-reason doctrine as it applies for all fundamental freedoms.[171]

In order to give a framework for those grounds of justification, I will begin with a brief description of the *Gebhard* case. Mr Reinhard Gebhard was a German national, however residing in Italy since 1978. In 1977, Mr Gebhard had been authorised to work as a lawyer, *Rechtsanwalt*. From 1978 he pursued his work as lawyer in Italy. Mr Gebhard used the title "*avvocato*". After complaints, the Milan Bar Council prohibited him from using the Italian title of "*avvocato*".

---

169 Van Thiel, *EU Case Law on Income Tax, Part 1*, IBFD, Amsterdam, 2001, pp. 102-115.

170 Case C-55/94 *Reinhard Gebhard v. Consiglio dell'Ordine degli Avvocati e Procuratori di Milano*.

171 The rule-of-reason doctrine as explained in the *Gebhard* case was also elaborated by the ECJ in case C-3/95 *Reisebüro Broede v. Sandker* regarding the freedom to provide services.

The European Court of Justice declared that the refusal of the right of Mr Gebhard to make use of the title "*avvocato*" was an infringement of the freedom of establishment and more precisely a non-discriminatory restriction. The Court formulated the basic steps of the rule-of-reason doctrine in the following way.

> "It follows, however, from the Court's case-law that national measures liable to hinder or make less attractive the exercise of fundamental freedoms guaranteed by the Treaty must fulfil four conditions: they must be applied in a non-discriminatory manner; they must be justified by imperative requirements in the general interest; they must be suitable for securing the attainment of the objective which they pursue; and they must not go beyond what is necessary in order to attain it (see case C-19/92 *Kraus v. Land Baden-Wuerttemberg*, [1993] ECR I-1663, paragraph 32)."[172]

Thus the "Gebhard test" specified that the following conditions shall be fulfilled if an obstacle to the four freedoms is to be justified. Accordingly, the national measure must:

- be applied in a non-discriminatory manner;
- be justified by imperative requirements in the general interest;[173]
- be suitable for securing the attainment of the objective which it pursues (the principle of proportionality); and
- not go beyond what is necessary in order to attain it.

3.8.4 The Principle of Proportionality

In the *Gebhard* case the proportionality requirement was defined in the following way. National measures that are liable to hinder or make less attractive the exercise of fundamental freedoms must not go beyond what is necessary in order to attain that freedom.[174] This is in line with the definition of the principle of proportionality contained in the EC Treaty. Article 5 of the EC Treaty provides that "[a]ny action by the Community shall not go beyond what is necessary to achieve the objectives of this Treaty". In order to establish what the principle means in reality it is, however, necessary to consider specific cases.

---

172 Case C-55/94 *Gebhard*, para. 37. The rule-of-reason doctrine has been confirmed in, for example, case C-212/97 *Centros*, para. 34.

173 The expressions "public interest" and "general interest" are synonymous.

174 Case C-55/94 *Gebhard*, para. 37.

The principle of proportionality has been at issue in several cases where the European Court of Justice has had to consider the compatibility of (national) anti-abuse legislation with fundamental freedoms. As subsequently will be discussed, national anti-abuse measures may be justified even if they constitute measures that are in conflict with fundamental freedoms. However, if such anti-abuse measures are not proportional, they are not justified according to the rule-of-reason doctrine. A first example is case C-28/95 *Leur-Bloem*. The case dealt with Dutch legislation on mergers through the exchange of shares and the relationship between national legislation and the Merger Directive. The Court declared that when applying specific criteria in national law, Member States should observe the principle of proportionality.[175] Furthermore, the Court stated that "the laying down of a general rule automatically excluding certain categories of operations from the tax advantage [according to specific criteria of national law] ... whether or not there is actually tax evasion or tax avoidance, would go further than is necessary for preventing such tax evasion or tax avoidance and would undermine the aim pursued by the Directive".[176]

Also in case C-250/95 *Futura Participations* the European Court of Justice applied a proportionality test. The case basically concerned the question of whether the need for fiscal supervision could justify an infringement in Luxembourg tax law of the freedom of establishment. The decisive importance of the proportionality test has also been confirmed by the Court in for example case C-415/93 *Bosman*[177] and case C-19/92 *Kraus*.[178]

In conclusion a national measure may be potentially justified by a ground of public interest, such as the effectiveness of fiscal supervision, but the measure at issue will anyway have to be proportionate in order to be finally justified according to the rule-of-reason doctrine. Hinnekens rightly points out: "Proportionality may therefore play a much more important role in finding a prohibited restriction irrespective of distinction on basis of nationality than in finding prohibited tax discrimination."[179]

3.8.5 Rule-of-reason Doctrine in Relation to Direct and Indirect Discrimination

A question which has been much discussed in recent years is to what extent the rule-of-reason doctrine also applies in relation to both direct and indirect discrimination.

---

[175] Case C-28/95 *Leur-Bloem*, para. 43.

[176] Case C-28/95 *Leur-Bloem*, para. 44.

[177] Case C-415/93 *Bosman*, para. 104.

[178] Case C-19/92 *Kraus*, para. 32.

[179] Hinnekens, "The Search for the Framework Conditions of the Fundamental EC Treaty Principles as Applied by the European Court to Member States' Direct Taxation", *EC Tax Review*, 2002, pp. 112-119, at p. 117.

One starting point for this discussion is the first step in the rule-of-reason doctrine as modelled in the *Gebhard* case. In order to be justified "national measures liable to hinder or make less attractive the exercise of fundamental freedoms guaranteed by the Treaty must fulfil four conditions, one being that: – they must be applied in non-discriminatory manner ...".[180] A literal interpretation of the words following the dash speaks, in my view, in favour of the opinion that only non-discriminatory measures – that is, measures constituting neither direct nor indirect discrimination – could be justified according to the rule-of-reason doctrine.

To begin with what is evidently clear: the rule-of-reason doctrine applies in relation to non-discriminatory restrictions. As previously mentioned, that follows from the mere wording in the *Gebhard* case. Moreover, there is strong reason to believe that the rule-of-reason doctrine also applies in relation to measures that constitute indirect discrimination, even if that could be doubtful in relation to the quoted phrase from the *Gebhard* case. The reason for this is that the Court in fact seems to have applied the rule-of-reason doctrine in at least one case of indirect discrimination, notably case C-204/90 *Bachmann*. The *Bachmann* case concerned the taxation in Belgium of a non-resident, Mr Bachmann, and his purported right in Belgium to make deductions for payments for sickness and invalidity insurance contracts, as well as life insurance contracts. According to Belgian law, residents in Belgium had that right of deduction for tax purposes, but non-residents had not. Finally, the difference in treatment in Belgian law was justified on the condition that it preserved the fiscal coherence of Belgian tax law. In my view, the Belgian tax legislation at issue in the *Bachmann* case was an example of indirect discrimination, had it not been justified.

Another reason in favour of the view that the rule-of-reason doctrine also applies in relation to measures of indirect discrimination, is that the Court considers grounds in the public interest in such cases, even if the Court later on rejects those conditions and judges them not to be applicable. It has been advanced that one should not put too much weight on the mere fact that the Court "considers" those grounds in the public interest. Such considerations do not necessarily mean that the Court will apply them. Wathelet, a judge of the European Court of Justice, expresses such a view in an article, where, however, he only expresses his personal views.[181] He claims that as regards direct discrimination, only express limitations and exceptions contained in the EC Treaty apply. Wathelet further explains that the Court, especially in relation to cases on direct taxation, after finding a difference in treatment, will first examine

[180] Case C-55/94 *Gebhard*, para. 37.

[181] Wathelet, "The Influence of Free Movement of Persons, Services and Capital on National Direct Taxation: Trends in the Case Law of the Court of Justice", in *Yearbook of European Law*, Eeckhout and Tridimas (ed.), Oxford University Press, Oxford, 2001, pp. 1-33, at pp. 15-16.

all justifications put forward, both statutory exceptions and limitations and grounds in the public interest "... without ruling whether or not the measures considered are discriminatory or not".[182] In general I agree with Wathelet's view, but there are two aspects where I slightly diverge. First, in my view the rule-of-reason doctrine applies also in relation to indirect discrimination. Secondly, I find somewhat strange the idea that the Court examines all justifications put forward irrespective of whether there is a case of discrimination or a non-discriminatory restriction. It seems irrational for the Court to consider grounds of justification in the public interest if they never could apply because there is a case of direct discrimination.

The view of some authors that the rule-of-reason doctrine and grounds of justification in the public interest did not even apply in cases of indirect discrimination seems to be losing ground.[183] In support of this change, Hakenberg states in a comment on the free movement of services: "In der Praxis wendet der EuGH allerdings heute in den überwiegenden Fällen den Ausnahme- bzw. Rechtfertigungstatbestand der 'zwingenden Gründe des Allgemeininteresses' an, der früher lediglich bei nicht-diskriminierenden Regelungen in Frage kam, nun jedoch auch diskriminierende Regelungen rechtfertigen kann."[184]

However, I would not go so far as to declare that the rule-of-reason doctrine also applies in relation to direct discrimination, not even considering shifts in the case-law of the Court. Case C-311/97 *Royal Bank of Scotland*, decided by the Court on 29 April 1999, dealt with a piece of Greek tax legislation that constituted direct discrimination. As a consequence the Court only considered express limitations and exceptions contained in the EC Treaty, and did not consider the rule-of-reason doctrine.[185]

Still, there are those who would like to see the rule-of-reason doctrine also applicable to measures constituting direct discrimination. Moreover, there are authors who believe that the European Court of Justice already has applied the rule-of-reason doctrine in occasional cases of direct discrimination. As previously noted, at the present stage

182 *Ibid.*, p. 16.

183 Cordewener considers the borderline between, on the one hand, statutory limitations and exceptions and, on the other hand, case-law based grounds of justification, to be dissolving. Cordewener, *Europäische Grundfreiheiten und nationales Steuerrecht*, Verlag Dr. Otto Schmidt, Cologne, 2002, p. 143.

184 "In practice, in the vast majority of cases, the ECJ correctly applies the rule-of-reason doctrine or such a justification as 'compelling reasons in the public interest'. This was previously only considered in the case of non-discriminatory regulations, but now can also justify discriminatory regulations." Hakenberg, in *EU- und EG-Vertrag*, Lenz and Borchardt (ed.), 3rd ed., Bundesanzeiger Verlagsgesellschaft mbH, Cologne, Art. 49/50, marg. no. 25,

185 The ECJ declared: "According to settled case-law, only an express derogating provision, such as Article 56 of the EC Treaty, could render such discrimination compatible with Community law ...". Case C-311/97 *Royal Bank of Scotland*, para. 32.

of development of case-law by the European Court of Justice, I do not think that the rule-of-reason doctrine applies in cases of direct discrimination, but I think it is still very important to consider the arguments put forward by those who consider that it should, or even does apply. AG Jacobs argued in his opinion[186] on case C-136/00 *Danner* that the traditional view of the Court has been that measures constituting direct discrimination cannot be justified according to the rule-of-reason doctrine.[187] However, AG Jacobs also identified a recent line of cases where he considers the Court to have applied the rule-of-reason doctrine also in cases of direct discrimination, but where the Court has not bothered to clarify whether there is a case of direct discrimination or not. As examples of cases where the Court has examined the national measure at issue according to the rule-of-reason doctrine, AG Jacobs refers to case C-200/98 *X and Y*, case C-55/98 *Vestergaard*, and case C-294/97 *Eurowings Luftverkehr*. However, one should in my view be well aware that in none of those cases did the Court consider the rule-of-reason doctrine to justify any of the disputed measures. As examples of cases where the Court in fact has applied the rule-of-reason doctrine and also found the disputed measure to be justified, AG Jacobs refers to the cases C-204/90 *Bachmann* and its parallel C-300/90 *Commission v. Belgium*. In this respect my analysis differs from the one of AG Jacobs, because I would categorise the measures at issue in those cases as constituting indirect discrimination. However, I do agree with AG Jacobs when he declares that in its recent case-law the Court has tended to avoid following the analysis to the end in order to discern whether there is a case of discrimination, be it either direct or indirect, or a measure constituting a non-discriminatory restriction.[188]

AG Jacobs considered it inappropriate to have different grounds of justification depending on whether a measure is discriminatory or constitutes a non-discriminatory restriction: "Once it is accepted that justifications other than those set out in the Treaty may be invoked, there seems no reason to apply one category of justification to discriminatory measures and another category to non-discriminatory restrictions."[189] He found no grounds for this distinction in the EC Treaty regarding the freedom to provide services, and moreover found it difficult to apply rigorously the distinction between discrimination and non-discriminatory restrictions. It is easy to agree with AG Jacobs in this view. Moreover, AG Jacobs considered grounds in the general interest, such as

186 It should be noted that AG Jacobs' opinion in case C-136/00 *Danner* was delivered on 21 March 2002.

187 Opinion of AG Jacobs' in case C-136/00 *Danner*, para. 35. Jacobs refers to the previously mentioned case C-311/97 *Royal Bank of Scotland*.

188 AG Jacobs puts it in the following way: "In most of the recent cases, however, involving national rules which might have been regarded as (directly) discriminatory, the Court has avoided assessing whether the rules in issue were discriminatory, and has examined grounds of justification not expressly mentioned in the Treaty." Opinion of AG Jacobs in case C-136/00 *Danner*, para. 36.

189 Opinion of AG Jacobs in case C-136/00 *Danner*, para. 40.

protection of the environment and consumer protection, to be legitimate even if they are not expressed in the EC Treaty. Finally, it would be the principle of proportionality that would decide whether a national measure were to be acceptable or not according to the rule-of-reason doctrine. The more discriminatory a measure is, the more likely it is that it will fail the proportionality test.[190]

It should be noted that the Court in its decision in case C-136/00 *Danner* did not answer AG Jacobs on how to apply the rule-of-reason doctrine in relation to measures that are discriminatory.[191] It is impossible to give any valid interpretation of the Court's silence, but one reason could be that the judges of the Court have diverging opinions.

In general, I think AG Jacobs has a strong point, but at the present stage the position of the Court must be interpreted in the way that direct discrimination cannot be justified according to the rule-of-reason doctrine. There is a problem here, and I have the impression that the Court feels bound to the traditional position, that when there is a measure of direct discrimination, the rule-of-reason doctrine does not apply. However, the Court in its recent case-law tries to avoid the problem that the rule-of-reason doctrine cannot be applied on measures constituting direct discrimination by avoiding to complete its analysis be declaring a measure to constitute direct discrimination. Instead it stops at the point where it can declare the measure to be an obstacle to the fundamental freedom at issue. At that stage it applies the rule-of-reason doctrine, even if the measure would have been considered to be a measure constituting direct discrimination, had it completed its analysis. In my view, this development is not satisfactory. The Court should be open and declare that the rule-of-reason doctrine also applies regarding measures constituting direct discrimination.

It should be noted that there are some authors who hold the position that the Court has in fact applied the rule-of-reason doctrine in relation to measures constituting direct discrimination.[192]

There have been scholarly attempts trying to reconcile the Court's recent practice of applying the rule-of-reason doctrine in relation to discriminatory measures with earlier case-law. Peters suggests that the condition that the measure must be applied in a non-discriminatory manner only means that a measure constituting direct discrimination

---

190 Opinion of AG Jacobs in case C-136/00 *Danner*, para. 40.

191 Cf. also Cordewener, "Case Note on C-136/00 Danner", *CML. Rev.* 2003, pp. 965-981, at pp. 969-970.

192 Barnard, "Fitting the Remaining Pieces into the Goods and Persons Jigsaw?", *EL Rev.*, 2001, pp. 33-59, p. 54. Barnard refers to case C-2/90 *Commission v. Belgium (Walloon Waste)*. The opinion that the ECJ applies the rule-of-reason doctrine also in relation to discriminatory national measures is also supported by Gundel, "Die Rechtfertigung von faktisch diskriminierenden Eingriffen in die Grundfreiheiten des EGV", *Jura*, 2001, pp. 79-85.

cannot be justified.[193] In contrast a measure constituting indirect discrimination can be justified, according to Peters. I agree with Peters' conclusion, but I do find it difficult to interpret "non-discriminatory" as encompassing indirect but not direct discrimination. Rather, it is the case-law of the Court that has evolved beyond what the Court once declared in the *Gebhard* case.

3.9 Direct Taxation and Grounds of Justification in the Public Interest Accepted in Principle

3.9.1 Introduction

As previously discussed, the European Court of Justice has developed the rule-of-reason doctrine, according to which indirect discrimination and non-discriminatory restrictions can be justified and thus acceptable. The purpose of this section is to introduce those grounds of justification. It should be noted, however, that some of the relevant cases deal with other fundamental freedoms than the ones in focus in this study. However, the principal analysis of the freedom of establishment and the free movement of capital will be made in Chapters 4, 5 and 6.

This section will focus on the following grounds of justification: (i) the effectiveness of fiscal supervision, (ii) coherence of the fiscal system, and (iii) the prevention of abuse. In this section it is my intention to introduce these grounds of justification. To illustrate the different grounds, I have chosen a few cases which will be discussed in some detail.

3.9.2 Effectiveness of Fiscal Supervision

3.9.2.1 Introduction

The effectiveness of fiscal supervision is of vital importance for the Member States and their tax authorities. Fiscal supervision is, in essence, collecting taxes on cross-border transactions. It should also be recalled that the area of fiscal supervision is one of the few areas where the Member States have reached unanimity on Community measures. In 1977 the Council adopted the Directive concerning mutual assistance by the competent authorities of the Member States in the field of direct taxation, known

193 Peters, "Non-discrimination: The Freedom of Establishment and European Tax Law", in *Legal Protection against Discriminatory Tax Legislation*, Gribnau (ed.), Kluwer Law International, London/The Hague/New York, 2003, pp. 101-122, at pp. 106-107.

as the Assistance Directive.[194] The Directive deals with the assessment, and not with the recovery of taxes. There is no limitation on the nationality or residence of the taxpayer in question. Any information which may enable national tax authorities to make a correct assessment must be exchanged. Moreover, special investigations shall be carried out by tax authorities if it is necessary in order to obtain the information required. It is for the "competent authorities" to make the exchange of information. Information may be exchanged (i) on request (Article 2), (ii) automatically (Article 3), and (iii) spontaneously (Article 4).

3.9.2.2 Case C-250/95 **Futura Participations** *(15 May 1997)*

The *Futura Participations*[195] case dealt with the freedom of establishment and the EC Treaty compatibility of Luxembourg legislation on corporate losses. Futura Participations SA (hereinafter Futura Participations) was a French company, which had its seat in Paris. Singer was the Luxembourg branch of Futura Participations. The question considered by the Court was whether Article 43 (ex Article 52) of the EC Treaty precluded a Member State from having tax legislation with the following characteristics. For a branch of a non-resident company to carry forward losses incurred, two conditions had to be fulfilled. First, the losses had to be economically related to the income earned by the taxpayer in the state of the branch, Luxembourg. Secondly, the taxpayer had to have kept and held in the state of the branch, in respect of the activities carried out there, accounts complying with the relevant rules of that state.

As regards the first condition, that losses carried forward must be economically linked with the income earned in the Member State where the tax was charged, the European Court of Justice did not consider it to constitute either a direct or an indirect discrimination.[196] The reason was that this piece of legislation was "... in conformity with the fiscal principle of territoriality".[197] The Court did not elaborate any further on the meaning of that principle of territoriality. A tentative conclusion is, at least in my view, that if a Member State bases a provision, or a set of provisions, on the fiscal principle of territoriality, such a provision does not in itself constitute an infringement of the freedom of establishment.

---

[194] Council Directive 77/799/EEC of 19 December 1977. This Directive was amended by Council Directive 79/1070/EEC of 6 December 1979, OJ L 331 of 27 December 1979, p. 8. With the amendment an extension of the scope was made to include also value added tax, and not only taxes on income and on capital.

[195] Case C-250/95 *Futura Participations SA and Singer v. Administration des contributions.*

[196] Case C-250/95 *Futura Participations*, para. 22.

[197] *Ibid.*

Regarding the second condition, to keep accounts complying with Luxembourg law for the taxable year when the losses were incurred, the Court was less accepting. The Court concluded that in practice the second condition meant that a company or firm resident in one Member State, France in this case, in addition to its own accounts, had to keep separate accounts for its branch in the other Member State, Luxembourg. Moreover, those separate accounts had to be held at the place of the branch, and not where the company or firm had its seat.[198] This condition was in conflict with the freedom of establishment, according to the Court.[199] In addition the Court tested whether this restriction was justified on the ground of "effectiveness of fiscal supervision". In effect the Luxembourg legislation at issue provided that for a foreign company or firm to carry forward losses incurred by its branch, two conditions had to be fulfilled. First, the company or firm had to keep separate accounts for its branch activities, and those accounts had to be kept in accordance with the law of the state where the branch was established. Secondly, those separate accounts had to be kept in the state where the branch was resident.

As previously noted, the Court found that the Luxembourg legislation at issue constituted a restriction on the freedom of establishment.[200] Such a measure could only be accepted if it "pursued a legitimate aim compatible with the Treaty and were justified by pressing reasons of public interest".[201] But even if that were the case, the measure would anyway have to be proportional: it had "... to ensure achievement of the aim in question and not go beyond what was necessary for that purpose".[202]

To begin with, the Court declared that it "repeatedly" had considered the effectiveness of fiscal supervision as a legitimate ground of justification for restrictions on fundamental freedoms guaranteed by the EC Treaty. Obviously, this ground applies not only for the freedom of establishment, which the present case concerned, but also on the free movement of goods, workers and capital.[203] The next issue for the Court to deal with was, of course, whether the second condition fulfilled the objectives of the ground of

---

198 Case C-250/95 *Futura Participations*, para. 25.

199 This provision must be characterised as a non-discriminatory restriction. The reason is that it did not make any difference in treatment on the basis of nationality or any similar criterion. The requirement to keep accounts in Luxembourg complying with Luxembourg law applied to all, residents and non-residents alike. However, the requirement was a detriment to non-residents who also had to keep accounts complying with the law of their state of residence.

200 Case C-250/95 *Futura Participations*, para. 25.

201 Case C-250/95 *Futura Participations*, para. 26.

202 *Ibid.* In support of considering the national measure's proportionality the ECJ referred to case C-55/94 *Gebhard*, para. 37; case C-19/92 *Kraus*, para. 32; and case C-415/93 *Bosman*, para. 104.

203 Case C-250/95 *Futura Participations*, para. 31. The Court made an explicit reference to Case 120/78 *Rewe-Zentral* (known as *Cassis de Dijon*), para. 8.

justification. To begin with, the Court found that there had presently been no provision made to harmonise national legislation of the Member States on how to determine the basis of assessment to direct taxes. Accordingly, in the view of the Court, Member States were free to decide their own rules in this field of law.[204]

The Court concluded that because accountancy rules in the Member States not necessarily are the same, there is no guarantee that the accounting where a company or firm is resident will be of any assistance when determining the chargeable income or the losses to be carried forward in the Member State where the branch is established.[205] Consequently, the Court in my view accepted the underlying purpose of the second condition that the accounts of the branch had to comply with Luxembourg law – the state of the branch.

However, the second condition also had to be proportional. Did the national requirements go beyond what was necessary in order to attain it? There was no general requirement in Luxembourg that non-residents had to keep proper accounts relating to their business activity in Luxembourg: such a requirement existed only regarding the carry forward of losses, as in the underlying case before the Luxembourg court. When the non-resident had met the requirement on the keeping of accounts, the Luxembourg tax authorities were only interested in those accounts in one aspect: that the amount of losses to be carried forward corresponded to the amount of losses actually incurred in Luxembourg by the taxpayer. If the taxpayer could demonstrate the amount of losses concerned, the Luxembourg tax authorities could not refuse him a carry forward of the losses. Thus the Court concluded that the *means* by which the taxpayer demonstrated the losses he sought to carry forward were not essential.[206] In support of this view the Court relied on the Directive 77/799/EEC, whereby the competent authorities of the Member States shall provide each other with the information required to make a correct tax assessment.[207]

3.9.2.3 Concluding Remarks

The effectiveness of fiscal supervision is a ground of justification recognised and accepted in principle by the European Court of Justice. The 1977 Directive on

[204] Case C-250/95 *Futura Participations*, para. 33. The ECJ did consider Article 54 (3) (g) [present Article 44 (2) (g)] of the EC Treaty, but found that measures for coordination stipulated there, were not relevant (para. 34).

[205] Case C-250/95 *Futura Participations*, para. 35.

[206] Case C-250/95 *Futura Participations*, para. 40.

[207] Case C-250/95 *Futura Participation*, para. 41.

mutual assistance in tax matters between Member States is, according to the Court, an important measure for Member States to acquire necessary information. Moreover, even if a national measure fulfils the purpose of guaranteeing the effectiveness of fiscal supervision, such a measure has to be proportional to its aims. In case C-250/95 *Futura Participations* a national measure for the carrying forward of losses by a non-resident, that he must have kept and held in that state accounts relating to his activities carried out there which also complied with the relevant national rules, was found not to be proportional.

3.9.3 Coherence of the Fiscal System

3.9.3.1 Introduction

Coherence of the fiscal system was accepted by the European Court of Justice in the cases C-204/90 *Bachmann* and C-300/90 *Commission v. Belgium*. This ground of justification has over the years been advanced by Member States and discussed by the Court in a large number of cases on matters of direct taxation. However, over the years the scope of application of fiscal coherence as a ground of justification has been considerably narrowed. Here I will introduce this ground by both discussing the *Bachmann* case, and a comparatively recent follow-up case, C-136/00 *Danner*.

3.9.3.2 Case C-204/90 **Bachman** *(28 January 1992)*

Today the *Bachmann*[208] case from 1992 is considered comparatively old in the Court's case-law on matters of direct taxation. However, in one aspect it is still important: the relevance of fiscal coherence, or simply coherence, as a ground for justifying infringements of fundamental freedoms.

The facts of the underlying case were the following. Mr Bachmann was a German national employed in Belgium. In Belgium, Mr Bachmann was refused deductions for contributions paid in Germany in respect of sickness and invalidity insurance contracts, as well as a life insurance contract. The insurances were taken out in Germany prior to his arrival in Belgium. Belgian legislation, however, stipulated limitations on the right to make deductions for insurance contributions. Only voluntary sickness and invalidity insurance contributions paid to a mutual insurance company recognised by Belgium, and pension and insurance contributions paid in Belgium could be deducted from occupational income.[209]

[208] Case C-204/90 *Hanns-Martin Bachmann v. Belgian State.*

[209] Case C-204/90 *Bachmann*, para. 2-3.

The European Court of Justice examined the compatibility of this provision of Belgian tax law with the free movement of workers. The Court maintained that there was a conflict between the national legislation at issue and the free movement of workers. The Court declared in its decision that the provisions in question "... may operate to the particular detriment of those workers who are, as a general rule, nationals of other Member States".[210] The reason was that workers from one Member State that were employed, or sought employment, in another Member State, would normally have concluded their pension and life insurance contracts or invalidity and sickness insurance contracts with companies established in the first Member State.[211] In my view this is an example of indirect discrimination.

The Court reasoned in the following way on the applicability of fiscal coherence. In Belgian law there was a connection between the deductibility of insurance contributions and the liability to tax on sums payable by the insurers under pension and life insurance contracts.[212] Belgian law provided that pensions, annuities, capital sums or surrender values under life insurance contracts were tax exempt on the condition that there had been no deduction of contributions.[213] The German national, Mr Bachmann, was denied deduction of his contributions in Belgium because the sums payable on his German insurances would not be taxable in Belgium. The Court declared: "The cohesion of such a tax system, the formulation of which is a matter for each Member State, therefore presupposes that, in the event of a State being obliged to allow the deduction of life insurance contributions paid in another Member State, it should be able to tax sums payable by insurers."[214]

Accordingly, the Court came to the final conclusion that legislation such as the Belgian laws on pensions and life insurance was justified by the need to preserve the coherence of the tax system.[215]

3.9.3.3 Case C-136/00 **Danner** *(3 October 2002)*

Case C-136/00 *Danner*[216] from 2002 is particularly related to the 1992 *Bachmann* case because it also dealt with insurance contributions and the coherence of the fiscal

[210] Case C-204/90 *Bachmann*, para. 9.

[211] *Ibid.*

[212] In this instance, the European Court of Justice referred to another case: C-300/90 *Commission v. Belgium*.

[213] Case C-204/90 *Bachmann*, para. 22.

[214] Case C-204/90 *Bachmann*, para. 23.

[215] Case C-204/90 *Bachmann*, para. 28.

[216] Case C-136/00 *Danner*.

system as a ground of justification. The fundamental freedom at issue was the freedom to provide services.

The basic facts of the underlying case were the following. Mr Danner was a medical doctor of both German and Finnish nationality. He appeared to have lived and worked in Germany until 1977, although from that year he established himself and his medical practice in Finland. In 1976 Mr Danner began to pay insurance contributions to two German insurance institutions: the *Bundesversicherungsanstalt für Angestellte* (BfA) and the *Berliner Ärzteversorgung*. Even after moving to Finland, Mr Danner continued to pay contributions according to the two insurance schemes. In his Finnish income tax return for 1996, Mr Danner deducted his German pension insurance contributions. However, the tax authorities only accepted a limited deduction with 10 per cent from his taxable income.

The question of whether this refusal was in line with Community law and fundamental freedoms came under the consideration of a Finnish administrative court. Eventually, the Finnish court asked the European Court of Justice for a preliminary ruling on the matter. The fundamental freedoms at issue were, as a starting-point, the freedom to provide services and the free movement of capital.

The European Court of Justice declared that it was undisputable that the Finnish legislation constituted a restriction: "… Article [49] of the Treaty precludes the application of any national legislation which has the effect of making the provision of services between Member States more difficult than the provision of services purely within one Member State…".[217] Furthermore, the Court stated that the Finnish legislation would dissuade individuals from taking out voluntary pension insurance with institutions in a Member State other than Finland. Likewise, the Finnish legislation would also dissuade foreign insurance institutions from establishing themselves in Finland.[218]

As regards possible grounds of justification, the Danish and Finnish governments submitted that the national measure had the purpose of maintaining fiscal coherence.[219] The Finnish government stated that in Finland pensions paid by Finnish and foreign institutions to both residents and non-residents were subject to tax. On the basis of this reasoning, the Finnish government made the following conclusion. On the one hand, if pension contributions were paid to a Finnish institution the pension would be taxed in Finland. On the other hand, if pension contributions were paid to a foreign institution and the receiver moved away from Finland, the pensions would not be

[217] Case C-136/00 *Danner*, para. 29.

[218] Case C-136/00 *Danner*, para. 31. The ECJ also refers to case C-118/96 *Jessica Safir*, para. 30.

[219] Case C-136/00 *Danner*, para. 33 and 34.

taxed in Finland. Consequently, Finnish legislation denied deductions in a case such as Mr Danner's.[220]

However, in contrast to case C-204/90 *Bachmann*, the European Court of Justice did in this case not accept coherence of the fiscal system as a ground of justification. According to the Court, the *Bachmann* case and *Commission v. Belgium* case were based on the fact that in the Belgian legislation there was a direct connection between the deductibility of contributions and the liability to tax on sums payable by insurers. The loss of tax revenue due to the deductions of pension contributions was countered by the taxation on the subsequent pensions, annuities and capital sums paid. If the contributions had not been deductible, the subsequent pensions and similar payments had not been taxable. However, in those cases there was a *direct link* between the deductibility and the taxation on the payable pensions. In the *Danner* case the Court, however, did not find that there was such a direct link in the Finnish tax system. According to the Finnish system, pensions payable from foreign institutions would be taxed irrespective of whether the insurance contributions were deductible or not deductible in Finland.[221]

In addition, the Court also took into consideration that there was a tax treaty between Finland and Germany. As a consequence, the Court declared that the reason of fiscal coherence had to be given a special meaning. Referring to case C-80/94 *Wielockx*, the Court stated: "[A]s a result of double taxation conventions like those which follow the model of the Organisation for Economic Cooperation and Development (OECD) … fiscal cohesion is no longer established in relation to one and the same person by a strict correlation between the deductibility of contributions and the taxation of pensions but is shifted to another level, that of the reciprocity of the rules applicable in the Contracting States, the principle of fiscal cohesion may not be invoked to justify the refusal of a deduction such as that at issue".[222]

In my view, the reasoning of the European Court of Justice is somewhat ambiguous regarding the ground of fiscal coherence. On the one hand, the Court declares that the Finnish legislation does not maintain the cohesion of the fiscal system, as was the fact in the *Bachmann* case. On the other hand, the existence of a tax treaty between Finland and Germany means that the cohesion reason cannot be advanced to justify the restriction.

220 Case C-136/00 *Danner*, para. 34.

221 Case C-136/00 *Danner*, para. 38.

222 Case C-136/00 *Danner*, para. 41.

3.9.3.4 Concluding Remarks

The need to preserve the fiscal coherence of a Member State's tax system is recognised by the European Court of Justice as a ground for justifying indirect discrimination. Formulating what constitutes "coherence of the fiscal system" is something for each Member State. However, the European Court of Justice will apparently test whether such coherence is at issue. In case C-204/90 *Bachmann* the question of coherence dealt with the deduction of insurance premiums and the taxation of sums payable from such insurances. Deduction was not allowed in a situation where the taxpayer was not liable to tax on the sums payable in the state denying the deduction, which served to preserve the fiscal coherence. Therefore the national measure was justified. Case C-136/00 *Danner* means that the question of fiscal coherence is transferred from the micro level of the national legislation of a Member State, to the macro level of the tax treaty between states. I further develop my view of the ground of fiscal coherence in Chapter 5 and Chapter 6.[223]

3.9.4 The Prevention of Abuse

3.9.4.1 Introduction

To the European Court of Justice the prevention of abuse is a recognised ground of justification. However, no case on direct taxation exists where that ground has been applied to justify infringements of the fundamental freedoms.[224] The prevention of abuse has still frequently been put forward in cases concerning direct taxation. It is my intention to use the case-law of the European Court of Justice in order to target the area where the ground of abuse does not apply and also identify where it might apply. In this section I will introduce this ground of justification with case C-212/97 *Centros*. The *Centros* case is not specifically a tax case, but the Court's general reasoning on the meaning of abuse as a ground of justification is relevant also for tax matters.

---

223 In Chapter 6 there is, for example, a discussion on the cases C-315/02 *Lenz* and C-319/02 *Manninen* (which both deal with the free movement of capital).

224 Cf. Terra and Wattel, *European Tax Law*, 3rd ed, Kluwer Law International, London/The Hague/New York, 2001, p. 77.

3.9.4.2 Case C-212/97 **Centros** *(9 March 1999)*

Case C-212/97 *Centros*[225] concerned the freedom of establishment, but from a company law perspective, and not from a tax-law perspective. The *Centros* case includes two important questions for this study.

First, does a situation where a company formed in accordance with the law of one Member State, and where that company wishes to establish a branch in another Member State, fall within the scope of Community law and, more particularly, the freedom of establishment? Secondly, to what extent can a Member State invoke a legislative objective such as preventing abuse, when justifying infringements on the freedom of establishment? In this section I will deal with the second of these two questions.

The circumstances of the underlying case before the Danish court had the following components. A Danish couple, Mr and Mrs Bryde, set up a private limited company in the United Kingdom, Centros Ltd. Centros Ltd applied to the Danish authorities for permission to establish a branch in Denmark, which, however, was denied by the Danish Department of Trade.

It was clear that Centros Ltd had not traded since it was established. United Kingdom law did not demand any minimum share capital and Centros Ltd's capital, GBP 100, had never been paid nor had it been made available to the company.[226] According to Danish law, Centros Ltd was regarded as a foreign limited liability company.

Article 117 of the Danish law on private limited companies (the *Anpartsselskabslov*) stipulated: private limited companies and foreign companies having a similar legal form, which are established in one Member State of the European Communities, may conduct business in Denmark through a branch. Centros Ltd, through Mrs Bryde, requested that the Danish authorities – the Board[227] – register a branch of Centros in Denmark.[228] The Board denied registration. The major reason was that Centros in fact was seeking to establish a principal establishment in Denmark and not a branch. Centros did not perform any activity in the United Kingdom. The Board believed that Centros was trying to circumvent, in particular, the Danish rules on the paying up of a minimum capital of DKK 200,000.[229]

The Court was asked whether it was contrary to Articles 43 and 48 (ex Articles 52 and 58) of the EC Treaty to refuse the establishment in one Member State (Denmark) of a

[225] Case C-212/97 *Centros Ltd v. Erhvers- og Selskabsstyrelsen.*

[226] Case C-212/97 *Centros*, para. 3.

[227] *Erhvervs- og Selskabsstyrelsen.*

[228] Case C-212/97 *Centros*, para. 5.

[229] Case C-212/97 *Centros*, para. 7.

branch of a company formed in another Member State (the United Kingdom) where it had its registered office, but where it did not carry on any business, which was intended to be exercised through the branch. That the more economically burdensome rules in Denmark for the formation of companies were avoided by the establishment, was added as a further circumstance.

The Court maintained that the provisions of the EC Treaty on the freedom of establishment are specifically intended to enable companies formed in accordance with the law of one Member State and having their registered office, central administration or principal place of business within the Community, to have activities in other Member States through an agency, branch or subsidiary.[230] In relation to this reasoning the Court finally declared: "That being so, the fact that a national of a Member State who wishes to set up a company chooses to form it in the Member State whose rules of company law seem to him the least restrictive and to set up branches in other Member States cannot, in itself, constitute an abuse of the freedom of establishment. The right to form a company in accordance with the law of a Member State and to set up branches in other Member States is inherent in the exercise, in a single market, of the freedom of establishment guaranteed by the Treaty."[231] The Court also declared that the fact that company law is not completely harmonised in the Community is of little consequence. The Court reiterated that Member States can, if they so wish, decide on a complete harmonisation in that field.[232]

Furthermore, the European Court of Justice declared that the right to form a company according to the law of one Member State and to establish branches in other Member States is inherent in the freedom of establishment guaranteed by the EC Treaty.[233]

With the support of the Court's decision in Case 79/85 *Segers*,[234] the Court stated that the fact that a company does not conduct any business in the Member State in which it has its registered office, and if it pursues its activities only in the Member State where its branch is established, that is not sufficient to prove the existence of abuse or fraudulent conduct which would entitle the branch state to deny the benefits of the freedom of establishment.[235]

---

230 Case C-212/97 *Centros*, para. 26.

231 Case C-212/97 *Centros*, para. 27.

232 Case C-212/97 *Centros*, para. 28.

233 Case C-212/97 *Centros*, para. 29.

234 Case 79/85 *Segers v. Bedrifsvereniging voor Bank- en Verzekeringswegen, Groothandel en Vrije Beroepen.*

235 Case C-212/97 *Centros*, para. 29.

In applying the rule-of-reason doctrine, the European Court of Justice also declared that combating fraud cannot justify the refusal to register a branch of a company which has its registered office in another Member State.[236]

3.9.4.3 Concluding Remarks

From case C-212/97 *Centros* one can make the following preliminary remarks on the prevention of abuse as a ground of justification in the public interest. First, it is important to note that the European Court of Justice recognises the prevention of abuse as a ground of justification. Secondly, for a national provision to fulfil that purpose one could infer the following characteristics from the Court's decision. The provision must have the specific purpose of preventing wholly artificial arrangements: the national legislation must have the sole purpose of preventing abuse and the arrangement in question must have the sole purpose of tax abuse.

---

236 Case C-212/97 *Centros*, para. 38.

4 The Freedom of Establishment and Direct Taxation

4.1 Introduction

4.1.1 Purpose and Outline

The general objective of this chapter is to systematise, analyse and evaluate the freedom of establishment as laid down in the EC Treaty and the case-law from the European Court of Justice. The emphasis will lie on the freedom of establishment in relation to direct taxation. It is also necessary to discuss matters of a general nature that do not particularly deal with taxation.

The outline of this chapter is, in the main, similar to the outline of Chapter 6 below on the free movement of capital. There is, however, one factor which gives this chapter a somewhat different outline: there is a large number of cases from the European Court of Justice on the freedom of establishment in relation to matters of direct taxation. The number of corresponding cases on the free movement of capital is much more modest.

The chapter has the following outline. The remaining part of *section 4.1* contains an overview of Articles 43 to 48 of the EC Treaty, which covers the freedom of establishment. The personal scope of the freedom of establishment and the meaning of "establishment" is discussed in *section 4.2*. Case-law from the European Court of Justice on this issue is discussed.

Section 4.3 contains an analytical framework for the following case-law analysis. Sections 4.4 to 4.7 contain the case-law analysis of the freedom of establishment in relation to direct taxation. *Section 4.4* deals with host state restrictions, and is divided into three different parts: companies establishing branches (*section 4.4.2*), companies establishing subsidiaries (*section 4.4.3*) and individuals establishing branches (*section 4.4.4*). *Section 4.5* deals with home state restrictions and is also divided into three major parts: companies establishing branches (*section 4.5.2*), companies establishing subsidiaries (*section 4.5.3*) and other cases (*section 4.5.4*). The pending case C-446/03 *Marks & Spencer* is the subject of *section 4.6*. Even if the *Marks & Spencer* case is only pending before the European Court of Justice, I have decided to discuss it quite thoroughly. There are two reasons for this. First, the case focuses on how one should define discrimination and how to make the comparison between different situations which result in an eventual discrimination. One could also add that the Court, in its recent case-law on matters of direct taxation, on several occasions has been less explicit on the issue of what constitutes discrimination. Secondly, the analysis made by the United Kingdom Special Commissioners is clear and thorough. *Section 4.7* deals with a case that emphasises the problem of making a clear distinction between the home and host state perspectives: Case C-307/97 *Saint-Gobain* could be labelled a borderline case between those two perspectives. In section 4.7 I also discuss the relation between fundamental freedoms and tax treaties, including some remarks on the question of whether Community law stipulates a most-favoured-nation requirement.

4.1.2 Overview of Articles 43 to 48 of the EC Treaty

Chapter 2 of Title III of the EC Treaty on the free movement of persons, services and capital deals with the freedom of establishment. The fundamental provision on the freedom of establishment is contained in Article 43, which provides:

> "Within the framework of the provisions set out below, restrictions on the freedom of establishment of nationals of a Member State in the territory of another Member State shall be prohibited. Such prohibition shall also apply to restrictions on the setting-up of agencies, branches or subsidiaries by nationals of any Member State established in the territory of any Member State.
>
> Freedom of establishment shall include the right to take up and pursue activities as self-employed persons and to set up and manage undertakings, in particular companies or firms within the meaning of the second paragraph of Article 48, under the conditions laid down for its own nationals by the law of the country where such establishment is effected, subject to the provisions of the Chapter relating to capital."[1]

Accordingly, Article 43 (1), the first sentence, of the EC Treaty provides that *restrictions* on the freedom of establishment of nationals of one Member State in the territory of another Member State shall be prohibited. The form of establishment referred to here is usually labelled "primary establishment", which would include, for example, the establishment of a new company formed under the legislation of the host state. The form of establishment referred to in Article 43 (1), the second sentence, covers the setting up of agencies, branches and subsidiaries. This form of establishment is usually called "secondary establishment" because it does not cover a "new" establishment, but is a "scion" of an establishment in another state.

Furthermore, Article 44 (1) of the EC Treaty stipulates that in order to attain the freedom of establishment, the Council shall act by means of directives. Thereby, the Council

1 According to the ECJ, Article 43 of the EC Treaty has direct effect, cf. e.g. Case 2/74 *Reyners v. Belgium*.

shall act in accordance with the procedure referred to in Article 251 of the EC Treaty and after hearing the Economic and Social Committee. A number of duties on the Council and Commission are set out in order to reach the freedom of establishment, and they are listed in Article 44 (2).

Limitations and exceptions to the freedom of establishment are stipulated in Articles 45 and 46, which will be dealt with more thoroughly below.

Certain areas where the freedom of establishment is important, and measures are required of the Council, are recognised in Article 47. The mutual recognition of diplomas, certificates and other evidence of formal requirements is the subject of Article 47 (1). Article 47 (2) deals, among other things, with measures by the Council concerning the taking up and pursuit of activities as self-employed persons. The final paragraph, Article 47 (3), covers the abolition of restrictions on the medical and allied and pharmaceutical professions.

Article 48 of the EC Treaty basically provides that companies and firms formed within the European Union shall be treated in the same way as natural persons (individuals) who are nationals of a Member State.

4.2 Personal Scope and the Meaning of "Establishment"

4.2.1 Introduction

Article 43 of the EC Treaty, which is the fundamental provision on the freedom of establishment, defines the personal scope of the freedom as covering "nationals of a Member State". Accordingly, all nationals of a Member State are covered by the freedom of establishment. Furthermore, the European Court of Justice has declared that where a national of a Member State at the same time is a national of a third state, he will all the same be covered by the freedom of establishment.[2]

In this section there will be an analysis of cases from the European Court of Justice which I consider to be especially interesting regarding the question of who is covered by the freedom of establishment. Accordingly, the decisive question is: what are the conditions for being covered by the freedom of establishment? It should be noted that the cases may have other parts, perhaps equally interesting, but they will largely be left out in this section.

---

2 The ECJ thus declared in case C-369/90 *Mario Vicente Micheletti and others v. Delegación del Gobierno en Cantabria* (para. 15): "... the provisions of Community law on freedom of establishment preclude a Member State from denying a national of another Member State who possesses at the same time the nationality of a non-member country entitlement to that freedom on the ground that the law of the host State deems him to be a national of the non-member country".

It should be underlined that the question of which factors that connect for example a company or an individual to a Member State, will not be discussed here. Instead, that question is specifically dealt with in the case-law analysis in the sections dealing with host and home state restrictions.[3]

4.2.2 Individuals and Firms

The term "nationals of a Member State" obviously covers individuals, "natural persons" to use Community terminology, but it also covers companies and firms.

In case C-112/91 *Werner* the freedom of establishment did not apply. The facts of the underlying case were the following. Mr Werner had a dental practice in Germany, where he also was a national. However, Mr Werner was resident for tax purposes in the Netherlands and not in Germany. Because of his status as non-resident in Germany, he was not allowed specific tax benefits there that only were granted to residents. The question was whether the denial of tax benefits in Germany was in conflict with the freedom of establishment. The Court answered that the freedom of establishment did not apply. The reason for this answer was presumably that the taxation of the German national Mr Werner was considered as a strictly internal German affair, and Mr Werner had not exercised the freedom of establishment when conducting his dental practice in Germany. The fact that he was resident in the Netherlands obviously did not affect the outcome.

Case C-107/94 *Asscher*[4] dealt with a Dutch national, Mr Asscher, who had immigrated to Belgium from the Netherlands. Mr Asscher worked as a self-employed person both in Belgium and in the Netherlands, even though he was resident in Belgium only. Because Mr Asscher was not resident in the Netherlands, he was taxed at a higher tax rate on the income earned in that state than if he had been resident there. The general question which the European Court of Justice was requested to answer was whether the higher taxation in the Netherlands of non-residents constituted an infringement of the freedom of establishment.

An initial and more particular question of relevance to this section was whether in a situation such as Mr Asscher's, it was possible to invoke the freedom of establishment regarding the tax treatment in the Netherlands, the state where Mr Asscher was a national.[5]

---

3 Sections 4.4 to 4.7.

4 Case C-107/94 *P.H. Asscher v. Staatssecretaris van Financiën.*

5 Case C-107/94 *Asscher*, para. 31.

Initially, and in line with case C-112/91 *Werner*, the European Court of Justice began by declaring that the freedom of establishment cannot be invoked in a situation which is "purely internal to a Member State".[6] However the Court also declared that the freedom of establishment cannot be interpreted in such a way as to exclude from that right "… a given Member State's own nationals from the benefit of Community law where by reason of their conduct they are, with regard to their Member State of origin, in a situation which may be regarded as equivalent to that of any other person enjoying the rights and liberties guaranteed by the Treaty".[7] This could be interpreted as an extension of the somewhat narrow scope given to the freedom of establishment in the *Werner* case.

Mr Asscher was a national of the Netherlands, but he was resident for tax purposes in Belgium. Moreover, and most importantly, Mr Asscher had income from activities in *both* Member States, income which influenced his taxation in the Netherlands. As a consequence, the Court considered that Mr Asscher had exercised rights and liberties recognised by the EC Treaty and more specifically the freedom of establishment. Mr Asscher was "… in a situation which may be regarded as equivalent to that of any other person relying as against the host Member State on the rights and liberties guaranteed by the Treaty".[8]

One conclusion of the *Asscher* case is that under certain conditions, it is possible to rely on the freedom of establishment also in relation to the Member State where the person in question is a national. What those conditions are, is somewhat more subtle. It is unquestionable that there has to be a cross-border element involved. In this case, Mr Asscher was resident in Belgium and exercised business activities in the Netherlands, which accordingly entitled him to be covered by the freedom of establishment. But suppose that Mr Asscher had not conducted any business in Belgium, would he then have been covered by the freedom of establishment when conducting business in the Netherlands? The decision by the Court does not explicitly answer that question, and perhaps rightly so since the facts of the case were different. However, by stressing the fact that Mr Asscher indeed was conducting business in both Belgium and the Netherlands, the impression is that Mr Asscher would not have been covered by the freedom of establishment if he had not conducted business in Belgium.[9]

---

6 Case C-107/94 *Asscher*, para. 32.

7 *Ibid.*

8 Case C-107/94 *Asscher*, para. 34.

9 Case C-107/94 *Asscher*, para. 33 and 34.

4.2.3 Companies

4.2.3.1 Articles 48 and 293 of the EC Treaty

The way in which a company is connected with a specific Member State is stipulated in Article 48 of the EC Treaty:

> "Companies or firms formed in accordance with the law of a Member State and having their registered office, central administration or principal place of business within the Community shall, for the purposes of this Chapter, be treated in the same way as natural persons who are nationals of Member States.
>
> 'Companies or firms' means companies or firms constituted under civil or commercial law, including cooperative societies, and other legal persons governed by public or private law, save for those which are non-profit-making."

The meaning of Article 48 (1) of the EC Treaty is that companies or firms which have been formed in accordance with the law of a Member State, and have their registered office, central administration or principal place of business within the Community, shall be treated in the same way as individuals who are nationals of a Member State. The European Court of Justice has declared that as regards companies it is their corporate seat that serves as the connecting factor with the legal system of a particular state, like nationality in the case of individuals.[10] It should be observed that when the Court in this context refers to a company's seat as the connecting criterion to a specific Member State, the Court's reference to "seat" includes all three connecting criteria mentioned in Article 48: registered office, central administration or principal place of business.[11]

Article 48 (2) declares that the expression "companies or firms" means companies or firms constituted under civil or commercial law, including cooperative societies, and other legal persons that are governed by public or private law, with the exception of those that are non-profit-making.[12] From this general requirement it is possible to

---

10 See for example Case 270/83 *Avoir fiscal*, para. 18; case C-330/91 *Commerzbank*, para. 13; and case C-264/96 *ICI*, para. 20. It should be noted that the ECJ in the English language version of the *Avoir fiscal* case referred to a company's registered office as its general connecting factor to a specific Member State (para. 18). That is, however, an incorrect translation. The French language version of the same paragraph refers to a company's "*siège*" – the seat of a company. Accordingly, it is a company's seat in the meaning of its registered office, central administration or principal place of business that serves as the connecting factor with the legal system of a particular Member State. This is a matter that I will consider in the following case-law analysis of this chapter, more precisely in sections 4.4 to 4.7.

11 Cf. Edwards, "Secondary Establishment of Companies – the Case Law of the Court of Justice", *Yearbook of European Law*, Oxford University Press, Oxford, 1998, pp. 221-257, at p. 226.

12 Legal entities which are non-profit-making are accordingly not covered by the EC Treaty Chapter on the freedom of establishment. Cf. also case C-182/83 *Fearon v. Irish Land Commission*, para. 8.

deduce two conditions.[13] The first condition is the "form and profit motive". According to Article 48 (2) "companies or firms" must be constituted according to civil or commercial law. The profit motive is considered as the most important one.[14]

The second condition concerns the nationality of a company or firm. Article 48 (1) stipulates that a company or firm must have its registered office, central administration or principal place of business within the Community to be covered by the freedom. Consequently, companies or firms from third countries are excluded from the freedom of establishment as manifested in Articles 43 to 48 of the EC Treaty. It is, of course, possible for nationals of third countries to establish firms and companies within the European Union, and the freedom of establishment will cover such firms and companies.

Finally, it should be noticed that it is possible for a national of a Member State to make a "U-turn establishment". Suppose that company P, a national of Member State X, establishes a business through a subsidiary, labelled Q, in Member State Y. The freedom of establishment entitles Q company to establish a branch in Member State X, home state of the parent company P.[15]

It is also important to note Article 293 of the EC Treaty which stipulates:

> "Member States shall, so far as is necessary, enter into negotiations with each other with a view to securing for the benefit of their nationals … the mutual recognition of companies or firms within the meaning of the second paragraph of Article 48, the retention of legal personality in the event of transfer of their seat from one country to another, and the possibility of mergers between companies or firms governed by the laws of different countries."

Accordingly, Member States should recognise companies formed under their national legislation, and should also secure the retention of legal personality when companies transfer their seat between Member States. It should, however, be underlined that the provision only obliges Member States to enter into negotiations on these issues.

---

[13] Kapteyn and VerLoren van Themaat, *Introduction to the Law of the European Communities*, 3rd ed., Kluwer Law International, London/The Hague/Boston, 1998, p. 733.

[14] An interesting case as regards non-profit-making entities and the freedom of establishment is case C-70/95 *Sodemare SA, Anni Azzurri Holding SpA and Anni Azzurri Rezzato Srl v. Regione Lombardia*. The ECJ stated in that case: "… Articles [43] and [48] of the [Treaty] do not preclude a Member State from allowing only non-profit-making private operators to participate in the running of its social welfare system …".

[15] Kapteyn and VerLoren van Themaat, *Introduction to the Law of the European Communities*, 3rd ed., Kluwer Law International, London/The Hague/Boston, 1998, p. 732. Cf. the situation in case C-212/97 *Centros*.

So far there have been no conventions between Member States on these issues.[16] In case C-208/00 *Überseering* the European Court of Justice declared that the exercise of the freedom of establishment was not dependent upon the actual adoption of the conventions that are referred to in Article 293 of the EC Treaty.[17] In other words, even if the Member States have not been able to conclude any conventions in the previously mentioned areas, they are nonetheless bound to comply with the freedom of establishment. The Court found that it was not necessary for the Member States to adopt a convention on the mutual recognition of companies that meet the conditions set out in Article 48 of the EC Treaty for them to exercise the freedom of establishment.[18]

4.2.3.2 The Incorporation Principle and the Seat Principle

The persons that benefit from the EC Treaty are those that are nationals of a Member State. As regards individuals it is their nationality of a Member State that serves as a connecting factor. When it comes to companies, Article 48, as previously mentioned, provides three different connecting criteria that all are alternative to each other: registered office, central administration or principal place of business. Companies formed in accordance with the law of a Member State and fulfilling one of the three criteria will be covered by the freedom of establishment.

As the wording of Article 48 implies, Member States apply different connecting criteria for companies to their legal system. In general, Member States apply either of two principles determining whether a company belongs to the legal system of that state: the incorporation principle and the real seat principle.

The incorporation principle means that the law of the state where a company is incorporated will govern the company and determine its legal capacity and personality. The real seat principle means that the state where a company has its "real seat" will govern the company and determine its legal capacity and personality. The meaning of "real seat" varies between different states, but will normally be where the company has its central management and control.[19]

The application of the different principles among Member States raises problems for Community law. A short example may illustrate that. Suppose that a company

16 Dyrberg, "Full Free Movement of Companies in the European Community At Last?", *EL Rev.*, 2003, pp. 528-537, at p. 529.

17 Case C-208/00 *Überseering*, para. 55.

18 Case C-208/00 *Überseering*, para. 60.

19 Dyrberg, "Full Free Movement of Companies in the European Community At Last?", *EL Rev.*, 2003, pp. 528-537, at p. 529. Cf. also Nelson, "Ursprungsstatens rätt bestämmer aktiebolags rätt till utlandsetablering", *Svensk Skattetidning*, 2003, pp. 138-153.

is registered in state X and situated there according to the incorporation principle. Company A transfers its central management and control to state Y, which applies the real seat principle. Thus it is possible that also state Y will consider the company to be situated in that state. However, it is also possible that state Y will consider the company as a foreign company because it in some way has not complied with the requirements of its company law, even if the company in effect has its seat there. One detrimental effect of that may be that the company cannot take part in legal proceedings in state Y as if it were a company situated in that state.

It has been argued that the incorporation principle favours the mobility of companies. A major reason for this is that there is no requirement to re-incorporate in another Member State, which could be both costly and time-consuming.[20] However, the application and recognition of the incorporation principle also opens up the possibility of fraudulent behaviour, for example the establishment of sham companies ("letter-box companies"). A sham company may have no substantial connection whatsoever with the state where it is incorporated. The real seat theory can mean that a company will have a more substantial connection to the state where it has its seat, for example in the form of its effective management and control. Even if there is such a connection, the entire business of a company may of course be conducted in other states than the state where it has its management and control.

Wymeersch traces the roots of the real seat theory to France ("*siège réel*") in the 19th century, where the criterion was introduced as a response to a situation where French companies emigrated to the "legally more clement climate" of Belgium.[21] Furthermore, Wymeersch notes that Member States hold different views on the possibility of the transfer of corporate seat: some states do not allow any transfer of seat (e.g. Germany and Austria), some states explicitly allow seat transfer (e.g. France and Italy), and some states have no explicit provisions on the issue (such as Belgium and Luxembourg).[22]

In an increasing number of cases, the European Court of Justice has considered the application by Member States of the incorporation principle and the real seat theory, as well as their mutual relationship and their compatibility with the freedom of establishment. In this section I will outline some of the issues considered by the European Court of Justice in a few important cases. The reason for this presentation is that in the tax law cases forming the core of this chapter, the Court refers to the different connecting criteria for a company to a specific Member State. Therefore I consider

20 Cf. Dyrberg, *op. cit.*

21 Wymeersch, "The Transfer of the Company's Seat in European Company Law", *CML Rev.* 2003, pp. 661-695, at p. 668.

22 *Ibid.*, p. 695.

it important to provide a general understanding of this issue. It should be noted that the relationship between the incorporation and real seat principles could be a subject for separate studies.

One early case[23] is C 81/87 *Daily Mail*. The case concerned a company, here called Daily Mail, which was incorporated in the United Kingdom, where it also had its registered office. Daily Mail applied to the United Kingdom authorities for consent to the transfer of its central management and control to the Netherlands. The reason for the transfer was that the unlimited tax liability in the United Kingdom was based on the fact that central management and control was exercised there. Moreover, by transferring central management and control to the Netherlands, Daily Mail would have avoided unlimited tax liability in the United Kingdom. The Court came to the conclusion that in the present state of Community law the transfer of a company's seat was something to be covered by future legislation or conventions. It should be underlined that the Court's answer mainly refers to the situation of the home state: in my view it hardly relates to the situation in the other state to which the transfer was to be made. Moreover, Daily Mail would have retained its status as a company incorporated in the United Kingdom, even if the seat was transferred to another Member State.[24] The Court decided that the freedom of establishment did not include a right for a company incorporated in one Member State to transfer its central management and control (as well as its central administration) to another Member State, while still having the status of an incorporated company in the first Member State.[25]

Case C-212/97 *Centros* is important in this context because the European Court of Justice recognised the registration of a company in another Member State, even if the reason for the foreign incorporation was to avoid a comparatively high minimum capital share holding. A Danish couple, Mr and Mrs Bryde, had established a company, Centros Ltd, in the United Kingdom. In turn, Centros Ltd wanted to establish a branch in Denmark. There was strong reason to believe that the major purpose for the establishment of the company in the United Kingdom was to avoid the capital requirement for establishing a company in Denmark: the paid-up of minimum capital was fixed at DKK 200,000. The corresponding payment in the United Kingdom was GBP 100.

---

[23] Another early case is C 79/85 *D.H.M. Segers v. Bestuur van de Bedrijfsvereniging voor Bank- en Verzekeringswezen, Groothandel en Vrije Beroepen* (usually referred to as "*Segers*"). In this case the ECJ considered that a Dutch social security organisation could not refuse social security benefits to the director of a company on the ground that the company had its registered office in the United Kingdom.

[24] The ECJ declared: "It must therefore be held that the Treaty regards the differences in national legislation concerning the required connecting factor and the question whether – and if so how – the registered office or real head office of a company incorporated under national law may be transferred from one Member State to another as problems which are not resolved by the rules concerning the right of establishment but must be dealt with by future legislation or conventions." Case 81/87 *Daily Mail*, para. 23.

[25] Case 81/87 *Daily Mail*, para. 24.

There was no substantial business carried on through Centros Ltd in the United Kingdom. The case has both outbound and inbound implications. From an outbound perspective the Danish Government argued that the establishment of a company in the United Kingdom did not amount to a "relevant external element in the light of Community law and, in particular, freedom of establishment".[26] The European Court of Justice took the opposite view. The Court even stated: "… it is immaterial that the company was formed in the first Member State only for the purpose of establishing itself in the second, where its main, or indeed entire, business is to be conducted".[27]

From an inbound perspective, however, the Court considered that the denial of the Danish authorities to register a Danish branch of Centros Ltd was an infringement of the freedom of establishment which could not be justified.

From the *Centros* case it is clear that the establishment in another Member State with the purpose to establish in the first state is, as a general rule, acceptable. An important result from the *Centros* case is, in my view, that the European Court of Justice seems to give much weight to the incorporation principle, even if there is good reason to believe that the effective management and control of a company will not be exercised in the state of registration.

A recent case in this area is the previously mentioned C-208/00 *Überseering*. Überseering BV ("Überseering") was a company incorporated under Dutch law and was registered with the register of companies of Amsterdam and Haarlem. Überseering purchased a piece of land in Germany, which was used for business purposes. It contracted a German company (NCC GmbH) to refurbish a garage and a motel on the site. Überseering complained that the paint work was defective, and claimed compensation. Ultimately, Überseering brought an action before a German court against NCC GmbH with a claim for compensation. However, two German nationals, resident in Düsseldorf, had acquired all shares in Überseering. Two German courts dismissed the action brought about by Überseering. The reason was that Überseering was considered to have transferred its actual centre of administration to Düsseldorf, and as a company incorporated in the Netherlands but with its centre of administration in Germany, Überseering did not have legal capacity in Germany and could accordingly not bring legal proceedings there. It follows from this that the *Überseering* case can, in principle, be regarded as an inbound case: it deals with the treatment in Germany of a Dutch company.

In the *Überseering* case, the European Court of Justice was asked, among other questions, whether the dismissal of the case in Germany was in conflict with the freedom of

[26] Case C-212/97 *Centros*, para. 16.

[27] Case C-212/97 *Centros*, para. 17.

establishment. The Court found that the consequence of the approach taken in German law and by the German courts was that a company validly incorporated in a Member State other than Germany had no alternative to reincorporation in Germany if it had the intention of using the German procedural system.[28] Überseering was incorporated and registered in the Netherlands, and was therefore entitled to exercise the freedom of establishment. In the view of the Court "[t]he requirement of reincorporation of the same company in Germany is therefore tantamount to outright negation of freedom of establishment".[29]

Consequently, the refusal in German law to recognise the legal capacity of a company incorporated in the Netherlands but with its centre of administration in Germany was considered a restriction on the freedom of establishment, which moreover could not be justified.[30]

Another recent case in this area of Community law is C-167/01 *Inspire Art*, which primarily is an inbound case, but also with outbound implications similar to the *Centros* case. The *Inspire Art* case deals with the treatment in the Netherlands of a company incorporated in the United Kingdom (England and Wales). Inspire Art Ltd ("Inspire Art") was a company governed by the law of the United Kingdom. It had a branch in Amsterdam, the Netherlands. Even though it was incorporated in the United Kingdom, Inspire Art traded exclusively in the Netherlands. Dutch legislation required that Inspire Art's branch in the Netherlands filed its registration with the Dutch commercial register and acquire the status of *formeel buitenlandse vennootschap* (formally foreign company). Inspire Art did not have that description attached to its registration in the commercial register. The Chamber of Commerce of Amsterdam applied to a Dutch court for a ruling that Inspire Art would have to acquire the previously mentioned status, because Dutch legislation prescribed this when a foreign company traded solely in the Netherlands.

---

28 Case C-208/00 *Überseering*, para. 79.

29 Case C-208/00 *Überseering*, para. 81.

30 Several Member States have various forms of "exit taxes" on the emigration of companies as well as individuals. The question arises as to whether such exit taxes are compatible with the freedom of establishment. So far, no such case concerning companies has been decided by the European Court of Justice. A critical point for this discussion is whether the emigrating company would be covered by the personal scope of the freedom of establishment. Weber argues that if a company transfers its central management and control ("seat") to another Member State, and as a consequence loses its legal personality in the state from which it emigrated, it would not be covered by the freedom of establishment because it no longer exists in that state. However, if the emigrating company continues to be resident in the original Member State, on the basis of incorporation, it would be covered by the freedom of establishment. Under such circumstances the legality of the exit tax could be tested against the freedom of establishment. Cf. Weber, "Exit Taxes on the Transfer of Seat and the Applicability of the Freedom of Establishment after Überseering", *European Taxation*, 2003, pp. 350-354.

The European Court of Justice found that Inspire Art was formed in the United Kingdom for the purpose of circumventing certain conditions of Dutch company law, in particular regarding the minimum capital and the paying up of shares. Those objectives of Inspire Art for incorporating in the United Kingdom instead of in the Netherlands did not mean that the establishment of a branch in the Netherlands was not covered by the freedom of establishment.[31] The effect of the registration of foreign companies with the Commercial Register was in fact that Dutch company law rules on minimum capital and directors' liability were applied mandatorily for foreign companies.[32] In the view of the Court those requirements constituted restrictions on the freedom of establishment. Moreover, no grounds of justification, either statutory or according to the rule-of-reason doctrine, applied.

4.2.4 The Meaning of the Term "Establishment"

The meaning of the freedom of establishment is the subject of Article 43 (2) of the EC Treaty. It is stipulated that the freedom of establishment shall include the right to take up and pursue activities such as those of self-employed persons. Furthermore, an "establishment" means the right to set up and manage undertakings, in particular companies or firms, as defined in Article 48 of the EC Treaty. The consequence of this freedom of establishment is, according to Article 43 (2), that the establisher is entitled to pursue his activities under the conditions laid down for the nationals of the Member State where the establishment is made, the "host state". The freedom of establishment is, however, subject to the provisions of the chapter of the EC Treaty relating to the free movement of capital.

It should be noted that a person may be established in more than one Member State. A common example is a company established in one Member State and having a branch in another Member State.

A well-known case on the freedom of establishment is C-55/94 *Gebhard*.[33] In that case, the European Court of Justice declared that the "concept of establishment" is broad.[34] More precisely, the Court stated that the concept of establishment allows a Community national to participate, on a stable and continuous basis, in the economic life of a Member State other than his state of origin and to make profit from the

---

31 Case C-167/01 *Inspire Art*, para. 98.

32 Case C-167/01 *Inspire Art*, para. 100.

33 Case C-55/94 *Gebhard*, para. 24.

34 Case C-55/94 *Gebhard*, para. 25.

establishment.[35] By doing so, the Court declared, the "establisher" contributes to the economic and social interpenetration within the Community in the sphere of activities as self-employed persons.

As previously mentioned, the freedom of establishment includes both primary and secondary establishment. The right of primary establishment is at present only partly provided for. It is, for example, possible for nationals of one Member State to establish a company in another Member State. However, there is no Community law permitting the transfer of a company from one Member State to another Member State. However, this is possible with the *societas europaea.*

Case C-251/98 *Baars* concerned what level of holding in a company established in another Member State is necessary for the freedom of establishment to apply. The issue was whether a specific holding required by Dutch legislation constituted a sufficient ownership in order to invoke the freedom of establishment.

In the *Baars* case the European Court of Justice began its reasoning by addressing the following question: was Mr Baars' ownership sufficient to give him the right to invoke the freedom of establishment?[36] The Dutch net wealth tax law defined the necessary requirement of a substantial holding as "a holding for the last five years of at least one third of the shares in a company and more than 7 per cent of paid-up nominal capital".[37] In the view of the European Court of Justice, such a holding was not necessarily equivalent with "control or management of the company", which are "... factors connected with the exercise of the right of establishment". In the present case, however, the control or management requirement was fulfilled because Mr Baars owned 100 per cent of the Irish company, "... which undoubtedly brings such a taxpayer within the scope of application of the Treaty provisions on the right of establishment".[38]

In my view, the conclusions of the *Baars* case regarding who is entitled to invoke the freedom of establishment are the following. First, "control or management" of a company are factors connected with the exercise of the freedom of establishment. Secondly, the holding of at least one third of the shares in a company and more than seven per cent of the paid-up nominal capital does not necessarily constitute the required "control or management".

I would, however, not make the assumption that it is necessary to have a holding exceeding one third of the shares and more than seven per cent of the paid-up nominal capital

---

35 *Ibid.*

36 Cf. case C-251/98 *Baars*, para. 19.

37 Case C-251/98 *Baars*, para. 20.

38 Case C-251/98 *Baars*, para. 21.

to be able to invoke the freedom of establishment. Whether "control or management" is fulfilled must, in my view, be decided in a case-by-case analysis. Suppose on the one hand that person A has one third of the shares in a company X, and that person B has two thirds of the shares. In this case, person A can hardly claim to have "control or management" of the company, which, however, person B can. Suppose on the other hand that person A still has one third (two sixths) of the shares in company X, but the other shares are owned with one sixth each by the persons B, C, D and E. In that case A has the individually largest holding, and he may also, in my view, exercise the "control or management" of the company. A shareholder contract between B, C, D, and E may, however, change such a position for person A.

4.3 Analytical Framework

4.3.1 Introduction

In this section the analytical framework will be presented that I will apply in the subsequent case-law analysis. There are two major issues that I will discuss in this section. To begin with, the neutrality between different forms of establishment. An establishment in another Member State may take several forms, for example a branch or a subsidiary. An important question is whether the freedom of establishment provides for tax neutrality between those different forms of establishment. Furthermore, is there any difference in a potential requirement for tax neutrality depending on whether the perspective is that of the host state or the home state? I will discuss these issues on the basis of case-law from the European Court of Justice.

Here I will also present the scheme which I will apply in the forthcoming analysis of cases decided by the European Court of Justice on the compatibility of national measures on direct taxation with the freedom of establishment.

4.3.2 Neutrality between Different Forms of Establishment

The starting point for a discussion on neutrality between different forms of establishment is of course the EC Treaty. Article 43 (1) of the EC Treaty provides that restrictions on the freedom of establishment of nationals of a Member State in the territory of another Member State shall be prohibited, which usually is labelled as the right of primary establishment. Secondary establishment is also permitted according to Article 43 (1): the prohibition against restrictions also applies to the setting up of agencies, branches or subsidiaries by nationals of any Member State established in the territory of any Member State.

Article 48 of the EC Treaty stipulates that the notion of nationality that applies to individuals shall also apply to companies or firms. More precisely, companies or firms that have registered office, central administration or principal place of business in a Member State shall be treated in the same way as individuals who are nationals of that Member State.

As previously discussed in Chapter 3, the European Court of Justice has decided that the freedom of establishment not only applies to treatment in the host state, but also applies in the home state.

From these starting points one could address the question of neutrality between legal forms from four different perspectives.[39]

(1) *Neutrality of legal form I*: Does the home state guarantee the free choice between carrying out economic activities in the host state through a branch or a subsidiary?

(2) *Neutrality of legal form II*: Does the host state treat a branch in the same way as a subsidiary?

(3) *Export neutrality of establishment*: Does the home state treat a foreign subsidiary in the same way as a resident subsidiary?

(4) *Import neutrality of establishment*: Does the host state treat a subsidiary of a non-resident parent company in the same way as a subsidiary of a resident parent company?

These questions will be addressed in the forthcoming case-law analysis. Even so I believe it necessary to make a few preliminary remarks on how the European Court of Justice has answered these questions so far. Regarding the neutrality of legal form I and whether the home state guarantees a free choice between carrying out activities in the host state through a branch and through a subsidiary, no cases have been decided so far. However, the *Marks & Spencer* case deals exactly with this issue, and I will discuss that case in section 4.6.

In contrast, neutrality of legal form II has been addressed by the Court in a number of cases on the relation between the freedom of establishment and national direct tax measures. In several cases the Court has decided that the host state is obliged to treat the branch of a non-resident company in the same way as a resident subsidiary, for example in Case 270/83 *Avoir fiscal*, C-330/91 *Commerzbank*, and C-250/95 *Futura Participations*. All three cases are discussed in this chapter.

I would like to note that both neutrality of legal form I and II focus on a discrimination approach to the understanding of the fundamental freedoms. As discussed in Chapter

39 Cf. Meussen, "The Marks and Spencer Case: Reaching the Boundaries of the EC Treaty", *EC Tax Review*, 2003, pp. 144-148, at p. 146 (with further references).

3, the comparison between different situations is vital for deciding whether or not discrimination is at issue. However, in its recent case-law the European Court of Justice has also applied a barrier approach – where it does not explicitly say what form of discrimination or restriction is at issue – regarding the freedom of establishment. But as Lang points out, even in the cases of "barriers" one could eventually find a point where a comparison between different situations could be made in order to establish that a difference in treatment is at issue.[40] In conclusion, I find it interesting to make a comparison between different forms of establishment even in those cases where the Court "only" comes to the conclusion that there is a case of non-discriminatory restriction.

Export neutrality and the question of whether the home state treats a foreign subsidiary in the same way as a resident subsidiary, have also been considered by the Court. Two cases of this category are C-251/98 *Baars* and C-168/01 *Bosal Holding*, both of which are discussed in this chapter. Import neutrality and the question of whether the host state treats a subsidiary of a non-resident parent company in the same way as the subsidiary of a resident parent company, has been addressed by the Court in the joined cases C-397/98 and C-410/98 *Metallgesellschaft and Others*, as well as case C-324/00 *Lankhorst-Hohorst*.

4.3.3 Preliminary Remarks on the Free Choice between a Branch and a Subsidiary

As regards secondary establishments, the freedom of establishment provides a national of a Member State with the right of establishing in another Member State a branch or a subsidiary, for example. According to the current understanding of the freedom of establishment, that right prohibits restrictions being applied either in the host state or the home state. But does the freedom of establishment guarantee identical treatment between the establishments of a branch compared with a subsidiary? This is a question that will be discussed in the subsequent case-law analysis, but due to the importance of the question, I consider it necessary to address it somewhat more deeply at this initial stage.

The primary tax consideration is, in my view, that the host state subsidiaries will be resident for tax purposes and subject to unlimited tax liability, whereas branches will be non-resident for tax purposes and subject to limited tax liability. As discussed in Chapter 3, the European Court of Justice has declared that the situations of residents and non-residents are not generally comparable. In cases relating to the freedom of establishment and the transfer of individuals, the Court has advanced as a reason for this difference between residents and non-residents, that there are objective differences

[40] Section 3.7.3.

between them from the point of view of the source of the income and the possibility of taking into account their ability to pay tax or their personal and family circumstances – the Schumacker doctrine.

However, when it comes to the comparison between, on the one hand, resident companies and, on the other hand, non-resident companies – branches – the Court has been less explicit on to what extent these two categories are comparable.

When discussing the freedom of establishment and the extent of the free choice between the establishment of a branch and a subsidiary, it is important to consider what in fact constitutes the two different forms of establishment. Of course, the terms "branch" and "subsidiary" have specific meanings in the private law as well as the tax law of the different Member States. What is of interest in this context is which meaning these terms have in the context of Community law and, more specifically in relation to the freedom of establishment. I will begin with the meaning of "subsidiary". According to Schön the meaning of "subsidiary" in the context of the freedom of establishment, implies that the participant in the common market has a substantial entrepreneurial influence on the management of the subsidiary which goes beyond the influence following from a mere capital investment according to the free movement of capital.[41] Such an "entrepreneurial influence" will of course be at hand when the shareholder has 100 per cent of the shares of the company, or where the shareholder has "real" influence over the business decisions of the company. Moreover, an entrepreneurial influence would also be assumed where the shareholder has at least 25 per cent of the nominal capital of the company,[42] which also would be in line with for example Article 3 of the Parent/Subsidiary Directive.[43]

A branch is, of course, not an independent legal entity; it is dependent on and forms part of the legal entity that has established it. In international tax law the term applied is "permanent establishment", which according to Article 5 (1) of the OECD MC means a fixed place of business through which the business of an enterprise is wholly

41 Schön, "The Free Choice between the Right to Establish a Branch and to Set-up a Subsidiary – a Principle of European Business Law", *EBOR*, 2001, pp. 339-364, at p. 345.

42 *Ibid.*

43 In case C-251/98 *Baars*, AG Alber in his opinion (para. 33) elaborates in a convincing way on the difference between the mere investment of capital in a company and actual establishment in another Member State. AG Alber states that the difference "… should probably be set at the point where a shareholder ceases to confine himself to the mere provision of capital in support of a particular business activity carried on by another person, and begins to become involved himself in conducting the business. Such involvement requires the shareholder to go beyond simply exercising his voting rights, and to participate in a way which will enable him to exercise real influence over the company's business decisions. In determining whether such is the case, regard should be had to the rules of the company law in the State in which the undertaking is established."

or partly carried on. According to the OECD MC a branch will constitute such a fixed place of business, but so will also, for example, a place of management, an office and a factory. The definition of permanent establishment in the OECD MC has had a tremendous impact not only on the definition of the term in the tax treaties of the world, but also on the definition contained in national tax legislation both within and outside the OECD area.

In general, a branch is less costly to establish and maintain than a subsidiary. A subsidiary will have to comply with more complicated formation procedures, as well as the requirements of everyday management.[44] In case C-212/97 *Centros*, AG Pergola in his opinion (para. 15) advanced the following characteristics for the subsidiary: a subsidiary is legally independent of the parent company by which it is controlled. A subsidiary can legitimately conclude contracts, though in some cases the parent company may intervene in the transaction as the contracting party. A subsidiary has its own funds to settle any debts it has contracted; the subsidiary with its own legal personality thus acts as a protective screen between parent company and creditors.

In my view there is a difference in degree of integration in the host country economy between a branch and a subsidiary, where a subsidiary is the more integrated entity.[45]

Already at this early stage I would like to draw one general conclusion from the previous discussion on the differences between branches and subsidiaries. I do not consider the freedom of establishment to include a formal requirement of identical treatment between branches and subsidiaries, neither from the host state perspective, nor from the home state perspective. The reason is simply that a branch and a subsidiary both constitute different degrees of integration in a state. In the national tax legislation of many states the varying degree of integration has been manifested in the difference between residents – such as resident subsidiaries – and non-resident branches. That a difference in treatment between residents and non-residents is permissible follows from the Schumacker doctrine of the European Court of Justice. However, there may be specific cases where branches and subsidiaries should, according to the freedom of establishment, be treated in the same way. So far the case-law of the European Court of Justice has been focused on similar treatment of a branch and a subsidiary in the host state, but there is reason to believe that in the near future the treatment of these entities in the home state will come into focus, for example through the Court's decision in the pending case C-436/00 *Marks & Spencer*.

---

44 Schön, "The Free Choice between the Right to Establish a Branch and to Set-up a Subsidiary – a Principle of European Business Law", *EBOR*, 2001, pp. 339-364, p. 346.

45 According to Schön, the EC Treaty contains the fundamental principle of permitting economic operators to choose different degrees of integration into the market in order to assure an optimal allocation of resources. Schön, *op. cit.*, p. 361.

4.3.4 Remarks on the Categorisation of the Case-law

I would like to make a few remarks on the categorisation of the case-law that is analysed in this chapter. The basic dividing line is between the host state perspective and the home state perspective. The case-law on the freedom of establishment in relation to matters of direct taxation developed regarding the host state perspective: how were the branches of foreign companies to be treated in the host state? Section 4.4 deals with the host state perspective. This section is divided into three major parts. Section 4.4.2 deals with companies establishing branches in the host state. Companies establishing subsidiaries in the host state is covered in section 4.4.3. Finally, individuals establishing branches in the host state is discussed in section 4.4.4.

The home state perspective is covered in section 4.5. In recent years the European Court of Justice has in several cases also decided that the freedom of establishment applies to measures of direct taxation taken by the home state. This section has a similar outline to section 4.4. In section 4.5.2 I deal with the treatment in the home state of a company that establishes a branch in another state. Section 4.5.3 deals with treatment in the home state of the company that establish a subsidiary in another state. Finally, section 4.5.4 covers other cases.

Section 4.6 deals with the decision by the Special Commissioners in the *Marks & Spencer* case. The case has been referred to the European Court of Justice but there is as yet no opinion of the Advocate General and, of course, no decision by the Court. I have anyway decided to discuss this case on the merits of its importance. It deals primarily with the treatment in the home state of a parent company establishing subsidiaries in other states. The case focuses on the meaning of discrimination, and is therefore of importance in this chapter. Finally, in one of the underlying national court decisions cases in the United Kingdom, the case has been decided by two leading experts on international tax law and Community law, John F Avery Jones and Malcolm Gammie.

Section 4.7 deals with case C-307/97 *Saint-Gobain*. From one perspective this case deals with the treatment in the host state of a branch of a foreign company. From another perspective the host state of the foreign company establishing the branch is also the home state of the branch when it conducts business in third states. This fact, and also the fact that the case emphasises the relationship between Community law and tax treaties, makes it suitable to deal with separately.

I would like to add that I began categorising the cases in a different way from the way previously described and actually chosen. My initial starting point for the categorisation was whether the cases at issue constituted direct discrimination, indirect discrimination or a non-discriminatory restriction. With such categorisation it turned out to be difficult to categorise recent cases from the European Court of Justice. The reason is that the

Court in the last five to seven years has avoided using clear language on what form of impediment the national legislation at issue raises to the freedom of establishment; in recent years the Court could be said to have applied a rather vague "barrier approach". I will of course discuss which form of restriction the national measures at issue constitute, but that will not form the basis of the categorisation.

There are problems with choosing the home and host state perspectives as the basis for the categorisation. One problem is that a case may be viewed from both the home and host state perspectives. A clear case of that is C-307/97 *Saint-Gobain*, which I accordingly will discuss separately (section 4.7). Even other cases are difficult to categorise with the method I have chosen, but they can predominantly be regarded from one perspective, for example case C-330/91 *Commerzbank*.

4.3.5 Analytical Scheme for the Case-law Analysis

When analysing the cases in sections 4.4 to 4.7 I will apply a scheme containing the following questions. It should be stressed that this schedule is specifically designed for the case-law on direct taxation and developed for the purposes of this study. Some of the questions will have evident answers, and I will deal with them shortly in the case-law analysis.

1. *Identification of the case.*

2. *The basic facts of the underlying case before the national court.* It is important to acquire a general knowledge of the facts of the underlying case. The first reason is that it facilitates the understanding of the legal issues to be decided by the European Court of Justice. The second reason is that it is not uncommon that the Court is influenced by those facts when deciding the case. As previously discussed in Chapter 1, the Court, in giving preliminary rulings, is only allowed to decide on matters of interpretation of Community law. Yet, as we shall see, the facts of the underlying cases may influence the Court when making such interpretations.

3. *The question asked by the referring national court.* It is of course necessary to refer to the question asked by the national court to the European Court of Justice. However, it is not uncommon that the Court decides to reformulate the question, for example by reason of misunderstandings made by the referring court. In such cases, I will in most cases only to refer the questions as expressed by the Court. The reason is simply that the answer given by the Court will be directed to the question in the form it has itself reformulated it.

4. *What does the national legislation at issue stipulate?* In principle, in its preliminary ruling the European Court of Justice will decide on the compatibility of national tax legislation with the fundamental freedoms at issue. The Court will often give a

thorough description of the national legislation applicable. It is not my objective to give an independent description of such national legislation: I will make use of the Court's description. It is of course possible that the Court's understanding of national legislation has either shortcomings or expresses misconceptions, or perhaps even both. That is a risk I have decided to take. What is in focus in my study is the Court's interpretation of the freedom of establishment and the free movement of capital. Even if the Court's understanding of the national legislation at issue is wrong, the Court's interpretation of those fundamental freedoms is valid.

5. *How is the person in question linked to a home Member State?* As regards individuals, the link with a Member State will often be on the basis of nationality or on a similar criterion such as residence for tax purposes. Regarding companies, the link with a Member State has traditionally been less evident, as the forthcoming case-law analysis will show. For example Article 48 of the EC Treaty stipulates, in short, that companies or firms formed in accordance with the law of a Member State and which have their registered office, central administration or principal place of business within the Community shall be treated as individuals who are nationals of Member States. The interpretation of this provision has, however, not been without difficulties.

6. *What is the basic cross-border element?* For the fundamental freedoms to apply there has to be some form of cross-border element, such as the establishment of a branch or the transfer of capital. In the case-law analysis this cross-border element will be identified, but it is often evident.

7. *How is the comparison made that establishes a potential discrimination?* In order to establish whether there is a case of discrimination, the European Court of Justice will make a comparison between different situations. How the Court makes this comparison in its case-law will be identified.

8. *What is the decision of the Court?*

4.4 Host State Restrictions

4.4.1 Introduction

In the following analysis I will discuss five cases: C 270/83 *Avoir fiscal*, C-330/91 *Commerzbank*, C-1/93 *Halliburton Services*, C-250/95 *Futura Participations* and C-311/97 *Royal Bank of Scotland*. The reason why I will deal with these four cases in the same section is that they all deal with the tax treatment of branches in the host state. All branches have been established by a company with its corporate seat in another Member State.

As we shall see, the five cases deal with different forms of restrictions. With the term "host state restrictions" I refer to the term "restriction" in a wide sense, in principle including both direct and indirect taxation, as well as non-discriminatory restrictions.

In the subsequent analysis I will basically follow the analytical framework as developed in section 4.3, even if the answer to some questions is so obvious that I will not specifically develop them.

4.4.2 Companies Establishing Branches

4.4.2.1 Case 270/83 **Avoir fiscal** *(28 January 1986)*

Case 270/83 *Avoir fiscal*[46] is one of the first cases of the European Court of Justice on the relationship between national tax legislation and the fundamental freedoms of the EC Treaty.[47] The case was one in a series of cases dealing with the treatment of foreign insurance companies in France. The *Avoir fiscal* case specifically dealt with the taxation of branches established in France by foreign insurance companies.

In this case it was the Commission that asked the Court for a declaration on whether France, by not granting the benefit of shareholders' tax credits to the branches and agencies in France of insurance companies established in another Member State on the same terms as those enjoyed by French companies, had failed to fulfil its obligations according to the EC Treaty, and in particular Article 43 (ex Article 52) of the Treaty.[48]

In France, the economic double taxation of company profits was limited according to an imputaton system called "*avoir fiscal*". In principle, economic double taxation consists in the taxation of company profits first at the company level in the form of company taxation, and second at the shareholder level in the form of dividend taxation. In France the shareholders were granted a tax credit – *avoir fiscal* – consisting of an amount equal to the tax paid by the dividend-distributing company. The shareholder could offset the *avoir fiscal* against the tax payable on the dividends received.[49]

---

46 Case 270/83 *Commission v. France*. The case is commonly referred to as the "*Avoir fiscal*" case.

47 The first case from the ECJ on the relation between fundamental freedoms and direct taxation was Case 18/84 *Commission v. France*, which dealt with the free movement of goods. See on this case Cordewener, *Europäische Grundfreiheiten und nationales Steuerrecht*, Verlag Dr. Otto Schmidt, Cologne, 2002, pp. 386-388.

48 Case 270/83 *Avoir fiscal*, para. 1.

49 Case 270/83 *Avoir fiscal*, para. 3.

However, the *avoir fiscal* was only granted to persons who had their habitual residence or registered office in France. If a foreign insurance company had a subsidiary in France which had its registered office there, the subsidiary would also be granted the *avoir fiscal*. However, the benefit of *avoir fiscal* would not be granted to secondary establishments, branches or agencies whose registered office was not in France.

The cross-border element of this case was the secondary establishment in France of branches or agencies of foreign, non-French, insurance companies. The freedom of establishment consists of the right of secondary establishment according to Article 43 (1) of the EC Treaty.

When deciding whether French law in this respect implied a difference in treatment, the Court made the following analysis. According to French law, insurance companies having their registered office[50] in France could benefit from the *avoir fiscal* on dividends stemming from shares held in French companies. In contrast, that tax benefit was not granted branches and agencies of insurance companies with their registered office in another Member State.[51] There is little elaboration on the subject of whether French companies are in an objectively comparable situation with foreign companies having a branch in France. It must be assumed that they are, because the Court in fact considers the French legislation at issue to be discriminatory.

The European Court of Justice, as well as the Commission, found that this difference in treatment constituted an infringement of the freedom of establishment according to Article [43] of the EC Treaty.[52] The Court accepted none of the grounds of justification put forward.

The question of neutrality between different forms of establishment was touched upon by the Court: "Acceptance of the proposition that the Member State in which a company seeks to establish itself may freely apply to it a different treatment solely by reason of the fact that its registered office is situated in another Member State would … deprive [Article 48 of the EC Treaty] of all meaning".[53] It seems here as if the Court in its interpretation of Article 48 aims at neutrality between the establishment of a branch of a non-resident company and that of a resident subsidiary of a foreign parent company. Whether that neutrality between different forms of establishment refers to the exact same treatment or not is not spelled out by the Court, but if it would have favoured identical treatment, it seems reasonable that the Court explicitly should have said so.

---

50 "Registered office" is used in the English language version, but the question is whether that is correct. See below and also section 4.2.3.1.

51 Case 270/83 *Avoir fiscal*, para. 16.

52 Case 270/83 *Avoir fiscal*, para. 27.

53 Case 270/83 *Avoir fiscal*, para. 18.

Advocate General Mancini states in his opinion that the freedom of establishment cannot be interpreted to mean that the three different forms of establishment mentioned in Article 43 – agencies, branches or subsidiaries – should be subject to "absolutely identical rules whether in regard to taxation or to anything else".[54]

The *Avoir fiscal* case is important from several aspects. First, the Court made it clear in this ruling from 1986 that also Member States' legislation in the field of direct taxation is subject to the prohibition against discrimination contained in the EC Treaty, and in this particular case, by the freedom of establishment. Secondly, the Court manifested its interpretation of Article 48 of the EC Treaty.[55] It is the seat of the company in the meaning of registered office, central administration or principal place of business that serves as the connecting factor with the legal system of a Member State.[56] In the view of the Court, the foreign insurance companies with branches in France could accordingly be said to have had a foreign "nationality", meaning that they had their registered offices in a country other than France. Because French tax legislation did not grant the *avoir fiscal* to such "foreign" branches, the French legislation should be considered as a case of direct discrimination.[57]

Also, in my view, this case has to be considered as a clear case of direct discrimination. The taxation in France was dependent on the nationality of the company: a company with its seat in France was granted the tax benefit, whereas a company with its seat in another state was not granted the benefit.

4.4.2.2 Case C-330/91 **Commerzbank** *(13 July 1993)*

Case C-330/91 *Commerzbank*[58] dealt with the compatibility with the freedom of establishment of United Kingdom legislation on the taxation of inbound interest received by a branch of a non-resident in that Member State. The *High Court of Justice* referred the matter of interpretation to the European Court of Justice.

The facts of the underlying case were the following. The German bank Commerzbank had a branch (permanent establishment) in the United Kingdom. Through its United Kingdom branch, Commerzbank issued loans to a number of companies in the United

---

54 Opinion of the AG Mancini in Case 270/83 *Avoir fiscal*, para. 11.

55 Case 270/83 *Avoir fiscal*, para. 18.

56 In fact the ECJ refers to "registration" instead of "seat" in the English language version of Case 270/83 *Avoir fiscal* (para. 18), but this is considered as a translation error, see on this issue section 4.2.3.1.

57 On the question of direct or indirect taxation, see Van Thiel, *EU Case Law on Income Tax, Part 1*, IBFD, Amsterdam, 2001, pp. 141-144.

58 Case C-330/91 *The Queen v. Inland Revenue Commissioners, ex parte Commerzbank AG.*

States. Commerzbank paid tax in the United Kingdom on the interest received from the United States on those loans.

Furthermore, Commerzbank applied to United Kingdom authorities for the repayment of the tax paid in the United Kingdom. Article 15 of the 1946 tax treaty between the United Kingdom and the United States provided that interest received was tax exempt in the United Kingdom, but on the condition that it was paid to a United Kingdom company or a company resident for tax purposes in the United Kingdom. Because Commerzbank was not resident in the United Kingdom, it could not benefit from the tax treaty, although as a compensation it would receive a refund of the overpaid tax. In addition, and vital in this case, the United Kingdom legislation on tax refunds granted an extra "repayment supplement" with 8.25 per cent per year. That supplement was, however, only granted to companies resident in the United Kingdom, which Commerzbank obviously was not.[59]

The European Court of Justice was asked to answer two principal questions. First, did the EC Treaty and the freedom of establishment prevent national legislation of a Member State from granting repayment supplement on overpaid tax to companies resident for tax purposes in that Member State, when at the same time it refused paying the supplement to companies which were resident in another Member State? Secondly, was such a rule still discriminatory if the exemption from tax, which gave the right to the refund, only applied to companies which were not resident for tax purposes in that Member State?[60]

Accordingly, the initial matter to be dealt with by the Court was whether the legislation at issue was discriminatory, and if so what form of discrimination it constituted. The Court referred to its interpretation of Articles 43 and 48 (ex Articles 52 and 58) in the previously discussed Case 270/83 *Avoir fiscal*.[61] The Court also stated that the rules on equal treatment "... forbid not only overt discrimination by reason of nationality or, in the case of a company, its seat, but all covert forms of discrimination which, by the application of other criteria of differentiation, lead in fact to the same result".[62] This is an important declaration by the Court. Companies may be subject to direct discrimination if the differentiation is based on the seat of the company. The seat of a company equals the nationality of an individual, in the view of the Court.

---

[59] Case C-330/91 *Commerzbank*, para. 6 and 8.

[60] Case C-330/91 *Commerzbank*, para. 12.

[61] Case C-330/91 *Commerzbank*, para. 13.

[62] Case C-330/91 *Commerzbank*, para. 14. In support of this view, the ECJ refers to Case 152/73 *Sotgiu v. Deutsche Bundespost*, para. 11.

In relation to this, the Court also considered the criterion "fiscal residence" which was used in the national legislation at issue. The Court concluded that fiscal residence applies independently from a company's seat.[63] As regarded the national legislation at issue, the Court came to the conclusion that a tax benefit only granted to those with fiscal residence in the United Kingdom was "… liable to work more particularly to the disadvantage of companies having their seat in other Member States".[64] It was not surprising that the European Court of Justice considered the national legislation in question to be discriminatory, and more precisely a case of indirect discrimination. If a non-resident company was denied the right to repayment, a right that a resident company had, then the non-resident company was by comparison in a disadvantageous situation. The fact that the exemption from tax, which gave rise to the refund, was available to non-residents only could not, in the view of the Court, justify a general rule that withheld the benefit.[65]

The reasoning of the European Court of Justice is relatively short and, in my view, a few subordinate questions remain unanswered. Obviously the Court has considered it possible in the present case that residents and non-residents can be in objectively comparable situations, but how that comparison was made more precisely is still a bit unclear. Furthermore, the Court did not address the question of whether the United Kingdom legislation at issue, beyond being discriminatory, also constituted a non-discriminatory restriction.[66]

In the United Kingdom the branches of foreign companies were subject to a more burdensome taxation than companies resident in the United Kingdom. From the perspective of the German company establishing itself in the United Kingdom, this is a case of indirect discrimination. From the perspective of the branch in the United Kingdom lending capital to persons resident outside of the United Kingdom it may also constitute a case of a home state restriction: the situation in the underlying case also has outbound implications. This question was, however, not separately addressed by the Court. In my view this case is also an example of the striving for neutrality between, on the one hand, a branch of a non-resident company, and, on the other hand, a resident subsidiary company.

---

63 Case C-330/91 *Commerzbank*, para. 15.

64 *Ibid.*

65 Case C-330/91 *Commerzbank*, para. 19.

66 This has been criticised by Van Thiel, *EU Case Law on Income Tax, Part 1*, IBFD, Amsterdam, 2001, p. 300.

4.4.2.3 Case C-1/93 **Halliburton Services** *(12 April 1994)*

Case C-1/93 *Halliburton Services*[67] was referred to the Court from the *Hoge Raad* of the Netherlands. The case concerned the compatibility of Dutch legislation on direct taxation with the freedom of establishment. More precisely, the facts of the underlying case were the following. Halliburton was an international group of companies. The parent company was Halliburton Inc., which was incorporated in the United States. Halliburton Inc. had all the shares in a German subsidiary (Halliburton GmbH) and a Dutch subsidiary (Halliburton BV). The German company Halliburton GmbH had a permanent establishment in the Netherlands. The group was subject to a reorganisation. Halliburton GmbH transferred and sold its permanent establishment in the Netherlands to the Dutch subsidiary Halliburton BV, which was a private limited company. The transfer included immovable property in the Netherlands. As a general rule in the Netherlands, the transfer of immovable property was subject to tax. There was, however, an exemption for transactions, which were carried out "as part of an internal reorganisation of public limited companies and private limited companies".[68]

From previous case-law it was clear that the Dutch *Hoge Raad* considered that, according to the principle of non-discrimination, as manifested in the US-Netherlands tax treaty, Halliburton BV could not be denied the benefit of the tax exemption in question on the ground that the parent company of the Halliburton Group was resident in the United States.[69] However, the non-discrimination article in the US-Netherlands tax treaty was not considered applicable when there was a transfer of immovable property between a German and a Dutch company. As a consequence, the tax exemption could not be extended to cover the transfer of immovable property in the present case. The compatibility of the denial of the tax benefit with the freedom of establishment was questioned before the *Hoge Raad*, which asked the European Court of Justice for a preliminary ruling.

The Court interpreted the question asked by the national court in the following way. Did Articles 43 and 48 (ex Article 52 and 58) of the EC Treaty preclude a Member State from granting tax exemption on the acquisition of immovable property situated in its territory or of rights *in rem* in relation to such property as part of an internal reorganisation, on the condition that the property was acquired from a company

---

[67] Case C-1/93 *Halliburton Services BV v. Staatssecretaris van Financiën*. The facts of the underlying case of the *Halliburton* case are complex, and I have chosen only to view it from the perspective of a company establishing a foreign branch.

[68] Case C-1/93 *Halliburton Services*, para. 5.

[69] Case C-1/93 *Halliburton Services*, para. 6.

constituted under its own law and not where it was acquired from a similar company constituted under the law of another Member State?[70]

By referring to its decision in case C-330/91 *Commerzbank*, the European Court of Justice confirmed that the rules on equal treatment forbid direct discrimination by reason of nationality or, in the case of a company, its seat. Furthermore, the Court declared that all indirect forms of discrimination are likewise prohibited, where the application of other criteria of differentiation in fact lead to the same result as if nationality or seat had been the criterion.[71]

The Court specifically noted that the tax exemption at issue only applied on transactions relating to immovable property between companies incorporated in the Netherlands. In contrast, companies incorporated in other Member States were excluded from the benefit.[72]

The Dutch government maintained that the legislation in question did not involve any discrimination, because the person liable to pay tax was a Dutch company: the situation was purely internal and would accordingly not affect Community law. This is clearly reasoning along the lines of the Court's decision in case C-112/91 *Werner*, where the German national Mr Werner, although a resident of the Netherlands, could be more heavily taxed in Germany than individuals resident there; there was no hindrance to a state treating its own nationals more harshly than non-nationals.[73] In conclusion: the Dutch government did not consider the case to include any relevant cross-border element for the freedom of establishment to apply.

The Court did not share the view of the Dutch government: the payment of tax on the sale of immovable property was a burden that made the conditions of the sale of the property more onerous and therefore had repercussions on the vendor, the German Halliburton GmbH. The Court clarified that the vendor was in a "distinctly less favourable position" than if it had chosen to form a Dutch public or private limited company instead of a branch (permanent establishment). This difference in treatment constituted an indirect discrimination of the freedom of establishment.[74]

[70] Case C-1/93 *Halliburton Services*, para. 13.

[71] Case C-1/93 *Halliburton Services*, para. 15.

[72] Case C-1/93 *Halliburton Services*, para. 17.

[73] See sections 3.4.2 and 4.2.2.

[74] Case C-1/93 *Halliburtion Services*, para. 19-20.

4.4.2.4 Case C-250/95 **Futura Participations** *(15 May 1997)*

The *Futura Participations*[75] case dealt with the compatibility of Luxembourg legislation on corporate losses with the freedom of establishment. Futura Participations SA (hereinafter Futura Participations) was a French company, and it had its seat in Paris. Singer was the Luxembourg branch of Futura Participations. The cross-border element of this case was the establishment by a French company of a branch in Luxembourg.

The main question considered by the Court was whether Article 43 (ex Article 52) of the EC Treaty precluded a Member State from having tax legislation with the following characteristics. For a branch of a non-resident company to carry forward losses incurred, two conditions had to be fulfilled. First, the losses had to be economically related to the income earned by the taxpayer in the state of the branch, Luxembourg. Secondly, the taxpayer had to have kept and held in the state of the branch, in respect of the activities carried out there, accounts complying with the relevant national rules.

As regards the *first condition*, that losses carried forward had to be economically linked with the income earned in the Member State where the tax was charged, the European Court of Justice did not consider it to constitute any prohibited difference in treatment.[76] The reason was that this condition was "… in conformity with the fiscal principle of territoriality".[77] The Court did not elaborate any further on the meaning of this principle of territoriality. It is, however, clear that a law provision containing a condition for the carrying forward of losses that those losses have to be economically linked with the income earned in that state, expresses the principle of territoriality as understood by the European Court of Justice. A possible conclusion is, at least in my view, that if a Member State bases a provision, or a set of provisions, on the principle of territoriality, such provisions do not constitute an infringement of the freedom of establishment.

Regarding the *second condition*, to keep accounts complying with Luxembourg law for the taxable year when the losses were incurred, the Court was less understanding. The Court concluded that in practice the second condition meant that a company or firm resident in one Member State, France in this case, in addition to its own accounts must keep separate accounts for its branch in the other Member State, Luxembourg. Moreover, those separate accounts must be held at the place of the branch, and not where the company or firm had its seat.[78] To begin with the Court considered this condition

[75] Case C-250/95 *Futura Participations SA and Singer v. Administration des contributions*. The case will be further examined in Chapter 5.

[76] Case C-250/95 *Futura Participations*, para. 22.

[77] *Ibid.*

[78] Cf. case C-250/95 *Futura Participations*, para. 25.

to be in conflict with the freedom of establishment and that it must be regarded as a non-discriminatory restriction.[79] Next the Court tested whether this restriction was justified on the ground of "effectiveness of fiscal supervision", an issue which I will return to in Chapter 5.

The case can be summarised in the following way.[80] First, it was not contrary to the freedom of establishment to request that in order to carry forward losses, the losses had to be economically related to the territory of the state where they were to be incurred. This stemmed from the principle of territoriality. Secondly, it was contrary to the freedom of establishment that the carrying forward of losses was subject to the condition that, in the year which the losses were incurred, the taxpayer had kept and held in the host state accounts relating to its activities there, where those accounts had to comply with national law in the host state.

4.4.2.5 Case C-311/97 **Royal Bank of Scotland** *(29 April 1999)*

Case C-311/97 *Royal Bank of Scotland* also dealt with the taxation of a branch (permanent establishment) of a foreign company and the freedom of establishment.[81] The Royal Bank of Scotland had its corporate seat in the United Kingdom. The bank carried on its business in Greece through a branch in Piraeus.

Greek tax law provided for a difference in taxation based on whether banks had their seat in Greece or in other countries. As regarded banks with their seat in Greece, two tax rates applied: either 40 per cent or 35 per cent.[82] Which rate to apply was decided by the tax subject's legal form and the nature of the shares it issued. However, as regarded banks with their seat in other countries only one tax rate applied, irrespective of their legal form and the nature of the shares which they issued.[83] Moreover, Greek legislation provided that a bank that had its seat in Greece was required to issue registered shares and would because of that be subject to the lower rate. The higher rate only applied to banks with their seat in another Member State and with a permanent establishment (branch) in Greece.[84]

---

79 Case C-250/95 *Futura Participations*, para. 26.

80 Case C-250/95 *Futura Participations*, para. 43.

81 Case C-311/97 *Royal Bank of Scotland plc v. Elliniko Dimosio (Greek State).*

82 Parts of the Greek legislation at issue dealt not only with banks but with company taxation in general. I will not cover that aspect any further. It is easy to agree with Terra and Wattel that the Greek legislation is difficult to grasp, Terra and Wattel, *European Tax Law*, 3rd ed., Kluwer Law International, London/The Hague/New York, 2001, p. 92.

83 Case C-311/97 *Royal Bank of Scotland*, para. 24.

84 Case C-311/97 *Royal Bank of Scotland*, para. 25.

In brief, the Court was asked the following question by the national Greek court. Assume that national legislation of a Member State grants special tax benefits for companies having their seat in that Member State. However, such tax benefits are not granted to companies that have their seat in another Member State and carry on their business through a permanent establishment in that other state.[85] Is such a provision of law compatible with the freedom of establishment?

The Royal Bank of Scotland was linked to Greece through a secondary establishment – a branch – in that Member State. The cross-border element consisted, obviously, of the establishment of a branch in Greece of a company with its seat in the United Kingdom.

The European Court of Justice began its reasoning by stating that in relation to companies it is their seat – in the meaning of their registered office, central administration or principal place of business – that serves as the connecting factor with the legal system of a particular state.[86]

The comparison establishing a case of discrimination is the comparison of the taxation of banks with their seat in Greece and banks with their seat in another Member State conducting business in Greece through a branch in that state.[87] In support of this methodology of deciding whether different situations are comparable or not, it is interesting to note that the Court finds support in its own case-law on the taxation of individuals, even if the present case deals with the taxation of companies. From the Court's reasoning and case-law references one can deduce that the Court considers the Schumacker doctrine to apply, to the extent possible, to cases on company taxation as well.[88]

The Court tested whether the situation of resident Greek banks and the branches in Greece of non-resident banks were objectively comparable, and decided that they were.[89] The Court declared that as regards individuals it had previously held that residents and non-residents are not in general in comparable situations.[90] There may, however, in the view of the Court, also be cases of discrimination in the different treatment of residents and non-residents "... where there is no objective difference such as to justify different treatment on this point as between the two categories of tax-

85 Case C-311/97 *Royal Bank of Scotland*, para. 18.

86 Case C-311/97 *Royal Bank of Scotland*, para. 23.

87 Case C-311/97 *Royal Bank of Scotland*, para. 26-27.

88 Case C-311/97 *Royal Bank of Scotland*, para. 26.

89 Cf. section 3.6.

90 Case C-311/97 *Royal Bank of Scotland*, para. 27. The Court referred to case C-279/93 *Schumacker*, para. 31-32; case C-80/94 *Wielockx*, para. 18; case C-107/94 *Asscher*, para. 41.

payers".[91] When it came to deciding the taxable base, Greek legislation made no difference between banks with their seat in Greece and foreign banks with branches in Greece. However, Greek banks were subject to unlimited tax liability in Greece, whereas foreign banks with branches in Greece were only subject to limited tax liability. The Court declared that this difference was a result of the limited fiscal sovereignty of the state where the income arose, compared to the state where the company has its seat. That difference "... is not such as to prevent the two categories of companies from being considered, all other things being equal, as being in a comparable situation as regards the method of determining the taxable base".[92] Consequently, the situations of resident banks, and non-resident banks with a branch in Greece, were objectively comparable.

To conclude, Greek legislation did not distinguish between Greek and foreign companies established in Greece through branches regarding the determination of the taxable base. However, only Greek companies could enjoy the lower tax rate. Accordingly, the legislation was discriminatory,[93] and it was a matter of direct discrimination: the preferential treatment was only given companies with their seat in Greece. The Court noted that only express derogations from the freedom of establishment could justify direct discrimination, notably Article 46 of the EC Treaty. The Greek government had not relied on any such grounds, and the Greek legislation in question was considered as discriminatory. Also in my view, this is a case of direct discrimination because the differentiating criterion for the tax benefit at issue was whether a bank had its seat in Greece or not.

Two important results follow from the *Royal Bank of Scotland* case. First, the Court confirmed the decision of the *Avoir fiscal* case that it is the seat of a company – in the meaning of its registered office, central administration or principal place of business – that decides in which state it has its "nationality". Secondly, event if it is not generally the case, the situation of, on the one hand, companies with their seat in a specific Member State, and, on the other hand, companies with their seat in another Member State established in the first-mentioned Member State through a branch, may be comparable. What was decisive for the situation of a Greek company to be comparable with the situation of a Greek branch of a foreign company, was that the taxable base was calculated in the same way in both situations.

In addition the *Royal Bank of Scotland* case also speaks in favour of neutrality between the branch of a foreign company and a company with its seat in the state at issue.

[91] Case C-311/97 *Royal Bank of Scotland*, para. 27, where the case also refers to *Schumacker* and *Asscher*.

[92] Case C-311/97 *Royal Bank of Scotland*, para. 29.

[93] Case C-311/97 *Royal Bank of Scotland*, para. 25.

4.4.2.6 Conclusion

In this section I will draw some general conclusions from the five cases previously analysed. The analysed cases have been C 270/83 *Avoir fiscal*, C-330/91 *Commerzbank*, C-1/93 *Halliburton Services*, C-250/95 *Futura Participations* and C-311/97 *Royal Bank of Scotland*. All five cases deal with the treatment in the host state of a branch of a company with its seat in another Member State. In all cases the foreign company has made use of its right of secondary establishment of a branch in another Member State. The right of secondary establishments is stipulated in Article 43 of the EC Treaty.

As regards a company's "nationality" according to Article 48 of the EC Treaty, the Court applies the seat criterion as the general term but recognises that the content of that criterion is something for the Member States to determine. Accordingly a company's seat refers to the connecting criteria stipulated in Article 48: registered office, central administration or principal place of business.

Four of the cases explicitly contain a "classic" discrimination analysis: *Avoir fiscal*, *Royal Bank of Scotland*, *Commerzbank* and *Halliburton*. In its analysis the Court made an express comparison between the taxation of resident companies and non-resident companies. In the early cases *Avoir fiscal*, decided 1986, and *Commerzbank*, decided 1993, the Court is not that explicit on the principal reasons for the comparison made. One should note that both of those cases were decided several years before the Court developed its Schumacker doctrine (case C-279/93), decided in 1995. However, in the *Royal Bank of Scotland* case, the Court explicitly refers to the comparison methodology developed in the *Schumacker* case, which dealt with the taxation of individuals. The Court states that in general the situations of residents and non-residents are not comparable. In the *Royal Bank of Scotland* case it is the fact that the tax base is calculated in the same way regarding residents and non-residents that makes the two categories comparable.

As regards the form of discrimination at issue, it is my view that both Case 270/83 *Avoir fiscal* and case C-311/97 *Royal Bank of Scotland* deal with direct discrimination. Direct discrimination in relation to companies is related to the "nationality" of the company. Furthermore, the Court declared in the *Avoir fiscal* case that if one accepted that the Member State in which a company wishes to establish itself could freely treat such a foreign company differently because it has its registered office in another Member State, that would deprive Article 48 of all meaning. The Court confirmed this interpretation in case C-311/97 *Royal Bank of Scotland*, with explicit references to the *Avoir fiscal* case.

In case C-330/91 *Commerzbank*, the Court stated that the rules on equal treatment not only forbid direct discrimination by reason of nationality, or, in the case of a company, its seat, but all indirect forms of discrimination which, by the application of other criteria of differentiation, in fact lead to the same result. Furthermore, the Court declared that the use of "fiscal residence" as a differentiating criterion applies independently of a company's seat. However, the criterion of fiscal residence in this case was likely to work more particularly to the disadvantage of companies having their seat in other Member States. Companies with their seat in other Member States also, most often, have their fiscal residence in other Member States. The Court considered the legislation at issue to constitute indirect discrimination. Also the *Halliburton* case deals with indirect discrimination, including a specific reference to the *Commerzbank* case.

Case C-250/95 *Futura Participations* is different from the others regarding the discrimination analysis. Finally, it was only the fact that branches of non-resident companies were obliged to keep accounts complying with the national Luxembourg legislation that constituted an infringement of the freedom of establishment. However, this law provision could hardly be said to be discriminatory. This law provision applied equally to residents and to non-residents. But it had the effect that non-residents, besides keeping their accounts according to French legislation, also had to keep accounts complying with Luxembourg legislation. In my view it has to be concluded that this legal rule constitutes a non-discriminatory restriction, and that is also generally accepted in the literature.[94]

In the five cases, the Court did establish a form of neutrality between the branch of a non-resident company and a resident company. The neutrality is, however, limited to specific tax benefits. The *Avoir fiscal* case deals with the benefit of a tax credit limiting the effects of economic double taxation. In the *Commerzbank* case it was the benefit of a repayment supplement on overpaid tax in the United Kingdom. The *Royal Bank of Scotland* case dealt with the higher tax rate that applied to the income of branches of non-resident banks compared with resident banks. In the *Halliburton* case it concerned a tax exemption in the Netherlands on inter-corporate reorganisations including immovable property, which was not granted where a non-resident German company took part.

The tax legislation at issue in the *Futura Participations* case is somewhat different from the other cases. The first provision at issue was that losses carried forward must be economically linked to the income earned in the Member State in which tax was charged. The second provision stipulated that accounts had to be kept according to the legislation of the host state, even if accounts also had to be kept according to the legislation of the home state. That condition constituted a non-discriminatory restriction.

94 Cf. e.g. Pistone, *The Impact of Community Law on Tax Treaties*, Kluwer Law International, The Hague/London/New York, 2002, p. 130.

4.4.3 Companies Establishing Subsidiaries

4.4.3.1 Introduction

In this section I will discuss two cases on the treatment in the host state of the establishment of a subsidiary. The establisher is a company with its seat in another Member State. There are comparatively few cases dealing with this situation, and here I will only deal with the joined cases C-397/98 and C-410/98 *Metallgesellschaft and Others* and case C-324/00 *Lankhorst-Hohorst.*

4.4.3.2 Joined Cases C-397/98 and C-410/98 Metallgesellschaft and Others *(8 March 2001)*

In general, the joined cases C-397/98 and C-410/98 *Metallgesellschaft and Others* concerned United Kingdom legislation on "Advance Corporate Tax" (ACT). The ACT was part of the imputation system in the United Kingdom for mitigating the effects of economic double taxation. The national legislation at issue is one of the more complicated ones dealt with in this study.

Before I go into details of the decision by the European Court of Justice, there will first be a description of the facts and the legislation at issue. I will limit the description to case C-397/98 (*Metallgesellschaft*), because I find it sufficient as a basis for the forthcoming analysis. There were several questions that the Court dealt with, but I will limit the discussion to the first issue, whether the lack of possibility to take advantage of the group income election was an infringement of the freedom of establishment.

Metallgesellschaft Ltd and the Metal and Commodity Company Ltd were companies resident in the United Kingdom. They paid dividends to their parent companies in Germany, Metallgesellschaft AG and Metallgesellschaft Handel & Beteiligungen AG. The parent companies hade their corporate seat in Germany. According to United Kingdom tax law, companies resident there had to pay corporate tax on their profits. Furthermore, a company resident in the United Kingdom that made distributions of, for example, dividends, was liable to pay ACT on the amount distributed. The ACT was not a withholding tax. Instead it was a corporation tax paid in full by the distributing company. The dividend-distributing company could set off the ACT paid against the mainstream corporation tax (MCT) it had to pay for every accounting period.

Moreover, a company resident in the United Kingdom was not liable to pay tax on dividends that it received from other companies resident in the United Kingdom. Consequently, when a company resident in the United Kingdom distributed dividends to another company resident in the United Kingdom, the distributing company was liable to pay ACT, but the receiving company was granted a tax credit against its MCT for the ACT paid by the distributing company. The tax credit was equal to the ACT paid.

In addition to the described system of taxation, there was also an exemption system regarding dividends received by a United Kingdom parent company from a subsidiary that also was resident in the United Kingdom.[95] Companies not resident in the United Kingdom and with no branch there, were not subject to corporate tax in the United Kingdom. Non-resident companies were, however, liable to tax on income such as dividends having its source in the United Kingdom.

Section 233 (1) of the Income and Corporation Taxes Act 1988 (ICTA) provided that if a non-resident parent company was not entitled to a tax credit in the absence of a tax treaty between the United Kingdom and another state, it was not subject to United Kingdom tax on dividends paid by its resident subsidiary. The opposite applied if a non-resident company was entitled to a tax credit according to a tax treaty between the United Kingdom and the state of residence of the parent company.

The 1970 tax treaty between the United Kingdom and Germany did not grant the right to a tax credit for companies resident in Germany which held shares in and received dividends from companies resident in the United Kingdom.[96] Consequently, a parent company which had its seat in Germany and received dividends subject to ACT from a subsidiary resident in the United Kingdom was not entitled to a United Kingdom tax credit corresponding to the ACT paid. Such a foreign parent company was furthermore not taxable in the United Kingdom on the dividends received from its resident subsidiary.[97] In contrast, if a non-resident parent company was entitled to a tax credit according to a tax treaty, that company could claim an offset of that credit against the income tax that it was liable to pay in the United Kingdom on the dividends received from its subsidiary resident there. Moreover, if the amount of tax credit exceeded the amount of the actual tax paid, the non-resident parent company was entitled to a repayment of the difference.[98]

United Kingdom tax legislation also contained a system called "group income election". According to Section 247 of the ICTA, two companies resident in the United Kingdom, where one company holds at least 51 per cent of the other, could make a group income election. Thus the meaning of the group income election was that the subsidiary would not pay any ACT on the dividends paid to its parent company. It was still possible to give a specific notice stating that one did not want to be covered by the group income election system. If a dividend was paid according to the group income election system by a subsidiary in the United Kingdom to its parent company,

---

95 According to section 231 (2) of the ICTA.

96 Joined cases C-397/98 and C-410/98 *Metallgesellschaft and Others*, para. 18.

97 Joined cases C-397/98 and C-410/98 *Metallgesellschaft and Others*, para. 19.

98 Joined cases C-397/98 and C-410/98 *Metallgesellschaft and Others*, para. 20.

also resident in the United Kingdom, the subsidiary was not liable to pay any ACT and the parent company was correspondingly not entitled to a tax credit.

In the underlying cases the German parent companies maintained that they suffered a cash flow disadvantage because their United Kingdom subsidiaries were not covered by the group income election system.[99]

The European Court of Justice was asked whether the benefit of not having to pay ACT according to the system of group income election was contrary to Articles 12, 43, 48 and/or Article 56 (ex Articles 6, 52, 58 and 73d).[100] Metallgesellschaft maintained that the United Kingdom legislation at issue tended to discourage companies resident in other Member States from establishing subsidiaries in the United Kingdom. The legislation at issue therefore constituted an unjustified restriction on the freedom of establishment, as well as the free movement of capital, in the view of Metallgesellschaft and Others.

Before entering the specific question of compatibility of the national legislation with those fundamental freedoms, the Court noted some fundamentals on the relationship between national measures of direct taxation and Community law.

First, the Court declared that even if direct taxation falls within the competence of the Member States, they must nevertheless exercise that competence in line with Community law and avoid discrimination on the basis of nationality.[101] Secondly, the Court stated that it follows from the case-law of the Court that the general prohibition against discrimination in Article 12 of the EC Treaty only applies to situations where Community law does not have a specific prohibition against discrimination.[102] Accordingly, the prohibition against discrimination contained in the provisions on the freedom of establishment applies before the principle of non-discrimination contained in Article 12, according to the Court.[103]

The European Court of Justice also repeated some now well-established interpretations of Article 43 of the EC Treaty. First, the Court declared that the freedom of establishment includes the right to take up and pursue activities as self-employed persons and to set up and manage undertakings under the conditions laid down for its own nationals according to the law of the country where such establishment is effected. Secondly, the Court declared that the abolition of restrictions on the freedom of establishment also applies to restrictions on the setting up of agencies, branches or subsidiaries by nationals

[99] Joined cases C-397/98 and C-410/98 *Metallgesellschaft and Others*, para. 30.

[100] Joined cases C-397/98 and C-410/98 *Metallgesellschaft and Others*, para. 35.

[101] Joined cases C-397/98 and C-410/98 *Metallgesellschaft and Others*, para. 37.

[102] Joined cases C-397/98 and C-410/98 *Metallgesellschaft and Others*, para. 38.

[103] Joined cases C-397/98 and C-410/98 *Metallgesellschaft and Others*, para. 39-40.

of any Member State established in the territory of another Member State.[104] Thirdly, in the view of the Court, Article 48 of the EC Treaty includes the right of companies or firms formed in accordance with the law of a Member State and having their registered office, central administration or principal place of business within the Community, to pursue their activities in a Member State through a branch or a subsidiary.[105]

Fourthly, the Court considered that the argument that the Member State in which a company seeks to establish itself may freely treat such a company differently because its registered office is in another Member State would deprive Article 43 of all meaning.[106]

After this rather lengthy analysis of the Court's previous case-law, the Court, in its decision, returned to deal with the specific question of whether an infringement of the freedom of establishment was at issue. The Court considered that the legislation in this context on group income election did in fact constitute a difference in treatment. The Court applied as the decisive criterion that of the corporate seat of the parent company.[107] Moreover, that difference in treatment constituted a cashflow advantage for parent companies resident in the United Kingdom: those companies would not have to pay ACT. More precisely the Court declared: "It is not disputed that this gives the subsidiary of a parent company resident in the United Kingdom a cashflow advantage inasmuch as it retains the sums which it would otherwise have had to pay by way of ACT until such time as MCT becomes payable, that is to say, for a period of between eight and a half months, at the least, and 17 and a half months, at the most, depending on the date of distribution. Where MCT is not payable at all for the accounting period in question, this entails an even longer period, since ACT can be set off against corporation tax due in respect of subsequent accounting periods."[108]

4.4.3.3 Case C-324/00 **Lankhorst-Hohorst** *(12 December 2002)*

In case C-324/00 *Lankhorst-Hohorst*[109] the European Court of Justice dealt with the compatibility of German legislation against thin capitalisation with the freedom of

[104] Joined cases C-397/98 and C-410/98 *Metallgesellschaft and Others*, para. 41.

[105] Joined cases C-397/98 and C-410/98 *Metallgesellschaft and Others*, para. 42.

[106] *Ibid.* The ECJ refers in support of this interpretation to Case 270/83 *Avoir fiscal*, para. 18.

[107] Joined cases C-397/98 and C-410/98 *Metallgesellschaft and Others*, para. 44.

[108] *Ibid.* A similar case is C-254/97 *Baxter* (decided 8 July 1999). It deals with French legislation on the deduction for tax purposes of expenditure on scientific and technical research. Baxter and others were French subsidiaries of foreign parent companies. The ECJ concluded that the tax legislation at issue was more likely to work to the detriment of those French subsidiaries that had foreign companies (cf. para. 13). Therefore the national legislation at issue was in breach of the freedom of establishment.

[109] Case C-324/00 *Lankhorst-Hohorst GmbH v. Finanzamt Steinfurt.*

establishment. The matter was referred to the European Court of Justice from the *Finanzgericht Münster* for a preliminary ruling.

The facts of the underlying case were the following. The German company Lankhorst-Hohorst GmbH ("Lankhorst-Hohorst") sold, among other things, boat equipment and goods for watersport activities. In August 1996 the share capital of the company was DEM 2,000,000. The only shareholder in Lankhorst-Hohorst was Lankhorst-Hohorst BV ("LH BV"), a company registered in the Netherlands. Furthermore, the only shareholder in LH BV was Lankhorst Taselaar BV ("LT BV"), which was a company also registered in the Netherlands. On 1 December 1996, an agreement was made according to which LT BV granted Lankhorst-Hohorst a loan of DEM 3,000,000, repayable over ten years in annual instalments of DEM 300,000 from 1 October 1998. The variable interest rate was 4.5 per cent until the end of 1997. LT BV received interest payments of DEM 135,000 in 1997 and DEM 109,695 in 1998. The loan was intended as a substitute for capital, and the loan was accompanied with a letter of support (*Patronatserklärung*), according to which LT BV waived repayment if third party creditors raised claims against Lankhorst-Hohorst.

The German tax authorities questioned the loan arrangement according to the German legislation on thin capitalisation. *Finanzamt Steinfurt* considered the interest paid from Lankhorst-Hohorst to LT BV as a covert distribution of profits within the meaning of Paragraph 8a of the *Körperschaftsteuergesetz* (KStG) and taxed Lankhorst-Hohorst on behalf of that distribution with 30 per cent.[110]

Paragraph 8a of the KStG stipulated the following. Compensation on a loan which a company limited by shares and subject to unlimited taxation had obtained from a shareholder not entitled to a specific "corporation tax credit", and where that shareholder had a substantial holding in its share or nominal capital, would be regarded as a covert distribution of profits.[111] A further requirement was that the repayment, calculated as a fraction of the capital was agreed upon and that the loan capital was more than three times the shareholder's proportional equity capital. There was an exception for the situation where the company limited by shares could have obtained the loan from a third party under otherwise similar circumstances or the situation where the loan constituted borrowing to finance normal banking transactions.[112]

It was clear that the lending Dutch company LT BV was not entitled to a corporation tax credit. According to German law there was no entitlement to corporation tax credit, first, for non-resident shareholders and, secondly, for corporations governed by German law which were exempt from corporation tax, which was not relevant in this case. The

[110] Case C-324/00 *Lankhorst-Hohorst*, para. 11.

[111] Case C-324/00 *Lankhorst-Hohorst*, para. 3.

[112] *Ibid.*

loan from LT BV enabled Lankhorst-Hohorst to reduce its bank borrowing from about DEM 3,700,000 to DEM 900,000, and, accordingly, to reduce its interest charges.

German tax authorities considered that Lankhorst-Hohorst was over-indebted and due to its inability to provide security, it could not have obtained a similar loan from an independent third party granted without security and covered by a *Patronatserklärung*.[113]

The case was to be decided by the *Finanzgericht Münster*, which referred the compatibility of the German tax law in question with the freedom of establishment to the European Court of Justice for a preliminary ruling.

The European Court of Justice declared that the previously referred provision in the KStG only applied to compensation in respect of loan capital which a company limited by shares subject to unlimited taxation had obtained from a shareholder not entitled to a corporation tax credit. This was, according to the Court, a restriction that caused a difference in treatment between resident subsidiary companies according to whether or not their parent company had its seat in Germany.[114] It was the Court's view that in the large majority of cases, resident parent companies would receive a tax credit, but, as a general rule, non-resident companies would not.[115] This difference in treatment between resident subsidiary companies according to the seat of the parent company, constituted an "obstacle" to the freedom of establishment and was prohibited, in principle, by Article 43 of the EC Treaty.[116] In my view, this obstacle must amount to discrimination in the host state, Germany. The difference in treatment is based on the seat of the foreign parent company.[117] Only if the parent company had its seat outside of Germany, did the less attractive taxation take place in Germany. The Court did, however, not use the term discrimination – even if the words "difference in treatment" were used.[118]

---

113 Case C-324/00 *Lankhorst-Hohorst*, para. 12.

114 Case C-324/00 *Lankhorst-Hohorst*, para. 27.

115 Case C-324/00 *Lankhorst-Hohorst*, para. 28. In exceptional cases, corporations incorporated in Germany were exempt from corporation tax, and consequently not entitled to tax credit. Such companies were essentially legal persons governed by public law and companies carrying on business in a specific field or performing tasks which would be encouraged. Companies with profit motives, such as Lankhorst-Hohorst, could not "validly" be compared to the previously mentioned companies with no such motives (*ibid.*).

116 Case C-324/00 *Lankhorst-Hohorst*, para. 32.

117 Gutmann and Hinnekens are critical of the loose terminology applied by the ECJ in its analsysis in recent cases on direct taxation. Instead of pointing out that there is a discrimination, the ECJ uses sweeping language. In their view the *Lankhorst-Hohorst* case is a case on indirect discrimination because the differentiating criterion is "residence for tax purposes". Gutmann and Hinnekens, "The Lankhorst-Hohorst Case. The ECJ Finds German Thin Capitalisation Rules Incompatible with Freedom of Establishment", *EC Tax Review*, 2003, pp. 90-97, at p. 93. I agree with their overall analysis. One could perhaps ask whether the *Lankhorst-Hohorst* case not is a case of direct discrimination because, according to the ECJ, the differentiating criterion is the seat of the parent company. According to Article 48 of the EC Treaty the seat of a company is one criterion that determines the "nationality" of a company.

118 Case C-324/00 *Lankhorst-Hohorst*, para. 32.

4.4.3.4 Conclusion

The *Metallgesellschaft* case dealt with German companies that had established subsidiaries in the United Kingdom. They had made use of the right of secondary establishment according to the freedom of establishment stipulated in Article 43 of the EC Treaty. In United Kingdom tax law there was a difference in treatment between subsidiaries having their parent companies resident in the United Kingdom, and those having their parent companies in other states, such as Germany. Subsidiaries with resident parent companies were entitled to group income election, whereas non-resident parent companies at issue were not. This ended up in a comparative cashflow disadvantage for those companies which had such a foreign connection. The Court is less explicit on what form of restriction this difference in treatment includes. In my view some form of discrimination would be probable: the seat of the parent company is the determining factor for the tax benefit at issue. Moreover the case is an expression of a desire to establish neutrality between subsidiaries in the host state irrespective of where the parent company has its seat, which is "seat" in the wide meaning applied by the Court on the basis of the different criteria enumerated in Article 48 of the EC Treaty.

The *Lankhorst-Hohorst* case verifies that the discrimination approach is still alive in the case-law of the Court, even if the Court has chosen not to use that terminology. It could be noted that the Court in *Lankhorst-Hohorst* tested a number of grounds of justification according to the rule-of-reason doctrine. I believe that this is the reason why the Court has chosen not to be explicit on the outcome that the case deals with a matter of, probably, direct discrimination on the basis of the seat of the parent company. The well-established rule-of-reason doctrine does not apply in cases of direct discrimination, whereas cases of indirect discrimination constitute a grey zone where it might be applicable. The Court has, however, advanced to a stage where in practice it is ready to apply the rule-of-reason doctrine in cases of direct discrimination as well. Instead of overtly changing its policy, it seems to have chosen to stop its discrimination analysis just before the conclusion that a case in fact deals with direct discrimination. The Court stops the analysis where it is established that the national measure at issue at least constitutes a restriction, in the wide sense, to the fundamental freedom at issue; by doing so, the Court feels free to apply the rule-of-reason doctrine.

4.4.4 Individuals Establishing Branches

4.4.4.1 Introduction

Even if this study is primarily focused on company taxation, there are two cases on individuals establishing foreign branches that I will discuss. They are cases C-80/94 *Wielockx* and C-107/94 *Asscher*. The discussion will be fairly short, because the *Asscher* case has been discussed previously on several occasions in relation to other specific questions, notably the question of who is covered by the EC Treaty and the freedom of establishment.

4.4.4.2 Case C-80/94 **Wielockx** *(11 August 1995)*

Case C-80/94 *Wielockx*[119] dealt with Dutch legislation on the deduction for tax purposes of pension premiums and its compatibility with the freedom of establishment. The basic facts of the underlying case were the following. Mr Wielockx was resident in Belgium, where he also was a national. Moreover, Mr Wielockx was a partner in a physiotherapy practice in the Netherlands, where he earned his total income and was liable to tax. However, in the Netherlands, Mr Wielockx was refused permission to deduct contributions to a pension reserve because he was not resident there.

The European Court of Justice was asked to give a preliminary ruling on, among others, the following question. Did Article 43 (ex Article 52) of the EC Treaty preclude a Member State from allowing residents to deduct from their taxable income business profits which they allocate to form a pension reserve, while denying that benefit to Community nationals liable to pay tax who, although resident in another Member State, receive all or almost all of their income in the first state?[120]

The cross-border element of this case is, of course, that Mr Wielockx, a national of and resident in Belgium, conducted business activities in the Netherlands.

Once again the Court declared that in general the situations of residents and non-residents are not comparable. The reason is that there are objective differences between the two categories as regards the source of the income, the possibility of taking account of their ability to pay tax, and their personal and family circumstances.[121] In the present case, however, there was a comparable situation. The Court declared that a non-resident taxpayer, whether employed or self-employed, who receives all, or almost all, of his income in the state where he works is objectively in the same situation "... in so far as concerns income tax as a resident of that State who does the same work there".[122]

The Court came to the conclusion that, in the actual situation, if a non-resident was not granted the same right to deductions as a resident, his personal situation would not be taken into account either by the state where he worked, because he was not resident there, or by his state of residence, because he received no income there.[123] Such a

[119] Case C-80/94 *G.H.E.J. Wielockx v. Inspecteur der Directe Belastingen*.

[120] Case C-80/94 *Wielockx*, para. 13.

[121] Case C-80/94 *Wielockx*, para. 18. The ECJ refers in this instance to case C-279/93 *Schumacker*.

[122] Case C-80/94 *Wielockx*, para. 20.

[123] Case C-80/94 *Wielockx*, para. 21-22.

taxpayer was subject to discrimination, because the difference in treatment was based on residence. It was a question of indirect discrimination because Dutch legislation granted the benefit to "residents", and that tax term is not necessarily equivalent to "national".[124]

Furthermore, the *Wielockx* case is important because of the role played by tax treaties in relation to "fiscal coherence" as a ground of justification. The Court rejected fiscal coherence as such a ground, and based its line of argumentation on the implications of a tax treaty based on the OECD MC. I will return to this matter in Chapter 5.

4.4.4.3 Case C-107/94 **Asscher** *(27 June 1996)*

Case C-107/94 *Asscher* dealt with Dutch taxation of non-residents and the compatibility with the freedom of establishment. Mr Asscher was a Dutch national. He worked in the Netherlands, but he was not resident there for tax purposes. In the Netherlands, Mr Asscher was the director of a private limited company, of which he was the sole shareholder. He also worked in Belgium, where he was the manager of a Belgian company. In 1986 he had left the Netherlands to live in Belgium, however, the migration did not change his professional activities either in the Netherlands or in Belgium.

Because Mr Asscher was not resident in the Netherlands, his Dutch salary was taxed at a higher rate than it otherwise would have been subject to. However, according to Dutch tax law, a non-resident could under specific circumstances be taxed according to the same more beneficial tax regime, which residents were subject to. A non-resident was treated as a resident if he could show that all or almost all – that is to say at least 90 per cent – of his worldwide income was taxable in the Netherlands. That condition was deemed to be fulfilled if the taxpayer in the Netherlands was subject to contributions according to the compulsory Dutch national social scheme.[125] For such taxpayers the tax rate in the first band of taxable income was 13 per cent. If the taxpayer was considered "foreign", the tax rate in the first band was 25 per cent.[126] The tax treaty between Belgium and the Netherlands provided that Mr Asscher's Dutch income was exclusively taxed in the Netherlands.

The question of whether Mr Asscher was part of the Dutch national insurance scheme was, as previously mentioned, important for the taxation of his Dutch income. Mr Asscher was insured with the Dutch insurance scheme until he emigrated to Belgium in 1986. After that he had not contributed to the Dutch scheme and had exclusively

[124] Cf. case C-80/94 *Wielockx*, para. 3.

[125] Case C-107/94 *Asscher*, para. 6.

[126] Case C-107/94 *Asscher*, para. 8.

been subject to Belgian social security legislation. Consequently, according to Dutch law, Mr Asscher was taxed at the higher rate of 25 per cent. The compatibility of this Dutch provision with fundamental freedoms of the EC Treaty was the subject of this preliminary ruling by the European Court of Justice.

The following questions, as interpreted by the Court, are of interest in this section.[127] First, was Article 43 (ex Article 52) of the EC Treaty to be interpreted as precluding a Member State from applying to a Community national who pursues an activity as a self-employed person within its territory, and at the same time pursues another activity as a self-employed person in another Member State, in which he resides, a higher rate of income tax than that which applies to residents pursuing the same activity?

Secondly, was the answer to the first question affected by the fact that less than 90 per cent of the taxpayer's worldwide income consists of earnings which may be taken into account for income-tax purposes by the state in which he works but where he does not reside? The second question will be subject to further consideration in Chapter 5 on possible grounds of justification, notably the ground of fiscal coherence.

In its answer to the first question the Court referred to the well-established Schumacker doctrine.[128] The Court explained that the situations of residents and non-residents are not, as a general rule, comparable. A different treatment of the categories is, accordingly, accepted under Community law.[129] However, a difference in treatment is not accepted if a Member State refuses to tax benefits linked to the taking into account of personal and family circumstances to a taxpayer who works but does not reside in its territory, but where resident taxpayers are granted those benefits.[130]

The Court added the following, which I find relevant to quote in full: "However, a Member State in which a non-resident taxpayer works may be justified in refusing him such tax benefits where he does not receive all or almost all of his income in that State, since comparable benefits are granted in the State in which he resides and which is responsible, under international tax law, for taking personal and family circumstances into account."[131] In this case, the 25 per cent tax rate was charged on the income of non-residents who received less than 90 per cent of their worldwide income in the Netherlands. In contrast, the rate was 13 per cent on those residing and pursuing the same activity in the Netherlands, even if the individual received less than 90 per cent of their worldwide income in that state.

---

[127] Case C-107/94 *Asscher*, para. 35.

[128] Case C-107/94 *Asscher*, para. 41-43.

[129] Case C-107/94 *Asscher*, para. 42.

[130] Case C-107/94 *Asscher*, para. 43.

[131] Case C-107/94 *Asscher*, para. 44.

The reason for the higher tax rate for non-residents was, according to the Dutch government, that some non-residents otherwise would escape the progressive nature of the tax because their tax obligations were restricted ("confined") to income received in the Netherlands.[132] The Court did not accept that reason.

As a basis for its line of reasoning the Court relied on Article 24 (2) (1) of the Belgium – Netherlands tax treaty,[133] providing exemption with progression as the means of mitigating international juridical double taxation: income received in the source state, the Netherlands, was exclusively taxed in that state and exempt in the state of residence, Belgium. Belgium, as the state of residence, could, however, take the exempted income into account when determining which progressive tax rate to apply.[134] Accordingly, non-residents in the Netherlands could not escape the tax progression, and the reason of justification declared by the Dutch government for the generally higher tax rate for non-residents, did not have any bearing, in the view of the Court. Both residents and non-residents were accordingly in comparable situations.

In conclusion the European Court of Justice found that the higher tax rate applied by the Netherlands to non-residents, and not to residents, constituted an indirect discrimination on the freedom of establishment.

4.4.4.4 Conclusion

Both cases deal with the taxation of individuals who are entrepreneurs and exercise the freedom of establishment in another Member State. In the first case, Mr Wielockx was resident in and national of Belgium. He was employed in the Netherlands, where he received all his income. However, in the Netherlands he was denied the right to deduct contributions to a pension reserve. Such deductions were only entitled residents in the Netherlands. Mr Asscher was a Dutch national, but he was resident in Belgium. He received income from professional activities in both Belgium and the Netherlands. In the Netherlands, Mr Asscher's income was taxed at a higher rate than if he had been resident there, which he was not. Both cases deal with indirect discrimination: tax benefits were denied because none of them was resident for tax purposes in the host state, which happens to be the Netherlands.[135]

In both cases the Court confirms the general status of the Schumacker doctrine. The situations of residents and non-residents are not generally comparable. The reason is

[132] Case C-107/94 *Asscher*, para. 46.

[133] Based on Article 23A (1) and (3) of the OECD MC.

[134] Case C-107/94 *Asscher*, para. 47.

[135] The question of why the "Werner doctrine" did not apply in the *Asscher* case, even if Mr Asscher was a national in the Netherlands, has been discussed in a previous section 4.2.2.

that there are objective differences between them from the point of view of the source of the income, the ability to pay tax and the possibility to take into account of personal and family circumstances. The situations between residents and non-residents may, however, according to the Schumacker doctrine, be comparable if a non-resident taxpayer, either employed or self-employed, receives all or almost all of his income in the state where he works and that state is the state where he is non-resident. In that case the situations of residents and non-residents are objectively the same as regarding income taxation.

In my view, the situation in the *Wielockx* case fulfils reasonably well the conditions of the Schumacker doctrine. The *Asscher* case is, however, somewhat different. In addition to the facts of the *Wielockx* case, Mr Asscher, a Dutch national, received income also in Belgium and he was covered by the social security system of that state. In the *Asscher* case the Court also made the important declaration that a Member State may be justified in denying a non-resident specific benefits if comparable benefits are granted in the state where he is resident, and if that state is responsible under international tax law to take personal and family circumstances into account. However, it is questionable whether "international tax law" imposes such an obligation, even if one resorts to the OECD MC.

4.5 Home State Restrictions

4.5.1 Introduction and Case 81/87 *Daily Mail* (27 September 1988)

Fundamental freedoms of the EC Treaty do not only prohibit discrimination based on nationality or on a similar criterion with the same effect, but also prohibit otherwise restrictive measures. In this section I will also deal with restrictions that take place not in the "host state", where the establishment is made when it comes to the freedom of establishment, but in the "home state", where the "establisher" is a national. For some time it was in doubt whether such "home state" restrictions were prohibited by the EC Treaty, and, as will be shown, the European Court of Justice has in several cases clarified this. In this section there is an analysis of cases from the European Court of Justice, primarily in the field of direct taxation, but to some extent also in the field of company law.

In general one could say that the perhaps most important aspect of Case 81/87 *Daily Mail*[136] was how the European Court of Justice defined the scope of the freedom of establishment. The principal question was whether the freedom of establishment also prohibited restrictions in the "home state". The basic facts of the underlying case

[136] Case 81/87 *The Queen v. H.M. Treasury and Commissioners of Inland Revenue, ex parte Daily Mail and General Trust plc.*

were the following. The companies Daily Mail and General Trust plc, subsequently only referred to as "Daily Mail", considered ceasing corporate residence in the United Kingdom and establishing residence in the Netherlands. It was clear that United Kingdom legislation permitted a company incorporated in the United Kingdom and having its registered office there, to establish its central management and control outside of the United Kingdom without ceasing its status as a company incorporated in the United Kingdom.[137]

Only companies resident in the United Kingdom were liable to corporation tax there. Furthermore, United Kingdom tax legislation stipulated that it was necessary to acquire the consent of the Treasury if a company wanted to cease corporate residence in the United Kingdom.[138] Daily Mail applied for such permission. It was common ground that the reason for the change of residence was to avoid taxation in the United Kingdom on gains from the alienation of shares. Negotiations with the Treasury for permission lasted for years.

However, before the United Kingdom authorities finally decided the matter, Daily Mail chose to establish an investment management company in the Netherlands. Daily Mail opened a case before the High Court of Justice, where it claimed that Articles 43 and 48 (ex Articles 52 and 58) of the EC Treaty gave it the right to transfer its central management and control to another Member State without prior consent or the right to obtain such consent unconditionally.[139] The cross-border element of this case was, accordingly, the transfer of a company's central management and control to another Member State.

The Court expressed its interpretation of Article 48 and the connecting factors for a company with a Member State. In the view of the Court, Article 48 placed on the same footing as connecting factors the registered office, the central administration and the principal place of business of a company.

In the Court's view, the freedom of establishment did not, however, confer a right for a company to transfer its central management and control and its central administration to another Member State, while still being incorporated in the first Member State.[140] The problems regarding the change of residence for companies was a question which, according to the Court, was not solved by the freedom of establishment, but was a question that had to be dealt with by future legislation or conventions.[141]

137 Case 81/87 *Daily Mail*, para. 3-4.

138 Case 81/87 *Daily Mail*, para. 6.

139 Case 81/87 *Daily Mail*, para. 8.

140 Case 81/87 *Daily Mail*, para. 24.

141 Case C- 81/87 *Daily Mail*, para. 23. This approach by the ECJ in matters of company law is not the more "activist" approach, which it has taken in the field of direct taxation.

In this seminal decision, the European Court of Justice declared in relation to Articles 43 and 48 of the EC Treaty: "Even though those provisions are directed mainly to ensuring that foreign nationals and companies are treated in the host Member State in the same way as nationals of that State, they also prohibit the Member States of origin from hindering the establishment in another Member State of one of its nationals or of a company incorporated under its legislation which comes within the definition of Article [48]."[142] Furthermore, the Court stated that the articles on the freedom of establishment would be meaningless if the Member State of origin could prohibit undertakings from leaving in order to establish themselves in another Member State.[143]

In conclusion, the most important result of the *Daily Mail* case is, of course, that the European Court of Justice clarified that the freedom of establishment not only applies in the host Member State, but also applies in the Member State of origin ("the home state"). The fact that company legislation of the Member States and the Community had not, and still has not, reached the stage where the cross-border transfer of corporate seat is possible, is another matter. Even if the *Daily Mail* case only implicitly dealt with matters of taxation, it was to be followed by a series of cases where the European Court of Justice acknowledged the prohibition against home state restrictions on the freedom of establishment in the field of direct taxation.

The following case-law analysis is divided into four different parts, each containing a distinct perspective. In *section 4.5.2* I deal with companies establishing branches, where case C-141/99 *AMID* is discussed. *Section 4.5.3* deals with companies establishing subsidiaries, and here I discuss the cases C-264/96 *ICI*, C-200/98 *X AB and Y AB*, and C-168/01 *Bosal Holding*. *Section 4.5.4* concerns "other cases" with a home state perspective. In this section there is an analysis of the cases C-251/98 *Baars*, C-436/00 X *and Y*, and C-9/02 *de Lasteyrie du Saillant*.

4.5.2 Companies Establishing Branches

4.5.2.1 Introduction

In this study there is only one case on home state restrictions dealing with the establishment by a company of a branch in another Member State, and that is case C-141/99 *AMID*. The *AMID* case is of interest also from the perspective that it is one in a row of cases dealing with the cross-border treatment of losses. Other notable cases in this particular field of law are C-250/95 *Futura Participations*, C-264/96 *ICI* and the pending case C-446/03 *Marks & Spencer*. The *AMID* case is different from all the

142 Case 81/87 *Daily Mail*, para. 16.

143 *Ibid.*

other cases because it combines the establishment of a foreign branch and the situation where the head office has the losses and the branch the profits.

4.5.2.2 Case C-141/99 **AMID** *(14 December 2000)*

Case C-141/99 *AMID* dealt with Belgian legislation on the treatment of losses in cross-border situations and the compatibility of the Belgian legislation at issue with the freedom of establishment. The basic facts of the underlying case were the following. AMID was a Belgian limited company with its seat and fiscal domicile in Belgium. AMID had a permanent establishment in Belgium. According to the tax treaty between Belgium and Luxembourg, the income from the permanent establishment was tax exempt in Belgium. In 1981 AMID made a loss in Belgium (BEF 2,126,926), whereas the permanent establishment in Luxembourg made a profit (LUF 3,541,118). According to Luxembourg tax legislation, it was not possible for AMID to set off the Belgian loss against the Luxembourg profit. Instead, AMID deducted its Belgian loss of 1981 from its Belgian profits of 1982. However, when applying the relevant tax legislation, the Belgian tax authorities denied AMID the deduction of the 1981 Belgian losses. The reason for the denial was that the 1981 losses should have been set off against the 1981 Luxembourg profits.[144] According to Belgian legislation loss carry-forward was not allowed if the losses were to be set off against the profits of a foreign branch. However, if it were the profits of a Belgian branch, such loss carry forward would have been possible under Belgian law.[145]

The matter was dealt with by Belgian courts and there was also a request for a preliminary ruling from the European Court of Justice. The question referred to the Court was the following. A company, AMID, was incorporated under national law in Belgium, where it also had its seat. AMID could for the purposes of corporation tax deduct a loss incurred the previous year from the taxable profits for the current year, but only on the condition that the loss could not be set off against the profit made during that same previous year by one of its permanent establishments in another state. However, the loss, although set off, could not be deducted from the taxable income in either of the states concerned. Moreover, the loss would have been deductible if the permanent

[144] This followed from the Belgian "Velasquez doctrine". According to de Broe, the Velasquez doctrine meant that losses realised in Belgium first had to be offset against profits realised in Belgium, secondly, against profits realised in countries with which Belgium had not concluded any tax treaty, and, thirdly and finally, against losses realised through a permanent establishment in a tax treaty country (Articles 75 and 78 of the Royal Decree implementing the Belgian Income Tax Code). See de Broe, "Cases Filed by Belgian Courts: the AMID Case", in *Direct Taxation: Recent ECJ Developments*, Lang (ed.), Linde Verlag, Vienna, 2003, pp. 11-33, at p. 11.

[145] Cf. Vanistendael, "The Compatibility of the Basic Economic Freedoms with the Sovereign National Tax System of the Member States", *EC Tax Review*, 2003, pp. 136-143, at p. 140.

establishment of AMID had been located in Belgium. Was this difference in treatment an infringement of the freedom of establishment?[146]

Before answering this particular question the Court recapitulated a few important steps from its previous case-law. First, as regards companies it is their corporate seat in the sense elaborated in previous case-law that serves as the connecting factor to the legal system of a particular state, like nationality in the case of individuals.[147] Secondly, Article 43 of the EC Treaty on the freedom of establishment also contains a prohibition against restrictions in the home state.[148] The cross-border element of the *AMID* case was the secondary establishment of a branch in another Member State.

Returning to the particular question referred, on the different treatment of losses from a cross-border situation compared with a purely Belgian situation, the Court argued in the following way. The case dealt with a company incorporated in one Member State and which made use of its freedom of establishment in another Member State through the creation of branches (permanent establishments). The legislation at issue limited the possibility of carrying forward losses incurred in that Member State during a previous tax period where, during the same period, that company made profits in another Member State through a permanent establishment. However, it would have been possible to offset the losses of such a permanent establishment, if it had been located in the same Member State as the company that established it and which it formed part of. In the view of the Court, the situation of a Belgian company which, having no establishment outside of Belgium, incurs a loss during a given tax year, finds itself, for tax purposes, in a comparable situation with that of a Belgian company which, having an establishment in Luxembourg, incurs a loss in Belgium and makes a profit in Luxembourg during that same tax year.[149]

The Belgian government did not consider the legislation at issue to be a hindrance to Article 43 of the EC Treaty. It did admit that in the specific situation at issue there was a disadvantage for AMID because the Belgian losses could not be offset against the Luxembourg profits.[150] In the opposite situation, the Belgian government maintained that the situation of a Belgian company with a foreign permanent establishment could be subject to more advantageous taxation than if the situation had been purely Belgian.

146 Case C-141/99 *AMID*, para. 17.

147 Case C-141/99 *AMID*, para. 20.

148 Case C-141/99 *AMID*, para. 21 (with further references).

149 Case C-141/99 *AMID*, para. 29. Hinnekens does not agree with the ECJ, and finds the situations not comparable. According to him the *AMID* situation is only comparable to the situation of a Belgian company that concentrates its business in Belgium and where the foreign branch profits are not considered. Hinnekens, "AMID: The Wrong Bridge or a Bridge Too Far? An Analysis of a Recent Decision of the European Court of Justice", *European Taxation*, 2001, pp. 206-210, at p. 208.

150 Case C-141/99 *AMID*, para. 24.

Such a more advantageous situation would occur if the Belgian company made a profit and the permanent establishment in Luxembourg made a loss: the Luxembourg loss would be set off in Belgium and it could also be set off in Luxembourg against subsequent profits of the permanent establishment.[151]

Furthermore, the Belgian government put forward the argument, in my view considerably more "hollow" than the previous one, that Belgian companies with a foreign permanent establishment were not comparable with Belgian companies only conducting business within Belgium.[152] Companies with their business concentrated to Belgium had all their income taxed at the Belgian tax rate. In contrast, Belgian companies with foreign permanent establishments were taxed according to the applicable tax treaty on the income of the permanent establishments.

The European Court of Justice did not accept any of the arguments put forward by the Belgian government. Even if it turned out that the Belgian tax system on cross-border losses more often than not would be more favourable to Belgian companies with foreign permanent establishments, that would not suffice. As long as there was one situation where it was disadvantageous to have a foreign permanent establishment when calculating losses, as compared with a strictly internal situation, that would be enough to constitute a disadvantageous difference in treatment and a hindrance to the freedom of establishment.[153]

As regards the second argument put forward by the Belgian government, the European Court of Justice could not find how that argument could explain the difference in treatment regarding losses.

The Court decided that Article 43 of the EC Treaty precluded legislation of a Member State where a company with its seat in that state, could, for the purposes of corporation tax, deduct a loss incurred the previous year from the taxable profit for the current year only on condition that that loss was not capable of being set off against the profit made during that same previous year by one of its permanent establishments situated in another Member State, to the extent that a loss thus set off could not be deducted from taxable income in either of the Member States concerned. In comparison according to the tax legislation of the same Member State, such a loss would have been deductible if the establishment of the company at issue was situated exclusively in the Member State in which it had its seat.

[151] Case C-141/99 *AMID*, para. 24.

[152] Case C-141/99 *AMID*, para. 25.

[153] Case C-141/99 *AMID*, para. 27. In support of this view the ECJ referred to Case 270/83 *Avoir fiscal*, para. 21.

4.5.2.3 Conclusion and the **Ritter** *Case*

The *AMID* case has two features that makes it special. First, according to the tax treaty between Belgium and Luxembourg, the income of a branch in Luxembourg was tax exempt in Belgium. Secondly, the losses were incurred in the same corporate body as where the profits arose. Luxembourg legislation did not permit the deduction of the Belgian losses from the Luxembourg profits. Avery Jones considers that to be in line with the Court's decision in the *Futura Participations* case and the fiscal principle of territoriality advanced in that case.[154] In the view of Avery Jones the obvious solution to the problem posed in the *AMID* case was to let the Belgian head office with its losses be granted the right to carry those losses forward to be deducted in a subsequent year. However, Belgian law did not accept that since the losses of one year were to be deducted against the profits of the Luxembourg branch of the same year.

The *AMID* case is a difficult case stemming from Belgian law, and I find it equally difficult to draw any general conclusions from the outcome. The subsequent *Marks & Spencer* case has similarities with the *AMID* case because it has partly been analysed from the head office – branch perspective. However, the question in the *Marks & Spencer* case is more straightforward, and I will deal with it in section 4.6.

At present there are several cases on the cross-border treatment of losses pending before the European Court of Justice. One such case is the German *Ritter* case.[155] In that case a German couple incurred a loss from immovable property in France. They were subject to unlimited tax liability in Germany and had employment income from sources in Germany. The tax treaty between France and Germany stipulated that income from immovable property was taxable only in the source state, which in this case was France. According to German practice, the application of the exemption method in tax treaties means that neither income nor losses are included in the German tax base (the residence state). Consequently, the French losses in the *Ritter* case were not included in the German tax base. This outcome was contested in German courts as being in conflict with fundamental freedoms. From a strict tax law perspective there is in my view nothing wrong with the German practice regarding the exemption method and the non-consideration of foreign losses. That stems from the widely accepted purpose of tax law to offer symmetric treatment of income and losses. If profits are taxable, corresponding losses are deductible, and vice versa. However, in the view of previous case-law there is reason to believe that the Court will not accept that argument.

154 Avery Jones, "A Comment on 'AMID: The Wrong Bridge or a Bridge Too Far?'", *European Taxation*, 2001, p. 251.

155 Preliminary ruling requested by the BFH, 13 November 2002. On this case see e.g. Cordewener, Dahlberg, Pistone, Reimer and Romano, "The Tax Treatment of Foreign Losses: Ritter, M & S, and the Way Ahead (Part One)", *European Taxation*, 2004, pp. 135-142.

The outcome of the *Bosal Holding* case is the main reason for this prediction. In that case the Court allowed the deduction of costs even though the income was not taxable in the Netherlands. Correspondingly, the ECJ might well allow the deduction of losses in Germany even if the French income would not have been taxable in Germany according to the exemption method.

4.5.3 Companies Establishing Subsidiaries

4.5.3.1 Introduction

There is a growing number of cases dealing with the taxation in the home state of companies establishing subsidiaries in other Member States. In this section I will deal with three such cases: C-264/96 *ICI*, C-200/98 *X AB and Y AB* and C-168/01 *Bosal Holding*. A specific point of interest regarding these cases is the way in which the Court identifies the infringement of the freedom of establishment. Already at this stage it could be noted that in several cases the Court has chosen a less explicit approach, merely concluding that the national measure constitutes a barrier or similar to the freedom.

4.5.3.2 Case C-264/96 **ICI** *(16 July 1998)*

Case C-264/96 *ICI*[156] also dealt with the interpretation of the freedom of establishment as manifested in the EC Treaty. Imperial Chemical Industries (ICI) and Wellcome Foundation Ltd were both resident in the United Kingdom and formed a consortium. The two companies beneficially owned 49 per cent and 51 per cent respectively of Coopers Animal Health (Holdings) Ltd, hereinafter "Holdings". Holdings had the purpose of holding shares in a total of 23 subsidiary companies, and they were located in several countries: four companies, including Coopers Animal Health Ltd (hereinafter Coopers), were resident in the United Kingdom, six companies were resident in other Member States, and 13 companies were resident in third (non-member) states.[157]

Coopers incurred losses on its trade in the United Kingdom. According to United Kingdom law, there was a possibility to set off incurred losses within a corporate group, a form of group relief. Accordingly, ICI wanted to incur those losses against its chargeable profits. However, the Inland Revenue of the United Kingdom denied ICI such a group relief. The reason was that the majority of Holding's subsidiaries,

---

156 Case C-264/96 *Imperial Chemical Industries plc (ICI) v. Kenneth Hall Colmer (Her Majesty's Inspector of Taxes).*

157 Case C-264/96 *ICI*, para. 3-4.

19 out of 23, were not resident in the United Kingdom. Therefore Holding could not be considered as such a holding company as was required by the United Kingdom legislation at issue.[158]

In principle, the European Court of Justice was requested to answer the following question. Was a national law, providing that a group income relief was permitted only if the business of a holding company consisted wholly or mainly in the holding of shares in subsidiaries established in the Member State in question, compatible with the freedom of establishment?[159] Evidently, a more general question contained in the previous question was whether the freedom of establishment also included a prohibition against restrictions in the home state. A prohibition against home state restrictions had already been discernible in the 1988 *Daily Mail* case, which the Court also noted in the present case.

The Court began its reasoning by declaring that Articles 43 and 48 also contain a right of secondary establishment. As regards companies, the Court stated, it is the corporate seat which serves as the connecting factor to a particular Member State.[160]

The Court confirmed the outcome of the *Daily Mail* case and declared that the freedom of establishment also contains a prohibition against restrictions in the home state: "It should also be pointed out that, even though, according to their wording, the provisions concerning freedom of establishment are directed mainly to ensuring that foreign nationals and companies are treated in the host Member State in the same way as nationals of that State, they also prohibit the Member State of origin from hindering the establishment in another Member State of one of its nationals or of a company incorporated under its legislation which comes within the definition contained in Article [48] (Case 81/87 *Daily Mail and General Trust* [1988] ECR 5483, paragraph 16)."[161]

The cross-border element of the *ICI* case was that the corporate group contained foreign subsidiaries, which had the consequence that group income relief was denied. The Court concluded its decision with the following.[162] The legislation at issue applied the test of the subsidiaries' seats to establish differential tax treatment of consortium companies in the United Kingdom. This tax benefit of consortium taxation was only available to

[158] Case C-264/96 *ICI*, para. 7.

[159] Case C-264/96 *ICI*, para. 18.

[160] Case C-264/96 *ICI*, para. 20. With the term "having their corporate seat" the ECJ means, in line with Article 48 of the EC Treaty, companies or firms formed in accordance with the law of a Member State and having their registered office, central administration or principal place of business within the Community (*ibid.*).

[161] Case C-264/96 *ICI*, para. 21.

[162] Case C-264/96 *ICI*, para. 22.

companies controlling, wholly or mainly, subsidiaries with their seats in the United Kingdom. Evidently, the Court considered the legislation at issue to constitute a restriction in the wide sense of the EC Treaty. Whether it also constitutes discrimination is not stated by the Court. That could very well be the case: a comparison could be made between, on the one hand, a consortium with resident subsidiaries only and, on the other hand, a substantial number of non-resident subsidiaries. In the first situation the tax benefit is granted, and in the second situation it is not. The distinguishing criterion is the seats of the subsidiaries. In my view that could amount to discrimination.

Pistone argues that the *ICI* case is the first case where the European Court of Justice has declared that "... economic crossing is no longer needed for the purpose of exercising the right of establishment".[163] Even if it is somewhat unclear what is meant by "economic crossing", I am willing to agree in one sense. In the *ICI* case the Court does declare that the freedom of establishment also covers the cross-border holding of shares: there is no requirement for an income to cross the border between Member States.

4.5.3.3 Case C-200/98 **X AB and Y AB** *(18 November 1999)*

Case C-200/98 *X AB and Y AB*[164] dealt with Swedish tax law on the organisation of corporate groups and the possibility for inter-corporate transfers of income: all in relation to the freedom of establishment. The case was referred to the European Court of Justice for a preliminary ruling by the Swedish Supreme Administrative Court (*Regeringsrätten*).

The facts of the underlying case were briefly the following. X AB was the parent company and Y AB was its subsidiary. Both companies were resident in Sweden for tax purposes. Swedish legislation provided that, under certain conditions, transfers of income between companies belonging to the same corporate group could benefit from a tax relief.[165] More specifically, it was provided that if a Swedish company owned more than 90 per cent of the shares in another Swedish company, intra-group transfers of income were treated as deductible expenses for the transferring company and as taxable income for the receiving company.[166] Subsequently, I will use the term "group contributions" (*koncernbidrag*) for this form of income distribution. The objective of the legislation on group contributions was to create neutrality between alternative ways

[163] Pistone, *The Impact of Community Law on Tax Treaties*, Kluwer Law International, The Hague/London/New York, 2002, p. 139.

[164] Case C-200/98 *X AB and Y AB v. Riksskatteverket.*

[165] Case C-200/98 *X AB and Y AB*, para. 4.

[166] *Ibid.*

of corporate structuring of business activities: on the one hand, business conducted through one company, and, on the other hand, business through a parent company with one or more subsidiary companies.[167]

The Court considered three different types of reorganisation.[168] In the first case, the shares in the subsidiary Y AB would be entirely owned by the parent X AB together with the other Swedish subsidiaries it owned. In the second case, the company Z BV, a Dutch subsidiary which X AB fully owned, would acquire 15 per cent of the shares in Y AB. Finally, in the third case, the Dutch Z BV and Y GmbH, that was a German subsidiary wholly owned by X AB, would each acquire 15 per cent of the shares in Y AB.[169] The question was whether it was possible to make group contributions and enjoy the special tax relief in these three different cases.

The Swedish Revenue Law Commission (*Skatterättsnämnden*) came to the conclusion that in the first case the tax relief would be granted according to Swedish tax law, and in the second case as well, in this case by applying the clause on non-discrimination contained in the Swedish-Dutch tax treaty. However, as regarded the third case, the tax relief on group contributions could not be granted. The reason for the denial was explained as case-law from the Supreme Administrative Court which prohibited the cumulative application of two tax treaties because such treaties were not considered to apply to business operations in third states.[170] X AB and Y AB appealed against this decision, claiming that the Swedish law was in conflict with both the freedom of establishment and the free movement of capital. In turn, the Supreme Administrative Court referred the question of compatibility of the Swedish legislation with Community law to the European Court of Justice.

The specific question which the European Court of Justice had to consider was the following. Did Articles 43 and 48 (ex Articles 52 and 58) of the EC Treaty on the freedom of establishment and Articles 56 and 58 (ex Articles 73b and 73d) of the EC Treaty on the free movement of capital preclude national provisions where in cases 1 and 2 intra-group transfers were permitted, while in case 3 intra-group transfers were prohibited?[171]

In relation to the freedom of establishment the European Court of Justice stated: "… it must be pointed out that, even though according to their wording, those provisions

---

[167] *Ibid.*

[168] Case C-200/98 *X AB and Y AB*, para. 7-10 (see also para. 24). I will here use the names applied by the Swedish court in the underlying case: X AB and Y AB.

[169] Case C-200/98 *X AB and Y AB*, para. 7.

[170] Case C-200/98 *X AB and Y AB*, para. 10.

[171] Case C-200/98 *X AB and Y AB*, para. 25.

are mainly aimed at ensuring that foreign nationals and companies are treated in the host Member State in the same way as nationals of that State, they also prohibit the Member State of origin from hindering the establishment in another Member State of one of its nationals or of a company incorporated under its legislation which comes within the definition contained in Article 58 of the Treaty (Case 81/87 *Daily Mail and General Trust* [1988] ECR 5483, paragraph 16 and Case C-264/96 *ICI* [1988] ECR I-4695, paragraph 21)."[172]

Accordingly, the European Court of Justice confirmed its home state restriction approach developed in the *Daily Mail* and *ICI* cases. The cross-border element in this case was of course the acquisition of a Swedish company by a company with its corporate seat in another Member State.

The European Court of Justice came to the conclusion that the Swedish legislation did constitute a violation of the freedom of establishment. The reason was that the Swedish legislation made a difference in treatment on the basis of the criterion of the subsidiaries' seats.[173] Swedish law did not grant the same tax relief for companies that in the third case decided to form subsidiaries in other Member States. The Court did not articulate whether this piece of legislation was discriminatory or constituted a non-discriminatory restriction. In my view, it could very well be argued that the Swedish legislation in fact was discriminatory, and even constituting a direct discrimination. The differentiating criterion for the tax benefit was the seat of the company owning one of the companies taking part in the group relief system. Furthermore, the Court also recognised that there was a "difference of treatment" based on the seat of the companies involved.[174] Another argument in favour of the consideration that it was direct discrimination is that the Swedish government did not advance any grounds of justification. It would probably be very difficult to justify a piece of tax legislation that is directly discriminatory with the exceptional grounds provided for in the EC Treaty.

The Swedish government even acknowledged that the legislation at issue was contrary to Article 43 of the EC Treaty. In view of the outcome, the Court did not find it necessary to consider whether there also was a breach of the free movement of capital.[175] The case is important in as much as it confirms previous practice of the Court where the freedom of establishment also is considered to comprise a prohibition against restrictions in the home state.

---

172 Case C-200/98 *X AB and Y AB*, para. 26.

173 Case C-200/98 *X AB and Y AB*, para. 28.

174 *Ibid.*

175 Case C-200/98 *X AB and Y AB*, para. 30.

4.5.3.4 Case C-168/01 **Bosal Holding** *(18 September 2003)*

Case C-168/01 *Bosal Holding* dealt with Dutch legislation on the right to deduct costs in the Netherlands. The general question was whether this provision was compatible with the freedom of establishment and the Parent/Subsidiary Directive.

The facts of the underlying case were the following. Bosal Holding BV ("Bosal") was a limited company with its seat in the Netherlands. Bosal had holdings in several Dutch and foreign companies. Moreover, the foreign companies were established both inside and outside of the European Union. The holdings ranged from 50 to 100 per cent of the share capital. Holding, financing and licensing activities were the business objectives of Bosal.

In 1993 Bosal incurred interest charges with NLG 3,969,339. The interest was connected with the financing of Bosal's corporate holdings outside of the Netherlands, but within the European Union. Bosal sought a deduction of those interest payments from its taxable profit in the Netherlands, even if Dutch tax legislation did not allow such a deduction. Bosal claimed that the tax legislation at issue was in conflict with the freedom of establishment.

The core provision of the Dutch tax legislation at issue was Article 13 (1) of the Dutch *Wet op de Vennotschapsbelasting* which read:

> "In determining profit no account shall be taken of gains acquired from a holding or of the costs relating to a holding, unless it is evident that such costs are indirectly instrumental in making profit that is taxable in the Netherlands (exemption relating to holdings). In any event, the interest on and costs of loans taken up in the six months preceding the acquisition of the holding shall, except where it is likely that these loans have been taken up for a purpose other than the acquisition of the holding, be regarded as costs relating to a holding."[176]

Accordingly, Article 13 (1) of the *Wet op de Vennootschapsbelasting* meant that costs relating to a holding could only be deducted if the costs were indirectly instrumental in making profit that was taxable in the Netherlands. Companies enjoying that right to deduct costs reduced their taxable income and, accordingly, the tax payable. In contrast, if a company did not enjoy that that right, because it had subsidiaries in countries other than the Netherlands, and those companies made their profit exclusively in countries other than the Netherlands, then the right to deduct such holding costs did not apply. The reason was that the income of the foreign subsidiaries was tax exempt in the

[176] Case C-168/01 *Bosal Holding*, para. 8.

Netherlands. In contrast, the income of Dutch subsidiaries was, of course, taxable in the Netherlands, because such companies were subject to unlimited tax liability there. Accordingly, the tax paid in the Netherlands by parent companies with foreign subsidiaries would exceed the tax paid by those parent companies which instead had Dutch subsidiaries and were entitled to the cost deduction at issue.[177]

The Dutch *Hoge Raad* asked the European Court of Justice for a preliminary ruling. The question referred was: Did Article 43 (ex Article 52) of the EC Treaty, in conjunction with Article 48 (ex Article 58), or any other rule of Community law, preclude a Member State from granting a parent company subject to tax in that Member State a deduction of costs relating to a holding owned by it, only if the relevant subsidiary made profits which were subject to tax in the Member State in which the parent company was established?[178] The European Court of Justice was also asked if it made any difference to the answer to this question whether or not the relevant Member State took account of the abovementioned costs in levying tax on the subsidiary, where the subsidiary was subject to tax based on its profits in the Member State concerned but the parent company was not.

Bosal, the Netherlands, the Commission and the United Kingdom submitted observations on the questions asked to the Court. The reasons for the opinion that there was no infringement varied from the view that there was no restriction, to the view that even if there was a restriction, it was justified.

The Parent/Subsidiary Directive is also of interest in this case. Article 4 (2) of the Directive stipulates that each Member State shall retain the option of providing that any charges relating to the holding, and any losses from the distribution of the profits of the subsidiary, may not be deducted from the taxable profits of the parent company. In a reading out of context of this provision of the Parent/Subsidiary Directive, one would come to the conclusion that the Dutch provision at issue was compatible with the Directive. That seems also to be the position of the Court.[179] The Court, however, declared that the possibility to make deductions for tax purposes according to the Directive must be made in compliance with the fundamental provisions of the Treaty, in this case Article 43 and the freedom of establishment.[180]

In the view of the Court, the denial according to Dutch law of deductions for the cost of financing the holding of foreign companies "... constitutes a hindrance to

177 Cf. also the opinion of AG Alber in case C-168/01 *Bosal Holding*, para. 45.

178 Case C-168/01 *Bosal Holding*, para. 12.

179 Case C-168/01 *Bosal Holding*, para. 25.

180 Case C-168/01 *Bosal Holding*, para. 26.

the establishment of subsidiaries in other Member States".[181] Moreover, "... a parent company might be dissuaded from carrying on its activities through the intermediary of a subsidiary established in another Member State since, normally; such subsidiaries do not generate profits that are taxable in the Netherlands".[182]

Apparently, the Court considered the Dutch legislation at issue to constitute a non-discriminatory restriction. On the face of it, I can agree with that view: the disputed provision did not make any distinction between residents and non-residents in the Netherlands. However, it is not difficult to continue the Court's reasoning and thus find that it was only where the subsidiaries were resident in other countries than the Netherlands (and their profit were not taxable in the Netherlands) that the cost deduction could not be made. Consequently, there is in fact a comparison made between the taxation of holdings in Dutch subsidiaries and in foreign subsidiaries. In my view the application of such a comparison is not far from showing a case of direct discrimination.[183]

Moreover, several grounds of justification in the general interest were put forward, most notably fiscal coherence, but all were rejected by the Court. I will deal with them in Chapter 5. Vanistendael considers the outcome of the case to be clear evidence that "... the Court is determined to march on in the direction of a fully integrated economic and monetary union consisting of a market without borders and with free and fair competition and that no one is going to derail it from its track".[184] The outcome of the *Bosal Holding* case is good reason for believing Vanistendael to be right.

4.5.3.5 Conclusion

Traditionally the prohibition against restrictions on the freedom of establishment in matters of direct taxation has been focused on unequal treatment in the host state, the state where the establishment was made. The first tax case where discrimination in the host state was prohibited was the 1986 *Avoir fiscal* case.[185] The *Avoir fiscal* case was to be followed by a number of cases also prohibiting discrimination in the host state, for example case C-330/91 *Commerzbank*, case C-80/94 *Wielockx* and case C-250/95 *Futura Participations*.

---

[181] Case C-168/01 *Bosal Holding*, para. 27.

[182] *Ibid.*

[183] Weber agrees with the Court's view that the national provision at issue constitutes a non-discriminatory restriction, such as in case C-415/93 *Bosman*. Weber, "The Bosal Holding Case: Analysis and Critque", *EC Tax Review*, 2003, pp. 220-230, at p. 223.

[184] Vanistendael, "Bosal?!", *EC Tax Review*, 2003, pp. 192-193, at p. 193.

[185] Case 270/83 *Avoir fiscal*.

But already in 1988 there was a clear statement from the European Court of Justice in the *Daily Mail* case that the freedom of establishment also prohibits unequal treatment in the host state. If such a prohibition of restrictions applied also in matters of direct taxation, this was not evident, however. Yet, in recent years there have been a number of cases confirming the assumption that the freedom of establishment also includes a prohibition against restrictions in the home state. The *ICI* case, from 1998, dealt with UK legislation providing for inter-corporate loss relief. Such loss relief according to national legislation was not permitted if foreign companies were part of the group. The European Court of Justice decided that such treatment constituted a (home state) restriction. Other cases concerning the freedom of establishment where the Court has recognised the prohibition against restrictions in the field of direct taxation are case C-200/98 *X AB and Y AB*, case C-251/98 *Baars* and case C-141/99 *AMID*.

As regards case-law on home state restrictions I have analysed three cases: C-264/96 *ICI*, C-200/98 *X AB and Y AB* and C-168/01 *Bosal Holding*. In my view, in all of these cases the Court has been less explicit on what form of restriction is constituted by the national legislation at issue. I have been open for the possibility that they all could be interpreted as constituting discrimination and not necessarily non-discriminatory restrictions. The Court has avoided taking such an explicit standpoint. A reason for that could be the difficulty in reconciling discrimination with the applicability of the rule-of-reason doctrine, which, for example, according to the *Gebhard* case, only applies to non-discriminatory restrictions.

The question of whether Article 43 of the EC Treaty on the freedom of establishment includes a prohibition against restrictions in the host state as well as the home state has previously been subject to discussion. In the seminal Case 81/87 *Daily Mail* the Court declared: "Even though those provisions [principally Article 43 and 48] are directed mainly at ensuring that foreign nationals and companies are treated in the host Member State in the same way as nationals of that State, they also prohibit the Member State of origin ["home state" in the terminology applied in this study] from hindering the establishment in another Member State of one of its nationals or of a company incorporated under its legislation which comes within the definition of Article [48]." This interpretation has been upheld by the Court in subsequent case-law, such as the cases C-264/96 *ICI*, C-200/98 *X AB and Y AB* and C-324/00 *Lankhorst-Hohorst*.

It should also be noted that in the previously analysed cases the Court has upheld its view on how a company acquires the "nationality" of a particular Member State: it is the "seat" in the meaning of the different connecting criteria mentioned in Article 48 of the EC Treaty, that is the determining factor.

As regards discrimination we learned from the *Schumacker* case and subsequent cases – "the Schumacker doctrine" – that the situations of residents and non-residents as a general rule are not comparable. However, if for example an individual received all or almost all of his income in the host state, his situation could be comparable with that of a resident. In the cases at issue the comparison made, or at least the more or less obvious comparison, is between companies with both their seats[186] and residence for tax purpose in the "home state". The difference in treatment in the home state occurs when the company instead of establishing a subsidiary in the home state, establishes a subsidiary in another state.

4.5.4 Other Cases

4.5.4.1 Introduction

In this study I have identified three cases where individuals have established their activities in another Member State: the cases C-251/98 *Baars*, C-436/00 *X and Y* and C-9/02 *de Lasteyrie du Saillant*.

4.5.4.2 Case C-251/98 **Baars** *(13 April 2000)*

In case C-251/98 *Baars*,[187] the European Court of Justice dealt with elements of Dutch wealth taxation and its compatibility with the freedom of establishment. Mr Baars was resident in the Netherlands. He owned all the shares in an Irish company, Ballyard Foods Limited ("Ballyard"). As a general rule, shares were subject to wealth taxation in the Netherlands. There was, however, under certain conditions an exemption for shares in companies if the shareholder had a substantial holding. There was a specific requirement for the exemption from wealth taxation, and that was that the shares were held in a company established in the Netherlands.

Accordingly, the Dutch tax authorities denied Mr Baars the otherwise applicable exemption from wealth taxation because he owned shares in a foreign company, even if the company had its corporate seat in another Member State. The Dutch tax authorities did not contest that Mr Baars' holding in Ballyard was "substantial". Mr Baars was of the meaning that the tax exemption denied was an infringement of both the freedom of establishment and the free movement of capital. The question was referred to the European Court of Justice by a Dutch Regional Court of Appeal for a preliminary ruling. The *Baars* case also contains an interesting discussion on the meaning of establishment, which I have dealt with in section 4.2.4.

186 "Seat" in the meaning of the ECJ's practice on the interpretation of Article 48 of the EC Treaty.

187 Case C-251/98 *C. Baars v. Inspecteur der Belastingdienst Particulieren/Ondernemigen Gorinchem.*

The cross-border element of the *Baars* case is the cross-border owning of shares.

As in previous cases the Court declared that Article 43 (ex Article 52) of the EC Treaty also prohibits home state restrictions: "... the Member State of origin, from hindering the establishment in another Member State of one of its own nationals".[188] The Court found the Dutch legislation to constitute a violation of the freedom of establishment because it made a difference between taxpayers, in matters of wealth taxation, by using the criterion of the seat of the companies of which the taxpayers were shareholders.[189]

Given its answer to the question of compatibility with the freedom of establishment, the Court did not answer the question of compatibility with the free movement of capital.[190]

It is clear that the restriction in the *Baars* case takes place in the home state, the state where the establisher has his origin. The national legislation at issue in the *Baars* case could be said to constitute discrimination. There are two situations compared: holding shares in national and in foreign companies. There is a difference in treatment between these situations.[191]

4.5.4.3 Case C-436/00 **X and Y** *(21 November 2002)*

Case C-436/00 *X and Y* concerned Swedish legislation that would not grant the benefit of tax deferral when transferring shares in companies under market value, if foreign legal persons were involved.[192] The European Court of Justice was asked for a preliminary ruling on the issue of whether this legislation was compatible with the freedom of establishment and the free movement of capital. In this section I will only deal with the relation to the freedom of establishment, while the issue of compatibility with the free movement of capital, which actually was considered in substance by the Court, is dealt with in Chapter 6.

X and Y were individuals with Swedish nationality, and they were also resident in Sweden for tax purposes. X and Y had shares in several companies. A corporate

[188] Case C-251/98 *Baars*, para. 28. In support of the prohibition against home state restrictions the ECJ refers to Case 81/87 *Daily Mail*, case C-264/96 *ICI*, and case C-200/98 *X AB and Y AB*.

[189] Case C-251/98 *Baars*, para. 30.

[190] See on this issue section 6.4.2.

[191] Cf. opinion of AG Alber in case C-251/98 *Baars*, para. 39.

[192] Case C-436/00 *X and Y* is discussed in e.g. Wiman, "Pending Cases Filed by Swedish Courts: the X and Y Case and the Skandia and Ola Ramstedt Case", in *Direct Taxation: Recent ECJ Developments*, Lang (ed.), Linde Verlag, Vienna, 2003, pp. 191-206.

reorganisation was being planned. A preliminary ruling on the tax implications was requested from the Swedish Revenue Law Commission (*Skatterättsnämnden).* The decision of the Revenue Law Commission was appealed against to the Supreme Administrative Court (*Regeringsrätten*). In turn, the compatibility of the applicable Swedish tax legislation with the fundamental freedoms of the EC Treaty was referred by the Supreme Administrative Court to the European Court of Justice for a preliminary ruling.

The basic facts of the underlying case were the following. X AB was the Swedish parent company in a group of companies. X AB was owned in equal shares by, on the one hand, the Swedish individuals X and Y, and, on the other hand, a Maltese company. X and Y had no proprietary interest in the Maltese company. Y SA, a Belgian company, was a parent company also owned by X and Y. The Swedish company Z AB was a subsidiary of Y SA.

The planned reorganisation had the following components. X and Y would transfer their shares in X AB to Z AB at the acquisition cost. Prior to the reorganisation X and Y had considered it convenient to transfer certain activities to Y SA.

Under specific circumstances Swedish legislation provided for a tax deferral on the capital gains realised from the inter-corporate transfer of shares. The European Court of Justice was asked to consider the following three different types of share transfers.[193]

(a) Transfers to a foreign legal person in which the transferor or his kin directly or indirectly had a holding (*type A share transfers*).

(b) Transfers to a Swedish limited company in which such a foreign legal person either directly or indirectly had a holding (*type B share transfers*).

(c) Transfers to a Swedish limited company other than those described in (b) and in which the transferor or his kin directly or indirectly had a holding (*type C share transfers*).

According to Swedish tax law, the tax consequences of these three types of transfers were the following. On the transfer of type C the Swedish law provided that the transferor's liability to capital gains tax was deferred, generally until the time when the transferor disposed of his holding in the transferee company. In contrast, the transferor was immediately liable to tax on capital gains from transfers of the A and B types.[194]

The Court first considered whether the rule on the freedom of establishment applied. The Swedish National Tax Board (*Riksskatteverket*) claimed that the EC Treaty had no bearing because the situation was purely internal, and referred in support of this view

[193] Case C-436/00 *X and Y*, para. 30.

[194] Case C-436/00 *X and Y*, para. 31.

to case C-112/91 *Werner*. The reason for the case being a strictly internal Swedish matter was that the national legislation at issue concerned an economic activity in Sweden that would continue to be pursued in Sweden even after the share transfer.[195] The Court did not accept that argument. In both type A and type B share transfers there were foreign elements. For type A transfers, the transferee company was established in another Member State. For type B transfers, a company established in another Member State had a holding in the transferee company. In both cases the foreign element was the basis for a difference in Swedish taxation.

Accordingly, the Court continued to examine the compatibility of the Swedish legislation with the freedom of establishment, beginning with type A transfers. The Court concluded that there was a difference in treatment in refusing the transferor the benefit of tax deferral on capital gains tax on shares transferred at undervalue where the transferee company, in which the transferor had a holding, was established in another Member State. As a consequence of the denied tax deferral, the transferor was subject to a cash-flow disadvantage. Denying the tax deferral on the ground that the transferee company was established in another Member State was, according to the Court, likely to have a "deterrent effect" on the exercise of the freedom of establishment.[196]

The type A transfers consisted of the transfer of shares to a foreign legal person in which the transferor or his kin directly or indirectly had a holding. In contrast to a type C transfer to a Swedish limited company, a type A transfer meant a denial of tax deferral on capital gains resulting from the transfer. In relation to type A transfers the Court concluded: "Such inequality of treatment thus constitutes a restriction on the freedom of establishment of nationals of the Member State concerned (and, moreover, on that of nationals of other Member States resident in that Member State), who have a holding in the capital of a company established in another Member State, provided that that holding gives them definite influence over the company's decisions and allows them to determine its activities …".[197]

The type B transfers consisted of transfers to a Swedish limited company in which such a foreign legal entity either directly or indirectly had a holding. In contrast to a type C transfer to a Swedish limited company with no such foreign holding, a type B transfer would mean a denial of tax deferral on capital gains from the transfer.

The Court considered that the difference in tax treatment between, on the one hand, type A and B transfers, and, on the other hand, type C transfers, constituted a restriction on the freedom of establishment according to Articles 43 and 48 of the EC Treaty. It

[195] Case C-436/00 *X and Y*, para. 33.

[196] Case C-436/00 *X and Y*, para. 36.

[197] Case C-436/00 *X and Y*, para. 37.

was a restriction on the freedom of establishment in the meaning of "… a company, established in another Member State (in the present case a Belgian limited company), and treated, within the meaning of Article 43 EC, in the same way as a natural person who is a national of that Member State who wishes to pursue his activities through the intermediary of a branch in the Member State concerned".[198] Furthermore, the Court stated that by refusing the transferor of the possibility of tax deferral on capital gains, the transferor was denied a cash flow advantage, "… by reason of the fact that the parent company of the transferee company is situated in another Member State".[199] According to the Court an acceptance of the denied cash-flow advantage would deprive Article 43 of the EC Treaty of all meaning.[200]

4.5.4.4 Case C-9/02 **de Lasteyrie du Saillant** *(11 March 2004)*

The Court delivered its decision in case C-9/02 *de Lasteyrie du Saillant* on 11 March 2004. The case concerned French legislation on "exit taxation" and its compatibility with the freedom of establishment. The case was referred by the French *Conseil d'État* as a request for a preliminary ruling from the European Court of Justice on the interpretation of the freedom of establishment.

The facts of the underlying case were the following. Mr de Lasteyrie du Saillant (subsequently Mr de Lasteyrie) was resident for tax purposes in France where he also was a national. He emigrated from France to Belgium in 1998. In France he held, or had held, at some time during the five years preceding his departure from France, either directly or indirectly with members of his family, securities conferring entitlement to more than 25 per cent of the profits of a company subject to corporation tax that was established in France. The reason for Mr de Lasteyrie moving to Belgium was, according to him, to carry out his profession there.

French tax legislation provided for "exit taxation" with the following general content. Taxpayers that had been resident in France for at least six of the ten previous years were taxable, at the date of their transfer of residence, on the increase in value of the

[198] Case C-436/00 *X and Y*, para. 38. In support of this view the ECJ referred to case C-250/95 *Futura Participations*, para. 24, and case C-307/97 *Saint-Gobain*, para. 35 (*ibid.*, para. 38).

[199] Case C-436/00 *X and Y*, para. 38. A recent parallel case is C-268/03 *De Baeck v. Belgium* (decided 8 June 2004 by order of the ECJ). It dealt with Belgian taxation on capital gains from the alienation of shares. In brief, capital gains from the alienation of shares in Blegian companies were tax exempt, whereas gains from the alienation of shares in foreign companies were subject to tax. The ECJ decided in line with the *X and Y* case that the Belgian legislation at issue was in breach of both the freedom of establishment and the free movement of capital.

[200] *Ibid.* The ECJ refers, in support of this view, to joined cases C-397/98 and C-410/98 *Metallgesellschaft and Others*, para. 42.

securities of the company at issue, according to Article 167 *bis* of the *Code Générale des Impôts* (CGI). Losses could not be offset against increases in value of the same kind that occurred elsewhere. There was a possibility for a suspension of the exit tax, also according to Article 167 *bis* of the CGI if the securities were part of the taxpayer's assets in a five-year period after the exit or if he returned to France during that period.[201] One of the conditions for a suspension was that the taxpayer made a declaration within a limited period of time designating a representative in France and offerering guarantees for the recovery of the tax.[202]

The Court found the French legislation at issue to be in breach of the freedom of establishment (ex Article 52 of the EC Treaty). In the view of the Court, the exit tax restricted the freedom of establishment and had at least a "dissuasive effect" on taxpayers wishing to establish in another Member State.[203] This wording permits the belief that the Court considered the legislation at issue to constitute a non-discriminatory restriction. However, the Court also made a comparison between the taxation of different investment (establishment) alternatives. The Court stated: "A taxpayer wishing to transfer his tax residence outside French territory, in exercise of the right guaranteed to him by Article 52 (present Article 43] of the Treaty, is subjected to disadvantageous treatment in comparison with a person who maintains his residence in France."[204] This comparison between different situations from the home state's perspective is seemingly an expression of a discrimination analysis.

4.5.4.4 Conclusion

In section 4.5.4 the cases C-251/98 *Baars*, C-436/00 *X and Y*, and C-9/02 *de Lasteyrie du Saillant* have been analysed. All three cases deal with the compatibility of law provisions with the freedom of establishment. In all three cases the Court has not been very outspoken on what form of hindrance to the freedom the national legislation at issue constituted. Even so, there is an inherent discrimination analysis in all three cases: it would be easy to formulate a comparison between a domestic establishment and a cross-border establishment.

It is worth noting that neither in the *Baars* case nor in the *de Lasteyrie du Saillant* case did the Court consider the free movement of capital, which in contrast was done in the *X and Y* case.

---

201 Case C-9/02 *de Lasteyrie du Saillant*, para. 16.

202 Case C-9/02 *de Lasteyrie du Saillant*, e.g. para. 56. Mutén considers the French legislation on exit taxation at issue in this case to be lenient in an international comparison. Mutén, "EG-domstolen och exitskatten", *Skattenytt*, 2004, pp. 294-300, at p. 295.

203 Case C-9/02 *de Lasteyrie du Saillant*, para. 45.

204 Case C-9/02 *de Lasteyrie du Saillant*, para. 46.

All three cases concern tax laws very different from each other. The *Baars* case deals with wealth taxation, the *X and Y* case deals with the taxation of corporate reorganisations and the *de Lasteyrie du Saillant* case deals with exit taxation of individuals.

4.6 Case C-446/03 *Marks & Spencer* (Pending)

4.6.1 Introduction

4.6.1.1 General

Case C-446/03 *Marks & Spencer* will undoubtedly turn out to be one of the leading cases of the European Court of Justice in the field of direct taxation and fundamental freedoms. Recently, the High Court of Justice has asked the European Court of Justice for a preliminary ruling on the interpretation of the freedom of establishment. Originally, the *Marks & Spencer* case was decided on 17 December 2002 by UK Special Commissioners John F. Avery Jones and Malcolm Gammie. The decision by Avery Jones and Gammie, well-known experts of international tax law and Community law, is both elaborate and of a high standard, which is why I find it adequate to analyse it in detail, even if there is as yet no Advocate General's opinion. It should be added that the junior counsel for the taxpayer was Paul Farmer, also a leading international expert in this field of law.

Here, only those parts of the decision by the Special Commissioners that I consider important for this part of my study will be referred to. While this is a major part, some other parts will be covered in other sections of this study.[205] The decision by the Special Commissioners was appealed to the United Kingdom High Court of Justice that has referred the case to the European Court of Justice for a preliminary ruling.[206]

4.6.1.2 Facts of the Underlying Case

The facts of the underlying case where the following. Marks & Spencer plc was a United Kingdom trading and holding company with a large number of foreign subsidiaries. The foreign subsidiaries made trading losses for the years that ended on 31 March

[205] In the decision by the Special Commissioners there is a discussion on the meaning of discrimination. That is a topic which I largely have dealt with in Chapter 3 of this study: for my position on the meaning of this term I therefore refer to that chapter.

[206] The reference to the ECJ is discussed by e.g. Dörr, "A Step Forward in the Field of European Corporate Taxation and Cross-border Loss Relief: Some Comments on the Marks and Spencer Case", *Intertax*, 2004, pp. 180-186.

1998 to 2001 (inclusive) in respect of which the parent company – Marks & Spencer – claimed group relief in the United Kingdom. The United Kingdom tax inspector denied the taxpayer's claims for group relief on the ground that the foreign subsidiaries were not resident in the United Kingdom, as required by section 413(5) of the Income and Corporation Taxes Act 1988. The requirement was repealed by the Finance Act 2000 so that, for accounting periods beginning on or after 1 April 2000, group relief was granted according to section 402(3A) and (3B) and section 403D(1)(a) of the 1988 Act where the loss-making company was either resident in the United Kingdom or carrying on a trade in the United Kingdom through a branch or a subsidiary. For that period the inspector denied group relief on the ground that the foreign subsidiaries met none of those conditions.

4.6.1.3 Questions of Community Law in Focus

The decision by the Special Commissioners is both thorough and elaborate. It would not be possible to analyse every detail of the decision in the present study. I would like to frame the main issues in the following way. The company Marks & Spencer was resident in the United Kingdom. It had subsidiaries in other Member States. The foreign subsidiaries had accumulated losses. Could those losses be deducted from the taxable profits in the United Kingdom by the parent Marks & Spencer? United Kingdom tax law denied Marks & Spencer the right to take those losses into account.

Did the refusal for Marks & Spencer to take the foreign losses into account constitute an infringement of the freedom of establishment? The case deals with the question of whether this denial was discriminatory or not. In order to establish whether or not it was discriminatory, a comparison between objectively comparable situations had to be made. The central issue of the case was: What constitutes objectively comparable situations in order to establish whether the United Kingdom legislation at issue was discriminatory or not?

There were two comparisons that seem to be the ones finally considered by the Special Commissioners.[207] In all compared situations the foreign entity, be it either a branch or a subsidiary, would have a loss that the United Kingdom entity sought to deduct. Because the different comparisons are important when trying to establish whether there is discrimination or not, I will be thorough when describing the different alternatives. It should be borne in mind that a comparison in a discrimination analysis consists of a comparison between two different situations.

[207] *Marks & Spencer*, decision by the Special Commissioners, para. 116 compared with para. 56. I would like to note that it is not easy to uncover the different comparisons made.

The *first comparison* was from the perspective of a United Kingdom parent company when it chose between the following situations. In the *first situation* the United Kingdom parent company (Marks & Spencer) had a United Kingdom subsidiary. The parent company wanted to claim the losses of the subsidiary, and these losses derived from the United Kingdom or from branches in France, Belgium or Germany. In the *second situation* the United Kingdom parent company (Marks & Spencer) had a foreign subsidiary in France, Belgium or Germany. In the first situation the parent company would be granted group relief on the foreign losses, whereas in the second situation group relief would not be granted on the foreign losses.

The *second comparison* was from the perspective of a United Kingdom subsidiary with a parent company also resident in the United Kingdom. The United Kingdom subsidiary chose between the following situations. In the *first situation*, the United Kingdom subsidiary established branches in France, Belgium or Germany. The subsidiary wanted to claim the losses of those foreign branches. In the *second situation*, the United Kingdom subsidiary established subsidiaries in France, Belgium or Germany. The subsidiaries claimed the losses of the foreign subsidiaries. In the first situation group relief would be granted, whereas in the second situation it would not.

When considering these different comparisons, the first question is whether the situations are objectively comparable or not. If they are objectively comparable, the second question is whether there is any difference in treatment. If there is a difference in treatment to the detriment of the appellant, that treatment is discriminatory and an infringement of the fundamental freedom at issue. Such a discriminatory difference in treatment may, however, be justified according to the rule-of-reason doctrine, using the terminology of this study.

4.6.1.4 Position of Marks & Spencer

Marks & Spencer appealed the decision by the tax inspector on the denial of group relief to the Special Commissioners. Marks & Spencer – the "appellant" – held that the United Kingdom legislation denying the group relief infringed the freedom of establishment as laid down in Article 43 of the EC Treaty. More precisely, Marks & Spencer advanced the following grounds for the purported infringement:

(i) by limiting the group relief for accounting periods ending before 1 April 2000 to companies resident in the United Kingdom, and for periods thereafter to companies which traded in the United Kingdom through a branch or agency, the group relief legislation made it less attractive to establish subsidiaries in other Member States than in the United Kingdom;

(ii) the inability of non-resident subsidiaries, as compared with resident subsidiaries, to surrender losses to the United Kingdom parents (or other members of its group with United Kingdom taxable profits) entailed a difference in tax treatment based on the residence or seat of the subsidiary; and

(iii) the United Kingdom rules hindered the freedom of establishment of United Kingdom companies by restricting the freedom to chose the most appropriate form for pursuing activities in another Member State; this arose because there was no provision for loss relief for foreign subsidiaries.

4.6.1.5 Background

Marks & Spencer had loss-making subsidiaries in Belgium, France and Germany. They all carried on business as general retailers selling clothing, food, home-ware and financial services. It is important to note the following parts of the United Kingdom legislation at issue. Corporation tax was charged on the profits of companies that were either resident in the United Kingdom or conducting business there through a branch or an agency. A resident company was liable to tax in the United Kingdom on its worldwide profits. In contrast, a non-resident company was only taxed in the United Kingdom on profits attributable to its United Kingdom branch or agency. The United Kingdom had tax treaties with all involved countries: Belgium, France and Germany.

The appellant, Marks & Spencer plc, was liable to tax in the United Kingdom on its worldwide income. For reasons of avoiding international double taxation (in the legal sense), the United Kingdom applied the credit system. It means that foreign profits were also taxable in the United Kingdom, but it was possible to make a credit against the United Kingdom tax for the tax paid in the other country.

The Special Commissioners emphasised two aspects of this system for the avoidance of double taxation that were important for this case.[208] Each aspect concerned a form of establishment in another Member State.

First, if a United Kingdom company chose to establish in the other Member State in the form of a branch, the profits of the branch would be taxable in the United Kingdom and the foreign tax paid on those foreign profits would be credited against the tax payable in the United Kingdom.[209] The trading profits of the branch would be calculated according to United Kingdom law. If there was a branch loss, that loss would be deductible against the profits of the United Kingdom company, Marks & Spencer plc. Moreover, if a loss could not be fully relieved in one fiscal year, it could be carried forward. The

[208] *Marks & Spencer*, decision by the Special Commissioners, para. 11-12.

[209] The possibility of cost deduction of the foreign taxes paid is not specifically considered here, and that method would in this respect make no principal difference. The Special Commissioners noted this alternative method, but put it within parentheses.

fact that the branch loss also could be relieved in the branch state would not inflict on the right to make a loss deduction in the United Kingdom.

Secondly, if a United Kingdom company would choose to establish in the other Member State in the form of a subsidiary, rather than a United Kingdom subsidiary, the following would apply. Dividends paid by the foreign subsidiary to the United Kingdom parent company would be taxed as profits. However, there would be a tax relief for the tax paid by the foreign subsidiary. Because the United Kingdom parent company and the foreign subsidiary were separate legal entities, the parent company would not be taxed on the (undistributed) profits of the subsidiary, and it would not be able to make any deductions for the losses incurred by the foreign subsidiary. There was one exception in the United Kingdom law where (undistributed) profits of a foreign subsidiary in fact were taxed in the hands of the parent company, and that was according to a specific form of anti-avoidance legislation, generally known as CFC legislation. The CFC legislation also provided relief in the United Kingdom for the foreign tax (if any) paid on the foreign profit at issue. The CFC legislation was not applicable in the underlying case.

The decision by the Special Commissioners is divided into the following sections, which I mainly will follow: (i) the principles applicable to Article 43, (ii) non-discriminatory measures liable to hinder or make less attractive the exercise of the Treaty freedoms, (iii) application of Article 43 EC discrimination principles to the appellant's case, (iv) justification for the United Kingdom provisions, and (v) conclusion. As regards justifications for the United Kingdom provisions, that issue is covered in Chapter 5. It could be noted already here that possible grounds of justification were less in focus in the decision by the Special Commissioners: the focus was rather on what constitutes a piece of discriminatory tax legislation.

4.6.2 The Principles Applicable to Article 43 of the EC Treaty

4.6.2.1 Differential Taxation by a Host State of Activities Conducted through a Branch or a Subsidiary

The first question that the Special Commissioners dealt with in relation to the principles following from Article 43 of the EC Treaty, was the differential taxation by a host state of activities conducted through a branch or a subsidiary. After having mentioned the definitions of direct and indirect discrimination, the Special Commissioners continued with the issue of what constitutes objectively comparable situations: a necessary step for deciding whether discrimination is at hand or not. The Special Commissioners stated, correctly in my view, that as a general rule the situations of residents and non-residents are not comparable depending on facts such as the possibility to take account of their ability to pay tax or of their personal and family circumstances.[210] However, as the Special Commissioners pointed out, the Court has in several cases concluded that the situations of branches and subsidiaries in the host state are comparable, for example in the *Avoir fiscal* case, the *Halliburton* case and the *Saint-Gobain* case. However, in my view one should note that the situations compared regarding companies are relatively limited. They only refer to the taxation of the income in question.

The Special Commissioners continued with a comparison between, on the one hand, the facts of the *Marks & Spencer* case, and, on the other hand, the *Royal Bank of Scotland* case and the *Futura Participations* case.[211] An unacceptable difference in treatment would occur in the host state ("France") regarding the computation of, or the relief granted by France for losses in a French branch as compared to losses arising in a French subsidiary, if France claimed the right to tax both the branch and the subsidiary in respect of the activities carried on there. The reason is that under those circumstances the situations of the branch and the subsidiary would be comparable. However, if the difference in treatment reflects the different basis for taxing the income or activities of resident and non-resident persons, the situations would not be comparable. In support of this view on "incomparability" the Special Commissioners referred to the *Futura Participations* case. In that case, as regarded non-residents, only those losses could be deducted in Luxembourg that were economically linked to income earned in Luxembourg and subject to tax there. In contrast, companies resident in Luxembourg, unless there was a tax treaty exception granting exemption, were taxed in Luxembourg on all foreign income. Moreover, the Special Commissioners especially noted that the Court found the previously related Luxembourg legislation regarding losses of a branch to be in conformity with the fiscal principle of territoriality. Moreover, they believed that what the Court meant in that case was that a state may choose to tax its companies on their worldwide income, but normally taxes non-resident companies only on income associated with their establishments within the state.[212]

It should be underlined that the present case is different from both the *Royal Bank of Scotland* case and the *Futura Participations* case by the fact that it deals with the taxation in the home state.

---

[210] References are made to Case C-279/93 *Schumacker* (para. 31) and Case C-311/97 *Royal Bank of Scotland* (para. 27).

[211] *Marks & Spencer*, decision by the Special Commissioners, para. 33.

[212] *Marks & Spencer*, decision by the Special Commissioners, para. 37.

4.6.2.2 Differential Tax Rules of a Home State Restricting the Freedom of Establishment Elsewhere in the Community

The Special Commissioners recognised that there have been a growing number of cases where the European Court of Justice has found national tax provisions of the state of origin ("home state" with the terminology applied in this study) to be in breach of the fundamental freedoms of the EC Treaty.[213] In this respect, the Special Commissioners said:

> "We think that it is important to recognise the basis upon which the Court of Justice decided that art 43 EC (or art 49 EC) operated in these cases to strike down the origin state's tax rule. All these decisions were dealing with a tax rule in the state of origin that was discriminatory as described in paragraph 30 above (namely, applying a different rule to objectively comparable situations or the same rule to different situations). In every case, the complaint involved a taxation measure, the effect of which was to treat a national of the state of origin concerned *less favourably* if he sought to exercise the Treaty freedom in question (i.e. by establishing abroad or by acquiring services from a service provider based in another member state) than was the case in the *comparable* domestic situation or provision when the freedom was not exercised."[214]

When the Special Commissioners came to the conclusion that, for example, the *AMID* and *Baars* cases constitute home state discrimination, they go a step further in their analysis than several other commentators have done.[215] The reason for the diverging terminology is how the European Court of Justice has decided to categorise the cases at issue. The Court is not as explicit as the Special Commissioners when they present their analysis. Rather, the Court applies a vague language when determining whether a specific case involves discrimination or a non-discriminatory restriction, or just simply a "barrier" or a "hindrance". The Court seems to avoid using the language required for pointing out that there is a case of home state discrimination. I will return to the question of whether the UK legislation can be said to constitute a case of non-discriminatory restriction.

---

[213] The Special Commissioners explicitly refer to case C-251/98 *Baars*; case C-264/96 *ICI*; case C-141/99 *AMID*; case C-55/98 *Vestergaard*; case C-294/97 *Eurowings*; case C-118/96 *Safir*; and case C-136/00 *Danner*.

[214] *Marks & Spencer*, decision by the Special Commissioners, para. 54.

[215] Cf. e.g. Vanistendael, "The Compatibility of the Basic Economic Freedoms with the Sovereign National Tax Systems of the Member States", *EC Tax Review*, 2003, pp. 136-143.

4.6.2.3 The Choice of Branch or Subsidiary from the Perspective of the Home State

As regards the question of the choice of either a branch or a subsidiary from the home state's perspective, the Special Commissioners made the following interpretation of the Court's case-law on Article 43 of the EC Treaty. Article 43, in their view, does not mean that the United Kingdom – as the home state – should apply the same tax rule to a French subsidiary as the tax rule it applies to the United Kingdom subsidiary in respect of its French branch.

Instead, Article 43 provides the following. First, it provides that the host state may not treat foreign nationals (for example a foreign branch) *less favourably* than it treats its own nationals in comparable situations. Secondly, the Special Commissioners advanced: "The counterpart of this principle is that a state of origin may not inhibit establishment outside the state of origin by treating its nationals (including their subsidiaries in other member states) less favourably if they establish abroad than it does in comparable origin state situations. In those terms, a state of origin does not inhibit establishment in another member state by treating its nationals established abroad (including foreign subsidiaries) *more* favourably than comparable domestic establishment."[216] None of these rules does, according to the Special Commissioners, mean that the state of origin should treat foreign branches and subsidiaries in the same way.

Were it not for the United Kingdom system of group relief, I would agree with the Special Commissioners. However, in the United Kingdom a parent company with a subsidiary with losses can make use of the group relief system. That puts the treatment of, on the one hand, a head office and a branch, and, on the other hand, a parent company with a subsidiary, on an equal footing as regards the treatment of losses. Gutmann argues, and I agree with him, that this means that the United Kingdom denial of group relief for losses of foreign subsidiaries is in breach of the freedom of establishment and the requirement of equal treatment in the state of origin, in this case the United Kingdom.[217]

Is *Marks & Spencer* as a home state case the mirror image of the host state *Futura Participations* case? That seems to be the view of the Special Commissioners. But then they do not seem to have reflected upon Gutmann's idea, that the group relief system equalises the treatment of foreign branches with foreign subsidiaries.

---

[216] *Marks & Spencer*, decision by the Special Commissioners, para. 58.

[217] Gutmann, "The Marks & Spencer Case: Proposals for an Alternative Way of Reasoning", *EC Tax Review*, 2003, pp. 154-158.

4.6.3 Non-discriminatory Measures Liable to Hinder or Make Less Attractive the Exercise of Treaty Freedoms

The Special Commissioners continue their reasoning by discussing the fact that the European Court of Justice has recognised that fundamental freedoms also include a prohibition against non-discriminatory measures liable to hinder or make less attractive the exercise of the Treaty freedoms. This means that a national provision may constitute a restriction on a fundamental freedom even if the provision applies equally to nationals of all Member States and is not as such discriminatory.[218]

The Special Commissioners note the divergence in terminology and classification in the case-law of the European Court of Justice. Moreover, they also explicitly state how they classify the cases concerning infringements of fundamental freedoms: "In this case, we consider that the appropriate way to classify (or to think about) the case is as we have done thus far, namely whether the cases involve the application of a host state tax rule to a national of another member state or the application of a state of origin's tax rules to its nationals, where in either case that gives rise to a *difference in treatment of comparable cross-border situations*."[219]

Furthermore, the Special Commissioners recognise a third category of infringement of fundamental freedoms of the EC Treaty, as outlined in cases such as C-19/92 *Gebhard*, C-415/93 *Bosman* and C-190/98 *Graf v. Filzmoser Maschinenbau GmbH*. In the way that infringements of fundamental freedoms were categorised in Chapter 3 of this study the referred cases involved prohibited non-discriminatory restrictions. What is typical for those cases is that the national law at issue does not distinguish on the basis of nationality, or any similar criterion: the legislation at issue covers all. However, an effect of the legislation is anyway that it infringes cross-border movements that are guaranteed by a fundamental freedom. It seems to me that the Special Commissioners apply a similar definition to the cases falling under this category. They do not consider the United Kingdom law rule at issue to fall under this category. The emphasis given by the Special Commissioners of the Court's reasoning in the *Futura Participations* case is noteworthy in this instance. They specifically quote the European Court of Justice in the *Futura Participations* case where it states that each Member State is free to draw up its own rules governing the determination of profits, income, expenditure and deductions, as well as amounts in respect of which of them can be included in the calculation of taxable income or of losses which may be carried forward.[220]

---

218 *Marks & Spencer*, decision by the Special Commissioners, para. 63.

219 *Marks & Spencer*, decision by the Special Commissioners, para. 64 (emphasis added).

220 Case C-250/95 *Futura Participations*, para. 33.

The conclusion of the Special Commissioners is that the case at issue cannot be classified as a non-discriminatory home state restriction.[221] In their view the restriction could better be regarded as a case of "dislocation" rather than a "neutral" tax rule.[222] The Special Commissioners hold the view, that what Marks & Spencer is "really" complaining about is the interaction of the tax system of the host state and the home state. According to them there is no case-law where the Court has considered such a "dislocation" to constitute a non-discriminatory restriction. The fact that by establishing foreign subsidiaries Marks & Spencer was subject to different tax rules was not a restriction on a fundamental freedom, but something following from the fact that the Member States had not been able to harmonise their corporate tax systems.[223]

The Special Commissioners are of course correct that if the Member States could have agreed upon, for example, a directive on the treatment of cross-border losses, the problem for Marks & Spencer would not have occurred. However, one might doubt whether the United Kingdom legislation at issue could not be regarded as constituting a non-discriminatory restriction. Vanistendael considers the United Kingdom legislation to constitute such a non-discriminatory restriction: "When … loss compensation is only available for activities carried out on the domestic territory and not for activities carried out abroad, there is a serious handicap to set up such operations abroad. Therefore there are good reasons to conclude that under the non-restriction approach there is indeed a violation of the right of establishment."[224]

4.6.4 Application of Art 43 EC Discrimination Principles to the Appellant's Case

The Special Commissioners rightly point out that the question of whether a breach of Article 43 is at issue in this case will depend on how one makes the comparison between different situations. Marks & Spencer advanced that a comparison should be made between, on the one hand, an establishment of a subsidiary in the United Kingdom – where group relief would be granted – and, on the other hand, an establishment in another country – where group relief would not be granted.[225] However, the reasoning by the Special Commissioners loses its direction somewhat here, because the Special Commissioners discuss the implications of the *AMID* case – which had been advanced

221 *Marks & Spencer*, decision by the Special Commissioners, para. 78.

222 *Marks & Spencer*, decision by the Special Commissioners, para. 75.

223 *Ibid.*

224 Vanistendael, "The Compatibility of the Basic Economic Freedoms with the Sovereign National Tax Systems of the Member States", *EC Tax Review*, 2003, pp. 136-143, at p. 140.

225 *Marks & Spencer*, decision by the Special Commissioners, para. 80.

by Marks & Spencer. The Special Commissioners correctly come to the conclusion that the *AMID* case is rather awkward in relation to the comparison between resident and non-resident subsidiaries: the *AMID* case deals with the taxation of losses in the hands of a head office vis-à-vis the profits of a non-resident branch. However, it is important to note that both the *AMID* and *Futura Participations* cases deal with the treatment of losses within the same company in the head office – branch constellation.

In their conclusions, the Special Commissioners return to the question of why a comparison between resident subsidiaries and non-resident subsidiaries is not a correct one. They conclude that the reason is that the foreign subsidiaries are outside the scope of the United Kingdom tax in respect of the activities concerned. In comparison, the activities of a resident subsidiary would, of course, be within the scope of United Kingdom tax jurisdiction. The application of different rules to different situations does not constitute discrimination. In my view, the Special Commissioners are right, but that is of course due to the comparison they chose to make: the comparable cross-border situation is a situation consisting of the establishment of a foreign branch.

The Special Commissioners also considered the United Kingdom system for group relief from the perspective of the foreign subsidiaries. They even considered that the system for group relief should properly be viewed from that perspective. That interpretation was underlined by the fact that the appellant would usually pay its subsidiaries the equivalent value of its tax savings by way of payment for group relief payment.[226] It goes beyond the scope of this study to evaluate whether the Special Commissioners' interpretation of the United Kingdom rule at issue is correct in this respect. Supposing that it is correct, the Special Commissioners put forward two strong reasons why the rule is in conformity with the freedom of establishment when viewed from the perspective of the foreign subsidiaries. First, as regards the host state of the secondary establishment in the form of a subsidiary, the freedom of establishment would only confer the right of equal treatment in that state. The way in which the United Kingdom formulates its tax legislation is, of course, beyond the powers of the host state. Secondly, as regards the United Kingdom legislation from the home state perspective, it is only nationals (or equivalent) of the home state that are covered by the scope of the fundamental freedom, not the subsidiary set up in another Member State.

Finally, the Special Commissioners also addressed the United Kingdom legislation at issue from the perspective of the appellant, Marks & Spencer.[227] Once more, the Special Commissioners expressed that they did not think that the legislation at issue should be regarded from the appellant's perspective: the tax rule at issue related to who

[226] *Marks & Spencer*, decision by the Special Commissioners, para. 90.

[227] *Marks & Spencer*, decision by the Special Commissioners, para. 93.

may surrender losses rather than who may claim them.[228] The rule at issue prevented the foreign subsidiaries from surrendering their losses. As I understand it, the Special Commissioners consider that the foreign subsidiaries cannot claim to be covered by the freedom of establishment in the home state. From the perspective of the home state it is only nationals (or the equivalents) that are protected by the fundamental freedom. Accordingly, the rule at issue could not be in breach of the freedom of establishment. However, if the appellant were considered to be targeted by the rule at issue, there would not be any breach of the freedom of establishment. The Special Commissioners understood the appellant as if it were only the denial of the right to claim losses of foreign subsidiaries that should be put in relation to the freedom of establishment. I interpret that in the following way. The appellant may claim losses of resident subsidiaries, but not of foreign subsidiaries. When those alternatives are compared it would be unfavourable to have foreign subsidiaries. But according to the Special Commissioners, it is not possible to make such an isolated comparison of the right to claim losses of subsidiaries – it is also necessary to consider how the profits of the subsidiaries are taxed and in which state. In the view of the Special Commissioners it was necessary to consider the treatment of both profits and losses: "Trading profits and losses are merely two sides of the same coin. No doubt the appellant hopes that the outcome of its trading operations is less a matter of chance than flipping a coin. Whatever the relative odds that attach to conducting business or flipping a coin, however, in any period the possibility exists of profit or loss; that the coin may land heads or tails up."[229]

From this I conclude that the Special Commissioners considered it impossible for the provision to be in breach of the freedom of establishment when considering the taxation of resident subsidiaries in comparison to foreign subsidiaries. The reason was that the profits of the foreign subsidiaries were not taxable in the United Kingdom. The Special Commissioners did, however, discuss whether the taxation of dividends from the foreign subsidiaries to its resident parent, and the CFC taxation of resident parents, could constitute the taxation in the United Kingdom of the profits of the foreign subsidiaries.

As regards the taxation of foreign dividends, their conclusion was that the taxation in the United Kingdom of dividends received by a resident parent company from a

---

228 There is a brief comparison with Case C-264/96 *ICI*. The Special Commissioners consider the rule at issue in the *ICI* case to be decisively different from the one in the *Marks & Spencer* case. In the *ICI* case the rule at issue concerned ICI's right to establish subsidiaries in other Member States, whereas in the *Marks & Spencer* case, the rule at issue concerned the identity of the loss-making company (*Marks & Spencer*, decision by the Special Commissioners, para. 94). I agree that the rules in the two cases are not the same, but they are in my view similar when regarding their effect. In both cases the existence of non-resident subsidiaries was decisive for the conclusion whether loss relief would be granted or not.

229 *Marks & Spencer*, decision by the Special Commissioners, para. 98.

foreign subsidiary could not in any relevant sense be said to constitute the taxation of the profits of the foreign subsidiary.[230] I agree with this view: the received dividends must, from a juridical viewpoint, be regarded as the profits of the receiving parent, even if they stem from the activity of the subsidiary. The answer may be different from an economic point of view, but that is another matter.

As regards the United Kingdom CFC legislation, the Special Commissioners did not think that it would apply to the appellant's foreign subsidiaries.[231]

4.6.5 Decision by the Special Commissioners

The Special Commissioners decided that the United Kingdom legislation on group relief did not constitute any discrimination or other infringement of the freedom of establishment. As previously noted the Special Commissioners considered two types of comparisons in order to test whether the legislation at issue was in breach of the freedom of establishment. Regarding the first comparison they decided that the United Kingdom was not required to accord the same group relief for losses of a United Kingdom subsidiary of the appellant and those of its foreign subsidiaries. The reason was that, according to them, Article 43 of the EC Treaty requires that the establishment in other Member States receive no less favourable treatment than the treatment granted nationals of that Member State. The United Kingdom, however, could treat the different forms of establishments in different ways.

As regards the second comparison, the Special Commissioners considered that the United Kingdom was free to treat the appellant's resident subsidiaries and foreign subsidiaries in different ways. The reason was that the foreign subsidiaries were outside of the scope of United Kingdom tax jurisdiction. Therefore, resident and foreign subsidiaries were not in objectively comparable situations. The application of different rules to situations that are not objectively comparable did not amount to a prohibited discrimination in the meaning of the EC Treaty, in their view.

Moreover, the United Kingdom legislation at issue did not constitute a non-discriminatory restriction in the view of the Special Commissioners. The reason was that the appellant's failure to gain loss relief on behalf of the foreign subsidiaries was based on the allocation of fiscal jurisdiction among Member States as well as the failure among the Member States to agree on measures for harmonisation of their tax systems in this respect.

230 *Marks & Spencer*, decision by the Special Commissioners, para. 103.

231 *Marks & Spencer*, decision by the Special Commissioners, para. 102.

Finally, even if there was a breach of the freedom of establishment, it could be justified according to the ground of fiscal coherence, which I will deal with in Chapter 5.

4.6.6 Concluding Remarks

The *Marks & Spencer* case is important for several reasons. The primary reason is that it targets the question of what constitutes discrimination. In its recent case-law, the European Court of Justice has refrained from applying a "discrimination analysis". Instead, the Court has stopped at a stage where it has been able to establish that the measure at issue constitutes an "obstacle" or a "barrier" to a fundamental freedom. There may be several reasons for this approach from the Court. In my view, a major reason may be the uncertainty regarding the application of the rule-of-reason doctrine in relation to indirect and also, perhaps, direct discrimination. If the Court followed its analysis to the end and established that in fact there were a case of discrimination, it would also have to deal with the controversial question of the rule-of-reason doctrine in relation to discriminatory measures. By applying the "obstacle" or "barrier" approach, the Court avoids that difficult issue. Because the *Marks & Spencer* case has been referred to the European Court of Justice for a preliminary ruling, the Court may be forced by the thorough discrimination analysis of the Special Commissioners to be more explicit on this issue. A second reason why the *Marks & Spencer* case is important is that it puts into question the extension of the freedom of establishment in the home state.

The comparisons considered by the Special Commissioners are complex. The reason is of course that they are formulated so as to target the application of the United Kingdom group relief system in different situations, all involving at least a parent and its subsidiary. If one only wishes to contrast the treatment of cross-border losses one can target the core problem of the *Marks & Spencer* case with less complex comparisons. I will formulate two such comparisons (in chronological order, comparisons three and four in relation to the two previous ones).

However, before I discuss those comparisons, I would like to raise a principle matter on what constitutes objectively comparable situations. Marks & Spencer had established foreign subsidiaries, and regarding the losses of those foreign subsidiaries, it could not make use of the United Kingdom system for group relief. In order to establish whether there is a case of discrimination, is it really the case that the only objectively comparable situation is that of another *cross-border* establishment? I doubt whether it is. Is not the internal market supposed to mean the abolishment of obstacles to the fundamental freedoms raised in order to deter cross-border movements? I believe it is. In my view, the establishment of a United Kingdom subsidiary is objectively comparable to that in another Member State. In this specific case an important feature is that even if the losses of the foreign subsidiaries could be taken into account in the United Kingdom, the profits of the foreign subsidiaries could not be taken into account from a juridical point of view. I will return to that issue in the subsequent analysis of two alternative comparisons where I will try to focus the main issues of the *Marks & Spencer* case.

The third comparison is between the following two situations. In the first situation there is a United Kingdom company with a foreign branch. The United Kingdom company wishes to deduct the losses of its foreign branch. In the second situation there is a United Kingdom company with a foreign subsidiary. The United Kingdom parent company wishes to deduct the losses of the foreign subsidiary. It is possible to deduct the foreign branch losses in the first situation. The reason is that the branch forms part of the company and that the United Kingdom applies the credit system. According to the credit system both branch profits and branch losses are taken into account in the United Kingdom. In the second situation the group relief system will not permit the foreign losses to be deducted by the United Kingdom parent company. The reason is that the subsidiary is foreign.

The major difference in this comparison lies in the fact that both the losses and profits of the foreign branch will be taken into account when determining the taxable income of the United Kingdom company. In contrast, neither the losses nor the profits of the foreign subsidiary will be taken into account when determining the taxable income of the United Kingdom parent company; as regards profits, at least not from a juridical point of view. From an economic point of view profits may be distributed from the subsidiary in the form of dividends, but from a juridical point of view those dividends are part of the profit of the parent company. In my view, these two situations are not objectively comparable. The difference is based on the fact that the foreign branch forms part of the United Kingdom company, whereas the foreign subsidiary is an independent legal entity from the United Kingdom parent company.

The fourth comparison is between the following two situations. In the first situation there is a United Kingdom parent company with a subsidiary also resident in the United Kingdom. In the second situation there is a United Kingdom parent company with a foreign subsidiary. The subsidiaries in both situations have losses that the parent company wishes to deduct according to the system of group relief. However, it is only in the first situation that losses will be deducted, because the group relief system will not accept losses from a foreign subsidiary.

From the perspective of the United Kingdom company standing between the two investment alternatives – either establish a subsidiary in the United Kingdom or in another Member State – I consider those two alternatives to be objectively comparable. The freedom of establishment is intended to abolish obstacles to cross-border establishments. The fact that United Kingdom tax law will not grant the benefit of group relief in respect of the losses of a foreign subsidiary must have a detrimental effect on those United Kingdom companies intending to establish subsidiaries with risky business activities in other Member States. The alternatives may, however, not be objectively comparable from the perspective of the United Kingdom government: even if the group relief is extended to foreign subsidiaries, the profits of those subsidiaries will not be taxable in the United Kingdom.

4.7 Border-line Cases between Home and Host State Restrictions

4.7.1 Introduction

For several reasons case C-307/97 *Saint-Gobain* will be dealt with separately in this section. The first reason is reflected in the title of this section: "Border-line Cases between Home and Host State Restrictions". In some other cases dealt with in this study, there have been more or less obvious signs that, in fact, the case could be viewed from the perspective of both the home state and the host state. In other words, the cases have had inbound and outbound implications. One such case, C-330/91 *Commerzbank*, dealt with the United Kingdom branch of a German company, where the branch had income from a third country, the United States. Another example of such a case previously discussed in this study are the joined cases C-397/98 and C-410/98 *Metallgesellschaft and Others*. The primary question of the last-mentioned case dealt with the United Kingdom subsidiaries of German parent companies, and the taxation of dividends distributed from subsidiaries to non-resident parent companies as compared with parent companies resident in the United Kingdom. In general, the *Metallgesellschaft* case can be viewed both from the perspective of the German company establishing a subsidiary in the United Kingdom and from the perspective of the United Kingdom subsidiary distributing dividends to its German parent company. Moreover, both the *Saint-Gobain* case and the *Commerzbank* case are examples of a well-known feature of international tax law labelled "triangular situations".[232]

A second reason why I have decided to treat the *Saint-Gobain* case separately is because it is one of the cases regarding the freedom of establishment where the question of access to treaty benefits of the host state is highlighted. This issue has been addressed in other cases, for example in the previously mentioned *Commerzbank* case. However, the issue is emphasised and further developed in the *Saint-Gobain* case. The importance of tax treaties in the *Saint-Gobain* case has also made it possible to consider the question of whether Community law includes a requirement for a Most-Favoured-Nation ("MFN") treatment of non-residents. I will briefly discuss that issue in the subsequent concluding remarks.

[232] I will not specifically deal with the problem of triangular situations in this study.

4.7.2 Case C-307/97 *Saint-Gobain* (21 September 1999)

Case C-307/97 *Saint-Gobain*[233] dealt with the compatibility of German tax legislation with the freedom of establishment. The basic facts of the underlying case were the following.

Saint-Gobain SA was a French company and Saint-Gobain ZN (*Zweigniederlassung Deutschland*) was the German branch (permanent establishment) of the French company. Saint-Gobain SA was incorporated in France, where it also had its seat. According to German tax law, Saint-Gobain ZN was treated as a permanent establishment of the French company in Germany and was only subject to limited tax liability there. The German tax authorities (*Finanzamt*) denied Saint-Gobain ZN certain tax concessions relating to the taxation of dividends from shares in foreign companies. The reason for the denial was that the tax benefits were restricted to companies subject to unlimited tax liability in Germany.[234]

Saint-Gobain SA owned, through its German branch, shares in a US company (Certain Teed Corporation and with a holding of 10.2 per cent) and in two German companies ("Grünzweig" and "Gevetex" with a holding of 98.63 per cent and 99 per cent respectively). Saint-Gobain ZN and the two companies Grünzweig and Gevetex had concluded an agreement (*Organvertrag*) according to which they were treated in Germany as a group of companies (*Organschaft*). A result of this was that the profits and losses of the minor companies, Grünzweig and Gevetex, were incorporated in the profits and losses of the dominant company, Saint-Gobain ZN, which was accepted according to German law even though Saint-Gobain ZN only was the permanent establishment of a foreign company. The profits of Grünzweig and Gevetex according to the *Organvertrag* were transferred to Saint-Gobain ZN, including group dividends distributed by foreign subsidiaries.[235]

According to German legislation and tax treaty law there were tax concessions in Germany applying to foreign dividends received that had already been taxed abroad. However, these tax concessions were only granted to German companies – resident for tax purposes – and not permanent establishments in Germany of foreign companies, which is why Saint-Gobain ZN was liable to tax in Germany on the received dividends. Consequently, the German tax authorities, the *Finanzamt*, denied Saint-Gobain SA the tax concessions in question. It was the denial of three different types of tax concessions that Saint-Gobain ZN challenged.

[233] Case C-307/97 *Compagnie de Saint-Gobain, Zweigniederlassung Deutschland v. Finanzamt Aachen-Innenstadt.*

[234] Case C-307/97 *Saint-Gobain*, para. 8.

[235] Case C-307/97 *Saint-Gobain*, para. 9-11.

First, Saint-Gobain ZN was denied the exemption from German corporation tax on dividends received from the United States and Switzerland. The reason was that the treaties limited the benefit of tax exemption to German companies and companies subject to unlimited tax liability in Germany. The tax concession was a form of international group relief (*internationales Schachtelprivileg*) which provided the exemption from tax on profits distributed between a parent company and its subsidiary.[236] Secondly, German tax law denied Saint-Gobain ZN the benefit of a tax credit for the foreign tax paid by the foreign subsidiaries and sub-subsidiaries of Saint-Gobain SA in the countries in which they were established. German law restricted the benefit of this indirect tax credit to companies that were subject to an unlimited tax liability in Germany.[237] Thirdly, Saint-Gobain ZN was denied an exemption from capital tax on its shareholding in the US company. The reason was that Saint-Gobain ZN was not a German company.[238]

Saint-Gobain ZN challenged this German legislation that denied it the tax concessions mentioned at the German *Finanzgericht Köln*.[239] Subsequently, the question of the compatibility of the legislation at issue with the freedom of establishment was referred to the European Court of Justice for a preliminary ruling.

Regarding all three tax issues the European Court of Justice made a comparison of the tax consequences for, on the one hand, a company having its seat outside of Germany, and, on the other hand, a company having its seat in Germany. It should be noted that according to German legislation a company with its seat in Germany was resident there for tax purposes and subject to an unlimited tax liability in Germany. The Court formulated the questions referred to it in the following way. Did Articles 43 and 48 (ex Articles 52 and 58) of the EC Treaty preclude the exclusion of a permanent establishment in Germany of a company limited by shares having its seat in another Member State ("the non-resident company") from the following tax benefits granted to companies which had their seat in Germany?[240]

(1) An exemption from corporation tax for dividends received from companies established in non-member countries (Switzerland and the United States), so called "corporation tax relief for international groups", provided for by a tax treaty with a non-member country.

[236] Case C-307/97 *Saint-Gobain*, para. 16.

[237] Case C-307/97 *Saint-Gobain*, para. 19

[238] Case C-307/97 *Saint-Gobain*, para. 21-22.

[239] Case C-307/97 *Saint-Gobain*, para. 15.

[240] Case C-307/97 *Saint-Gobain*, para. 32.

(2) The crediting against German corporation tax of the corporation tax levied in a state other than Germany on the profits of a subsidiary established there, provided for by German legislation.

(3) An exemption from capital tax for shareholdings in companies established in non-member countries (capital tax relief for international groups), also provided for by German legislation.[241]

To begin with, the European Court of Justice once again confirmed that it is the corporate seat, in the meaning of companies or firms formed in accordance with the laws of a Member State and having their registered office, central administration or principal place of business within the Community, that serves to determine, like the nationality for individuals, their connection to a Member State's legal order.[242]

Furthermore, the European Court of Justice found that the refusal to grant tax concessions to permanent establishments of foreign companies in Germany "… makes it less attractive for those companies to have inter-corporate holdings through German branches, since under German law and double-taxation treaties the tax concessions in question can only be granted to German subsidiaries which, as legal persons, are subject to unlimited tax liability which thus restricts the freedom to choose the most appropriate legal form for the pursuit of activities in another Member State which the second sentence of the first paragraph of Article 52 [present Article 43] of the Treaty expressly confers on economic operators."[243]

Thus, the Court explicitly recognised the right of a national of a Member State to choose the legal form of a secondary establishment in another Member State. The German legislation made a difference in taxation of resident companies and permanent establishments of non-resident companies.

In addition, the Court declared that "[t]he difference in treatment to which branches of non-resident companies are subject in comparison with resident companies as well as the restriction of the freedom to choose the form of secondary establishment must be regarded as constituting a single composite infringement of Articles 52 and 58 [present Articles 43 and 48] of the Treaty".[244]

---

[241] It was not completely clear whether this rule in fact contained a difference in treatment between companies with their corporate seat in Germany and companies not having their seat there. Cf. case C-307/97 *Saint-Gobain*, para. 41.

[242] Case C-307/97 *Saint-Gobain*, para. 34 and 35. In support of this interpretation, the ECJ also referred to case C-264/96 *ICI*, para. 20 (with further references).

[243] Case C-307/97 *Saint-Gobain*, para. 42.

[244] Case C-307/97 *Saint-Gobain*, para. 43.

I regard this as unusually strong language from the European Court of Justice compared to other recent cases: even if the general term "restriction" is used, there is reason to consider the difference in treatment to constitute a case of direct discrimination. If one compares this case with the *Avoir fiscal* case and the *Royal Bank of Scotland* case, previously discussed in this chapter, which generally are considered to be cases of direct discrimination, the *Saint-Gobain* case could also be considered as one of direct discrimination. I will return to this issue below, because the Court also considered an argument from the German government that the situation of a resident company and a non-resident company as a general rule are not comparable: permanent establishments of non-resident companies and resident companies are in situations that are *objectively different*. The reason was plainly that non-resident companies were only subject to limited tax liability in Germany, whereas companies resident in Germany were subject to unlimited tax liability.[245] In its response to the question of comparability the Court narrowed the actual elements of the comparison to consist of (i) the liability to tax on dividend receipts in Germany from shares in foreign subsidiaries and sub-subsidiaries, and (ii) the taxation of the holding of such shares.

When comparing, on the one hand, companies not resident in Germany but having a permanent establishment there, and, on the other hand, companies resident in Germany, the Court considered the different situations to be comparable.[246] In addition, the Court considered the taxation to be even more comparable since the difference in treatment applied only as regards the grant of the tax concessions, which allowed resident companies either to deduct from corporation tax the amount of foreign tax levied on dividends from shareholdings in foreign companies, or to exclude those dividends or holdings from their income and from their global assets which were taxable in Germany.[247] As regarded non-residents with a permanent establishment in Germany, the non-residents were denied those concessions, making them liable to tax in Germany on the foreign dividends and shareholdings at issue.[248]

The comparison made between the branches of a non-resident and a resident company was accordingly not made on the basis of the overall tax situation of the two, but on specific items of income and the taxation of them. This is a more limited comparison than the comparison elaborated by the European Court of Justice in relation to the taxation of individuals according to the previously discussed Schumacker doctrine.

245 Case C-307/97 *Saint-Gobain*, para. 45-46.

246 Case C-307/97 *Saint-Gobain*, para. 47.

247 Case C-307/97 *Saint-Gobain*, para. 48.

248 Cf. Terra and Wattel, *European Tax Law*, 3rd ed., Kluwer Law International, London/The Hague/New York, 2001, p. 89.

The final conclusion of the Court was that Articles 43 and 48 of the Treaty precluded the exclusion of a permanent establishment in Germany from the tax concessions that were at issue in this case. All grounds of justification advanced were rejected by the Court, among them that there would be a reduction in tax revenue in Germany, that counter-balancing advantages were granted to permanent establishments in Germany of non-resident companies and that tax benefits at issue were granted according to bilateral tax treaties.

I now return to the question whether the *Saint-Gobain* case and the German legislation at issue in fact constituted direct discrimination, or if it in fact (also) included home state restrictions.[249] This case includes two cross-border elements, and therefore I would like to categorise it as a cross-border case between discrimination and home state restrictions. First, the case concerns the establishment in Germany of a French company through a branch. Secondly, it also contains the holding of the French company through the German branch of shares in companies with their seat in both Germany and the United States. There are several basic similarities with the *Avoir fiscal* case and the *Royal Bank of Scotland* case. Both of those cases dealt with the taxation in the host state of non-resident companies established through branches (permanent establishments). The non-resident companies were not granted the same tax treatment as companies with their corporate seat, which are resident companies for tax purposes, in the host state. I consider such difference in treatment on the basis of the corporate seat to constitute direct discrimination, which is supported by the previously mentioned case-law of the Court.

However, the German branch, Saint-Gobain ZN, was in fact receiving dividends from other countries. Could not the denial of German tax concessions on those foreign dividends from companies in other Member States, be considered as a home state restriction of the freedom of establishment? The fact that only companies resident in Germany would receive the tax concessions in question could be regarded as a restriction on the right to choose the legal form of a secondary establishment. There is reason to believe that the Court in fact considered the German difference in treatment from this two-fold perspective. As previously noted the Court stated: "The difference in treatment to which branches of non-resident companies are subject in comparison with resident companies *as well as the restriction* of the freedom to choose the form of secondary establishment must be regarded as constituting a single composite infringement of Article [43] and [48] of the Treaty."[250] It may even be argued that the

[249] Cf. Pistone, *The Impact of Community Law on Tax Treaties*, Kluwer Law International, The Hague/London/New York, 2002, p. 148.

[250] Case C-307/97 *Saint-Gobain*, para. 43 (emphasis added). Confer also AG Mischo's opinion in this case, for example para. 102-104.

Court tries to "amalgamate" the discrimination approach and the restriction approach into one united prohibition against breaches of the freedom of establishment. I am, however, less certain regarding that conclusion.

The relation between Community law and tax treaty law was also addressed by the Court and the subject of considerable attention. The relation was addressed due to a suggested ground of justification put forward by the German and Swedish governments. I will deal with this in Chapter 5 of this study, but will here discuss it from one specific angle: does Community law prescribe a most-favoured-nation treatment of non-nationals?

As a ground of justification the German government advanced that the conclusion of bilateral tax treaties with third countries does not come within the sphere of Community competence. Furthermore, there had been no Community harmonisation in this area, a reference to the failure to reach a multilateral tax treaty within the European Community. The German government also considered that an eventual extension to non-residents of tax concession according to tax treaties with third countries would not be compatible with the division of competences under Community law.[251]

The Swedish government took an even narrower approach than the German government: tax treaties are based on the principle of reciprocity and that balance would be disturbed if the benefit of the treaties were extended to companies established in Member States not party to the treaties.[252]

The Court recognised that there had been no unifying measures adopted in the area of tax treaty law, even though such an objective was set out in Article 293 (ex Article 220) of the EC Treaty. Moreover the Court noted that, in the framework of bilateral tax treaties, Member States were to determine the connecting factors when allocating taxing powers according to the tax treaty.[253] The Court continued: "As far as the exercise of the power of taxation so allocated is concerned, the Member States nevertheless may not disregard Community rules."[254] In addition, the Court repeated its well-known position that even if direct taxation is a matter for the Member States, they must nevertheless exercise their taxation powers in consistency with Community law. In my view, one has to interpret this statement in this context in the way that tax treaties of the Member States must be drafted in a way that is consistent with Community law. In line with that view, the Court declared: "In the case of a double-taxation treaty concluded between a Member State and a non-member country, *the national treatment principle* requires

251 Case C-307/97 *Saint-Gobain*, para. 54.

252 Case C-307/97 *Saint-Gobain*, para. 55.

253 Case C-307/97 *Saint-Gobain*, para. 56 with reference to Case C-336/96 *Gilly*, para. 24 and 30.

254 Case C-307/97 *Saint-Gobain*, para. 57.

the Member State which is party to the treaty to grant to permanent establishments of non-resident companies the advantages provided for by that that treaty on the same condition as those which apply to resident companies."[255]

In the view of the Court, the balance and the reciprocity of Germany's tax treaties with Switzerland and the United States "could not be called into question" by a unilateral extension on the part of Germany, because such an extension "would not in any way affect the rights of the non-member countries which are parties to the treaties and would not impose any new obligation on them".[256]

From a strict tax treaty law perspective, this outcome is almost sensational. As a general rule, tax treaties are limited only to residents of the contracting states. The result of the *Saint-Gobain* case is, however, that tax treaties concluded by Member States with third countries also include non-resident branches, established in a signatory Member State, of companies resident in other Member States.

4.7.3 Conclusion

4.7.3.1 General Conclusions from the Saint-Gobain *Case*

In my view the *Saint-Gobain* case can be regarded from different perspectives: both from the perspective of Germany as the host state of the branch established by the French company, and from the perspective of the home state of the French branch making investments in third countries. The differentiating criterion of the German legislation at issue was the seat of a company: if a company had its seat in Germany it was granted specific tax concessions, however, if a company had its seat in another Member State and it was merely established in Germany through a branch, those tax concessions were not granted. The nationality of a company is determined according to its "seat", in the meaning of registered office, central administration or principal place of business. Even if it is not articulated by the European Court of Justice there is reason to believe that the German legislation at issue constituted direct discrimination. However, this did not hinder the Court from considering the rule-of-reason doctrine and discussing a number of justifications in the public interest.

The case also highlights the question of neutrality between the establishment of different legal forms, notably the establishment of either a subsidiary or a branch. The Court declared in the *Saint-Gobain* case that the difference in treatment between branches of non-residents and resident companies also constituted "a restriction to choose the

[255] Case C-307/97 *Saint-Gobain*, para. 58 (emphasis added).

[256] Case C-307/97 *Saint-Gobain*, para. 59.

form of secondary establishment". This is clear language, and from this I would infer that there should be neutrality in the host state between different forms of secondary establishments. However, whether this neutrality would include a requirement for the exact same treatment of branches of non-residents compared with resident companies is not necessarily the outcome. There are still major differences between establishing a branch and establishing a subsidiary, one being that the first group is subject to limited tax liability and the other to unlimited tax liability.[257]

4.7.3.2 Tax Treaties and Community Law

Article 293 of the EC Treaty prescribes that the Member States shall so far as is necessary enter into negotiations with each other in order to secure the abolition of double taxation within the Community. This provision has long been interpreted as an impetus for Member States to conclude a multilateral tax treaty between the Member States of the Community. No such treaty has been signed. In the *Saint-Gobain* case the Court declared that the Member States remain competent to determine the criteria for taxation of income and wealth in order to eliminate double taxation. In the *Saint-Gobain* case the Court also refers to the previous *Gilly* case, where the Court declared that Member States are, within the framework of bilateral tax treaties, free to determine the connecting factors for the purposes of allocating powers of taxation between them. In my view, it seems clear that the Court recognises that in general, the area of tax treaty law is an area of competence of the separate Member States, at least until the time when joint Community measures have been taken according to Article 293 of the EC Treaty.[258]

But even so, the Court also declared that Member States are obliged according to "the national treatment principle" to grant permanent establishments of non-resident companies such advantages of their tax treaties as are granted to resident companies.

[257] Kostense formulates the general question following from the *Saint-Gobain* case as whether the case means that the host state should grant the branch full resident status or should only grant the same treaty benefits as resident companies are entitled to. This is a way of formulating the question of the extension of neutrality of legal form in the host state. Kostense's answer is that the case is more a sign of evolution, and that it provides a solution similar to the one contained in Article 24 para. 4 of the OECD MC. Kostense, "The Saint-Gobain Case and the Application of Tax Treaties. Evolution or Revolution?", *EC Tax Review*, 2000, pp. 220-232, at p. 220.

[258] One should in this context also note Article 307 of the EC Treaty. It stipulates that rights and obligations from agreements, such as tax treaties, concluded before 1 January 1958 or, for acceding states, before the date of their accession, between one or more of Member States on the one hand, and one or more third countries on the other, shall not be affected by the EC Treaty. If such treaties are incompatible, Member States shall take steps to eliminate those incompatibilities. Moreover, Member States shall in such cases adopt a "common attitude".

In the view of the Court this unilateral extension of the tax treaties of Member States does not inflict upon the balance and reciprocity of Member States' tax treaties. I do not completely agree with this view. When a state enters a bilateral tax treaty with another state the traditional approach is that only residents of the treaty-concluding states are covered by the scope of the treaty. Nearly all Member States of the European Union are Members of the OECD, and they all follow the OECD MC rather closely when concluding tax treaties.[259] Article 1 of the OECD MC limits the personal scope of the treaty to residents of the contracting states. Residence in the sense of a tax treaty based on the OECD MC refers, according to Article 4 of the MC, to such persons which are subject to an unlimited tax liability of a treaty-concluding state. When the European Court of Justice in the *Saint-Gobain* case places non-residents (branches) equally with residents (subsidiaries) regarding tax treaty benefits, there is a deviation from the general approach taken in tax treaties based on the OECD MC.

A result of this approach by the European Court of Justice is that when Member States conclude bilateral tax treaties, they should be aware that the benefits of their residents also include non-resident branches of companies having their seat in other Member States. It is not unimaginable that this widened personal scope on the side of Member States of the European Union may have implications on the willingness to conclude tax treaties, from the perspective of Member States.

Offermanns and Romano pose the question of whether the *Saint-Gobain* decision forces Member States to renegotiate their tax treaties.[260] In their opinion that is not the case because the decision does not in itself inflict upon the tax treaties at issue. I agree in principle with that view. However, Member States are obliged to confer tax concessions such as the ones at issue in the *Saint-Gobain* case to branches of non-resident companies. In view of that, one could legitimately ask if it would not be preferable to a multilateral tax treaty for the European Union or, at least a Model Convention for the European Union where these problems are dealt with.[261] Pistone has developed an interesting proposal for a Model Tax Convention for the European Community (EC MC). Member States would be obliged to follow the model because

[259] The OECD MC is, of course, only a model treaty. Member States of the OECD are at liberty to deviate from the MC. The broad outline of the MC and its general structure is, however, followed by the Member States.

[260] Offermanns and Romano, "Treaty Benefits for Permanent Establishments: the Saint-Gobain Case", *Bulletin*, 2000, pp. 180-189, at p. 188.

[261] Pistone lists six different proposed solutions to solve conflicts between tax treaties and Community law: (i) the application of a most-favoured-nation doctrine, (ii) the purely international solution, (iii) the purely Community law solution based on Article 94 of the EC Treaty, (iv) strengthening source taxation, (v) a multilateral tax treaty, and (vi) a model tax convention. The two last methods would be based on Article 293 of the EC Treaty. Pistone, *The Impact of Community Law on Tax Treaties*, Kluwer Law International, The Hague/London/New York, 2002, p. 207.

it would be a treaty based on Article 293 of the EC Treaty.[262] This makes it different from the OECD MC, which has a more "loose legal binding effect". I will here only discuss Article 1 of Pistone's proposal, which reads:

> "1. This convention shall apply to persons who are residents of one or both of the Contracting States.
>
> 2. However, also EU nationals who are residents of other Member States may claim the benefits of this treaty, provided that they prove an effective link with at least one Contracting State."

Paragraph 1 is identical with the corresponding provision in the OECD MC. As can be seen, the OECD MC is focused on protecting the benefits of residents of the contracting states. However, paragraph 2 extends the personal scope to nationals of the European Union who also are residents of Member States other than the treaty-concluding states. This is a way of manifesting by treaty the results of the European Court of Justice in the *Saint-Gobain* case. In my view this method would make the position of the Court more easily understandable to the ordinary taxpayer, compared with relying on case-law from the Court.

Finally, I will also briefly discuss the existence of a most-favoured-nation obligation in Community law regarding tax treaty benefits. The notion of most-favoured-nation treatment stems from international trade law. The idea is that by applying a most-favoured-nation treatment, trade barriers on the transfer of goods will be eliminated: there will at least be the same tariff applicable for goods irrespective from where they originate. There are examples of most-favoured-nation clauses in tax treaties, for example in the treaty between Sweden and Namibia and in the treaty between Austria and Germany.

Rädler has argued in favour of the existence of a most-favoured-nation requirement within the Community in the field of direct taxation. In support thereof, he has advanced case C-279/93 *Schumacker* and the court hearings of that case.[263] The case dealt with the taxation in Germany of the non-resident Mr Schumacker. He was a national of and resident in Belgium. Because he was non-resident in Germany he was not subject to certain benefits according to German law. At the court hearings it was asked (i) whether there would have been a case if Mr Schumacker had instead lived in the Netherlands because of more favourable treatment according to the tax treaty between the Netherlands and Germany. Furthermore it was asked (ii) if the first question was answered in the affirmative would that have been acceptable under Community law?

---

[262] Pistone, *op. cit.*, p. 237.

[263] Rädler, "Most-favoured-nation Clause in European Tax Law?", *EC Tax Review*, 1995, pp. 66-67.

According to Rädler the first question seemed to be answered in the affirmative by everybody, whereas the second question was "evaded". In his view, a most-favoured-nation requirement would favour a "level playing field" and capital import neutrality. In principle, I agree with Rädler's conclusion that such a level playing field would be the outcome. However, in my view there is so far no ground to consider that Community law stipulates a most-favoured-nation treatment, at least not from the case-law of the European Court of Justice.

Van Thiel recognises that there is no explicit ruling of the European Court of Justice that confirms the existence of a most-favoured-nation requirement.[264] However, he assumes that the EC Treaty does prescribe an "intra-Community most-favoured-nation-treatment" in the meaning that a Member State (or the Community) may not treat a product or a national of another Member State worse than a product or a national of a third Member State. Moreover, Van Thiel considers there to be a Member State/third country most-favoured-nation treatment, in the meaning that a Member State (or the Community) may not treat a product or a national of a third country better than the product or national of another Member State. In support of this position Van Thiel advocates, for example, that the internal market requires it and that the wording of the EC Treaty allows it.

I agree that there is no support in the case-law of the Court of the existence of a most-favoured-nation requirement, even if the Court was in the periphery of the issue in the *Saint-Gobain* case. Moreover, one must recognise the administrative difficulties Member States would encounter if the Court were to rule that there is a most-favoured-nation requirement in their tax treaty law.[265] Soon there may be decisions by the European Court of Justice on the existence of a most-favoured-nation requirement. One pending case is the "D case", and has been referred by a Dutch court. D was resident in Germany where he also was a national. He had property in the Netherlands. One issue of the case was whether D could invoke a more beneficial treatment following from the Netherlands-Belgium tax treaty as compared with the Netherlands-Germany treaty. At the time of writing there is no AG opinion.[266]

264 Van Thiel, *EU Case Law on Income Tax*, IBFD, Amsterdam, 2001, pp. 92-102.

265 Kemmeren finds support in Case C-204/90 *Bachmann* (para. 26) that the Court in fact already has rejected the existence of a most-favoured-nation requirement. The Court's declaration seems to concern Member States' sovereignty in the area of tax treaties and direct taxation. Kemmeren, "The Termination of the 'Most Favoured Nation Clause' Dispute in Tax Treaty Law and the Necessity of a Euro Model Tax Convention", *EC Tax Review*, 1997, pp. 146-152, at p. 148.

266 On this case (C-376/03) see Van der Linde, "Some Thoughts on Most-favoured-nation Treatment within the European Community Legal Order in Pursuance of the D Case", *EC Tax Review*, 2004, pp. 10-17.

5 Grounds of Justification: Accepted and Rejected Grounds

5.1 Introduction

In my analysis of the case-law of the European Court of Justice, I have identified several grounds of justification that, in principle, have been accepted by the Court. It should be underlined that the Court only accepts these grounds *in principle*. As will become clear, the Court rarely considers them applicable in its case-law. The grounds of justification accepted in principle that I have identified regarding the freedom of establishment in the field of direct taxation are (i) the prevention of abuse, (ii) the preservation of fiscal coherence and (iii) the effectiveness of fiscal supervision. There is also a fourth category which I have labelled potential grounds of justification. Basically, it only contains one ground, namely the fiscal principle of territoriality.

The following analysis in *section 5.2* will focus on these grounds of justification. In respect of each ground I will refer to and discuss relevant cases from the European Court of Justice. Occasionally, there will be references made to cases on matters of direct taxation but in relation to other fundamental freedoms. The reason for that is simply that the ground of justification I am dealing with has been elaborated upon in those cases and that the result is important also in the present context of the freedom of establishment.

Furthermore, the Court has also rejected a number of grounds which have been invoked in cases on direct taxation and the freedom of establishment. I will deal with such rejected grounds in *section 5.3*.

5.2 Grounds of Justification Accepted in Principle

5.2.1 Prevention of Abuse and Related Grounds

5.2.1.1 Introduction

It is necessary to begin with some terminological remarks. I have chosen to label this ground of justification "the prevention of abuse". With that term I refer to a situation where national law serves the purpose of preventing the abuse of law: such legislation may constitute an accepted ground of justification, which will be discussed subsequently. As will become clear, it is my view that the European Court of Justice only recognises a narrow scope of measures directly aimed at preventing abuse as a ground of justification according to the rule-of-reason doctrine.

The terminology is not clear on what constitutes abuse of tax law, neither in the case-law of the European Court of Justice, nor in national legislation. There are several terms that may be interpreted differently, and that, in the view of some, even overlap. Such related terms are "tax evasion" and "tax avoidance", which could in general be described in the following way. Tax avoidance includes schemes for tax planning that have as a main purpose to avoid taxation, be it in the home state or the host state. In principle, tax avoidance is tolerated by states, even if they may enact legislation trying to prevent tax avoidance schemes. Such legislative measures are often designed to target specific measures of tax avoidance. Tax evasion, however, is generally considered unacceptable by most states: it includes measures that are in obvious breach of national tax legislation and its objectives.

Rädler has pointed out the problems arising from the fact that Community law applies diverging terminology on what constitutes abuse of tax law and the simultaneous application of terms such as tax evasion and tax avoidance.[1] Moreover, Rädler identifies the use of terms with different meanings in the English and German language versions of Community acts such as the Merger Directive.[2]

It should be underlined that it is not possible to give any generally accepted definition of the discussed terms. The meaning changes, for example, between different jurisdictions, as well as over time. However, in the following case-law analysis I will try to unveil how the European Court of Justice understands these terms in its case-law.

In the case-law analysis of this chapter I will deal with the question of whether in national legislation, primarily in the field of direct taxation, law rules which constitute a hindrance to the freedom of establishment may be justified on the ground that they prevent the abuse of law. I will not specifically deal with the question of abuse of the fundamental freedom at issue, even if I touch upon this issue in relation to a few cases. A further remark on terminology is required. In its case-law the European Court of Justice has applied a variety of terms. When analysing the cases, I will refer to the different terms used by the Court.

---

1 Rädler, "Do National Anti-abuse Clauses Distort the Internal Market", *European Taxation*, 1994, pp. 311-313. See also Farmer, "National Anti-abuse Clauses and Distortion of the Single Market: Comments on Prof. Rädler's Article", *European Taxation*, 1994, p. 314. Farmer advocates a Community law understanding of what constitutes abuse.

2 Rädler, *ibid.*

Prevention of tax avoidance as a ground of justification was advanced already in Case 270/83 *Avoir fiscal*. The Court stated that this ground could not be accepted "in this context".[3] Furthermore, the Court declared that the Treaty did not permit any derogation from the fundamental principle of freedom of establishment on such a ground. One may wonder whether the Court is referring to the fact that there are no express limitations or exceptions to the freedom of establishment on the ground of preventing tax avoidance, or that the case-law based on the rule-of-reason doctrine does not permit the prevention of tax avoidance as a ground of justification. It is difficult to say for certain what the Court actually meant.

In the foregoing, the analysis of the ground of prevention of abuse in Chapter 3 was introduced with case C-212/97 *Centros*, which is a case on company law instead of tax law. In that case the European Court of Justice made the interesting declaration of principle that national courts may, case by case, take into account – on the basis of objective evidence – abuse or fraudulent conduct on the part of the persons concerned, with a view to denying them the benefits of Community law which they seek to rely upon.[4] Three tax cases will here be analysed more in detail: case C-264/96 *ICI*, case C-324/00 *Lankhorst-Hohorst* and case C-436/00 *X and Y*. In the concluding discussion several other cases from the European Court of Justice, including the *Centros* case, will be discussed as well. It should be underlined that all these cases, with the exception of *Centros*, have been thoroughly discussed in Chapter 4 regarding, for example, the basic underlying facts and the compatibility of the national measure with the freedom of establishment.

5.2.1.2 Case C-264/96 ICI *(16 July 1998)*

As previously referred, case C-264/96 *ICI* dealt with the possibility of cross-border loss compensation within a group of companies. United Kingdom tax legislation denied inter-corporate loss compensation if the United Kingdom holding company did not have as its main purpose wholly or mainly holding shares in subsidiaries established in the United Kingdom. The European Court of Justice came to the conclusion that the legislation at issue was in breach of the freedom of establishment.[5] The next step for the Court was to consider whether any grounds of justification applied. The first ground of justification that the Court considered was whether the prevention of tax avoidance could justify the national piece of legislation at issue.[6]

---

3 Case 270/83 *Avoir fiscal*, para. 25.

4 Case C-212/97 *Centros*, para. 25.

5 Case C-264/96 *ICI*, para. 23.

6 Case C-264/96 *ICI*, para. 25-27.

The United Kingdom government argued that this law provision was designed to reduce the risk of tax avoidance, where members of a consortium channelled the deficits of non-resident subsidiaries to a subsidiary resident in the United Kingdom. Furthermore, the profit would, according to that government, accrue to non-resident subsidiaries, and thereby not be subject to tax in the United Kingdom. The purpose of the United Kingdom was to prohibit such tax avoidance.[7]

In response to the ground of preventing tax avoidance, the European Court of Justice "noted" that the piece of legislation at issue did not have the specific purpose of preventing "wholly artificial arrangements" that had been set up to circumvent its tax legislation.[8] Instead the legislation in question applied generally to all situations in which the majority of a group's subsidiaries are established, for whatever reason, outside the United Kingdom.[9]

Furthermore the Court explained: "However, the establishment of a company outside the United Kingdom does not, of itself, necessarily entail tax avoidance, since that company will in any event be subject to the tax legislation of the State of establishment." From this statement one could possibly infer that the establishment in a "pure" tax haven could constitute "tax avoidance" because the established company would not be subject to any actual taxation in such a state. Moreover, the Court uses the term "tax avoidance" and one may in that respect wonder whether the Court considers national measures directly applicable against tax avoidance schemes as legitimate grounds of justification. No definite answer is given by the Court. Even so, one should not make too much of the fact that the Court uses such a vague term as "tax avoidance".

To conclude, what would in the view of the Court characterise a law provision that has the purpose of preventing abuse? First, it must have the specific purpose of preventing wholly artificial arrangements. Secondly, the purpose of the targeted transaction should be to circumvent the tax legislation of the state where the company had its corporate seat, the United Kingdom in this specific case. Thirdly, it may not generally apply to all situations in which the majority of a group's subsidiaries are established, for whatever reason, outside the United Kingdom.

I agree in principle with the position expressed by the Court. If cross-border transactions in themselves were considered as an indication of tax avoidance, the Community

---

7 Case C-264/96 *ICI*, para. 25.

8 In the English language version of case C-264/96 *ICI*, the ECJ uses the expression "the risk of tax avoidance" (para. 26). The equivalent expression in the French language version is "*le risque d'évasion fiscale*". In general one could say that "tax avoidance" refers to measures which are "unacceptable" or "illegitimate", while "tax evasion" refers to measures which are "unlawful". On this issue cf. the *International Tax Glossary* published by the IBFD, Larking (ed.), 4th ed., Amsterdam, 2001.

9 Case C-264/96 *ICI*, para. 26.

economy and the internal market would be in danger, to say the least. Moreover, the risk of charges being transferred to other states than the United Kingdom was entirely dependent on whether or not all subsidiaries were in fact resident in the United Kingdom.

5.2.1.3 Case C-436/00 **X and Y** *(21 November 2002)*

Case C-436/00 *X and Y* dealt with Swedish legislation on the inter-corporate transfer of assets (shares) made below market value. According to specific conditions, such transfers could be made without any immediate tax consequences in the form of capital gains taxation. However, Swedish legislation did not allow such a preferential transfer if it was made to a foreign legal person in which the transferor or his kin directly or indirectly had a holding, referred to as "type A share transfer".

Moreover, the benefit of tax deferral on such inter-corporate transfers of shares was denied if the transfer was made to a Swedish limited company in which a foreign legal person either directly or indirectly had a holding (type B share transfer). Transfers to other Swedish legal persons than the previously mentioned could, however, be made with the benefit of tax deferral (type C share transfer).

The National Tax Board (*Riksskatteverket*) advanced that the difference in treatment between, on the one hand, A and B type share transfers and, on the other hand, type C share transfers, was justified by reasons of overriding public interest such as the prevention of tax avoidance and the effectiveness of fiscal supervision.[10]

Even if the Swedish National Tax Board actually used the term "tax avoidance",[11] the European Court of Justice did not when it referred to the reasoning of the Board. Instead, the Court referred to "tax evasion".[12] This lack of consequence by the Court in its use of terminology strengthens my view that one should not put too much weight to the choice of term made by the Court. The national provision sought to ensure both the effective taxation of the capital gains concerned and the effectiveness of the supervision of such taxation. When the Court considered whether the provision at issue was aimed at preventing tax avoidance, it seemed to follow the same reasoning as in the previously discussed *ICI* case. It stated that the provision "... is not specifically designed to exclude from a tax advantage purely artificial schemes designed to circumvent Swedish tax law ...".[13] In the view of the Court the provision applied in

10 Case C-436/00 *X and Y*, para. 48. Other grounds of justification were also advanced, but they will not be addressed here.

11 Case C-436/00 *X and Y*, para. 48.

12 Case C-436/00 *X and Y*, para. 60.

13 Case C-436/00 *X and Y*, para. 61.

general to any situation where, for whatever reason, a transfer at undervalue is made to a company established in another Member State, or, for that matter, to a branch in Sweden of such a foreign company.[14]

In line with this reasoning, the Court declared that tax evasion or tax fraud could not be deduced from the fact that the transferee company or its parent company is resident in another Member State.[15] Finally, the Court in its reasoning on the prevention of tax evasion as a ground of justification considered whether the disputed measure was proportionate or not.[16]

According to the Court, the objective of the Swedish measure was to ensure that the transferor was actually taxed in Sweden on gains from the transfer of shares. That was especially the case if the transfer was made before his definite transfer abroad. The Court concluded that the national measure in question was not capable of achieving that objective in either A or B type transfers. Accordingly, this piece of legislation did not meet the test of proportionality.

In my view it is somewhat superfluous to discuss the proportionality of the measure when the Court already has decided that it goes way beyond the mere prevention of tax evasion. Perhaps it is an expression of methodological thoroughness by the Court.

5.2.1.4 Case C-324/00 **Lankhorst-Hohorst** *(12 December 2002)*

In case C-324/00 *Lankhorst-Hohorst* the European Court of Justice came to the conclusion that German legislation on thin capitalisation was in breach of the freedom of establishment. The Court continued with the question whether the restriction was justified by "pressing reasons of public interest",[17] and among other grounds the one of preventing abuse.

The German, Danish and United Kingdom governments, as well as the Commission claimed that the German legislation at issue was intended to combat *tax evasion* in the form of "thin capitalisation" or "hidden equity capitalisation".[18] In general, thin capitalisation means that a company is "thinly" capitalised by having a high proportion of debt capital in relation to its equity capital. There would in effect be a shifting of

---

14 *Ibid.*

15 Case C-436/00 *X and Y*, para. 62. In support, the ECJ refers to case C-478/98, *Commission v. Belgium*, para. 45 (*ibid.*).

16 Case C-436/00 *X and Y*, para. 63.

17 Case C-324/00 *Lankhorst-Hohorst*, para. 33.

18 Case C-324/00 *Lankhorst-Hohorst*, para. 34.

taxable income from the borrower to the lender of capital, because the borrower would have the right to make a deduction for interest paid. In principle the interest would be taxable for the lender in its state of residence, but typically the taxation would be minimal in comparison with the taxation in the state of the borrower. The borrower and the lender would normally be related, that is corporate entities of the same group of companies.

The European Court of Justice stated that it is "settled law that reduction in tax revenue does not constitute an overriding reason in the public interest which may justify a measure which is in principle contrary to a fundamental freedom".[19] In relation to the ground of preventing tax evasion, the Court stated:

> "As regards more specifically the justification based on the risk of tax evasion, it is important to note that the legislation at issue here does not have the specific purpose of preventing wholly artificial arrangements, designed to circumvent German tax legislation, from attracting a tax benefit, but applies generally to any situation in which the parent company has its seat, for whatever reason, outside the Federal Republic of Germany. Such a situation does not, of itself, entail a risk of tax evasion, since such a company will in any event be subject to the tax legislation of the State in which it is established ..."[20]

There are several important conclusions to be drawn from this statement when trying to find the answer the question: how should a piece of legislation be designed in order to meet the requirements of prohibiting abuse, and as such serve as a ground of justification for the restriction such a measure otherwise would constitute?

First, the anti-abuse legislation should be targeted against "tax evasion". Secondly, to constitute acceptable anti-abuse legislation according to the Court, the legislation has to have the specific purpose of preventing "wholly artificial arrangements" and to be designed to circumvent the (tax) legislation of the Member State in question. The German legislation in question applied, according to the Court, to any situation in which the parent company had its seat, for whatever reason, outside of Germany.

Thirdly, the European Court of Justice considered that the situation in question did not in itself include a risk for tax evasion, because the company would in any event be subject to the tax legislation in the state where it was established. The reasoning of the Court in the present case is well in line with the reasoning in the previously mentioned *ICI* case.

---

[19] Case C-324/00 *Lankhorst-Hohorst*, para. 36. For support of this opinion the ECJ referred to case C-264/96 *ICI*, para. 28; case C-35/98 *Verkooijen*, para. 59; joined cases C-397/98 and C-410/98 *Metallgesellschaft and Others*, para. 59; and case C-307/97 *Saint-Gobain*, para. 51.

[20] Case C-324/00 *Lankhorst-Hohorst*, para. 37. In support the ECJ referred to case C-264/96 *ICI*, para. 26.

The European Court of Justice made a further remark, which differs from the previous abstract reasoning. The Court noted that in the specific case no abuse had been proved, and one has to assume that the reason in the Court's view is that the loan was made in order to assist Lankhorst-Hohorst by reducing the interest burden from its bank loan. Moreover, Lankhorst-Hohorst made a loss in the financial years of 1996, 1997 and 1998, and its loss exceeded the interest paid to LT BV.[21] In my view it is interesting to note that the Court considers the actual circumstances of the underlying case before the national court, even if its ruling in principle only deals with the compatibility of national law with Community law.

5.2.1.5 Conclusion

In this section on the prevention of abuse as a ground of justification in the public interest, the Court's reasoning in three cases has been examined: C-264/96 *ICI*, C-436/00 *X and Y*, and C-324/00 *Lankhorst-Hohorst*. In Chapter 3, the prevention of tax evasion as a ground of justification was introduced with an analysis of case C-212/97 *Centros*.

The Court's reasoning is fairly consistent in all four cases. For a national measure to constitute a measure aimed at preventing abuse one could conclude that the following conditions have to be met. First, it has to have the specific purpose of preventing wholly artificial arrangements. Secondly, it may not apply in general so that it covers both arrangements with solid business reasons and arrangements with the mere purpose of abuse. Thirdly, the mere establishment in another Member State is not enough to constitute abuse. Finally, even if a national measure aims at preventing abuse and meets the previously mentioned conditions, the measure must also comply with the test of proportionality. The measure must be proportionate in relation to the objective it is intended to accomplish.

The terminology of the Court is, however, not consistent when addressing this ground of justification. In my view, tax law abuse, as generally understood in international tax law, would be the most suitable one.

There are several non-tax law cases from the European Court of Justice where the compatibility of national anti-abuse legislation with fundamental freedoms has been the issue. One notable case is C-221/89 *Factortame*.[22] The case dealt with a particular piece of anti-abuse legislation in the United Kingdom and its compatibility with the freedom of establishment. The law provision in question stipulated specific require-

21 Case C-324/00 *Lankhorst-Hohorst*, para. 38.

22 Case C-221/89 *The Queen v. Secretary of State for Transport, ex parte Factortame Ltd and Others.*

ments for foreign fishing vessels to acquire registration in the United Kingdom and the right to use that Member State's fishing quotas. These requirements included for example that the legal and beneficial owners and the managers of the vessels had to be nationals of the United Kingdom. Regarding companies, at least 75 per cent had to be owned by nationals of the United Kingdom and at least 75 per cent had to be managed by directors from the United Kingdom. The objective of this provision was the prevention of "quota shopping": the use of a Member State's fishing quota by nationals of another Member State. The Court decided that the national requirements at issue were discriminatory. However, the Court explained that the freedom of establishment involves the actual pursuit of an economic activity through a fixed establishment in another Member State for an indefinite period of time. In the view of the Court, the requirements of the United Kingdom legislation at issue coincided with the actual concept of establishment; it followed that the freedom of establishment could not preclude such requirements. Pinto interprets the *Factortame* case as stipulating that a requirement for the freedom of establishment to apply is integration by the legal or natural persons with a Member State's economic activity through a fixed establishment for an indefinite period.[23] Moreover, Pinto contrasts the *Factortame* case with the *Centros* case, and targets the seemingly diverging approaches taken by the Court in those two cases.[24] As may be recalled, the Court in the *Centros* case accepted the registration of a company in the United Kingdom, even if it was apparent that no substantial business activity was to be conducted in that Member State, but instead in Denmark. The purpose of the registration in the United Kingdom was to avoid the more burdensome company registration in Denmark, where the founders also were nationals. In my view, it is difficult to reconcile these two decisions with each other. I think one has to bear in mind that they deal with different areas of law: one case deals with fishing quotas and the other with the registration of companies. The potential abuse objective is no doubt in common to both cases, but the areas of law are different. Fishing quotas have long been a politically sensitive area, albeit not to the same degree as the area of company law. In my view it is easier to reconcile the *Centros* decision with the tax law cases discussed in this study. In the *Centros* case the Court took the same narrow approach to the meaning of abuse as in the tax law cases.

The purpose of preventing abuse is of course not unknown in other areas of Community law dealing with matters of direct taxation. Both the Parent/Subsidiary Directive[25]

---

[23] Pinto, *Tax Competition and EU Law*, Kluwer Law International, The Hague/London/New York, 2003, p. 308.

[24] *Ibid.*, p. 308 *et seq.*

[25] Council Directive of 23 July 1990 on the common system of taxation applicable in the case of parent companies and subsidiaries of different Member States (90/435/EEC).

and the Merger Directive[26] contain anti-abuse provisions. An interesting case on this matter is C-28/95 *Leur-Bloem*. The case dealt with the interpretation of Article 11 of the Merger Directive.[27] According to this Article a Member State may deny the benefits of the Directive where the transaction, or "operation", in question has "as its principal objective or as one of its principal objectives tax evasion or tax avoidance".

It is interesting to note that a possible presumption on what constitutes tax evasion or tax avoidance is spelled out in Article 11 of the Merger Directive. It is stipulated that if an operation is not carried out for valid economic reasons, such as the restructuring or rationalisation of the activities of the companies participating in the operation, that may constitute a presumption that the operation has tax evasion or tax avoidance as its principal objective or as one of its principal objectives.[28]

The clarification in the Merger Directive of what constitutes tax evasion or tax avoidance coincides reasonably well with how the Court has defined it in the previously analysed tax cases. Perhaps the Court's case-law definition is somewhat narrower than the one contained in the Merger Directive. The Court relates to "wholly artificial arrangements", whereas the Directive in its definition also targets operations that have tax evasion or tax avoidance "as one of its principal objectives".

5.2.2 Fiscal Coherence

5.2.2.1 Introduction

Fiscal coherence as a ground of justification has been considered by the European Court of Justice in a large number of cases on direct taxation. Most notably, the Court considered and accepted this ground of justification in two parallel cases decided in 1992, cases C-204/90 *Bachmann* and C-300/90 *Commission v. Belgium*. Both cases concerned measures of indirect discrimination on the free movement of workers.

---

[26] Council Directive of 23 July 1990 on the common system of taxation applicable to mergers, divisions, transfers of assets and exchange of shares concerning companies of different Member States (90/434/EEC).

[27] The case was an internal one, but the ECJ still decided to interpret the Directive although it did not formally apply.

[28] Whether the establishment of a company in a state that applies a low tax rate amounts to abuse in the meaning of the ECJ, should certainly be answered in the negative. First, this isolated circumstance does not in itself meet the requirements of the tax law cases analysed in this section. Secondly, in case C-294/97 *Eurowings* the ECJ declared in relation to an Irish company (enjoying "Shannon privileges") which was subject to a company tax rate of 10 per cent (para. 21) that "[a]ny tax advantage resulting for providers of services from the low taxation to which they are subject in the Member State in which they are established cannot be used by another Member State to justify less favourable treatment in tax matters given to recipients of services in the latter State ..." (para. 44).

In this section there will be an analysis of cases where the Court has discussed the meaning of fiscal coherence. A limited number of these will be dealt with more thoroughly, while others will be referred to in less detail in a concluding subsection. Some cases where fiscal coherence has been advanced will be left out from the discussion, the reason being partly the lack of space, partly that they do not contribute in any substantial way to my analysis.

As previously noted, the Court accepted the ground of fiscal coherence in the *Bachmann* case. The *Bachmann* case has been thoroughly introduced in Chapter 3. However, the basic facts of that seminal case are these. Mr Bachmann was a German national employed in Belgium. In Belgium he tried to deduct insurance contributions which he had paid in Germany. He had taken out the insurance prior to his arrival in Belgium. However, he was denied the deductions in Belgium. Belgian law only accepted the deduction of contributions paid to Belgian insurance institutions. The Court recognised that it would normally be the case for foreign nationals who were employed in another Member State to have taken out such insurances in the Member State where they were nationals. In view of that, this Belgian law provision would seemingly, in the view of the European Court of Justice, constitute indirect discrimination. The Court did, however, accept this difference in treatment. According to Belgian tax law, pensions, annuities, capital sums or surrender values under life assurance contracts were tax exempt on the condition that there had been no deduction of contributions paid. Mr Bachmann was denied deduction in Belgium of his contributions, because the sums payable on the insurances would not be taxable in Belgium. The Court considered that Belgium was entitled to deny the deduction because that denial served to preserve the coherence of the Belgian tax system. It should be observed that the Court declared that the coherence of a tax (fiscal) system was something for the Member States themselves to define.[29]

The Court's decision in the *Bachmann* case and the application of fiscal coherence as an accepted ground has been subject to severe criticism. An early critic was Knobbe-Keuk,[30] and it seems that the Court in its subsequent case-law had adhered to her comments. It is unquestionable that the Court has limited the applicability of fiscal coherence as a ground of justification. Knobbe-Keuk considered the meaning of "coherence" as vague and arcane.[31] She posed the question of whether coherence means that

[29] Case C-204/90 *Bachmann*, para. 23.

[30] Knobbe-Keuk, "Restrictions on the Fundamental Freedoms Enshrined in the EC Treaty by Discriminatory Tax Provisions – Ban and Justification", *EC Tax Review*, 1994, pp. 74-85.

[31] See also Reimer, "Die Auswirkung der Grundfreiheiten auf das Ertragssteuerrecht der Bundesrepublik Deutschland – Eine Bestandsaufnahme", in *Grundfreiheiten im Steuerrecht der EU-Staaten*, Lehner (ed.), Münchener Schriften zum Internationalen Steuerrecht, Heft 23, pp. 39-101, at pp. 60-62.

deductions in computing income or corporate tax are possible only if the payments are taxable in the same state. If that was a correct interpretation, that would according to Knobbe-Keuk mean that, for example, a cost deduction for interest payments could not be made in one state when the payment was made to a non-resident who would not be taxable in that state on the interest received.[32] In addition, according to Knobbe-Keuk, the *Bachmann* decision was built on a misunderstanding. She understood the Court to have considered that the tax on the capital sums payable under the insurance contracts at issue was owed by the insurance company.[33] Knobbe-Keuk advanced three more inconsistencies of the *Bachmann* case.[34] First, the coherence of the Belgian tax system was set aside by Belgium itself in its tax treaties with all Member States, including Germany where Mr Bachmann was a resident. According to the Belgian tax treaties, Belgium waived the right to tax private pensions, including the life insurance contracts of the specific case, when the beneficiary of the capital sums payable was resident in the other signatory state. In the *Bachmann* case it was accordingly Germany that would tax the capital sums, according to the Belgium-Germany tax treaty. Secondly, the Belgian tax code contained a different treatment of insurance payments made by French, Dutch and Luxembourg employees working in Belgium for branches or subsidiaries of companies resident in those states. In such cases cost deduction for the insurance payments was allowed under Belgian law. Thirdly, even if the contributions were made to a Belgian insurance company – and the contributions accordingly would have been deductible also for Mr Bachmann – there was no guarantee that the capital sums in fact would be taxable in Belgium. According to tax treaty law it would be the state of residence (according to the tax treaty) that would exclusively tax the capital sums paid: either according to Article 18 of the OECD MC if paid as an annuity, or according to Article 21 if paid as capital instead of pension.

Returning to what the Court actually stated in the *Bachmann* case, two declarations are especially important. First, the Court declared that a principle such as coherence of the fiscal system was for the Member States to formulate. Secondly, if a state allows the deduction of insurance contributions paid in another state, it should also be able to tax the sums payable from those insurances.

In *sections 5.2.2.2* to *5.2.2.5* there will be an analysis in chronological order of the following cases: case C-107/94 *Asscher*, case C-251/98 *Baars*, joined cases C-397/98 and C-410/98 *Metallgesellschaft and Others*, case C-436/00 *X and Y*. Additional cases will be discussed in *section 5.2.2.6*.

32 Knobbe-Keuk, "Restrictions on the Fundamental Freedoms Enshrined in the EC Treaty by Discriminatory Tax Provisions – Ban and Justification", *EC Tax Review*, 1994, pp. 74-85, at p. 80.

33 *Ibid.*

34 Knobbe-Keuk, *op. cit.*, p. 80-81.

It should be noted that the facts of each case were subject to a more thorough analysis in Chapter 4. In order to facilitate the understanding of the Court's reasoning on the ground of fiscal coherence, there will be minor recapitulations of some vital facts of the referred cases. The purpose is to provide basic facts of the cases without forcing the reader to return to a previous section. General conclusions on fiscal coherence will be presented in *section 5.2.2.7*.[35]

5.2.2.2 Case C-107/94 **Asscher** *(27 June 1996)*

The basic underlying facts of case C-107/94 *Asscher* were the following. Mr Asscher was a Dutch national, and he had for some time been resident for tax purposes in Belgium. He was not resident in the Netherlands. However, he conducted business as a self-employed person in both Belgium and the Netherlands. In the Netherlands, Mr Asscher's income was taxed at a rate that was higher than it would have been if he had been resident in that state. Moreover, the social security regime which Mr Asscher was subject to was also of importance when analysing the reasoning of the Court in relation to fiscal coherence. He was covered by the Dutch social security system until he moved to Belgium in 1986. From that time, he was not obliged to make any contributions to the Dutch system, and only made contributions to the equivalent Belgian system. It is important to note that the Dutch tax legislation at issue contained a reference to the Dutch system of social insurance schemes. A non-resident taxpayer was treated as a resident taxpayer if at least 90 per cent of his worldwide income was taxable in the Netherlands. That condition was deemed to be fulfilled if he was subject in the Netherlands to contributions according to the national compulsory social insurance scheme.[36] For such taxpayers the tax rate would be 13 per cent instead of 25 per cent.

The Court came to the conclusion that the Dutch legislation at issue constituted indirect discrimination on the freedom of establishment. One of the grounds of justification which the Court considered was the ground of fiscal coherence.

The Court began its analysis by recapitulating what it considered to be the main conclusions from the 1992 cases, *Bachmann* and *Commission v. Belgium*. The Court emphasised the following. In those two cases there was a direct link between the right to deduct contributions and the taxation of sums payable from insurance contracts.[37] In this case the Court considered whether there was a direct link between, on the one

[35] Fiscal coherence was also discussed in case C-136/00 *Danner*. In that case the implications of a tax treaty were considered by the ECJ, cf. section 3.9.3.3.

[36] Case C-107/94 *Asscher*, para. 6.

[37] Case C-107/94 *Asscher*, para. 58.

hand, the application of a higher tax rate on income of some residents who received less than 90 per cent of their worldwide income in the Netherlands, and, on the other hand, the fact that no social security contributions were levied on the income of such non-resident individuals from sources of income in the Netherlands.[38] The Court did not accept any correspondence between these two factors: the application of a higher tax rate in the Netherlands did not provide any social security contribution.[39] Accordingly, there was no direct link between the higher tax rate and the levy of social security contributions.

Moreover, the Court also considered the fact that there is a binding system in Community law on the application of social security schemes regarding employed persons and their families moving within the Community.[40] In relation to this the Court referred to its own case-law where it had decided that Member States do not have the right to determine the extent to which their own legislation or that of another Member State applies where they are obliged to comply with Community law, such as the previously mentioned Council Regulation on social security schemes.[41] Consequently, in the view of the Court, this Community measure in the area of social security schemes precluded a Member State from using a tax measure to make up for the situation that the taxpayer was neither insured with, nor had to pay contributions to the social security scheme.[42]

5.2.2.3 Case C-251/98 **Baars** *(13 April 2000)*

Case C-251/98 *Baars* concerned Dutch wealth taxation and the freedom of establishment. More favourable wealth taxation on shares was only available on shares constituting a substantial holding in companies established in the Netherlands and not in other states. The Dutch government held that the need to preserve the fiscal coherence of the Dutch tax system justified the difference in treatment.[43]

---

38 Case C-107/94 *Asscher*, para. 59.

39 Case C-107/94 *Asscher*, para. 60.

40 Council Regulation (EEC) No 1408/71 of 14 June 1971 on the application of social security schemes to employed persons and their families moving within the Community (OJ, English Special Edition 1971 (II), p. 416).

41 Case C-107/94 *Asscher*, para. 60. In support of this view, the ECJ refers (*ibid.*) to Case 276/81 *Sociale Verzekeringsbank v. Kuijpers* [1982] ECR 3027, para. 14; Case 302/84 *Ten Holder v. Nieuwe Algemene Bedrijfsvereniging* [1986] ECR 1821, para. 21; Case 60/85 *Luijten v. Raad van Arbeid* [1986] ECR 2365, para. 14.

42 Case C-107/94 *Asscher*, para. 61.

43 Case C-251/98 *Baars*, para. 33-35.

According to the Dutch government the exemption from wealth tax on shares in Dutch companies was designed to mitigate the effects of economic double taxation that would arise when a company's profit was subject to corporation tax and the assets invested by the shareholder in that company were subject to wealth tax. The Dutch government advanced that there was coherence between, on the one hand, the taxation of the profits of Dutch companies, and, on the other hand, the exemption from wealth taxation on shares in Dutch companies.[44]

The following reasoning was behind the difference in treatment, according to the Dutch government.[45] Only assets invested in shares in companies established in the Netherlands were exempt from wealth tax, and the reason was that only the profits of such companies was subject to company taxation in the Netherlands. Consequently, assets in the form of shares in foreign companies should be subject to wealth tax in the Netherlands, because the profit of such companies was not subject to tax in the Netherlands. The exemption from wealth tax in the Netherlands had the objective of mitigating the effects of double taxation of company profits, a double taxation consisting of, first, the taxation of company profits, and, secondly, the wealth taxation of shares.

The European Court of Justice did not accept this line of reasoning, and gave a short and clear explanation why.[46] First, there was no double taxation of profits, not even in economic terms.[47] The case concerned wealth taxation. The question whether or not the company made any profit did not affect the liability to pay tax. Secondly, in the *Bachmann* and *Commission v. Belgium* cases there was a direct link between the deductibility of pension and life assurance contributions and the taxation of the sums payable from such contracts. There was no such direct link in the *Baars* case.[48] The reason was that the case concerned two separate taxes levied on different taxpayers. It was, consequently, irrelevant whether shareholders in Dutch companies were granted an exemption from wealth taxation and that companies established in states other than the Netherlands were exempt from corporate taxation in the Netherlands.

[44] Case C-251/98 *Baars*, para. 34.

[45] Case C-251/98 *Baars*, para. 35.

[46] The ECJ once more referred to its decision in case C-204/90 *Bachmann*, and case C-300/90 *Commission v. Belgium*, where the ground of fiscal coherence was accepted, see case C-251/98 *Baars*, para. 37.

[47] Case C-251/98 *Baars*, para. 39.

[48] Case C-215/98, *Baars*, para. 40.

5.2.2.4. Joined Cases C-397/98 and C-410/98 **Metallgesellschaft and Others** *(8 March 2001)*

The judgment of the European Court of Justice in the joined cases C-397/98 and C-410/98 *Metallgesellschaft and Others*, including the facts of the underlying case, has been thoroughly discussed in Chapter 4. Some facts are, however, necessary to recapitulate.

The United Kingdom applied an imputation system to mitigate the effects of double taxation. A company resident in the United Kingdom which paid dividends to its shareholders had to pay Advance Corporation Tax (ACT). The ACT was not a withholding tax, rather it was a corporation tax borne by the company distributing the dividends. The dividend-distributing company could later set the ACT off against its Mainstream Corporation Tax (MCT). Moreover, a company resident in the United Kingdom was not liable to pay corporation tax on dividends it received from another company resident in the United Kingdom. Any distribution of dividends subject to ACT made by one resident company to another resulted in a tax credit for the company receiving the dividends. That tax credit was equal to the ACT paid by the distributing company on those dividends.

United Kingdom tax legislation also contained a system called "group income election". According to this system, if two companies were resident in the United Kingdom, and one company held at least 51 per cent of the other, they could opt for a group income election. The consequence was that the subsidiary did not have to pay ACT on the dividends it paid to its parent company, which would anyway have been deductible against the MCT later on.[49] However, the group income election system only applied to companies resident in the United Kingdom.

In the present case, the United Kingdom subsidiaries of German parent companies could not opt for the group income election because the parent companies were resident in Germany. Consequently, the subsidiary of a parent company resident in Germany had a cash-flow disadvantage in comparison to the situation where the parent company had been resident in the United Kingdom. This difference in treatment was in breach of the freedom of establishment, according to the Court.

One of the grounds of justification which the Court considered was whether the national legislation at issue could be justified by the need to preserve the coherence of the United Kingdom tax system. The United Kingdom government argued in the following way. The objective of the ACT was to mitigate economic double taxation by exempting corporate shareholders from corporation tax on dividends that they received from

[49] It was, however, possible for the subsidiary to give a specific notice that it did not want the election system to apply on a specific distribution of dividends.

resident subsidiaries: the exemption was offset by the ACT levied on the payment of dividends by subsidiaries to their parent companies.[50] The United Kingdom government held that there was a direct link between the exemption from corporation tax granted a parent company in respect of dividends received from its resident subsidiary and the liability of that subsidiary to ACT when it paid those dividends.[51] The condition that ACT was paid by the dividend distributing company was essential to ensure that, before the granting of any exemption on dividends received, the distributing company was taxed on those dividends. In an internal United Kingdom situation where group income election applied, the ACT would be paid by the parent company when it in turn distributed dividends to its shareholders, and that would offset the exemption of the parent company from corporation tax on the dividends that the parent company had received.[52] If ACT were not payable on dividends from United Kingdom subsidiaries to non-resident parent companies, the consequence would be that the tax exemption granted to the parent company would not be offset by any tax levied on the payment of those dividends. According to the United Kingdom government, that would be incompatible with the coherence of the fiscal system of the United Kingdom.[53]

However, the European Court of Justice did not accept to that reasoning. The Court began by declaring that in the *Bachmann* case and the *Commission v. Belgium* case, there was a direct link between, on the one hand, the deductibility of contributions paid for old-age and life assurance contracts, and, on the other hand, the taxation of sums payable from such contracts. That link had to be preserved in order to guarantee the coherence of the fiscal system.

The Court reasoned that in the present case there was no such direct link between, on the one hand, the refusal to exempt subsidiaries in the United Kingdom of non-resident parent companies from ACT under the group income election regime and, on the other hand, the fact that parent companies which had their corporate seat in another Member State and received dividends from their United Kingdom subsidiaries were not liable to corporation tax in the United Kingdom.[54] According to the Court it was irrelevant that the exemption was intended to eliminate double taxation of the profits of subsidiaries in the United Kingdom, if the dividends were subject to a "comparable tax" in the Member State where the parent companies were established.[55]

---

[50] Joined cases C-397/98 and C-410/98 *Metallgesellschaft and Others*, para. 62.

[51] *Ibid.*

[52] Joined cases C-397/98 and C-410/98 *Metallgesellschaft and Others*, para. 64.

[53] Joined cases C-397/98 and C-410/98 *Metallgesellschaft and Others*, para. 65.

[54] Joined cases C-397/98 and C-410/98 *Metallgesellschaft and Others*, para. 69.

[55] Joined cases C-397/98 and C-410/98 *Metallgesellschaft and Others*, para. 70.

But what if the taxation in the Member State where the parent company was established were not "comparable"? The Court did not explicitly answer that question. Perhaps one could infer from the judgment that in such a situation the United Kingdom could have been justified by the need to preserve the coherence of the fiscal system. Still, in retrospect it is doubtful that the Court today would have accepted that. Fiscal coherence is not accepted when it comes to the taxation of two different entities, even if it is a parent-subsidiary constellation.

Moreover, the Court noted that the only way in which a non-resident parent company was liable to tax in the United Kingdom in respect of dividends received, was via income tax. That tax liability was, however, linked to the possible grant of tax credits provided for in the applicable tax treaty.[56] Under that tax treaty between the United Kingdom and Germany, parent companies resident in Germany were not liable to income tax in the United Kingdom on dividends from subsidiaries in the United Kingdom. The reason was that the treaty did not provide for the grant of tax credits corresponding to ACT paid by subsidiaries. As a consequence, the Court concluded, the refusal to grant subsidiaries resident in the United Kingdom of parent companies in another Member State like Germany the right to make a group income election, could not be justified on the ground of preserving the coherence of the United Kingdom fiscal system.[57] It seems that this reasoning was enough for the Court to come to the conclusion that fiscal coherence could not justify the national measure at issue. However, the Court also advanced further reasons. It noted that the United Kingdom during the procedures had abolished the system with ACT, and in the view of the Court that "… suggests that its payment [of ACT] was not essential to the proper functioning of the corporation tax system in the United Kingdom".[58] This is a rather odd legal argument. Presumably, it was advanced to support the previous reasoning in the way that it supposedly discloses the objectives of the United Kingdom legislator.

5.2.2.5 Case C-436/00 **X and Y** *(21 November 2002)*

The facts of case C-436/00 *X and Y* have been thoroughly discussed in Chapter 4. The case dealt with Swedish law on the transfer of shares at a value below market value. In a strictly domestic Swedish situation the inter-corporate transfer of shares could be made at a value below market value without any immediate taxation of the difference between market value and transfer value. If the transfer of shares was made to a foreign entity or to a Swedish limited company in which a foreign entity had either a direct

56 Joined cases C-397/98 and C-410/98 *Metallgesellschaft and Others*, para. 71.

57 Joined cases C-397/98 and C-410/98 *Metallgesellschaft and Others*, para. 73.

58 Joined cases C-397/98 and C-410/98 *Metallgesellschaft and Others*, para. 74.

or an indirect holding, the Swedish transferor was denied the benefit of tax deferral and liable to pay Swedish capital gains tax immediately. In contrast, if the transfer was made to a Swedish company the transferor had no immediate liability to pay tax on the amount constituting the undervalue of the transferred assets. In that case the transferor had the benefit of tax deferral.

The Court came to the conclusion that this difference in treatment constituted an infringement of the freedom of establishment. One of the grounds of justification considered was fiscal coherence. Once again, the Court began its reasoning by relating to its decisions in the *Bachmann* and *Commission v. Belgium* cases.[59] The Court repeated that in those cases it considered it important that there was a direct link between the deductibility of contributions and the taxation of sums payable by insurers under pension and life assurance contracts. That link was considered necessary to preserve the coherence of the fiscal system.[60]

Both the Swedish National Tax Board (*Riksskatteverket*) and the Dutch government maintained that the Swedish legislation at issue served to preserve the coherence of the fiscal system. Their reasoning is both adequate and interesting.[61] The National Tax Board focused on the general system for taxing capital gains in Sweden: the granting of the benefit presupposes that the capital gain on which a deferral is granted remains taxable in Sweden.[62]

According to the Dutch government the present case was analogous to the *Bachmann* case, and it reasoned convincingly that both cases concerned a temporary "exemption" offset by subsequent taxation.[63] In the *Bachmann* case, the exemption from taxation consisted of the deduction of insurance contributions offset by the subsequent taxation of insurance payments.[64] In the *X and Y* case, the temporary tax exemption – in the form of deferral of capital gains taxation – would end with the eventual disposal of the shares held by the taxable person in the transferee company.[65] Moreover, in the view of the Dutch government there was a direct link between the temporary exemption and the subsequent taxation: it included the levying of the same tax on the same taxable person but with deferral.[66]

---

59 Case C-436/00 *X and Y*, para. 52.

60 *Ibid.*

61 Opinion of AG Mischo in case C-436/00 *X and Y*, para. 33-41.

62 Opinion of AG Mischo in case C-436/00 *X and Y*, para. 35.

63 Opinion of AG Mischo in case C-436/00 *X and Y*, para. 36.

64 *Ibid.*

65 Opinion of AG Mischo in case C-436/00 *X and Y*, para. 37.

66 Opinion of AG Mischo in case C-436/00 *X and Y*, para. 39.

In the present case there was a circumstance that motivated a different decision from the *Bachmann* and *Commission v. Belgium* cases: the impact of a tax treaty between the Member States in question. According to the Court, the tax treaty between Sweden and Belgium had the following impact. There was no fiscal coherence in relation to any one taxpayer when trying to establish a strict correlation between the deferral of capital gains tax and the final taxation of that gain. In addition the Court declared:

> "Coherence is at another level, namely, the reciprocity of the rules applicable in the Contracting States in terms of the convention on the basis of connecting factors for the purposes of apportioning competence in tax matters. This the Member States remain free to determine in the absence of Community measures, as here …".[67]

The Court focused on two provisions in the tax treaty between Sweden and Belgium: Article 13 (4) and Article 13 (5). Article 13 (4) was identical with the corresponding provision in the OECD MC, while Article 13 (5) was typical for Swedish tax treaty policy.

Article 13 (4) provided that a state taxes all capital gains received by transferors resident in its territory. Moreover, a state does not tax capital gains that are made by transferors resident in the other treaty-concluding state.[68] If Article 13 (4) were applied to the situation in this specific case – that is a situation consisting of the transfer of shares to a foreign legal person – Sweden would not tax the capital gains from the eventual alienation of those shares by the foreign legal person: the state where that person was resident would have the right to tax. Moreover, Article 13 (4) was reciprocal between Sweden and Belgium, the signatory states.

Article 13 (5) dealt specifically with capital gains from the alienation of shares. Article 13 (5) covered the situation of a transfer of shares within the same jurisdiction in which the company in question was resident, and where the transfer was made to nationals of that state. Under those circumstances the state in question lost its right to tax share transfers that took place more than five years after the definite departure of the transferor. After that time, the right to tax would go to the other treaty-concluding state.

One can summarise the tax treaty implications in the following way. According to the treaty, capital gains from the alienation of shares would, as a general rule, be taxable in the state where the person who alienated the shares was resident, which in this specific

[67] Case C-436/00 *X and Y*, para. 53. In support of this view the ECJ referred to, for example, case C-80/94 *Wielockx*, para. 24; and case C-307/97 *Saint-Gobain*, para. 57 (*ibid.*).

[68] Case C-436/00 *X and Y*, para. 54.

case would be Belgium. The argument that Sweden should tax the capital gains in order to preserve fiscal coherence had no bearing when the tax treaty designates the other state to tax those capital gains. In effect, the reciprocal tax treaty had, in the view of the Court, provided a different level for determining fiscal coherence.

Furthermore, the Court declared that the denial of tax deferral of type A and type B share transfers "... is not necessary and proportionate to the objective it pursues ...".[69] In support the Court reasoned that in the *Bachmann* and *Commission v. Belgium* cases, payments were considered likely to escape from any taxation in the state which provided for the advantage. The legislation at issue in the present case rather served the purpose of defending the general tax base.[70] In the view of the Court, the coherence of the fiscal system could be achieved with less restrictive measures.

Finally, I would like to give a few general remarks on this case. First, the case indicates that fiscal coherence is still – in principle – accepted by the Court as a ground of justification. Secondly, it seems that the Court accepts that the national measure in question, at the strict level of national law, serves the purpose of safeguarding fiscal coherence. Thirdly, tax treaties may, on their basis of reciprocity, constitute a breach of the comparison at the national level which forms the ground for the evaluation of whether the national measure serves the purpose of preserving fiscal coherence or not. Fourthly, even if the tax treaty between Sweden and Belgium constituted such a breach in the evaluation of fiscal coherence of the national measure, the Court anyway discussed whether the national measure was proportionate or not. Finally, however, one should of course note that the Court did not accept fiscal coherence as a ground of justification in this case, as it has not done since the *Bachmann* case.

5.2.2.6 Other Cases on Fiscal Coherence

There is an important case from the European Court of Justice where the relationship between the preservation of fiscal coherence and tax treaty law. The case is C-80/94 *Wielockx* and it concerned Mr Wielockx, a Belgian national who was also resident in Belgium. He received his entire income in the Netherlands, where he also was liable to tax. In the Netherlands he wished to deduct contributions to a pension reserve, which he was, however, denied. According to Dutch law it was because Mr Wielockx was non-resident in the Netherlands that he was not granted the right to deduct the contributions. This difference in treatment was discriminatory according to the rule on freedom of establishment. The next step was whether it could be justified or not.

69 Case C-436/00 *X and Y*, para. 57.

70 Case C-436/00 *X and Y*, para. 58.

The Dutch government advanced that it could be justified by the need to preserve the coherence of the fiscal system.

The Dutch government claimed that the discrimination was justified by the "principle of fiscal cohesion" as elaborated in case C-204/90 *Bachmann*:[71] there must be a correlation between the sums deducted from the taxable income and the sums subject to tax. According to the tax treaty between the Netherlands and Belgium, the pensions paid would not be taxed in the Netherlands and as a symmetrical consequence Dutch legislation did not permit the deduction of contributions to the pension schemes.

However, the tax treaty between Belgium and the Netherlands was reciprocal in this relation to residents of those two states and the Court emphasised that it followed the OECD MC.[72] Persons from both states were taxed in their state of residence irrespective of where the contributions had been paid. The European Court of Justice concluded: "Fiscal cohesion has not therefore been established in relation to one and the same person by a strict correlation between the deductibility of contributions and the taxation of pensions but is shifted to another level, that of the reciprocity of the rules applicable in the Contracting States."[73] The Court considered that the tax treaty secured fiscal coherence and that the maintaining of such coherence could not be invoked in order to justify the refusal of deduction for pension scheme contributions in this case.[74] It should be noted that the Court referred to Article 18 of the OECD MC of 1977 which stipulated that pensions and similar remunerations should be taxable in the state of residence only.[75]

The *Wielockx* case is important because it was the first in a series of cases where the Court has distinguished the *Bachmann* case and denied the application of the ground of fiscal coherence, because a tax treaty shifts the basis for deciding coherence to another level than the national level: the tax treaty level.

Also in case C-324/00 *Lankhorst-Hohorst* the European Court of Justice discussed whether the ground of fiscal coherence could justify the infringement that the German thin capitalisation rules caused on the freedom of establishment.[76] The German and United Kingdom governments submitted that the thin capitalisation rule at issue was

---

71 Case C-80/94 *Wielockx*, para. 23.

72 Case C-80/94 *Wielockx*, para. 24.

73 *Ibid.*

74 *Ibid.*

75 Case C-80/94 *Wielockx*, para. 8. Furthermore, the ECJ noted that Article 14 of the Netherlands-Belgium tax treaty in addition provided that the source state could tax profit and income if there was a permanent establishment there (para. 9).

76 The underlying facts of case C-324/00 *Lankhorst-Hohorst* are discussed in Chapter 4.

in accordance with the arm's length principle, which is an internationally recognised principle manifested in, for example, Article 9 of the OECD MC.[77] The arm's length principle would mean that the conditions by which capital is borrowed must be compared with the conditions on which the company could have obtained such a loan from a third party. The Court concluded that the conditions in the *Bachmann* and *Commission v. Belgium* cases were not relevant in this case. The Court underlined that in those two cases there was, regarding one and the same person, a direct link between the deductibility of pension and life assurance contributions and the taxation of sums received under those contracts.[78] According to the European Court of Justice, there was no such direct link in the *Lankhorst-Hohorst* case. The German thin capitalisation rule had the consequence that the (German) subsidiary of a non-resident parent company suffered less favourable tax treatment, and the German government had not pointed to any tax advantage to offset such a treatment.[79]

Fiscal coherence as a ground of justification was also discussed in the *Marks & Spencer* case. It should be repeated that the Special Commissioners did not consider the United Kingdom tax law to be either discriminatory or to constitute a non-discriminatory restriction. Even so, fiscal coherence was subject to analysis. The Special Commissioners found that there was a direct link between the group relief granted for losses incurred by a surrendering company and the taxation of profits by the claimant company.[80] Moreover, there was a direct link between the withholding of group relief regarding losses incurred by the surrendering company and the exclusion ("exoneration") from taxation of eventual profits made by that company – the residence state of Marks & Spencer does not have any taxing power over French subsidiaries.[81] There is, however, a major problem with this elegant reasoning on fiscal coherence: the coherence relates to the taxation of two separate entities. The case-law of the European Court of Justice clearly states that coherence must be established regarding one and the same taxpayer. This problem was also acknowledged by the Special Commissioners.[82] In my view it makes the ground of fiscal coherence inapplicable to the *Marks & Spencer* case. If the Court were to accept fiscal coherence in the *Marks & Spencer* case it would have to abolish the requirement that it only applies regarding one taxpayer.

77 Case C-324/00 *Lankhorst-Hohorst*, para. 39.

78 Case C-324/00 *Lankhorst-Hohorst*, para. 42.

79 *Ibid.*

80 *Marks & Spencer*, decision by the Special Commissioners, para. 111.

81 *Ibid.*

82 *Marks & Spencer*, decision by the Special Commissioners, para. 112.

5.2.2.7 Conclusion

The preservation of fiscal coherence was accepted by the European Court of Justice as a ground of justification in two seminal cases: case C-204/90 *Bachmann* and case C-300/90 *Commission v. Belgium*. The *Bachmann* case concerned a German national, Mr Bachmann, who was resident for tax purposes in Belgium, but was denied the right to deduct pension contributions in that state. The Belgian government justified the denial with the reasoning that in Belgian law there was a connection between the deductibility of contributions and the liability to tax of sums payable by the insurers under pension and life assurance contracts. If Mr Bachmann would have been denied the deduction of contributions paid, the sums payable from the insurances would in that particular case not have been taxable in Belgium.

In its subsequent case-law the Court refers to its reasoning in the *Bachmann* case while consistently distinguishing it. It seems to me that the *Bachmann* case and the ground of fiscal coherence are still, in principle, valid. However, another perspective has been added in recent case-law that puts new light on fiscal coherence: the existence of tax treaties.

It is the following considerations in the *Bachmann* case that the Court in case after case refers to when referring to the reasoning of that case:

(a) There has to be a direct link between, for example, the deduction of an insurance contribution, and the taxation of the sums payable from that insurance, and that link has to be preserved.

(b) It has to be the same taxpayer at issue regarding, for example, the deduction granted and the sums payable.

In case C-80/94 *Wielockx*, the Court declared its position on how fiscal coherence should be considered in a situation where the taxation at issue was governed by tax treaty law. The effect of a tax treaty was that fiscal coherence could not be established in relation to one and the same person by a strict correlation between the deductibility of contributions and the taxation of pensions. The meaning of fiscal coherence was shifted to another level: the reciprocity of the rules of the tax treaty that applied between the contracting states. In other words, fiscal coherence was considered by the Court to be secured by the tax treaty. The *Wielockx* approach on fiscal coherence has been confirmed by the Court in several other cases including for example *Metallgesellschaft and Others*, *Danner*,[83] and *X and Y*. In relation to tax treaty law, the question may be asked whether the Court seeks to preserve coherence at the tax treaty level. It seems that the answer, at least so far, is no. What the Court has done could perhaps be concluded in the following way.

[83] See Chapter 3.

In the *Bachmann* case it recognised the preservation of fiscal coherence as a legitimate ground of justification of the national tax system. In later cases the Court recognised that states in their tax treaties have bilaterally agreed on a "coherent" taxation of the income covered by the treaty. Thus the matter of fiscal coherence has been shifted to another level, the tax treaty level. It seems that the Court does not wish to interfere at the tax treaty level, at least in this respect. An important conclusion from the *Wielockx* case is evidently the importance of tax treaties when deciding whether coherence is present. If tax treaties are taken into account, coherence cannot be established in relation to one and the same person by a strict correlation between the deductibility of contributions and the taxation of pensions. Instead the issue of coherence is shifted to another level, "the reciprocity of the rules applicable in the Contracting States". The reason why the European Court of Justice has taken this view seems to be that the existence of a tax treaty in itself is an expression of fiscal coherence between the signatory states. It seems that the Court has adhered to the criticism put forward by, among others, Knobbe-Keuk, which has previously been discussed in this chapter.

Lang discusses the possibility of invoking the preservation of fiscal coherence of the tax treaty.[84] He is sceptical. If Member States conclude tax treaties that do not follow the OECD MC there is, evidently, no uniform Community policy, and in Lang's view one cannot in such a situation invoke the preservation of fiscal coherence at the tax treaty level with any effect. He recognises that the situation is more difficult in relation to tax treaties with third countries. The question is whether it would endanger the coherence of the tax treaty system if the treaty benefits of one Member State's treaty with a third country was also granted to a national of another Member State.

In relation to the reasoning by Lang, one could add the following comments. If one considers the case-law of the Court, it is only in relation to a national tax system that the Court has accepted the ground of the preservation of fiscal coherence. If the Court has accepted it in relation to a national system, it is natural to ask whether the ground also applies on the treaty level. Treaties are bilateral, and in exceptional cases multilateral. They are concluded on the basis of negotiations between the concluding states where they "give and take" taxing rights on a mutual basis. As a result of those negotiations the treaty could be considered as "coherent" in the view of the treaty-concluding states. Moreover, most Member States of the European Union are members of the OECD and follow the OECD MC when concluding tax treaties. The OECD MC has a strong impact on the tax treaties of the OECD Members, even if at least recent amendments to it cannot be considered to have a strong binding effect on the Members.

---

84 Lang, "The Binding Effect of the EC Fundamental Freedoms on Tax Treaties", in *Tax Treaties and EC Law*, Gassner (ed.), Kluwer Law International, Series on International Taxation No 16, London/The Hague/Boston, 1997, pp. 17-31, at p. 29-30 (with further references to Hinnekens, *EC Tax Review*, 1995, p. 206).

When Member States conclude tax treaties they exercise the sovereignty they have in the field of direct taxation, which is also recognised by the European Court of Justice in its case-law. Primarily on the basis of the fact that tax treaties between Member States are bilateral agreements, they include *per se* a coherent taxation of the income category at issue. Secondly, the fact that the Member States of the European Union follow the OECD MC could be interpreted as implying that they conclude tax treaties in a "coherent" way, but that is, of course, in a rather broad meaning of the word.

Lang also discusses the relation to tax treaties with third countries and the preservation of fiscal coherence but that was before the Court's ruling in 1999 in case C-307/97 *Saint-Gobain*. In that case the benefits of German tax treaties with third countries were extended to branches of companies resident in other Member States of the European Union. In the *Saint-Gobain* case the Court merely concluded that the national treatment principle obliged Member States to extend the treaty benefits to such persons. Moreover, in the view of the Court, the balance and reciprocity of the treaty was not altered by such a unilateral extension by a Member State.

The Court seems to consider fiscal coherence to be secured at the tax treaty level. In practice the *Bachmann* ruling is obsolete if the tax treaty level is taken into account. However, the Court's decision in the *Saint-Gobain* case means that treaty benefits of a Member State can be extended to branches of non-residents in that state.

A final remark is that the meaning of fiscal coherence is unclear. It was applied in the *Bachmann* case in 1992, but has not been considered applicable in any case afterwards. The European Court of Justice still refers to it as valid, but one may seriously doubt if it will ever again be applied. Too much time has passed since 1992, at least in this field of Community law.[85]

5.2.3 Effectiveness of Fiscal Supervision

5.2.3.1 Introduction

The effectiveness of fiscal supervision as a ground of justification has been accepted by the Court, most notably in case C-250/95 *Futura Participations*, but also recognised

[85] Case C-136/00 *Danner* has been discussed in Chapter 3. It has been held that the *Danner* case is (almost) an overruling of the coherence argument applied in the *Bachmann* case, see e.g. von Quitzow, "Exit Bachmann, bienvenue Danner? – Eller när en dom har blivit så urholkad att den nästan får anses vara 'overruled'", *Skattenytt*, 2003, pp. 89-92. It is of course correct that after the *Bachmann* case (and the *Commission v. Belgium* case) there has been no case where the ECJ has applied fiscal coherence as a ground of justification. In addition, later case-law has provided further conditions for the justification to apply. However, the ECJ still refers to fiscal coherence as a valid ground of justification even if it does not find it applicable. In my view, fiscal coherence could still apply, at least in principle.

in a number of other cases in the field of direct taxation. The *Futura Participations* case has been more thoroughly examined in Chapter 3. Therefore, there will be only a reference to the facts of that case. The *Futura Participations* case is covered in *section 5.2.3.2*. Other cases where the effectiveness of fiscal supervision has been at issue are discussed in *section 5.2.3.3*. Some general conclusions are given in *section 5.2.3.4*.

5.2.3.2 Case C-250/95 **Futura Participations** *(15 May 1997)*

Case C-250/95 *Futura Participations* dealt with the freedom of establishment and Luxembourg legislation with conditions for determining the tax base of foreign companies with branches in Luxembourg. Futura Participations SA was a French company with its seat in Paris. The company had a branch in Luxembourg.

Luxembourg tax law provided the following situation. Resident taxpayers could deduct losses carried forward from previous years under the condition, however, that they had kept "proper accounts" during the year in which the losses were incurred.[86] Non-resident companies with a branch in Luxembourg were subject to tax in Luxembourg only on income earned, directly or indirectly, by their Luxembourg permanent establishment. Moreover, non-resident companies were not obliged to keep separate accounts on their Luxembourg activities. If they did not keep such accounts they could determine their Luxembourg income according to an "apportionment method". That method meant that according to a specific calculation, a proportion of the non-resident company's income would be treated as deriving from the Luxembourg branch.

Under special circumstances, non-resident companies were, however, also entitled to carry forward losses incurred by their Luxembourg branch. Conditions for this were that the losses were economically related to income received in Luxembourg and that the accounts were kept in Luxembourg. Furthermore, the accounts relating to the activities had to comply with relevant Luxembourg law. The Luxembourg branch of Futura Participations, Singer, determined its taxable income according to the apportionment method. It also requested to offset losses incurred in previous years, which the Luxembourg tax authorities refused.

The European Court of Justice was asked whether it was in accordance with the freedom of establishment for a non-resident company with a branch to stipulate the conditions that (i) the losses must be economically related to the income earned by the taxpayer in the state of the branch, and (ii) during the financial year in which the losses were incurred, the taxpayer must have kept and held in respect of the activities carried out there, accounts complying with relevant national rules in the state of the branch.

86 Case C-250/95 *Futura Participations*, para. 6.

As regards the first condition, the existence of an economic link, the Court answered that such a condition was in compliance with the fiscal principle of territoriality. Because of that there could be no form of discrimination.[87]

The second condition, however, the keeping of accounts, was in the view of the Court, in principle prohibited by the freedom of establishment. This condition meant that a company that wished to carry forward losses had to keep – in addition to the accounts kept in its home state complying with the legislation of that state – accounts in the state of the branch, which complied with the legislation of *that* state.[88]

The Court continued by examining whether there were any grounds of justification that could justify the second condition – the keeping of accounts – that, in principle, was in breach of the freedom of establishment. The Luxembourg government maintained that this condition was necessary to ascertain that the losses which the taxpayer wished to deduct had in fact arisen in Luxembourg and that the amount deducted corresponded with the losses incurred in Luxembourg. Moreover, the condition that the non-resident taxpayer had to hold proper accounts in Luxembourg was motivated by the wish for Luxembourg tax authorities to inspect them at any time.

The Commission recognised that the objectives of the second condition were legitimate. However, in the view of the Commission, Luxembourg tax authorities could have ascertained the amount of the losses incurred by the Luxembourg branch by checking the accounts held by the non-resident company in its state of residence – France. Moreover, the Commission pointed out that Directive 77/799/EEC of 19 December 1977 concerning mutual assistance by the competent authorities of the Member States in the field of direct taxation provided the possibility of obtaining required information from tax authorities in other Member States.

In its response, the Court initially recognised that the effectiveness of fiscal supervision was in fact an accepted ground of justification. In support, the Court referred to Case 120/78 *Cassis de Dijon*. Furthermore, the Court declared that a Member State has the right to apply measures which would "... enable the amount of both the income taxable in that State and of the losses which can be carried forward there to be ascertained clearly and precisely".[89]

In response to the reasoning by the Commission, the Court did not consider the second condition of Luxembourg law to be fulfilled by referring to the accounts kept according to the legislation of another Member State.[90] In the view of the Court there

[87] Case C-250/95 *Futura Participations*, para. 22.

[88] Case C-250/95 *Futura Participations*, para. 25.

[89] Case C-250/95 *Futura Participations*, para. 31.

[90] Case C-250/95 *Futura Participations*, para. 32.

was no guarantee that the accounts prepared in the Member State where the company, or firm for that matter, had its seat (France), would provide sufficient information concerning the amount of income chargeable to tax and of the losses which can be carried forward.[91]

To conclude, the Court seems to accept, in principle, that a Member State can stipulate a condition on the proper keeping of accounts in the state of the branch for the carry forward of losses in that state. However, such a condition must also comply with the test of proportionality: "… do the requirements of the second condition go beyond what is necessary to enable the amount of losses deductible from income earned by a taxpayer during a financial year subsequent to that which the losses were incurred to be ascertained".[92] In its previous case-law, in relation to the proportionality test, the Court declared that the measure was designed "… to ensure achievement of the aim in question and not go beyond what was necessary for that purpose".[93]

In general, Luxembourg law did not oblige non-residents to keep accounts on their activities in Luxembourg. It was only when a non-resident asked to carry forward losses that such Luxembourg accounts were required. The purpose of this obligation was to make it possible for Luxembourg tax authorities to ascertain that the losses the taxpayer wanted to be carried forward, clearly and precisely corresponded with losses actually incurred in Luxembourg.

The Court declared that the directive on the exchange of information makes it possible for the tax authority ("competent authority") of one Member State to ask the tax authority in another Member State to provide the information required to make a correct assessment of the amount of income tax payable.[94] Moreover, the Court considered that the fact that a Member State permits a non-resident to make use of an inexact apportionment method does not mean that it has to accept losses to be calculated according to an apportionment method as well.

In conclusion the Court found that the freedom of establishment precluded that the carrying forward of losses was made subject to the condition that in the year in which the losses were incurred, the taxpayer must have kept and held in that Member State accounts relating to his activities carried on there complying with the relevant national rules. The second condition, albeit accepted in principle, did not meet the proportionality test.

---

91 Case C-250/95 *Futura Participations*, para. 35.

92 *Ibid.*

93 Case C-250/95 *Futura Participations*, para. 26. In support of considering the national measure's proportionality the ECJ referred to case C-55/94 *Gebhard*, para. 37; case C-19/92 *Kraus*, para. 32; and case C-415/93 *Bosman*, para. 104.

94 Case C-250/95 *Futura Participations*, para. 41.

5.2.3.3 Other Cases on the Effectiveness of Fiscal Supervision

The ground of the effectiveness of fiscal supervision has been advanced in several other cases concerning direct taxation. There are few cases in addition to the one previously discussed, where this ground of justification has been more closely elaborated upon.

The first case to be discussed is C-1/93 *Halliburton Services*. The facts of the underlying case were in short the following. Halliburton was an international group of companies. The parent company was Halliburton Inc., resident in the United States. The parent company had one Dutch subsidiary and one German subsidiary. A reorganisation was planned to take place. The German subsidiary had a Dutch branch, containing immovable property, which it sold to the Dutch subsidiary. The transfer of the immovable property was subject to tax in the Netherlands. By contrast, if it had been a branch of a Dutch company or a US company, the transfer would have been exempt from tax in the Netherlands. This difference in treatment constituted an indirect discrimination on grounds of nationality, according to the European Court of Justice.

The Dutch government maintained that this discrimination was justified because it served the purpose of facilitating the effectiveness of fiscal supervision. More precisely, the government argued that the restriction was necessary "... because the competent tax administration is unable to check whether the legal forms of entities constituted in other Member States are equivalent to those of public and limited companies within the meaning of the relevant national legislation."[95]

The Court did not accept that argument. The reason was that, in the view of the Court, characteristics of the forms in which companies may be constituted in other Member States can be obtained through the application of Council Directive 77/799/EEC of 19 December 1977 on mutual assistance by the competent authorities of the Member States in the field of taxation. Article 1 (2) of the Directive provides that the system of exchanging information applies to taxes on the disposal of movable and immovable property. Moreover, Article 1 (1) provides for the exchange of information necessary to enable the competent authorities to make a correct assessment of taxes referred to by the Directive.

The reasoning of the Court, accordingly, follows the same lines as the previously discussed case C-250/95 *Futura Participations*. One should of course note that the Halliburton case was decided prior to the *Futura Participations* case. In both cases the possibility of exchanging information according to the Directive on that matter was considered sufficient to meet the requirement of effectiveness of fiscal supervision.

A recent example of a case where the Court has discussed the ground of effectiveness of fiscal supervision in matters of direct taxation is case C-324/00 *Lankhorst-*

[95] Case C-1/93 *Halliburton Services*, para. 21.

Hohorst.[96] The case dealt with the compatibility with the freedom of establishment of German tax rules against thin capitalisation. The European Court of Justice came to the conclusion that they were in breach of the freedom of establishment. One of the grounds considered was whether the national legislation served the objective of ensuring the effectiveness of fiscal supervision.[97] The Court simply declared that no argument had been put forward to show how the classification rule at issue enabled the German tax authorities "to supervise the amount of taxable income".[98]

5.2.3.4 Conclusion

The effectiveness of fiscal supervision is an accepted ground of justification also in matters of direct taxation. In general, this ground of justification was accepted already in Case 120/78 *Cassis de Dijon*. According to this ground, a Member State may apply measures which enable it to ascertain clearly and precisely the amount of both the income taxable in the state and of the losses which can be carried forward there.

Council Directive 77/799/EEC of 19 December 1977 provides for the exchange of information between the competent authorities of the Member States. According to this Directive it is possible, at least in the view of the Court, to acquire the necessary information to guarantee the effectiveness of fiscal supervision. On the basis of this Directive, the Court found in both case C-1/93 *Halliburton* and C-250/95 *Futura Participations* that measures in national legislation with the objective of safeguarding the effectiveness of fiscal supervision were not required or did not meet the test of proportionality. Terra and Wattel note that the Member States left with the Directive for obtaining information will in practice not always acquire it.[99]

5.2.4 Potential Grounds of Justification

In this section one potential ground of justification will be discussed. "Potential" ground because there is some uncertainty as to whether it actually is accepted by the European Court of Justice. This ground is the fiscal principle of territoriality. In case C-250/95 *Futura Participations* the Court considered the following question, among others. Regarding the right for a branch of a non-resident company to carry forward

---

[96] Case C-324/00 *Lankhorst-Hohorst* is discussed in detail in the previous section 5.2.1.4 dealing with the ground of prevention of abuse.

[97] Case C-324/00 *Lankhorst-Hohorst*, para. 43.

[98] Case C-324/00 *Lankhorst-Hohorst*, para. 44.

[99] Terra and Wattel, *European Tax Law*, 3rd ed., Kluwer Law International, London/The Hague/New York, 2001, p. 77.

losses there had to be an economic link between the losses and income earned in the Member State in which tax was charged. The Court accepted that requirement, and it seems that the reason according to the Court was that such a system was in conformity with the fiscal principle of territoriality.[100]

The Court returned to the principle of territoriality in case C-168/01 *Bosal*. The case concerned the right of a company resident in the Netherlands to deduct financing costs of subsidiaries. If the subsidiaries were resident in the Netherlands the parent could make a deduction for the costs in its Dutch tax return. However, if the subsidiaries were non-resident in the Netherlands (and with no branch there) such a cost deduction could not be made. Was this denial of deduction in conformity with the principle of territoriality on the ground that the Netherlands could not tax the profits of the non-resident subsidiaries? The Court cannot have had that view, because the Court decided that a Dutch parent was also entitled to deduct the financing costs of foreign subsidiaries. However, the Court's reasoning on the territoriality principle is not quite explicit.

In conclusion, the territoriality principle was accepted in the *Futura Participations* case regarding losses but not in the *Bosal* case regarding costs.

The *Marks & Spencer* case is similar to both the *Futura Participations* and *Bosal* cases. In principle it concerns the question of whether a company resident in the United Kingdom could take into account losses incurred by a foreign subsidiary. United Kingdom legislation would only allow losses of domestic subsidiaries to be taken into account. In the decision by the Special Commissioners the issue was discussed, and considered essential that the United Kingdom did not have the right to tax the profits of the foreign subsidiaries. The Special Commissioners primarily tackled this issue when considering whether the United Kingdom legislation was discriminatory or not, but considered it also in relation to the question of coherence.[101] As previously explained in this study "coherence" is a vague term. There is another expression in tax law that is more directly applicable to the taxation of profits and losses and that is the fiscal principle of reciprocity.[102] The tax issue in *Marks & Spencer* is in my view more precisely a question of whether the symmetric taxation of profits and losses should be maintained in the same Member State that taxes the profits of the parent company. However, the use of a more adequate terminology does not in itself solve the problem posed to the European Court of Justice. When considering the Court's decision in the *Bosal* case, one must be somewhat sceptical on whether the Court will consider the United Kingdom difference in treatment to be justified by the need to preserve "fiscal coherence". The reason is that the Court did not adhere to the territoriality argument,

---

100 Case C-250/95 *Futura Participations*, para. 18-22.

101 *Marks & Spencer*, decision by the Special Commissioners, para. 110-115.

102 Lodin, Lindencrona, Melz and Silfverberg, *Inkomstskatt*, 9th ed., Studentlitteratur, Lund, 2003, p. 39.

although it had been accepted in the *Futura Participations* case. It may be that the fiscal integrity of the territory of a Member State has been extended to the integrity of the territory of the European Union. Even if the profits of the parent company are taxed within the territory of the United Kingdom, the same Member State will anyway have to take into account losses incurred within the territory of the European Union.

5.3 Rejected Grounds of Justification

5.3.1 Introduction

A number of grounds of justification have been put forward before the European Court of Justice that the Court has considered unacceptable, even as such, and accordingly rejected. The following rejected grounds will be discussed: the lack of tax harmonisation (*section 5.3.2*), counterbalancing advantages (*section 5.3.3*), a new form of establishment that would mean equal treatment (*section 5.3.4*), lack of Community competence in the field of tax treaties (*section 5.3.5*) and loss of tax revenue (*section 5.3.6*).

As previously noted, there will be no general description or analysis of the cases involved. Facts of the different cases will only be discussed to the extent that it is necessary to facilitate the understanding of each rejected ground of justification. Already at this stage it is interesting to note that several of the grounds of justification subsequently discussed, and rejected by the Court, were rejected already in the 1986 *Avoir fiscal* case. However, that has not prevented Member States from returning to the very same grounds in a number of subsequent cases.

5.3.2 The Lack of Tax Harmonisation

As previously discussed in Chapter 2, there has been comparatively modest Community harmonisation in the field of direct taxation, if compared with the field of, for example, value added taxation. Member States still protect, with some persistency, their sovereignty in the field of direct taxation, a sovereignty which was advanced in Case 270/83 *Avoir fiscal*. That case dealt with the system in France for avoiding economic double taxation of corporate profits. Branches of foreign companies were not entitled to the "*avoir fiscal*", which was a payment to limit the effects of economic double taxation. The French government argued that the difference in treatment was caused by characteristics of and differences between the tax system of different Member States, as well as by tax treaty implications.[103]

[103] Case 270/83 *Avoir fiscal*, para. 23.

In addition, the French government argued that because the legislation at issue had not been harmonised, different measures were necessary in each case in order to take into account differences between Member States. Therefore those national measures were justified according to Article [43] of the EC Treaty.[104] The Court responded that even the fact that this specific part of the tax legislation of the Member States had not been harmonised "… cannot justify the difference of treatment of this case".[105] Furthermore, the Court declared that in the absence of harmonisation in the field of taxation, a company's tax position depends on the tax system of the Member States, and those systems must comply with the freedom of establishment.[106]

Finally, a comparison with the Court's reasoning in Case 81/87 *Daily Mail* is of interest. Primarily the *Daily Mail* case concerned the compatibility of United Kingdom company legislation with the freedom of establishment. A vital issue in this case was whether it was possible for a company to transfer its central management and control to another Member State. The Court concluded that the national laws of the Member States were different on this matter. Was it possible for a company registered in one Member State to transfer its central management and control to another Member State, considering the freedom of establishment as stipulated in the EC Treaty? The Court came to the conclusion that the EC Treaty did not decide on this matter that "must be dealt with by future legislation or conventions".[107]

Did the Court declare contradictory approaches regarding, on the one hand, tax legislation – which must comply with the freedom of establishment even if the level of harmonisation is low – and, on the other hand, company legislation – which need not comply with the freedom of establishment even if the level of harmonisation also is low? My answer is no, there is no contradiction. As regards the specific issue of company law – the transfer of central management and control – the EC Treaty is itself open to different national solutions as it makes clear in Article 48 of the Treaty, at least in the wording of the article.[108] That is not the case for the tax issues discussed in the cases referred to in this chapter; rather, the EC Treaty is silent on these specific issues of direct taxation in the Member States' national laws.[109]

---

[104] *Ibid.*

[105] Case 270/83 *Avoir fiscal*, para. 24. One may wonder whether the ECJ, with this way of expression, opens the door to a difference in treatment regarding tax legislation in other cases. The answer must be no. National law has to comply with the fundamental freedoms of the EC Treaty. Only grounds of justification expressively stated in the EC Treaty or in the case-law of the ECJ may justify a difference in treatment.

[106] *Ibid.*

[107] Case 81/87 *Daily Mail*, para. 23, cf. also para. 24.

[108] Cf. section 4.2.3.

[109] With the notable exception of Article 58 of the EC Treaty, which is discussed in Chapter 6.

5.3.3 Counterbalancing Advantages

5.3.3.1 Introduction

When the European Court of Justice considers whether a national measure constitutes a restriction, the Court makes a comparison between different situations to establish the difference in treatment. One initial step is to find out whether the situations compared are "objectively comparable". The meaning of objectively comparable situations was introduced in section 3.6 above. As a general rule, the European Court of Justice does not consider residents and non-residents to be in comparable situations. In specific cases, however, they may very well be in comparable situations, as shown in a number of Court cases.

If the situations are objectively comparable, can counterbalancing advantages justify discriminatory disadvantages? In the following section this question will be discussed in relation to three cases: Case 270/83 *Avoir fiscal*, case C-330/91 *Commerzbank* and case C-307/97 *Saint-Gobain*.

5.3.3.2 Case-law of the European Court of Justice

In Case 270/83 *Avoir fiscal*, the French government argued that the difference in tax treatment of branches of foreign companies was compensated by various advantages over French companies which balanced out the disadvantages.[110] The Court did not accept this argument. Even if such advantages existed, the Court reasoned, they could not justify a breach of the obligation under Article 43 (ex Article 52) and the freedom of establishment when branches of foreign companies were not granted the benefit of tax credit – the *avoir fiscal*.[111]

Also in case C-330/91 *Commerzbank*, the argument of counterbalancing advantages was raised. In the United Kingdom branches of foreign banks were not granted special benefits that resident companies were granted. The tax benefit denied consisted of a "repayment supplement" on taxes paid in the United Kingdom on interest received from the US by a branch in the United Kingdom of a German company ("Commerzbank"). The United Kingdom government argued that far from suffering discrimination, non-resident companies in Commerzbank's situation enjoyed privileged treatment.[112] The

[110] Case 270/83 *Avoir fiscal*, para. 17. The disadvantage in question was the failure in French law to grant the branches of non-resident companies the same tax credit ("*avoir fiscal*") as resident companies were granted.

[111] Case 270/83 *Avoir fiscal*, para. 21.

[112] Case C-330/91 *Commerzbank*, para. 16.

reason was that such non-resident companies were exempt from tax normally payable by resident companies. According to the United Kingdom government, resident and non-resident companies were treated differently because, for the purpose of corporation tax, they were in different situations. However, the European Court of Justice did not accept this argument on counterbalancing privileges. The Court declared that residents and non-residents were subject to unequal treatment: non-resident companies were not entitled to the repayment supplement, which resident companies were. The fact that non-resident companies, in contrast to resident companies, were exempt from the tax which gave rise to the refund could not "justify a rule of a general nature withholding the benefit".[113]

The referred decisions by the European Court of Justice in the *Commerzbank* case and the *Avoir fiscal* case are supported by a number of other cases such as case C-307/97 *Saint-Gobain*. In the *Saint-Gobain* case the Court also firmly declared that the difference in tax treatment between resident companies and branches (permanent establishments of non-resident companies) cannot be justified by other advantages that branches enjoy in comparison with resident companies.[114]

5.3.3.3 Conclusion

The subject of this section has been whether counterbalancing advantages can justify disadvantages. For example, if a non-resident company according to a specific law rule is treated less favourably than a resident company, can another law rule which is more favourable for non-residents outweigh the first difference in treatment? The case-law is clear. The answer is no, a counterbalancing advantage in one area of tax law cannot outweigh a disadvantage in another area. The reason for this approach by the Court might have the following basis. First, the Court is only asked to answer whether a specific piece of legislation constitutes discrimination or a restriction. Secondly, it would be difficult for the Court to take into consideration a country's tax system as a whole when deciding whether a national measure complies with the fundamental freedoms of the EC Treaty. Rather, such considerations are for the individual Member States or the Council and the Parliament to make.

5.3.4 New Form of Establishment Would Mean Equal Treatment

As previously mentioned on several occasions, Case 270/83 *Avoir fiscal* dealt with the tax treatment in France of branches of non-resident insurance companies. The branches

[113] Case C-330/91 *Commerzbank*, para. 19.

[114] Case C-307/97 *Saint-Gobain*, para. 53.

of non-resident companies were not granted the elimination of economic double taxation in the form of a tax credit – "*avoir fiscal*" – as resident companies were.

As a ground for justifying this difference in treatment between resident and non-resident companies, the French government argued that the non-resident companies could avoid those disadvantages by setting up a subsidiary in France.[115] A subsidiary resident in France would, of course, have enjoyed the tax credit system, since it would have been a French company. The Court did not accept this argument. The fact that a company with a registered office in another Member State could establish a subsidiary in France was not sufficient as a ground of justification. According to the Court, Article [43] (1) leaves traders free to choose the appropriate legal form in which to pursue their activities in another Member State, and among them the establishment of a branch.[116]

5.3.5 Lack of Community Competence in the Field of Tax Treaty Law

5.3.5.1 Introduction

Tax treaties are international agreements in public international law concluded by sovereign states. The existence of tax treaties has in several aspects been taken into account in the judgments of the European Court of Justice in relation to both the freedom of establishment and the free movement of capital. As previously discussed, the existence of tax treaties has strongly influenced how the Court decides on the ground of fiscal coherence.

An important and even more basic issue has been whether Community law has any impact on the tax treaties of the Member States. Some of the principal arguments have been the following. Member States still have the competence to decide on matters of taxation. Therefore Community law should have no impact on the tax treaties of the Member States, especially not treaties concluded with third countries. The European Court of Justice seems to have taken another position. Case-law from the European Court of Justice will be discussed in *section 5.3.5.2*. Conclusions are given in *section 5.3.5.3*.

5.3.5.2 Case-law of the European Court of Justice

Case 270/83 *Avoir fiscal* already contained a discussion on the competence of the European Court of Justice and Community law in the field of direct taxation.

[115] Case 270/83 *Avoir fiscal*, para. 17.

[116] Case 270/83 *Avoir fiscal*, para. 22.

In the *Avoir fiscal* case the French government argued that the situation relevant for the case concerned activities governed by tax treaties.[117] However, what the case in fact dealt with was the system in France for the elimination of economic double taxation of corporate profits. The Court's reasoning on this issue could perhaps have been more thorough. However, the Court rightly concluded that the difference in treatment that was at issue was not caused by a tax treaty. The question of economic double taxation is normally peripheral in tax treaties based on the OECD MC.[118]

In addition the Court explained that the rights conferred by Article [43] of the EC Treaty were unconditional "... and a Member State cannot make respect for them subject to the contents of an agreement concluded with another Member State".[119] Finally, the Court declared: "In particular, that does not permit those rights to be made subject to a condition of reciprocity imposed for the purpose of obtaining corresponding advantages in other Member States."[120]

Case C-307/97 *Saint-Gobain* touches the interesting question of tax treaties between Member States in relation to third countries. In the *Saint-Gobain* case the German government claimed that tax concessions granted according to bilateral tax treaties with non-Member States do not fall within the competence of the Community.[121] In support of this view, the Swedish government observed that tax treaties are based on the principle of reciprocity and that this balance would be disturbed if the benefit of the provisions were extended to companies established in Member States which were not.[122] The Court acknowledged that Member States remain competent to determine the criteria for eliminating international juridical double taxation through, for example, tax treaties. However, the Court also declared that "[a]s far as the exercise of the power of taxation so allocated is concerned, the Member States nevertheless may not disregard Community rules".[123] In addition, the Court repeated the well-known position that although direct taxation is a matter for Member States, they must nevertheless exercise their taxation powers consistently with Community law (with a reference to, among others, case C-264/96 *ICI*).[124] The conclusion according to the Court is that "...the *national treatment principle* requires the Member State which is party to the

[117] Case 270/83 *Avoir fiscal*, para. 23.

[118] Case 270/83 *Avoir fiscal*, para. 26.

[119] *Ibid.*

[120] *Ibid.* The ECJ refers to the freedom of establishment.

[121] Case C-307/97 *Saint-Gobain*, para. 54.

[122] Case C-307/97 *Saint-Gobain*, para. 55.

[123] Case C-307/97 *Saint-Gobain*, para. 57.

[124] *Ibid.*

treaty to grant to permanent establishments of non-resident companies the advantages provided for by that treaty on the same conditions as those which apply to resident companies".[125]

5.3.5.3 Conclusion

Tax treaties are international agreements concluded between sovereign states. Member States are sovereign in the area of taxation, and that applies also in the field of tax treaties.

To some extent tax treaties, or at least the benefits granted according to them, are also subject to the fundamental freedoms of the EC Treaty, which follows from the *Saint-Gobain* case. The national treatment principle requires the Member State that is party to a treaty to grant permanent establishments of non-resident companies the advantages provided for by that treaty on the same condition as those which apply to resident companies.

5.3.6 Loss of Tax Revenue

5.3.6.1 Introduction

The loss or reduction of tax revenue as a ground for justification has been advanced in several cases on the freedom of establishment in relation to direct taxation. In the view of many Member States, national legislation against tax avoidance or abuse includes the purpose of securing the tax base and preventing the loss of tax revenue. The European Court of Justice has not accepted such "general purpose" legislation. As previously discussed, pure anti-abuse legislation has in principle been accepted by the Court as a legitimate ground of justification. Loss of tax revenue is in my view very similar to the ground "erosion of the tax base". In my view the argument of reduction (or loss) of tax revenue is in effect equivalent to the argument of erosion of the tax base. If the tax base erodes, there will also be a reduction of tax revenue.

In the following *section 5.3.6.2* there will be an analysis of cases where the Court has rejected the ground of loss of tax revenue as a ground of justification. Conclusions are given in *section 5.3.6.3*.

[125] Case C-307/97 *Saint-Gobain*, para. 58 (emphasis added).

5.3.6.2 Case-law of the European Court of Justice

Case C-264/96 *ICI* dealt with United Kingdom legislation on the off-setting of inter-corporate losses. The off-setting of such losses was denied in the United Kingdom on the basis that the ICI group included foreign subsidiaries. The United Kingdom government advanced that the denial of off-setting of losses was necessary to prevent the reduction of tax revenue caused by the mere existence of non-resident subsidiaries.[126] However, the European Court of Justice did not accept that argument.[127] First, the Court noted that the loss of revenue was not one of the exceptions listed in Article [46] of the EC Treaty. Secondly, the loss of revenue could not be regarded as a matter of overriding general interest, which could be relied upon to justify unequal treatment that was, in principle, incompatible with Article [43] of the EC Treaty.

Case C-307/97 *Saint-Gobain* dealt with the taxation of dividends and shares in Germany. Companies resident in Germany were entitled to tax concessions to which German branches of non-resident companies were not. As a ground of justification the German government declared that if the tax concessions in question were also granted to permanent establishments of non-resident companies, the loss of revenue could not be compensated by other taxes.[128] The Court, however, stated that this argument of compensation was not among the reasons mentioned in Article [46] of Treaty. Furthermore, the argument "… cannot be regarded as a matter of overriding general interest which may be relied upon in order to justify unequal treatment that is in principle incompatible with Article 52 of the Treaty".[129]

The loss of tax revenue was also advanced as a ground of justification in the joined cases C-397/98 and C-410/98 *Metallgesellschaft and Others*, and, as in the *ICI* case, it was advanced by the United Kingdom. The Court simply replied that it was enough "… to point out that it is settled case-law that diminution of tax revenue cannot be regarded as a matter of overriding general interest which may be relied upon in order to justify a measure which is, in principle, contrary to a fundamental freedom".[130]

Also in case C-324/00 *Lankhorst-Hohorst*, the Court confirmed that it was settled case-law that the reduction in tax revenue is not accepted as a ground of justification.[131] Case C-9/02 *de Lasteyrie du Saillant* dealt with French exit taxation on the holding of

[126] Case C-264/96 *ICI*, para. 25.

[127] Case C-264/96 *ICI*, para. 28.

[128] Case C-307/97 *Saint-Gobain*, para. 49.

[129] Case C-307/97 *Saint-Gobain*, para. 50.

[130] Joined cases C-397/98 and C-410/98 *Metallgesellschaft and Others*, para. 59. In support of this declaration the Court referred to case C-264/96 *ICI* (*ibid.*).

[131] Case C-324/00 *Lankhorst-Hohorst*, para. 36 (with further references).

shares. As a ground of justification it was argued that this piece of legislation served the objective of preventing erosion of the French tax base.[132] The Court declared that it "is sufficient to recall that, in accordance with settled case-law, diminution of tax receipts cannot be regarded as a matter of overriding general interest which may be relied upon in order to justify a measure which is, in principle, contrary to a fundamental freedom ...".[133]

5.3.6.3 Conclusion

The loss of tax revenue has often been advanced in conjunction with the objective of preventing tax evasion and tax avoidance. Those grounds of justification were covered separately in a previous section. The case-law of the European Court of Justice is decisive on this matter: the prevention of the loss of tax revenue does not constitute an acceptable ground of justification.

From the previous analysis of the ground of preventing tax evasion, it followed that this ground in principle was accepted, even if no cases seem to have been decided by the Court. In conclusion, the Court does not view the loss of tax revenue and the prevention of tax abuse as, if the reader permits the metaphor, different sides of the same coin.

---

132 Case C-9/02, *de Lasteyrie du Saillant*, para. 59.

133 Case C-9/02, *de Lasteyrie du Saillant*, para. 60.

6 The Free Movement of Capital and Direct Taxation

6.1 Introduction

The general purpose of this chapter is to systemise, analyse and evaluate the free movement of capital and payments as manifested in the EC Treaty and the case-law from the European Court of Justice. The emphasis will be, as in Chapter 4 on the freedom of establishment, on the relationship between this fundamental freedom and national measures of direct taxation. As regards the free movement of capital and payments there are still comparatively few cases, both in general and regarding the compatibility with national tax measures. This situation is, however, changing. The free movement of payments will be left out of this study. The main reason is that I consider it more likely that national measures of direct taxation are in breach of the free movement of capital. Moreover, there is nowadays a high degree of consistency between the free movement of capital and the free movement of payments, manifested not the least by Article 56 of the EC Treaty, a fact which permits the focus on the free movement of capital.

This chapter deals with the following main issues. First, there is an analysis of the central Articles 56 and 58 of the EC Treaty. Article 56 gives the principal declaration on the meaning of the free movement of capital. Article 58 stipulates limitations to that freedom, also in the area of taxation. The scope of this limitation is important to this study. Secondly, there is an analysis of case-law where the European Court of Justice has considered the compatibility of national tax legislation with the free movement of capital. In contrast to the case-law on the freedom of establishment, in this single chapter I will deal with both the question of what constitutes a restriction, and which grounds of justification the Court has considered. The reason for this approach is two-fold. To begin with, there is a considerable degree of convergence between the different fundamental freedoms of the EC Treaty, both regarding the question of what constitutes a restriction (in the broad sense) and regarding the applicability of grounds of justification. Accordingly, one could, for example, have had a joint discussion on the grounds of justification applicable for both the freedom of establishment and the free movement of capital. However, even if the degree of convergence between the two freedoms is high, they are not necessarily identical. Moreover, there are few cases on the free movement of capital in relation to direct taxation. The few cases that exist are all the more important, and should not be allowed to "disappear" in the mass of cases on the freedom of establishment.

The free movement of capital was previously dealt with in Articles 67 to 73 of the EEC Treaty. In general, one could say that those provisions were less final and demanding than the present provisions on the free movement of capital. Article 67 (1) stipulated an obligation to progressively abolish restrictions on capital movements during the transitional period. However, that was only necessary to the extent that it ensured the proper functioning of the common market. Similarly, Article 68 (1) required Member States to be as liberal as possible when granting exchange authorisation. Article 71 stipulated that Member States should endeavour to avoid the introduction of new currency exchange restrictions on capital movements. Several directives have been adopted to ensure the free movement of capital. The most notable in this context is Council Directive 88/361/EEC.

According to Usher, Article 67 of the EEC Treaty was not a straightforward rule that could be applied by a national court, or by the European Court of Justice.[1] From 1960, there have been several directives on the liberalisation of capital markets within the Community.[2] However, it was not until Directive 88/361 that the basic principle of free movement of capital was established in Community law. This Directive took effect for most Member States from 1 July 1990. Article 1 (1) of the Directive stipulated that Member States should abolish restrictions on movements of capital taking place between persons resident in the Member States. There was an Annex no. 1 with the Directive which contained a non-exhaustive list of what was included in the meaning of capital movements. Even today, this list is an important means of interpretation, which I subsequently will return to.

The provisions of the EC Treaty dealing with the free movement of capital were subject to considerable changes with the Maastricht Treaty. These rules still apply, and will also be subject to further discussion. Two important differences to the prior Article 67 of the EEC Treaty, now Article 56 of the EC Treaty, should be mentioned already at this stage. First, Article 56 has direct effect and, secondly, it applies according to its wording also in relation to third countries.

This chapter has the following outline. *Section 6.2* contains an overview of Articles 56-60 of the EC Treaty. Several general issues on the free movement of capital and Article 56 of the EC Treaty are dealt with in *section 6.3*. That includes for example the meaning of the term "capital". Moreover, the direct effect and personal scope of Article 56 is discussed. In *section 6.4* the subject is the relation between the free movement of capital and other fundamental freedoms. Statutory limitations and exceptions to the free movement of capital contained in Article 58 of the EC Treaty is the subject

1 Usher, *The Law of the Money and Financial Services in the EC*, 2nd ed., Oxford University Press, Oxford, 2000, p. 16. See also Case 203/80 *Casati*.

2 On the historical development see Usher, *op. cit.*, pp. 17-22.

of *section 6.5*. Article 58 is of special interest in this study because it strictly refers to the compatibility of national measures of taxation.

In relatively few cases the European Court of Justice has considered whether national measures on direct taxation are in conformity with the freedom of establishment. In *section 6.6* there is an analysis of such cases, and the analysis is focused on what constitutes a restriction. In addition, accepted and rejected grounds of justification according to the rule-of-reason doctrine are the subject of *section 6.7*. The question to what extent the free movement of capital applies in relation to third countries is discussed in *section 6.8*. Concluding remarks are made in *section 6.9*.

6.2 An Overview of Articles 56-60 of the EC Treaty

The free movement of capital and payments is covered by Chapter 4 of Title III[3] of the EC Treaty. Article 56 (1) of the EC Treaty contains the fundamental provision on capital movements: within the framework of the provisions set out in that Chapter of the Treaty, all restrictions on the movement of capital between Member States and between Member States and third countries shall be prohibited.

Accordingly, Member States are prohibited from having or taking legislative or other measures that restrict the free movement of capital. The prohibition targets the movement of capital between Member States as well as between Member States and third countries. Typically, legislative measures in a Member State that restrict its residents from taking loans or making investments in other Member States might constitute a restriction on the free movement of capital.

Articles 57 and 58 both provide for limitations on the free movement stipulated in Article 56. Article 57 could be labelled a "grandfather clause": infringements of the freedoms are tolerated under certain statutory conditions. Specifically, Article 57 (1) provides that the freedoms of Article 56 shall be without prejudice to the application to third countries of any restrictions which existed as of 31 December 1993. Such restrictions may be contained in national or Community law and adopted in respect of the movement of capital to or from third countries. The tolerated measures according to national or Community law are also pointed out in a general way: direct investment – including in real estate – establishment, the provision of financial services or the admission of securities to capital markets. A more general provision providing for limitations is Article 57 (2). The Council may, acting by a qualified majority, and on a proposal from the Commission, adopt measures that restrict the free movement of capital. Unanimity is, however, required if the measure constitutes a "step back in

3 Title III of the EC Treaty deals with the free movement of persons, services and capital.

Community law" as regards the liberalisation of the movement of capital to or from third countries.

Further limitations on the free movement of capital and payments are stipulated in Article 58.[4] In general, Article 58 of the EC Treaty has the following components.

Article 58 (1)(a) provides that Member States are free to apply relevant provisions of tax law that distinguish between taxpayers who are not in the same situation with regard to their place of residence or with regard to the place where their capital is invested. Article 58 (1)(b) stipulates that Member States are free:

- to take all requisite measures to prevent infringements of national law and regulations, *in particular in the field of taxation*[5] and the prudential[6] supervision of financial institutions; or
- to lay down procedures for the declaration of capital movements for purposes of administrative or statistical information; or
- to take measures which are justified on grounds of public policy or public security.

Article 58 (2) deals with the relationship between the free movement of capital and payments and the freedom of establishment. It stipulates that the provisions of Chapter 4 on capital and payments shall be without prejudice to the applicability of restrictions on the freedom of establishment which are compatible with the EC Treaty.

A prohibition against arbitrary discrimination or a disguised restriction on the free movement of capital and payments according to Article 56 is contained in Article 58 (3).

Article 59 contains a safeguard in exceptional circumstances on the protection of the economic and monetary union. The Council may take safeguard measures with regard to the movement of capital to or from third states. Such measures may only be taken in situations of serious difficulty for the operation of the economic and monetary union. In that event, the Council shall act by a qualified majority on the proposal from the Commission and after consulting the European Central Bank (ECB).

The possibility to impose economic sanctions against third states is stipulated in Article 60, which, however, goes far beyond the scope of this study.

---

4 This Article is especially important for the following analysis of the national tax measures in relation to the free movement of capital, and it will accordingly be discussed more extensively in section 6.5.

5 Emphasis added.

6 The *Concise Oxford English Dictionary*, 10th ed., Oxford University Press, Oxford, 2002, defines "prudential" as "involving or showing care and forethought, typically in business".

6.3 General Issues on the Free Movement of Capital

6.3.1 Article 56 of the EC Treaty

Article 56 of the EC Treaty is the cornerstone provision of the free movement of capital, as well as the free movement of payments. It stipulates:

> "1. Within the framework of the provisions set out in this Chapter, all restrictions on the movement of capital between Member States and between Member States and third countries shall be prohibited.
>
> 2. Within the framework of the provisions set out in this Chapter, all restrictions on payments between Member States and between Member States and third countries shall be prohibited."

According to its wording this provision prohibits "restrictions", which is a term that includes direct and indirect discrimination, as well as non-discriminatory restrictions.[7] This is somewhat different from the language of the previous Article 67 of the EEC Treaty, which stipulated the abolition of *all restrictions* on the movement of capital as well as *any discrimination* based on the nationality or on the place of residence of the parties or on the place where such capital is invested.

Regarding the Court's general case-law on the free movement of capital, Barnard concludes that most cases concern measures of direct discrimination.[8] However, she also identifies cases where the ECJ has considered provisions of national law to constitute non-discriminatory restrictions, and thus exemplifies with case C-98/01 *Commission v. the United Kingdom.*[9] In this case the Court declared: "[A]lthough the relevant restrictions on investment operations apply without distinction to both residents and non-residents, it must none the less be held that they affect the position of a person acquiring a shareholding as such and are thus liable to deter investors from other Member States from making such investments and, consequently, affect access to the market …".[10]

---

7 See also von Wilmowsky, "Freiheit des Kapital- und Zahlungsverkehr", in *Europäische Grundrechte und Grundfreiheiten*, Ehlers (ed.), de Gruyter Recht, Berlin, 2003, pp. 290-317, at p. 295 (cf. also section 3.2).

8 Barnard, *The Substantive Law of the EU. The Four Freedoms*, Oxford University Press, Oxford, 2004, p. 466. Barnard exemplifies with case C-367/98 *Commission v. the Portuguese Republic* the discrimination approach taken by the ECJ in some of its cases. This case concerned Portuguese company law, which precluded investors from other Member States from acquiring more than a given number of shares in newly privatised Portuguese companies (this case is one of the "golden-shares cases" decided by the ECJ).

9 Barnard, *op. cit.*, p. 467.

10 Case C-98/01 *Commission v. the United Kingdom*, para. 47.

In its case-law the Court has in several cases used the same "barrier" approach as has been identified in the late case-law on the freedom of establishment discussed in Chapter 4 of this study.

For a capital movement to be covered by the free movement of capital there has to be some form of cross-border movement at issue, which follows directly from the wording of Article 56. According to Article 56 there are two types of cross-border movements: movements between different Member States, and movements between Member States and third countries. In practice, the cross-border movement may take many forms. An obvious situation is of course the cross-border transfer of money.[11] Another situation can be where the debtor leaves his home state and moves to another state. Moreover, a cross-border movement of capital may also be at issue where the holding of the capital is changed from an individual or a company in Member State X to one in Member State Y.

Von Wilmowsky gives two interesting examples where he considers the free movement of capital to be at hand. The first situation deals with a German individual who owns real property in Austria. The German individual disposes of the Austrian real property to another German individual. The second situation consists of a German person who has borrowed capital in a bank and asks his bank to take his financial instruments deposited in a Luxembourg bank as security for the loan in the German bank.[12] In neither of these situations there has been a cross-border "transfer" of the person owning the capital, nor any concrete cross-border transfer of the capital itself. However, von Wilmowsky suggests that in both situations there has been a transfer of capital and that the transfer has affected persons resident in different states. I agree with von Wilmowsky that the spirit of the free movement of capital also would cover these two situations. There is a considerable "foreign" element in both situations, and that should be enough for the freedom to apply here.

6.3.2 Direct Effect

In general, it is clear from the case-law of the European Court of Justice that Community law, such as treaty provisions and directives, may have direct effect. Case-law from the European Court of Justice provides three conditions for a rule of Community law to have direct effect:[13]

(i) The content of the obligation must be clear and precise.

---

[11] Cf. e.g. joined cases C-163/94, C-165/94 and C-250/94 *Sanz de Lera and Others*.

[12] Von Wilmowsky, "Freiheit des Kapital- und Zahlungsverkehr", in *Europäische Grundrechte und Grundfreiheiten*, Ehlers (ed.), de Gruyter Recht, Berlin, 2003, pp. 290-317, p. 294.

[13] Direct effect in general has been discussed in Chapter 1.

(ii) The wording of the provision must make the obligation unconditional and unqualified.

(iii) There can be no discretion in the implementation of obligations.[14]

As previously mentioned, Article 56 (1) of the EC Treaty (partly) stipulates: "Within the framework of the provisions set out in this chapter, all restrictions on the movement of capital between Member States and between Member States and third countries shall be prohibited." It is clear already from the wording of Article 56 (1) that it fulfils the conditions to have direct effect. In contrast, Article 67 (1) of the EEC Treaty did not have direct effect.[15]

The Court has also decided that provisions on the free movement of capital in Directive 88/361/EEC have direct effect. In the *Bordessa* case the Court declared that Article 1 in conjunction with Article 4 of the Directive on liberalised capital movements 88/361/EEC had direct effect.[16] Article 1 of the Directive was the previous equivalent of the present Article 56 of the EC Treaty, even if the provision of the Directive was less clear than Article 56.[17]

Furthermore, in the joined cases C-163/94, C-165/94 and C-250/94 *Sanz de Lera and Others* the Court declared that the previous Article 73b (1) had direct effect also in relation to third state capital movements. The Court declared that the provision[18] "... lays down a clear and unconditional prohibition for which no implementing measure is needed".[19]

---

14 Cf. e.g. Kapteyn and VerLoren van Themaat, *Introduction to the Law of the European Communities*, 3rd ed., Kluwer Law International, London/The Hague/Boston, 1998, pp. 529-542.

15 Article 67 (1) of the EEC Treaty read: "During the transitional period and to the extent necessary to ensure the proper functioning of the common market, Member States shall progressively abolish between themselves all restrictions on the movement of capital belonging to persons resident in Member States and any discrimination based on the nationality or on the place of residence of the parties or on the place where such capital is invested."

16 Joined cases C-358/93 and C-416/93 *Bordessa and Others*, para. 35.

17 Article 1 of Directive 88/361/EEC reads: "Without prejudice to the following provisions, Member States shall abolish restrictions on movements of capital taking place between persons resident in Member States. To facilitate application of this Directive, capital movements shall be classified in accordance with the Nomenclature in Annex I."

18 The present Article 56 (1) of the EC Treaty.

19 Joined cases C-358/93 and C-416/93 *Bordessa and Others*, para. 41.

6.3.3 The Meaning of "Capital"

6.3.3.1 The EC Treaty and Directive 88/361/EEC

There is no definition in the EC Treaty of what constitutes "capital".[20] However, there are some indications on the meaning of the term. Article 57 deals with the applicability of the free movement of capital in relation to third countries and the admissibility of restrictions which existed on 31 December 1993. Such restrictions are allowed if they concern the following:

- direct investment – including in real estate;
- establishment;
- the provision of financial services; or
- the admission of securities to capital markets.

A more illuminating explanation of the meaning of capital is provided in Directive 88/361/EEC of 24 June 1988. This Directive was issued to implement a provision on liberalised capital movements in the outdated EEC Treaty, Article 67. The explanation contained in the Directive is still useful as a means of interpretation, according to the European Court of Justice.[21] There is an important Annex (I) to the Directive containing a non-exhaustive nomenclature of the capital movements referred to in Article 1 of the Directive. The Annex contains thirteen headings, among which are (i) direct investments, (ii) investments in real estate and (iii) operations in securities normally dealt in on the capital market.[22] It should be stressed that heading (xiii) is "other capital movements" that ends with the non-exhaustive example "F – Miscellaneous".

Flynn describes capital with regard to the rule on freedom of capital as those resources used for, or capable of, investment intended to generate revenue.[23] That is a good

---

[20] On the meaning of capital in Article 67 of the EEC Treaty see Mohamed, *European Community Law on the Free Movement of Capital and the EMU*, Kluwer Law International, The Hague/London/Boston, 1999, esp. pp. 46-55.

[21] See e.g. case C-35/98 *Verkooijen.*

[22] The other headings of the annex to Directive 88/361/EEC are (iv) operations in units of collective investment undertakings, (v) operations in securities and other instruments normally dealt in on the money market, (vi) operations in current and deposit accounts with financial institutions, (vii) credits related to commercial transactions or to the provision of services in which a resident is participating, (viii) financial loans and credits, (ix) sureties, other guarantees and rights of pledge, (x) transfers in performance of insurance contracts, (xi) personal capital movements, (xii) physical import and export of financial assets and, finally, (xiii) other capital movements.

[23] Flynn, "Coming of Age: the Free Movement of Capital Case Law", *CML Rev.*, 2002, pp. 773-805, at p. 776.

description, which is relevant to keep in mind when dealing with the case-law of the European Court of Justice on this freedom. In the following a few cases from the Court will be referred to where the meaning of capital was at issue.

6.3.3.2 Case C-222/97 **Trummer and Mayer** *(16 March 1999)*

Case C-222/97 *Trummer and Mayer*[24] concerned the compatibility with the free movement of capital of Austrian legislation on conditions to enter in the land register a mortgage denominated in German marks.[25] Austrian legislation required the mortgage to be denominated in Austrian schillings. The European Court of Justice declared that the EC Treaty does not define the terms "movement of capital" and "payments".[26] In interpreting the meaning of movement of capital the Court applied Directive 88/361/EEC in spite of the fact that it was adopted on the basis of Articles 69 and 70 (1) of the former EEC Treaty.

The Court declared: "... the nomenclature in respect of movements of capital annexed to Directive 88/361 still has the same indicative value, for the purposes of defining the notion of capital movements, as it did before the entry into force of Article 73b *et seq.* ...".[27] The Court decided that a mortgage must be regarded as constituting an "other guarantee" within the meaning of heading (sometimes also referred to as "point") (ix) of the nomenclature, entitled "Sureties, other guarantees and rights of pledge". The general importance of the case is, of course, that the Annex to Directive 88/361/EEC can and should be used to interpret the meaning of both capital and payments as understood in the EC Treaty.[28]

6.3.3.3 Case C-35/98 **Verkooijen** *(6 June 2000)*

Case C-35/98 *Verkooijen*[29] will in subsequent sections be dealt with more thoroughly, and I will here only discuss it in relation to the meaning of "capital". Briefly, however, the facts of the underlying case were the following. Mr Verkooijen was resident in the Netherlands and was employed by a Dutch company, Fina Nederland BV. Mr Verkooijen took part in an employees' savings plan (*werknemersspaarplan*), through

24 Case C-222/97 *Manfred Trummer and Peter Mayer*.

25 Cf. case C-222/97 *Trummer and Mayer*, para. 2.

26 Case C-222/97 *Trummer and Mayer*, para. 20.

27 Case C-222/97 *Trummer and Mayer*, para. 21.

28 Cf. e.g. joined cases C-515/99, C-519/99 to C-524/99 and C-526/99 to C-540/99 *Hans Reisch and Others*.

29 Case C-35/98 *Statssecretaris van Financiën v. B.G.M. Verkooijen*.

which he acquired shares in a Belgian company that indirectly controlled the Dutch company. According to Dutch law, Mr Verkooijen was not entitled to tax exemption on the dividends stemming from his shares in the Belgian company, which he would have been if the company had been Dutch.

This dispute arose before the entry into force of the EC Treaty and regarding the free movement of capital it was Article 67 of the EEC Treaty that applied. Directive 88/361/EEC was one of the directives that implemented Article 67 of the EEC Treaty.[30] Therefore the Court considered whether Article 1 (1) of Directive 88/361/EEC precluded the following provision of national legislation of a Member State. According to the national piece of legislation at issue, the benefit of exemption from income tax on dividends paid to individuals who were shareholders was subject to the condition that those dividends were paid by a company whose seat was in the same Member State that granted the benefit.[31] An initial question of interest in this section was whether the cross-border distribution of dividends was covered by Directive 88/361/EEC.[32]

The Court confirmed that the EEC Treaty did not define capital, and sought guidance in the Annex to the Directive. Even if the receipt of dividends was not expressively mentioned in the Annex, the Court considered that it necessarily presupposes participation in new or existing undertakings referred to in Heading I (2) of the nomenclature,[33] and that it accordingly was covered by the Directive.

6.3.3.4 Concluding Remarks

The general conclusion to be drawn is, of course, that where the EC Treaty gives little guidance on the meaning of capital, Directive 88/361/EEC provides authoritative support for the interpretation of the expression. In my view, the meanings of capital and capital movements are to a large extent connected.

What constitutes capital (movements) has been addressed by the European Court of Justice in several other cases than the previously referred. In case C-302/97 *Konle* the Court declared that capital movements include investments in real estate on the

30 Article 67 of the EEC Treaty was amended and replaced through the Amsterdam treaty by the present Article 56 of the EC Treaty.

31 Case C-35/98 *Verkooijen*, para. 25.

32 Case C-35/98 *Verkooijen*, para. 26.

33 Case C-35/98 *Verkooijen*, para. 28. According to the Court, there was also a link to Acquisition by residents of foreign securities dealt in on a stock exchange, referred to in Heading III.A(2) of the Annex (cf. case C- 35/98 *Verkooijen*, para. 29).

territory of a Member State by non-residents. As a basis for that decision the Court advanced the Annex to Directive 88/361/EEC.[34]

An additional question that has been heavily debated is whether the nomenclature in the Annex to the Directive not only covers the flow of funds, but whether it also covers the transactions by which the funds are generated.[35] According to the introduction to the nomenclature, the capital movements listed are taken to cover:

> "... – all the operations necessary for the purposes of capital movements: conclusion and performance of the transaction and related transfers. The transaction is generally between residents of different Member States although some capital movements are carried out by a single person for his own account (e.g. transfers of assets belonging to emigrants),
>
> – operations carried out by any natural or legal person including operations in respect of the assets or liabilities of Member States or of other public administrations and agencies ...".

Flynn accordingly finds support for the view that such transactions are covered by the free movement of capital. He notes, however, that the Court has not always supported it.[36]

6.3.4 Personal Scope

The personal scope of the free movement of capital is wide. In fact, Article 56 of the EC Treaty does not refer to any specific group of persons that may invoke the freedom. In my view that means that any person with legal capacity could invoke the free movement of capital. Article 56 only refers to the object of the freedom – capital movements. In both case C-484/93 *Svensson and Gustavsson* and the joined cases C-358/93 and C-416/93 *Bordessa*, the free movement of capital was invoked by nationals of third states.[37] The previous Article 67 of the EEC Treaty required nationality of a Member State to apply, but that condition was abolished with the Maastricht Treaty.

34 Case C-302/97 *Konle*, para. 22. Cf. also joined cases C-515/99, C-519/99 to C-524/99 and C-526/99 to C-540/99 *Hans Reisch and Others*, para. 30.

35 Cf. Flynn, "Coming of Age: the Free Movement of Capital Case Law", *CML Rev.*, 2002, pp. 773-805, at p. 777.

36 Flynn, *op. cit.*, pp. 777-778.

37 Case C-484/93 *Svensson and Gustavsson,* and joined cases C-358/93 and C-416/93 *Bordessa and Others*.

6.4 Relation to the Freedom of Establishment and Other Freedoms

6.4.1 Introduction

The relation between the free movement of capital and other fundamental freedoms is of significance to this study, which also deals with the freedom of establishment. In several of the cases on the freedom of establishment dealt with in Chapters 4 and 5, the European Court of Justice was also asked to consider the national measure at issue in relation to the free movement of capital. In most cases the Court decided not to consider the compatibility with the free movement of capital, once it came to the conclusion that the measure was incompatible with the freedom of establishment.

One principal question dealt with in this section is whether the free movement of capital is equal to the other freedoms, or whether it only has an ancillary function to them.

6.4.2 Relation to the Freedom of Establishment

A starting point for the discussion of the relation between the freedom of establishment and the free movement of capital are Article 43 (2) and Article 58 (2) of the EC Treaty.

Article 43 (2), relating to the freedom of establishment, stipulates that the right of secondary establishment of for example a branch or a subsidiary in a Member State, is "subject to the provisions of the Chapter relating to capital".[38] From a textual point of view that provision seems to mean that if, for example, a national measure was in conformity with the the free movement of capital, it would also be in conformity with the freedom of establishment. Following from this, the opposite situation would also be true if the previous interpretation were true: if a national measure violated the free movement of capital it would also be violating the freedom of establishment.

Article 58 (2) stipulates: "The provisions of this Chapter shall be without prejudice to the applicability of restrictions on the right of establishment which are compatible with this Treaty." From a textual point of view this provision seems to mean that if for example a national measure were found to be in accordance with the freedom of establishment, it would also be in accordance with the free movement of capital, even if in principle it constitutes a restriction on the freedom of establishment. In my view the opposite would also be true if the first interpretation is true: if a national measure

[38] Article 43 (2) stipulates (emphasis added): "Freedom of establishment shall include the right to take up and pursue actvities such as self-employed persons and to set up and manage undertakings, in particular companies or firms within the meaning of the second paragraph of Article 48, under the conditions laid down for its own nationals by the law of the country where such establishment is effected, *subject to the provisions of the Chapter relating to capital.*"

is in breach of the freedom of establishment and not compatible with the Treaty, the measure will not be compatible with the free movement of capital.

This textual interpretation speaks in favour of the theory that the rules on the freedom of establishment and on the free movement of capital can be simultaneously applicable. This view also has substantial support in legal doctrine. Schön, for example, argues: "Dieser Gesetzgeberische Vorbehalt macht deutlich, daß die unternehmerische Niederlassung in einem anderen Mitgliedstaat gleichermaßen als Ausübung beider Grundfreiheiten verstanden werden kann."[39] Consequently, Schön considers that none of the freedoms can be regarded as *lex specialis* to the other.[40] Rather, the different freedoms protect different dimensions of the same activity or event: "Vielmehr schützt jede Grundfreiheit eine andere inhaltliche Dimension desselben Vorgangs – die Niederlassungsfreiheit die Ausübung eines Berufs, die Kapitalverkehrsfreiheit den Transfer geldwerter Güter. Dem Marktbürger steht es daher frei, sich auf jede dieser Grundfreiheiten zu berufen."[41]

However, there are authors who take another view and advocate a theory of exclusivity regarding the application of the fundamental freedoms.[42] As regards the relationship between the freedom of establishment and the free movement of capital, Article 43 (2) and the previously discussed expression "subject to the provisions of the chapter relating to capital" have been seen as argument for the exclusivity of the free movement of capital. It is difficult to agree with that interpretation. Rather, the quoted phrase means that if a measure has been either approved or disapproved according to the rules on the free movement of capital, there is no need to the test the compatibility with the freedom of establishment, even if that freedom in principle were applicable. If the measure has been tested according to the free movement of capital it has also been tested according to the rules on the freedom of establishment in the area where those two freedoms overlap. In conclusion, one must agree with von Wilmowsky that: "Die Exklusivitätstheorie verdient keine Gefolgschaft."[43]

---

39 "This legal reservation makes it clear that the establishment in another Member State can equally be regarded as exercising both fundamental freedoms." Schön, "Europäische Kapitalverkehrsfreiheit und nationales Steuerrecht", in *Gedächtnisschrift für Knobbe-Keuk*, Schön (ed.), Verlag Dr. Otto Schmidt, Cologne, 1997, pp. 743-777, at p. 749.

40 Schön, *op. cit.*, p. 749.

41 "Furthermore, each of the basic rights protects another included feature of the same activity – the freedom of establishment protects the pursuit of a profession, the free movement of capital protects the transfer of goods of monetary value. The citizen of the common market is therefore able to claim each of the basic freedoms." Schön, *op. cit.*, pp. 749-750 (with further references).

42 Cf. von Wilmowsky, "Freiheit des Kapital- und Zahlungsverkehr", in *Europäische Grundrechte und Grundfreiheiten*, Ehlers (ed.), de Gruyter Recht, Berlin, 2003, pp. 290-317, at pp. 292-293 (with further references).

43 "The exclusivity theory is not worth pursuing." Von Wilmowsky, *op. cit.*, p. 293.

It should be underlined that the freedom of establishment and the free movement of capital do not cover identical areas. The scope of application of the free movement of capital is wider than the scope of the freedom of establishment. It is difficult to imagine an entrepreneurial establishment in another Member State without any cross-border transfer of capital. It is difficult to imagine a situation where the freedom of establishment applies and the free movement of capital does not apply. In contrast, the opposite may very well occur, namely that the free movement of capital applies, but not the freedom of establishment: the free movement of capital has a wider scope of applicability than the freedom of establishment. In order to determine which freedom applies to a specific situation, one has to consider what form of activity is conducted. Article 43 of the EC Treaty on the freedom of establishment focuses on entrepreneurial activity. Article 56 of the EC Treaty on the free movement of capital focuses on the mere transfer of capital that may very well be an investment of some form, but not necessarily including the exercise of an entrepreneurial activity covered by the freedom of establishment. Moreover, the transfer of capital that forms part of an entrepreneurial activity will be covered by both the freedom of establishment and the free movement of capital.

In a number of cases the European Court of Justice has been asked whether a specific national tax measure is compatible with both the freedom of establishment and the free movement of capital. In general the Court has been unwilling to consider the compatibility with the free movement of capital. If the measure has been decided to be in breach of the freedom of establishment, the Court has not bothered to consider the compatibility with the free movement of capital. A reason for this may perhaps be reluctance on the side of the Court to step into the relatively unknown territory of the free movement of capital and to deal with the results unknown, at least at the time, which could follow. Moreover, when a measure has been found to be incompatible with the freedom of establishment, the Court may also have found it sufficient and has spent the time it otherwise would have dealt with the free movement of capital on the accumulating workload of new and undecided cases.

The Court's way of applying the freedoms seems to be in line with the view that the wider free movement of capital is parallel to the freedom of establishment. It should be noted that the Advocate General in his opinion also has more frequently considered the compatibility of a national tax measure with the free movement of capital.[44]

[44] Ståhl also advocates a high degree of convergence between the free movement of capital and the freedom of establishment. Ståhl, "Beskattning av fria kapitalrörelser – inom EU och mot tredje land", in *Festskrift till Gustaf Lindencrona*, Arvidsson, Melz and Silfverberg (ed.), Norstedts Juridik, Stockholm, 2003, pp. 493-512, esp. pp. 496-498.

One example is AG Mischo in his opinion in case C-436/00 *X and Y* where he declared it necessary to consider the national measure at issue in relation to the free movement of capital, even if he did so only for the sake of completeness.[45]

In AG Alber's opinion in case C-251/98 *Baars* he developed a theory on the relationship between the freedom of establishment and the free movement of capital. In his view the European Court of Justice in its case-law applied in parallel the free movement of capital and the freedom to provide services as well as the freedom of establishment.[46] In addition AG Alber states: "The underlying principle is that the rules on capital movements only preclude the parallel application of other fundamental freedoms in situations where the rules in question specifically regulate the flow of capital."[47] The conclusion is that the case-law of the Court is incompatible with the view that the rules on the free movement of capital are generally mutually exclusive in relation to other fundamental freedoms.[48] In determining the applicability of the free movement of capital and the freedom of establishment AG Alber postulates the following three "rules":[49]

(i) Where the free movement of capital is directly restricted such that only an indirect obstacle to establishment is created, only the rules on capital movements apply.

(ii) Where the freedom of establishment is directly restricted such that the ensuing obstacle to establishment leads indirectly to a reduction of capital flows between Member States, only the rules on the freedom of establishment apply.

(iii) Where there is a direct intervention affecting both the free movement of capital and the freedom of establishment, both fundamental freedoms apply, and the national measure must satisfy the requirements of both.

In general the three postulates formulated by AG Alber seem to reflect the attitude of the Court, although it is hard to find a case where the Court has applied the third postulate and applied the two freedoms simultaneously. Evidently, the postulates are generally formulated and may give rise to difficulties of interpretation.

A possible indication that the Court might disagree with the third postulate is case C-436/00 *X and Y*. As regards the compatibility with the free movement of capital the European Court of Justice declared that this question "... need be considered

[45] Opinion of AG Mischo in case C-436/00 *X and Y*, para. 74-82.

[46] Opinion of AG Alber in case C-251/98 *Baars*, esp. para. 14-15.

[47] Opinion of AG Alber in case C-251/98 *Baars*, para. 15.

[48] Opinion of AG Alber in case C-251/98 *Baars*, para. 22.

[49] Opinion of AG Alber in case C-251/98 *Baars*, para. 26-30.

only to the extent that, in the light of the latter provisions [i.e. the Treaty provisions on freedom of establishment], the national provision at issue is such as to involve a separate restriction, where the Treaty provisions concerning freedom of establishment do not apply".[50] The Court had previously concluded that a type B share-transfer would entail an unjustified restriction on the freedom of establishment. As regards a type A share-transfer, the Court considered it clear that Article 43 precluded the national provision at issue only to the extent that the holding that the transferor had in the transferee company, established in another Member State, gave him "definite influence" over that company's decisions and allowed him to determine its activities.[51] Even so, I find it hard to draw any general conclusions from this case.

In case C-302/97 *Konle* the Court did not make a simultaneous application of the free movement of capital and the freedom of establishment. The case concerned Austrian legislation that stipulated prior authorisation for foreigners wishing to acquire land for a secondary establishment in Austria. The Court decided that such a law provision was in breach of the free movement of capital, and as a consequence did not find that there was a "need" to examine the national measure in relation to the freedom of establishment.[52] It is worth noting that AG La Pergola took the opposite approach and tried the compatibility of the measure with the freedom of establishment while not considering the compatibility with the free movement of capital.

In conclusion, the free movement of capital has been shown to be in principle parallel to the freedom of establishment. In case of both freedoms being applicable, the Court has resorted to the better known content of the freedom of establishment rather than dealing with the unknown "territory" of the free movement of capital.

6.4.3 Relation to Other Freedoms

The European Court of Justice has dealt with the distinction between the free movement of capital and the free movement of goods. An early case on this matter is Case 7/78 *Thompson*.[53] The principal question that the Court dealt with was whether the EC Treaty provisions on the free movement of goods or those on capital applied to the cross-border movement of coins and similar assets. The conclusion of the Court can be divided into two parts. First, if the coins, or banknotes and similar means of payment, are legal tender, then it is a matter of money transfer and the free movement of goods

[50] Case C-436/00 *X and Y*, para. 66. Cf. also section 4.5.4.3.

[51] Case C-436/00 *X and Y*, para. 67.

[52] Case C-302/97 *Klaus Konle v. Republik Österreich*, para. 55.

[53] Case 7/78 *Regina v. Thompson and Others*.

does not apply.[54] Alternatively, if the coins and similar assets were legal tender, then the provisions on the free movement of goods should not apply.[55]

Also the joined cases C-358/93 and C-416/93 *Bordessa and Others* give support for the distinction made in the *Thompson* case. *Bordessa and Others* concerned the transfer of banknotes. Mr Bordessa was an Italian national resident in Italy. He was apprehended in Spain by the Spanish customs when travelling to France. Mr Bordessa's car contained ESP 38 million. According to Spanish law, there was a requirement for a prior customs declaration if one were to transfer banknotes, coins and similar assets out of Spain. As regards the relation with the free movement of goods, the Court declared, thus relating to the *Thompson* case, that the transfer of legal tender was not covered by this freedom.[56]

Already in case C-204/90 *Bachmann*, the Court considered whether the free movement of capital applied to a national provision dealing with the deductibility of insurance and pension contributions. However, the Court found that there was a breach of the free movement of workers and the freedom to provide services. The free movement of capital as manifested in Article 67 (1) of the EEC Treaty did not apply.[57]

The relation between the freedom to provide services and the free movement of capital was also discussed in case C-484/93 *Svensson and Gustavsson*. Mr and Mrs Svensson-Gustavsson were resident in Luxembourg. There they were refused an interest rate subsidy for dependent children on a loan for the construction of a house in Luxembourg. The loan was issued by a bank which was established in Belgium, where it also had its head office.[58] The case was decided before the entry into force of the Maastricht Treaty, and therefore the Court only considered whether this law provision was in conflict with Directive 88/361/EEC on liberalised capital movements. To begin with the Court found that the legislation at issue was an obstacle to the free movement of capital.[59] The Court also examined whether it was in conflict with the freedom to provide services. The Court concluded that the legislation was discriminatory against credit institutions in other Member States and was therefore in conflict with the freedom to provide services as manifested in Article 59 of the EEC Treaty.[60] AG Elmer wanted to decide the matter solely in relation to the freedom to provide services. He advanced: "The

[54] Case 7/78 *Thompson and Others*, para. 28.

[55] Case 7/78 *Thompson and Others*, para. 34.

[56] Joined cases C-358/93 and C-416/93, *Bordessa and Others*, para. 12.

[57] Case C-204/90 *Bachmann*, para. 34.

[58] Case C-484/93 *Peter Svensson and Lena Gustavsson v. Ministre du Logement et de l'Urbanisme*, para. 2.

[59] Case C-484/93 *Svensson and Gustavsson*, para. 10.

[60] Case C-484/93 *Svensson and Gustavsson*, para. 12.

essential point with regard to the national subsidy system described in the judgment of reference is, on the contrary, that the system makes it economically less attractive to raise the loan in a financial institution which is not established in the Member State in question and so to undertake a cross-frontier performance of services in the form of a housing loan."[61] AG Elmer concluded therefore that the national legislation in question should not be discussed in relation to rules of Community law on capital transactions.[62] The European Court of Justice did not explicitly deal with this matter and the Court only stated that both the free movement of capital and the freedom to provide services were affected, and the Court accordingly discussed the relation between the national legislation and those freedoms.

Case C-118/96 *Safir*[63] is in this respect similar to the *Svensson and Gustavsson* case. This case dealt with Swedish taxation of savings in the form of capital life insurances. Swedish tax law made a distinction between capital life insurances taken out with, on the one hand, Swedish insurance companies and, on the other hand, foreign insurance companies. As regards capital life insurances taken out with Swedish insurance companies, it was the insurance company in question that was liable to tax on the yield of the insurance capital.[64] Capital life insurances taken out with foreign, non-Swedish, insurance companies were taxed in a different way. Article 1 of the Swedish Premium Tax law stipulated that individuals or legal entities domiciled or permanently resident in Sweden who had taken out life assurance with companies not established in Sweden had to pay a special state tax on the premiums paid. The tax was 15 per cent of the amount of the premium.[65] On the request of the policyholder (the insured person), it was possible to reduce the tax or even grant an exemption from the tax. A precondition was that the company with which the insurance was taken out was subject, in the state where it was established, to revenue tax comparable to that payable by insurance companies established in Sweden.[66] This option for tax reduction was intended to equalise the taxation of savings between domestic and foreign insurance companies. The Court concluded that the Premium Tax Law regarding foreign insurance companies contained "... a number of elements liable to dissuade individuals from taking out capital life assurances with companies not established in Sweden and liable to dissuade insurance companies from offering their services on the Swedish

[61] Opinion of AG Elmer in case C-484/93 *Svensson and Gustavsson*, para. 8.

[62] Opinion of AG Elmer in case C-484/93 *Svensson and Gustavsson*, para. 11.

[63] Case C-118/96 *Jessica Safir v. Skattemyndigheten i Dalarnas Län, formerly Skattemyndigheten i Kopparbergs Län*.

[64] Case C-118/96 *Safir*, para. 4.

[65] Case C-118/96 *Safir*, para. 9.

[66] Case C-118/96 *Safir*, para. 11.

market".[67] Finally the Court stated that it was not necessary to determine whether the legislation was also incompatible with Articles 6, 73b and 73d of the EEC Treaty: the relation to the free movement of capital was accordingly not discussed.

AG Tesauro was of a slightly different opinion. In his opinion there was no reason to examine the compatibility of the national law in question with more than the freedom to provide services. The reason was that it was not possible to make such an examination with both the freedom to provide services and the free movement of capital.[68] He stated: "... the compatibility with Community law of the national legislation at issue should – unless it simultaneously hinders both the free provision of services and the free movement of capital – be examined under either Article 59 *et seq.* [the freedom to provide services] or under Article 73b *et seq.* [the free movement of capital]". The Advocate General found support for this approach in earlier case-law from the Court.[69] The previously referred *Svensson and Gustavsson* case, however, marked a change of policy, because the measure in national legislation was examined both in relation to the freedom to provide services and the free movement of capital.[70] The Advocate General also proposed a method for deciding when to consider the different freedoms. The free movement of capital (ex Article 73 *et seq.*) would apply "... if the measure at issue directly restricts the transfer of capital, rendering it impossible or more difficult, for example by subjecting it to mandatory authorisation or in any event by imposing currency restrictions".[71] In contrast, the freedom to provide services would apply if the measure "... only indirectly restricts movement of capital and primarily constitutes a non-monetary restriction on the freedom to provide services, then Article 59 *et seq.* [the freedom to provide services] will apply".[72] The Advocate General, however, recognised that both sets of provisions apply *together*, but only in relation to national measures that simultaneously restrict, "although from different angles", the provisions of both services and capital.[73]

---

67 Case C-118/96 *Safir*, para. 30. The Court notes four major reasons why the treatment of foreign insurance companies constituted an obstacle to the freedom to provide services, cf. para. 26-29.

68 AG Tesauro declared, rightly, that an examination according to the general prohibition against discrimination, contained in Article 6 of the EEC Treaty, was not relevant. The reason was that it is settled case-law that Article 6 of the EEC Treaty would apply only to situations governed by Community law in regard to which the Treaty lays down no specific prohibition of discrimination (cf. para. 8 in the opinion of AG Tesauro in case C-118/96 *Safir*).

69 Case 15/78 *Société Générale Alsacienne de Banque v. Koestler*; Case 203/80 *Casati*; joined cases C-358/93 and C-416/93 *Criminal proceedings against Bordessa and Others*.

70 Cf. opinion of AG Tesauro in case C-118/96 *Safir*, para. 14.

71 Opinion of AG Tesauro in case C-118/96 *Safir*, para. 17.

72 *Ibid.*

73 *Ibid.* A recent tax case dealing with both the freedom to provide services and the free movement of capital is C-334/02 *Commission v. France*. The case dealt with French taxation of income received by individuals in the form of interest and similar income from Government securities, bonds, equities, bills and other debt

6.5 Article 58 of the EC Treaty – Statutory Limitations and Exceptions

6.5.1 Introduction

Article 58 of the EC Treaty (ex Article 73d) was added with the 1992 Maastricht Treaty. It has been argued that this Article constitutes a statutory response to the case-law of the European Court of Justice where national tax legislation has been found to violate the fundamental freedoms of the EC Treaty.[74] This section will deal with Article 58 (1) and (3), whereas Article 58 (2), concerning the relationship between the free movement of capital and the freedom of establishment, is discussed in the previous section 6.4.2.

In the earlier discussed case C-35/98 *Verkooijen*, the European Court of Justice also dealt with the interpretation of Article 58 of the EC Treaty. That aspect of the *Verkooijen* case will be discussed in section 6.5.3. In case C-478/98 *Commission v. Belgium* the Court further clarified the relation between Article 58 of the EC Treaty and the rule-of-reason doctrine. This case is the subject of section 6.5.4. Case C-436/00 *X and Y* also contains further elaboration of Article 58 and is commented in section 6.5.5. Concluding remarks are given in section 6.5.6.

6.5.2 Generally on Article 58 (1) and (3) of the EC Treaty

Article 58 of the EC Treaty stipulates that, irrespective of the freedoms granted by Article 56, Member States are free to take certain national measures, especially in the area of taxation.

More specifically, Article 58 (1)(a) provides that Member States have the right to apply tax legislation which distinguishes between taxpayers who are not in the same situation with regard to (i) their place of residence, or (ii) the place where their capital is invested.

According to Article 58 (1)(b), Member States are also entitled to take "all requisite measures" to prevent infringements of national law and regulations. This applies particularly in the field of taxation and in the "prudential supervision" of financial institutions. Article 58 (1)(b) also provides for the right of Member States to lay down procedures

---

instruments, If the debtor was resident in France he could elect for a specific levy in discharge of income tax on the income concerned. The rate of the fixed levy was generally lower than the regular income taxation. The more beneficial taxation for French residents was, according to the ECJ, a restriction on the freedom to provide services. The reason was that it had the effect of discouraging taxpayers who were resident in France to enter into such loan contracts with companies established in other Member States (para. 23). The French law was also a restriction on the free movement of capital because it prevented companies established in other Member States from raising loan capital in France (para. 24). It is interesting to note that the ECJ considered the French law to be simultaneously in breach of both the freedom to provide services and the free movement of capital.

[74] Terra and Wattel, *European Tax Law*, 3rd ed., Kluwer Law International, London/The Hague/New York, 2001, pp. 40-41.

for the declaration of capital movements for purposes of administrative or statistical information. In addition, the same provision stipulates that Member States are free to take measures, which are justified on grounds of public policy or public security.

A general safe haven clause is contained in Article 58 (3) of the EC Treaty. It provides that the national measures and procedures that are referred to in Article 58 (1)-(2) shall not constitute "… a means of arbitrary discrimination or a disguised restriction on the free movement of capital and payments as defined in Article 56".

6.5.3 Case C-35/98 *Verkooijen* (6 June 1999)

The general issue in case C-35/98 *Verkooijen* was the compatibility of a specific provision of Dutch tax law on dividend taxation, with Article 1 (1) of Council Directive 88/361/EEC of 24 June 1988. That Article stipulated the abolishment of restrictions on capital movements and is similar to Article 56 of the EC Treaty. In brief, the Dutch legislation at issue provided that for an individual resident in the Netherlands to be granted tax exemption on received dividends, the distributing company had to have its seat in the Netherlands and not in another Member State, such as Belgium, as in the underlying case before the national court.

The Court came to the conclusion that a law rule such as the Dutch provision in question constituted a restriction on capital movements and was prohibited by Article 1 (1) of Directive 88/361/EEC.[75]

The case was decided before the Treaty of the European Union entered into force. Because of that, the Court found it necessary only to consider the compatibility of the legislation in question with the EEC Treaty and Directive 88/361/EEC.[76] Despite this, the Court considered Article 58 (ex Article 73d) of the Treaty, containing provisions added in the Maastricht Treaty, and elaborated *obiter dictum* on this provision.

The Court declared that the new provision in Article 58 (1)(a), stating the possibility for Member States to distinguish in tax legislation between taxpayers according to their place of residence or the place where the capital is situated, had already been upheld by the Court in its case-law.[77] The Court explained: "According to that case-law, before the entry into force of Article 73d (1)(a) [present Article 58 (1)(a)] of the Treaty, national tax provisions of the kind to which that Article refers, in so far as they establish certain distinctions based, in particular, on the residence of taxpayers, could be compatible with Community law provided that they applied to situations which were

[75] Case C-35/98 *Verkooijen*, para. 36.

[76] Case C-35/98 *Verkooijen*, para. 42.

[77] Case C-35/98 *Verkooijen*, para. 43.

not objectively comparable (see, in particular, Case C-279/93 *Schumacker* [1995] ECR I-225) or could be justified by overriding reasons in the general interest, in particular in relation to the cohesion of the tax system (Case C-204/90 *Bachmann v. Belgian State* [1992] ECR I-249 and Case C-300/90 *Commission v. Belgium* [1992] ECR I-305)."[78] To conclude, the Court was of the view that Article 58 (1)(a) only confirms what the Court already had maintained in previous case-law. One has to interpret the Court in the way that it considers Article 58 (1)(a) to be the Treaty manifestation of the case-law evolved under the "Schumacker doctrine". Moreover, the Court repeats the essence of its rule-of-reason doctrine in the field of direct taxation: even if the situations of residents and non-residents are objectively comparable, a difference in treatment may be justified by grounds of justification in the public interest.

The Court also examined the meaning of Article 58 (3) in relation to Article 58 (1)(a). Article 58 (3) states that the *measures and procedures* referred to in Article 58 (1) and (2) shall not constitute a means of arbitrary discrimination or disguised restriction on the free movement of capital and payments as defined in Article 56. However, Article 58 (1)(d) refers to *the relevant provisions* of Member States' tax law distinguishing between taxpayers by reason of residence or where their capital is invested.

Because Article 58 (3) refers to "measures and procedures" and Article 58 (1) refers to "provisions", it could be advocated, however, that Article 58 (3) does not have any limiting effect on the right of the Member States according to Article 58 (1). The European Court of Justice did, however, make it quite clear that such an interpretation is wrong. The fact that different terms are used is, according to the Court, "irrelevant".[79] The Court justifies that view with the fact that it is difficult to distinguish between "measures and procedures" and "provisions" and that the term "measures and procedures" is not mentioned in Article 58 (2), even if Article 58 (3) expressly refers to Article 58 (2).[80] Accordingly, Article 58 (3) applies also on Article 58 (1). This interpretation must be seen as reasonable.

Article 58 (3) has the appearance of a safe haven clause: Article 58 (1)(a) states that Article 56 on the free movement of capital shall not constitute an obstacle for Member States to apply provisions of their tax legislation that differentiate between resident and non-resident taxpayers. However, Article 58 (3) limits the opportunity for Member

[78] *Ibid.* Sedlaczeck concludes on the interpretation of Article 58 (1)(a) of the EC Treaty: "It merely provides in an explicit treaty provision what the ECJ ruled in the cases cited above [author's note: e.g. the cases *Avoir fiscal*, *Commerzbank* and *Schumacker*]: national tax law based on residence and non-residence is not as such discriminatory." Sedlaczeck, "The Prohibition of Discrimination and Restrictions", *European Taxation*, 2000, pp. 14-27, at p. 23. In view of the *Verkooijen* case one definitely has to agree with Sedlaczeck.

[79] Case C-35/98 *Verkooijen*, para. 45.

[80] *Ibid.*

States to make such differences between taxpayers, if they constitute a "means of arbitrary discrimination or disguised restriction" on the free movement of capital.[81]

6.5.4 Case C-478/98 *Commission v. Belgium* (26 September 2000)

Case C-478/98 *Commission v. Belgium* primarily concerned the interpretation of Article 56 (ex Article 73 (b)) and Article 58 (1)(b) (ex Article 73d (1)(b)). The Belgian Minister of Finance had contracted a loan of DEM 1,000 million on the Eurobond market. This loan from banks resident in Germany could be subject to swap transactions. Belgian law provided that withholding taxes on interest payments were waived in Belgium. However, subscription to the loan by others than banks, financial intermediaries and institutional investors was not permitted in Belgium. The Commission put into question whether the exclusion of other Belgian residents was in breach of the free movement of capital.

The European Court of Justice came to the conclusion that the national measure constituted a restriction on the free movement of capital.[82] The Belgian government invoked a number of justifications. The justifications invoked were the need to: (i) prevent tax evasion, (ii) preserve fiscal coherence, and (iii) ensure the effectiveness of fiscal supervision. All these grounds have been accepted in principle by the Court; see the analysis in Chapters 3 and 5. It seems to me that both the Belgian government and the European Court of Justice consider these grounds to be covered by the scope of Article 58 (1)(b) of the EC Treaty. This view is supported by the Court's reasoning in this case in as much as it declared: "It follows that in the present case the fight against tax evasion and the effectiveness of fiscal supervision may be relied on under Article 73d (1)(b) [present Article 58 (1)(b)] of the Treaty to justify restrictions on the free movement of capital between Member States."[83] Regarding the need to preserve fiscal coherence the Court's reasoning seems somewhat vaguer on whether that ground can be invoked according to Article 58 (1)(b) of the Treaty. Albeit the Court considered fiscal coherence, and rejected it in this specific case because there was no direct link between a fiscal advantage and a corresponding fiscal disadvantage. Still, the Belgian government relied on Article 58 (1)(b) when invoking fiscal coherence, and there is in my view little reason not to believe that the Court also considered that provision in the Treaty as a basis for invoking fiscal coherence.

---

81 Peters discusses the meaning of "arbitrary discrimination" and especially how the adjective "arbitrary" should be interpreted. She notes that Article 30 (ex Article 36) of the EC Treaty, dealing with the free movement of goods, which also contains a prohibition against "arbitrary discrimination". This provision is in turn based on Article XX of GATT, and she is hesitant to draw any analogies to the area of free movement of capital as provided for in the EC Treaty. Peters, "Capital Movements and Taxation in the EC", *EC Tax Review*, 1998, pp. 4-12, at pp. 10-12. In my view it seems clear that the in tax law common distinction between resident and non-resident never itself can be considered as "arbitrary".

82 Case C-478/98 *Commission v. Belgium*, para. 27.

83 Case C-478/98 *Commission v. Belgium*, para. 39.

When the Court considered the applicability of the grounds of preventing tax evasion and fiscal supervision it also considered whether the measure complied with the principle of proportionality.[84] In the view of the Court the measure was not proportionate to its objectives accepted in principle, and could therefore not be covered by Article 58 (1)(b) of the EC Treaty.

A general conclusion from this case is that the Court considers Article 58 (1)(b) as a reference to the grounds of justification in the public interest, constituting a part of the rule-of-reason doctrine, which the Court has developed over the years in its case-law, primarily in the field of other fundamental freedoms. Article 58 (1)(b) seems to be a Treaty manifestation of the Court's case-law, and those who believed the provision to add something new to the free movement of capital must be considered to have been wrong.

Finally, it should be observed that the Court considered none of the grounds of justification to apply.

6.5.5 Case C-436/00 *X and Y* (21 November 2002)

Case C-436/00 *X and Y* has been discussed in several parts of this study.[85] The case dealt with Swedish legislation on corporate reorganisations. The question was whether the denial of specific tax benefits on cross-border transactions was in breach of the freedom of establishment and the free movement of capital. The Court considered that the national legislation at issue constituted a restriction on the freedom of establishment and no ground of justification according to the rule-of-reason doctrine applied. The Court considered the need to preserve fiscal coherence, the risk of tax avoidance and the effectiveness of fiscal supervision.[86] In relation to the free movement of capital, the Swedish National Tax Board also advanced Article 58 of the EC Treaty as ground for justifying the Swedish legislation at issue, and it thereby essentially referred to the previously mentioned grounds according to the rule-of-reason doctrine.

Regarding the grounds of justification in the public interest (the rule-of-reason doctrine) in relation to Article 58 (1)(a) of the Treaty (ex Article 73d (1)(a)) the Court referred to its decision in the *Verkooijen* case, previously discussed in this study.[87] The Court did not find those grounds applicable, and referred to the reasoning applied regarding the freedom of establishment. It seems to me that the Court considers there to be a high degree of convergence between the rule-of-reason doctrine developed regarding, on the

---

84 Case C-478/98 *Commission v. Belgium*, para 41.

85 Cf. Chapters 4 and 5.

86 Case C-436/00 *X and Y*, para. 48.

87 Case C-436/00 *X and Y*, para. 72.

one hand, the freedom of establishment and, on the other hand, the free movement of capital. Article 58 (1)(a) seems to add nothing new in substance to the already developed rule-of-reason doctrine.

6.5.6 Concluding Remarks

Article 58 (ex Article 73d) was introduced with the 1992 Maastricht Treaty. According to its wording, Article 58 sets limitations on the free movement of capital. In addition, Article 58 is special because it explicitly refers to tax legislation of the Member States. Not many provisions in the EC Treaty do that. In my view it seems clear that the European Court of Justice considers that the rule-of-reason doctrine as developed regarding the other fundamental freedoms also applies – as a general phenomenon – to the free movement of capital. In support of this view, the following argument could be made.

Article 58 (1)(a) specifically provides that Member States are free to apply relevant provisions of their tax law that distinguish between resident and non-resident taxpayers and to make similar distinctions on where the capital is invested. In the *Verkooijen* case, which dealt with the free movement of capital, the Court declared that in its previous case-law it already had come to the conclusion that Member States had the right to treat nationals differently on the basis of their residence, provided that the situations of residents and non-residents were not objectively comparable. In this study the term the "Schumacker doctrine" has been used for this position developed and taken by the Court. It also follows from the Court's reasoning in the *Verkooijen* case that if the situation of residents and non-residents are objectively comparable, the difference in treatment may anyway be justified according to imperative reasons in the general interest. It seems that the Court infers this from Article 58 (1)(a), but if one considers other cases on the free movement of capital it is more likely that such grounds of justification according to the rule-of-reason doctrine follow from Article 58 (1)(b).

Article 58 (1)(b) gives Member States the right to take measures against, for example, infringements of national tax law. In case C-478/98 *Commission v. Belgium* the Court stated that this provision (ex Article 73d (1)(b)) refers to the right of Member States to take measures in the field of taxation to prevent tax evasion and ensures the effectiveness of fiscal supervision.[88]

Article 58 (1)(a) and (b) refers, according to the Court, to the rule-of-reason doctrine. More specifically, lit. (a) refers to the Schumacker doctrine, and lit. (b) refers to grounds of justification in the public interest that may be relied upon. The Court is not always clear on this issue, but this is a reasonable interpretation.

88 In support of this standpoint, the ECJ in case C-478/98 *Commission v. Belgium*, para. 38-39, refers to its decision in the joined cases C-358/93 and C-416/93 *Bordessa and Others*.

In addition, according to Article 58 (3) national measures taken according to Article 58 (1)(a) and (b) shall not constitute a means of arbitrary discrimination or a disguised restriction. This speaks in favour of the opinion that Article 58 (1) does not inflict upon the rule-of-reason doctrine.

In a fairly recent decision by the European Court of Justice in case C-367/98 *Commission v. Portugal* (4 June 2002), the Court made the following declaration on the status of the rule-of-reason doctrine in the area of the free movement of capital:

> "The free movement of capital ... may be restricted only by national rules which are justified by reasons referred to in Article 73d (1) [present Article 58 (1)] of the Treaty or by overriding requirements of the general interest and which are applicable to all persons and undertakings pursuing an activity in the territory of the host Member State. Furthermore, in order to be so justified, the national legislation must be suitable for securing the objective which it pursues and must not go beyond what is necessary in order to attain it, so as to accord with the principle of proportionality ..."[89]

I would say that it is clear that the rule-of-reason doctrine also applies to the free movement of capital. The inclusion of Article 58 in the Maastricht Treaty has not altered that. Moreover, it is my view that neither Article 58 (1)(a) nor (b) adds anything new to the practice developed by the Court in the field of direct taxation in the case-law on the other fundamental freedoms, predominantly the ones on persons and services.[90] The quoted declaration by the Court in case C-367/98 on company law seems to suggest that the rule-of-reason doctrine applies in parallel with the limitations and exceptions contained in Article 58. This probably does not apply in practice, at least not in the area of direct taxation.[91]

---

89 Case C-367/98 *Commission v. Portugal*, para. 49. In support of this declaration the ECJ refers to joined cases C-163/94 C-165/94 and C-250/94 *Sanz de Lera and Others*, para. 23, and case C-54/99 *Église de Scientologie*, para. 18.

90 It is primarily case C-35/98 *Verkooijen* that has brought light upon the interpretation of Article 58 of the EC Treaty. Prior to this case there were considerable doubts on its interpretation, see e.g. Mohamed, *European Community Law on the Free Movement of Capital and the EMU*, Kluwer Law International, The Hague/London/Boston, 1999, pp. 147-148.

91 Mohamed discusses the meaning of Declaration (No 7) on Article 73d of the Treaty establishing the European Community, which was annexed to the Treaty in the Maastricht agreement. The Declaration states that the right to differentiate between taxpayers applies only to those measures which were in force at the end of 1993 and only to operations concerning residents of other Member States. It has been interpreted as preventing Member States from retaining or introducing liberal tax laws with the objective of attracting capital from other Member States. Mohamed, *European Financial Integration Law*, Jure, Stockholm, 2001, p. 33. In my view, this Declaration seems to have had little influence on the cases decided by the ECJ, at least in the field of direct taxation.

Terra and Wattel submit three reasons why the new provisions of Article 58 of the EC Treaty were introduced:

(i) To lift the fears of Member States applying an imputation system of taxation to distributed company profits that the European Court of Justice might hold the discriminatory effects of such systems incompatible with the free movement of capital. According to the authors, Article 58 of the EC Treaty permits Member States that apply an imputation system to continue to make a distinction between resident and non-resident taxpayers.

(ii) To lift the fears of Member States that they might be restricted in their efforts to combat tax fraud, evasion and avoidance.

(iii) To secure room for the Member States to distinguish, for tax purposes, between resident taxpayers (subject to world-wide taxation) and non-resident taxpayers (only subject to source-country taxation).

As regards the first objective, the case-law of the European Court of Justice has made it difficult for Member States to maintain their imputation systems, even after the 1992 Maastricht Treaty where Article 58 was introduced: the outcome of the *Verkooijen* case is one example. Regarding the second objective, there have been difficulties for the Member States to maintain their legislation on the prevention of tax avoidance, irrespective of Article 58. The third objective – to distinguish between residents and non-residents – is, in the view of the Court, something which the Court itself has manifested in the Schumacker doctrine. The conclusion of Terra and Wattel is that Article 58 of the EC Treaty does in effect not have any substantial impact on the case-law from the European Court of Justice, with which I agree.[92]

6.6 Measures on Direct Taxation Constituting Restrictions on the Free Movement of Capital

6.6.1 Introduction

In this section there will be an analysis of restrictions prohibited by the European Court of Justice in cases dealing with national tax legislation of the Member States. If compared with the case-law on the freedom of establishment, there are only a few cases in this area. The analysis of the case-law will follow the same general pattern as the analysis in Chapter 4 on the freedom of establishment. Furthermore, in several

[92] Terra and Wattel, *European Tax Law*, 3rd ed., Kluwer Law International, London/The Hague/New York, 2001, pp. 19-20.

cases the Advocate General has discussed the compatibility of national tax legislation with the free movement of capital, but that angle has not been considered by the Court. A few such cases will also be discussed.

6.6.2 Case C-35/98 *Verkooijen* (6 June 1999)

Case C-35/98 *Verkooijen* concerned the compatibility of Dutch legislation on tax-exempt dividends with the free movement of capital. In 1991 Mr Verkooijen was both resident in and a national of the Netherlands, where he was employed by the Dutch company, Fina Nederland BV. Fina Nederland BV distributed petroleum products, and Petrofina NV, which was established in Belgium, where it also was quoted on the stock exchange, controlled the Dutch company.[93] Through an employee's savings plan (*werknemersspaarplan*), Mr Verkooijen acquired shares in Petrofina NV. In 1991 a dividend was paid to Mr Verkooijen on behalf of those shares. The dividend amounted to about NLG 2,337. In Belgium, there was a tax deduction at source of 25 per cent. In his tax return for 1991, Mr Verkooijen included the dividends as part of his taxable income.[94] Dutch tax law denied Mr Verkooijen a tax exemption on the received dividends. The reason for the denied exemption was that the Belgian company Petrofina NV had not been subject to Dutch dividend taxation.

The question considered by the European Court of Justice was whether Article 1 (1) of Directive 88/361/EEC precluded a legislative provision of a Member State which, like the provision at issue, made the grant of exemption from income tax payable on dividends paid to individuals who are shareholders subject to the condition that those dividends were paid by a company whose seat was in that Member State.[95]

The relevant Dutch tax legislation had the following characteristics.[96] Income tax was levied under the *Wet op de Inkomstenbelasting* 1964 (1964 Law on Income Tax, hereinafter called the "Income Tax Law"). According to Article 24 of the Income Tax Law, income from assets, such as dividends and other payments due to the holding of shares, was subject to income tax. Only individuals were subject to Dutch income tax (*inkomstenbelasting*). Dividends distributed by companies established in the Netherlands were subject to a deduction at source of income tax. That tax was labelled "dividend tax". The rules on the deduction of dividend tax were found in Article 1 (1) of the *Wet op de Dividendbelasting 1965* (the 1965 Law on the Taxation of Dividends).

---

[93] Case C-35/98 *Verkooijen*, para. 12.

[94] Case C-35/98 *Verkooijen*, para. 13.

[95] Case C-35/98 *Verkooijen*, para. 25.

[96] Case C-35/98 *Verkooijen*, para. 3-10.

This provision stipulated, in brief, that dividend tax was charged for all persons who received income in the form of dividends, and other such securities. The dividend may have been a definitive tax, which was particularly so where dividends on shares in a company established in the Netherlands were paid to a person who was not subject to Dutch income tax. However, if the dividends were paid to a person resident in the Netherlands, the dividend tax constituted a payment on account (*vorheffing*) of income tax. According to Article 15 of the *Algemene Wet inzake Rijksbelastingen* (General Law on State Taxes) that payment on account was set off against the tax payable on aggregate income, when tax on aggregate income was assessed. Income from shares up to a certain amount was exempted from tax by Article 47b of the Income Tax Law. The exemption applied to income from shares on which Dutch dividend tax had been levied, which, according to Article 1 (1) of the Dividend Tax Law, was income from shares in companies established in the Netherlands. The initial exemption of NLG 500 was raised to NLG 1,000 and an exemption of NLG 2,000 was available for married persons.

The exemption on dividends from companies established in the Netherlands fulfilled two underlying objectives.[97] First, the exemption was intended to raise the level of equity capital in undertakings and to stimulate interest on the part of private individuals in Dutch shares. Secondly, the exemption was intended to compensate to some extent for the double taxation which otherwise would result under the Dutch tax system, from the levying of corporation tax on company profits and tax on the income of private shareholders imposed on the dividends distributed by companies. The second objective applied in particular to small investors. The cross-border element of the case was, of course, the cross-border distribution of dividends.

The dispute in the main proceedings arose before the entry into force of the Treaty of the European Union. As a consequence it was Article 67 of the EEC Treaty[98] on the free movement of capital that applied. Article 67 was implemented by several directives and among them Directive 88/361/EEC, which was in force at the time of the proceedings. As may be recalled, Article 1 (1) of the Directive read: "Without prejudice to the following provisions, Member States shall abolish restrictions on movements of capital taking place between persons resident in Member States. To facilitate application of this Directive, capital movements shall be classified in accordance with the Nomenclature in Annex I."

---

97 Case C-35/98 *Verkooijen*, para. 11.

98 Article 67 of the EEC Treaty read: "During the transitional period and to the extent necessary to ensure the proper functioning of the common market, Member States shall progressively abolish between themselves all restrictions on the movement of capital belonging to persons resident in the Member States and any discrimination based on the nationality or on the place of residence of the parties or on the place where such capital is invested."

The first question put to the European Court of Justice was, in the Court's own way of formulating it, the following. Did Article 1 (1) of Directive 88/361/EEC preclude a legislative provision of a Member State that, like the provision at issue in the main proceedings, made the grant of exemption from income tax payable on dividends paid to individuals who are shareholders subject to the condition that those dividends were paid by a company whose seat was in that Member State?[99]

First, the Court considered whether the Directive covered dividend payments – a question answered in the affirmative and previously dealt with in this study.[100] Secondly, and the main subject of this section, did the refusal of a Member State to exempt its taxpayers who received dividends on shares in a company whose seat was in another Member State from liability to tax on those dividends, constitute a restriction of capital movements within the meaning of Article 1 (1) of the Directive?[101]

The Court concluded that the national legislation at issue did constitute a restriction of the free movement of capital.[102] The Court declared that the national legislation had "... the effect of dissuading nationals of a Member State residing in the Netherlands from investing their capital in companies which have their seat in another Member State".[103] The Court advanced the legislative history of the provisions: they were intended to promote investment by individuals in companies established in the Netherlands in order to increase their equity capital.[104] Secondly, it had a restrictive effect on companies established in other Member States because it constituted an obstacle to the raising of capital in the Netherlands. The reason was, of course, that the dividends that such foreign companies paid to individuals resident in the Netherlands were treated less favourably for tax purposes than dividends from companies resident in the Netherlands.[105]

Accordingly, the legislation was a restriction on capital movements prohibited by Article 1 (1) of Directive 88/361/EEC.[106] The outcome of the case is clear. There was a difference in taxation in the Netherlands depending on where the company in which one had shares had its seat: there was a more beneficial taxation if the company was Dutch than if it was foreign.

---

99 Case C-35/98 *Verkooijen*, para. 25.

100 Section 6.3.3.

101 Case C-35/98 *Verkooijen*, para. 31.

102 Cf. case C-35/98 *Verkooijen*, para. 34-36.

103 Case C-35/98 *Verkooijen*, para. 34.

104 *Ibid.*

105 Case C-35/98 *Verkooijen*, para. 35.

106 Case C-35/98 *Verkooijen*, para. 36.

6.6.3 Case C-439/97 *Sandoz* (14 October 1999)

Case C-439/97 *Sandoz* concerned the compatibility with the free movement of capital of Austrian legislation imposing a stamp duty on loan agreements. The case is important to this study, even if it does not deal with direct taxation. The *Sandoz* case does not deal with direct taxation on income. However, it is still interesting in this context because it is one of the rare cases dealing with matters of taxation in relation to the free movement of capital. There will be no discussion of the *Sandoz* case in section 6.7 on rejected and accepted grounds of justification, because it is difficult to draw a clear line in this case between the issues of whether there is a restriction and whether such a restriction can be justified. Similarly, in the *Sandoz* case the Court also interprets Article 58 of the EC Treaty, which is primarily dealt with in section 6.5 of this chapter. However, because it is difficult to isolate that question from the other questions dealt with in the *Sandoz* case, it will also be covered in this section.

The underlying case before the national court rested on the following facts. In January 1995 the Austrian company Sandoz (hereinafter "Sandoz (Austria)") contracted a loan of ATS 220 million with Sandoz Management Services SA, a company with its corporate seat in Belgium. No written loan instrument was issued, but Sandoz (Austria) entered the loan in its accounts. On 18 December 1995, Austrian authorities requested Sandoz (Austria) to pay stamp duty on the basis of the "equivalent" of a loan document (*Ersatszbeurkundung*), at a rate of 0.8 per cent of the amount of the loan in accordance with the first sentence of the fourth subparagraph of Article 33 *Tarifpost* (TP) 8 of the *Gebührengesetz* (Law on Duties – hereinafter "GebG").

Austrian legislation provided for a stamp duty tax on all loans, irrespective of whether they were taken out in Austria or abroad. There was, however, a distinction made between domestic and foreign loans[107] regarding the chargeable event. On the one hand, if the document was drawn up in Austria, stamp duty was payable according to Article 16 (1) of the GebG, either on the date the document was signed by both parties, or on the date of delivery or dispatch of the document by the sole signatory.[108] On the other hand, if the document was drawn up outside of Austria, duty was payable on conclusion of the written agreement or, on the date on which the document was brought into Austria; all according to Article 16 (2) of the GebG. The situation where a loan was granted by a lender that was not domiciled or did not have a registered office in Austria, and were the loan was not recorded in a special instrument, the loan agreement was covered by a special provision, Article 33 TP 8 of the GebG. This

[107] "Domestic" and "foreign" loan on the basis whether the document was drawn up in Austria or another country. See case C-439/97 *Sandoz*, para. 9.

[108] Case C-439/97 *Sandoz*, para. 10.

provision stipulated that where such a loan was entered into the books and records of account of the Austrian borrower, it should be deemed to constitute a written loan instrument. In Austria, the legislator considered it a risk that if loans were taken abroad, the loan instrument would remain with the foreign lender and thus lead to a situation where the Austrian borrower would not pay the stamp duty. Accordingly, this provision sought to ensure that loans to Austrian residents were granted under the same conditions from the tax point of view, irrespective of whether the lender was Austrian or foreign.[109]

The European Court of Justice was asked among other questions whether Article 56 (1) (ex Article 73b (1)) and Article 58 (1)b (ex Article 73d (1)(b)), as well as Article 58 (3) (ex Article 73d (3)) precluded the levying of the Austrian stamp duty on loans contracted in a Member State other than Austria.[110]

The European Court of Justice initially declared that Article 56 (1) covers all restrictions on movements of capital between Member States and between Member States and non-Member States.[111] Regarding the Austrian legislation on stamp duty the Court declared that it "... deprives residents of a Member State of the possibility of benefiting from the absence of taxation which may be associated with loans obtained outside the national territory".[112] Furthermore, the Court found that such national measures were likely to deter residents from obtaining loans from persons established in other Member States, and in support referred to case C-484/93 *Svensson and Gustavsson*.[113] The Austrian legislation at issue constituted, in the view of the Court, an obstacle to the free movement of capital as manifested in Article 56 (1) (ex Article 73b (1)).[114] In the view of the Austrian government, the taxing of loans taken out abroad was justified by the need to observe the principle that residents should be treated equally for tax purposes.[115] The Court accepted this line of reasoning. It declared that the Austrian legislation at issue prevented taxable persons from evading the requirement of domestic tax legislation through the exercise of the free movement of capital. In addition, the legislation in question was essential in order to prevent infringements of national tax law, as provided for in Article 58 (1)(a) (ex

[109] Case C-439/97 *Sandoz*, para. 15.

[110] Case C-439/97 *Sandoz*, para. 17.

[111] Case C-439/97 *Sandoz*, para. 18.

[112] Case C-439/97 *Sandoz*, para. 19.

[113] *Ibid.*

[114] Case C-439/97 *Sandoz*, para. 20.

[115] Case C-439/97 *Sandoz*, para. 23.

Article 73d (1)(b)).[116] Furthermore, the Court examined whether the legislation at issue constituted a means of arbitrary discrimination, prohibited according to Article 58 (3) (ex Article 73d (3)). The Court simply concluded that the legislation applied to all borrowers resident in Austria without distinction to nationality or the place where the loan was contracted. This interpretation of Article 58 (3) seems reasonable: the national legislation at issue applies without distinction to factors such as residence, and Article 58 (3) prohibits "arbitrary discrimination". The Austrian rule at issue is neither "arbitrary", nor "discriminatory". In conclusion, the Court considered the Austrian legislation in question to be in conformity with the requirements of Article 56 (1), Article 58 (1)(b) and Article 58 (3) of the EC Treaty.

The second question that the Court considered was whether Article 56 (1) (ex Article 73b (1)) and Article 58 (3) (ex Article 73d (3)), as well as Article 1 (1) and 4 of Directive 88/361/EEC precluded a provision of Austrian law[117] with the following content. On the one hand, if a legal entity or an individual resident in Austria concludes a contract for a loan not manifested in a written instrument and the existence of the loan is recorded by an entry in the borrower's books and accounting, the Austrian borrower is liable to pay duty tax.[118] On the other hand, if a loan was contracted in Austria, and not manifested in writing, Austrian law required that the loan was registered in the accounting. However, such an "Austrian" loan was not subject to duty tax according to Austrian law.[119] In the view of the Court, such a distinction according to the place where the loan was contracted constituted a restriction on the free movement of capital as manifested in Article 56 (1) (ex Article 73b (1)). The next step of the Court was to consider whether this restriction could be justified according to Article 58 (1)(b) (ex Article 73d (1)(b)) of the EC Treaty. First, the Austrian government advanced that this difference in treatment was intended to ensure equal tax treatment for Austrian residents, regardless of the borrower's nationality, and the placer were the loan was contracted. The Court did not accept that justification. The reason was that the law rule at issue was discriminatory; there was a difference in taxation on the basis whether the loan was taken out in Austria or abroad.[120] Secondly, the Austrian government advanced that the objective behind the legislation at issue was to overcome fraudulent concealment of loans taken out abroad. However, the Court replied that the legislation at issue was "... not apt to prevent fraud by borrowers resident in Austria".[121] Consequently, the

---

116 Case C-439/97 *Sandoz*, para. 24.

117 Article 33 TP 8 of the GebG.

118 Case C-439/97 *Sandoz*, para. 29.

119 Article 33 TP 8 of the GebG, see case C-439/97 *Sandoz*, para. 30.

120 Cf. case C-439/97 *Sandoz*, para. 34.

121 Case C-439/97 *Sandoz*, para. 35.

difference in treatment could not be justified by Article 58 (1)(b) of the EC Treaty. This outcome made it, in the view of the Court, not necessary to consider whether Article 58 (3) applied or not. This has to be interpreted to imply that the legislation at issue was not a means of "arbitrary discrimination". It is easy to agree with that opinion: the difference in treatment was based upon the fact of whether the loan was taken in Austria or abroad, which seems a "logical", albeit unlawful, form of discrimination.

It is the former question dealt with by the Court that is the more interesting, at least when considering the answer by the Court. Austrian stamp duty on loans taken out abroad was in line with the free movement of capital even if no stamp duty was taken out in the foreign country. The reason was that this provision was aimed at establishing a form of tax neutrality between loans taken out in Austria and in other countries. One could perhaps say that the Austrian legislation in question sought to establish capital export neutrality. This was an objective covered by Article 58 (1)(b) of the EC Treaty. Perhaps this outcome could be applied as an argument in favour of the view that some forms of anti-avoidance legislation are accepted according to the rule-of-reason doctrine and Article 58 (1)(b) of the EC Treaty. For example, the *Sandoz* case has been advanced by the Swedish government in support of a reformed CFC legislation.[122] To simplify the line of argumentation used, the Swedish CFC legislation is aimed at achieving neutrality in taxation between income derived from abroad and income having its source in Sweden. In my view this reasoning may have some bearing. But the fact remains that Swedish CFC taxation means taxation at an earlier point in time than if the foreign profits would have distributed as dividends (if ever); the CFC legislation is still detrimental to the domestic taxpayer.

6.6.4 Case C-436/00 *X and Y* (21 November 2002)

Case C-436/00 *X and Y* concerned the compatibility with the freedom of establishment and the free movement of capital of a Swedish rule that refused the benefit of tax deferral upon the transfer of shares in companies at undervalue if foreign legal persons were involved.

The individuals X and Y had Swedish nationality and were resident in Sweden. They owned shares in companies both in Sweden and in other states. Referring to a scheduled business reorganisation, X and Y asked the Swedish Revenue Law Commission (*Skatterättsnämnden*) for a preliminary ruling on the tax consequences. The reorganisation had the following basic characteristics. X and Y would transfer their shares in the Swedish company X AB at their acquisition cost. The shares would be

[122] Government bill, prop. 2003/04:10 *Ändrade regler för CFC-beskattning*, p. 110.

transferred to Z AB, another Swedish company, which in turn was a subsidiary of a Belgian company, Y SA. X and Y owned Y SA.

The facts of this case are dealt with more thoroughly in Chapter 4 on the freedom of establishment. However, the Court also considered the compatibility of the Swedish rule at issue with the free movement of capital. It should first be noted that the European Court of Justice considered that the national provision at issue constituted an unjustifiable obstacle to the freedom of establishment.

According to the Court, the free movement of capital was relevant only in respect of the situations where Article 43 of the EC Treaty did not apply to a type A share-transfer, because of the insufficient level of participation of the transferor in the transferee company, which was established in another Member State.[123]

The Court declared that the national measure could not be considered as a purely internal measure because it concerned movements of capital between Member States. That was the case when a transfer was made of shares at undervalue by a resident of a Member State to a company established in another Member State in which the transferor or his kin directly or indirectly had a holding.[124]

The Court considered it as "common ground" that the national provisions at issue were liable to dissuade those liable to Swedish tax on gains from transferring shares at undervalue to transferee companies established in another Member State in which they directly or indirectly had a holding.[125] Accordingly, the national provisions constituted a restriction on the free movement of capital.[126] It seems apparent that it concerned a restriction from the home state perspective.

6.6.5 Case C-242/03 *Weidert and Paulus* (15 July 2004)

Case C-242/03 *Weidert and Paulus* dealt with Luxembourg law provisions granting tax benefits on the investment in companies established in Luxembourg. The facts of the underlying case were basically the following. The couple Mr Weidert and Mrs Paulus (subsequently Mr and Mrs Weidert-Paulus) was resident for tax purposes in Luxembourg. Luxembourg tax law covered individuals resident for tax purposes in Luxembourg who acquired shares representing cash contributions in companies resident in Luxembourg. The tax relief consisted of a relief for investment in personal property.[127]

123 Case C-436/00 *X and Y*, para. 68.

124 Case C-436/00 *X and Y*, para. 69.

125 Case C-436/00 *X and Y*, para. 70.

126 *Ibid.*

127 Case C-242/03 *Weidert and Paulus*, para. 3.

Mr and Mrs Weidert-Paulus had made such an investment in a company established in Belgium, and claimed the same tax relief in Luxembourg as if the company had been established in that state. The question was referred to the European Court of Justice whether this limitation was compatible with the free movement of capital.

The Court considered the national law from both an inbound and an outbound perspective. From an outbound perspective it had the effect of discouraging nationals of Luxembourg from investing their capital in companies in other Member States.[128] From an inbound perspective it had the effect of restricting companies established in other Member States from raising capital in Luxembourg.[129] In conclusion, the Luxembourg law constituted a restriction on the free movement of capital. The decision by the Court is unquestionable and is in line with previous case-law of the Court, perhaps most notably the decision in the *Verkooijen* case.

6.6.6 Case C-319/02 *Manninen* (7 September 2004)

Case C-319/02 *Manninen* concerns the Finnish imputation system, in which the opinion of AG Kokott was delivered on 18 March 2004[130] and the decision by the Court was delivered on 7 September 2004. The Finnish imputation system had the following basic features. The corporate tax rate was 29 per cent, shareholders receiving dividends would accordingly receive 71 cent for a distributed profit of 100 cents. Shareholders were also entitled to a credit consisting of 29/71 of the dividend. Because the tax rate on received dividends including the credit also was 29 per cent, the economic double taxation of corporate profits is eliminated at the shareholder level. When dividends were distributed from a Finnish company to a non-resident shareholder, the system for elimination of economic double taxation did not work satisfactorily.

In the underlying case before the Finnish Supreme Administrative Court (*Korkein Hallinto-Oikus*) a Finnish national, Mr Manninen, had shares in a Swedish company. Mr Manninen was subject to unlimited tax liability in Finland, and a limited tax liability in Sweden on the dividend distributions from the Swedish company. The dividend distributing company in Sweden had to pay a Swedish withholding tax ("coupon tax") on the received dividends, nominally 30 per cent. Mutén calculates a net intake in the hands of Manninen of 51.2 cents[131] on profits distributed from a Swedish company,

---

128 Case C-242/03 *Weidert and Paulus*, para. 13.

129 Case C-242/03 *Weidert and Paulus*, para. 14.

130 For a thorough analysis of the opinion of AG Kokott in case C-319/02 *Manninen*, see Mutén, "ECJ Advocate General Issues Opinion on Finland's Imputation System", *Tax Notes International*, 29 March 2004, pp. 1154-1157.

131 With a corporate profit of 100 cents.

compared with 71 per cent on dividends from a Finnish company.[132] The Finnish Supreme Administrative Court asked the European Court of Justice for a preliminary ruling on the compatibility of this difference in treatment with the free movement of capital. AG Kokott found that the less favourable treatment of foreign dividends was a limitation on the free movement of capital. In addition, she also considered the treatment to make the acquisition of capital in the Finnish market more difficult for foreign corporations than for Finnish corporations. There was a restriction on the free movement of capital. The reasoning of AG Kokott on the meaning of fiscal coherence as a ground of justification is a matter which will be discussed in section 6.7.

The Court begins by dealing with the question as to whether the Finnish law provision at issue constituted a restriction on the free movement of capital as contained in Article 56 of the EC Treaty. The objective of the Finnish law was, according to the Court, to prevent the double taxation of company profits. In effect, the system for the taxation of corporate profits meant that dividends were tax exempt in the hands of the shareholder. Regarding the Finnish law at issue, the Court concluded that it only applied to dividends paid by companies established in Finland. In addition, the law at issue was disadvantageous in relation to individuals subject to unlimited tax liability in Finland who received dividends from foreign companies. Dividends from foreign companies were for such individuals subject to income taxation at 29 per cent. This difference in tax treatment on the basis of whether the dividend distributing company was established in Finland or not, was considered by the Court from both an inbound and an outbound perspective. From an outbound perspective the Finnish law at issue had the effect of "deterring" fully taxable persons in Finland (i.e. subject to unlimited tax liability) from investing their capital in companies established in another Member State.[133] From an inbound perspective the law at issue had a restrictive effect on the raising of capital in Finland by foreign companies. The Finnish law made it unattractive for Finnish tax subjects to invest in foreign companies compared to investments in Finnish companies.[134] In conclusion the Court found that the Finnish law at issue constituted a restriction on the free movement of capital. The next issue is whether the legislation can be justified according to the provisions of the EC Treaty, but that will be dealt with subsequently.

Case C-315/02 *Lenz* is similar to the *Manninen* case and should be mentioned in this context.[135] It deals with an Austrian imputation system and the compatibility with the

[132] Mutén, "ECJ Advocate General Issues Opinion on Finland's Imputation System", *Tax Notes International*, 29 March 2004, pp. 1154-1157, at p. 1154.

[133] Case C-319/02 *Manninen*, para. 22.

[134] Case C-319/02 *Manninen*, para. 23. In support of this view the ECJ refers to case C-35/98 *Verkooijen* and C-334/02 *Commission v. France*.

[135] The ECJ delivered its decision in case C-315/02 *Lenz* on 15 July 2004.

free movement of capital. On the corporate level the ordinary tax rate was 34 per cent.[136] When corporate profits were distributed as dividends the company had withheld 25 per cent on account of the shareholder, which for an individual taxpayer had the effect of a final and definite tax. According to Schuch, the average individual taxpayer had to pay dividend tax at a rate of about 30 to 35 per cent.[137] As an alternative, the taxpayer could elect to be taxed on domestic source dividends at half of his average income tax rate. In general, that would amount to a maximum tax rate of 25 per cent. Foreign source dividends were treated less favourably according to the Austrian system. Dividends received by an individual resident in Austria deriving from shares in non-resident corporations were in general subject to a progressive income tax rate of up to 50 per cent.[138] The European Court of Justice considered this difference in treatment to be in conflict with the free movement of capital.

6.6.7 Opinion of the Advocate General in Case C-200/98 *X AB and Y AB* (3 June 1999)

In is not uncommon that the Advocate General's opinion makes an analysis of a restriction in relation to the free movement of capital, and yet the European Court of Justice decides not to consider this freedom, at least not in its written decision. In this section one such opinion will be discussed.

The *X AB and Y AB* case dealt with the compatibility of the Swedish law on intra-group transfers of income (*koncernbidrag*) with the freedom of establishment.[139] The Court did not to consider the free movement of capital in its decision. The Swedish Supreme Administrative Court (*Regeringsrätten*) had asked whether the national provision at issue was compatible with both the freedom of establishment and the free movement of capital. The Advocate General came to the same conclusion as the European Court of Justice: the national provision was not compatible with the freedom of establishment. For the sake of completeness, however, the Advocate General also considered the compatibility of the national provisions with the free movement of capital.

On this matter AG Saggio concluded that there is no definition of "capital" in the EC Treaty. Therefore he took guidance in the Annex to Directive 88/361/EEC. He

---

136 On this issue see Schuch, "Pending Cases Filed by Austrian Courts: the Lenz Case", in *Direct Taxation: Recent ECJ Developments*, Lang (ed.), Linde Verlag, Vienna, 2003, pp. 137-152, at pp. 140-141.

137 Schuch, *op. cit.*, p. 141.

138 *Ibid.*

139 Case C-200/98 *X AB and Y AB*. The case has been more closely examined in Chapter 4 on the freedom of establishment.

quoted points 1 and 2 of section I, Direct investments, of the Annex to the Directive.[140] According to this capital movements include: "1. Establishment and extension of branches or new undertakings belonging solely to the person providing the capital, and the acquisition in full of existing undertakings; 2. Participation in new or existing undertakings with a view to establishing or maintaining lasting and economic links." According to the Advocate General, the present case concerned the acquisition and sale of shares in foreign companies. Furthermore, he correctly advanced that the European Court of Justice previously had held that various operations constitute capital movements, including the export of bank notes, the deposit of securities abroad, investing in foreign companies, and mortgage and financial guarantees denominated in the currencies of other Member States.[141] Consequently, the acquisition by a Swedish company of shares or investments in other companies established in another Member State could be classified as capital movements according to the EC Treaty and Directive 88/361/EEC. Moreover, the Swedish provision at issue was also a restriction on the free movement of capital, according to the Advocate General.[142]

6.6.8 A Case from the EFTA Court

The EFTA Court has decided a case on the compatibility of national Icelandic legislation on guarantee fees on loans with the free movement of capital.[143] Even if the case is not strictly a case on direct taxation, it is interesting to see how the EFTA Court interprets the free movement of capital. According to Icelandic law there was a state guarantee on loans taken by banks, credit funds, financial institutions and others. Such entities had to pay a state guarantee fee as a compensation for the guarantee. For loans taken abroad, the fee was 0.0625 per cent every three months, and for loans taken domestically the corresponding fee was 0.0375 per cent. The EFTA Court considered this difference in treatment to be in breach of the free movement of capital.[144] The approach applied by the EFTA Court to the interpretation of the free movement of capital in this case, is in conformity with the approach taken by the European Court of Justice.

---

140 Opinion of AG Saggio in case C-200/98 *X AB and Y AB*, para. 30.

141 *Ibid.* The AG in this instance quotes the following case-law on the free movement of capital: judgments in Case 203/80 *Casati*, Case 157/85 *Brugnoni and Ruffinengo*, Case C-148/91 *Vereniging Veronica*, and Case C-118/96 *Safir*.

142 Opinion of AG Saggio in case C-200/98 *X AB and Y AB*, para. 32.

143 Case E-1/00, *State Debt Management Agency v. Íslandsbanki-FBA hf* on the interpretation of Articles 4, 40, 42 and 61 of the EEA Agreement. Decided on 14 July 2000.

144 On this case see Mattsson, "Är de svenska CFC-reglerna förenliga med EG-rätten?", *Skattenytt*, 2004, pp. 165-191, at pp. 180-181.

6.7 Accepted and Rejected Grounds of Justification

6.7.1 Introduction

As discussed in Chapter 3, the European Court of Justice has developed the rule-of-reason doctrine, according to which national measures constituting indirect discrimination or non-discriminatory restrictions can be justified and thereby accepted even if they infringe on fundamental freedoms of the EC Treaty. The rule-of-reason doctrine was first developed regarding the free movement of goods, but has been recognised and applied by the Court regarding the free movement of services, workers and the freedom of establishment. To what extent the rule-of-reason doctrine also applies regarding the free movement of capital has been subject to debate.

The rule-of-reason doctrine means that a national measure that is liable to hinder or make less attractive the exercise of fundamental freedoms of the EC Treaty will still by justified if certain conditions are fulfilled. For the rule-of-reason doctrine to apply, the national measure must fulfil four general conditions: (i) it must be applied in a non-discriminatory manner, (ii) it must be justified by overriding reasons based on the general interest, (iii) it must be suitable for securing the attainment of the objective which it pursues, and (iv) it must not go beyond what is necessary in order to attain that objective.

An important question is whether the grounds of justification developed by the European Court of Justice and expressed for example in case C-55/94 *Gebhard* on the freedom of establishment, also apply for restrictions on the free movement of capital. Different opinions have been put forward by Advocates General in the case-law of the European Court of Justice.[145]

In case C-222/97 *Trummer and Mayer*, which dealt with the Austrian system for mortgages and the free movement of capital, the European Court of Justice referred to the public interest.[146] Further evidence that the Court does accept the rule of reason also regarding the free movement of capital are the joined cases C-515/99, C-519

[145] Cf. AG Alber's opinion (para. 56) in case C-251/98 *Baars*, and AG Saggio's opinion (para. 17 and 22) in case C-54/99 *Église de Scientologie*. See also Flynn, "Coming of Age: the Free Movement of Capital Case Law", *CML Rev.*, 2002, pp. 773-805, at p. 800.

[146] The ECJ declared in case C-222/97 *Trummer and Mayer*, para. 30: "It should be noted that a Member State is entitled to take the necessary measures to ensure that the mortgage system clearly and transparently prescribes the respective rights of mortgagees inter se, as well as the rights of mortgagees as a whole vis-à-vis other creditors. Since the mortgage system is governed by the law of the State in which the mortgage property is located, it is the law of that State which determines the means by which the attainment of that objective is to be ensured."

– 524/99 and C-526 – 540/99 *Reisch and Others*[147] and case C-302/97 *Konle*. In the last-mentioned case the European Court of Justice declared: "… the restrictive measure … can be accepted only if it is not applied in a discriminatory manner and if the same result cannot be achieved by other less restrictive procedures".[148]

In my view it is clear that the rule-of-reason doctrine also applies regarding the free movement of capital. In the *Gebhard* case, the Court declared that the basic components of the rule-of-reason doctrine apply for *all* fundamental freedoms. What is a matter of question, however, is which grounds of justification in the public interest apply regarding the free movement of capital. In my view it is not evident that grounds of justification that have been accepted regarding other fundamental freedoms should apply also to the free movement of capital. The primary reason for that is that the fundamental freedoms are different and there is no declaration by the Court that if a ground of justification has been accepted regarding one freedom, it should also apply to the other freedoms.

In this section there will be a discussion on the question of how the European Court of Justice has applied the rule-of-reason doctrine to the relationship between the free movement of capital and direct taxation.

6.7.2 Case C-35/98 *Verkooijen* (6 June 1999)

In case C-35/98 *Verkooijen*, the European Court of Justice came to the conclusion that Dutch tax legislation which denied tax exemption on dividends from foreign companies, but granted tax exemption on dividends from Dutch companies, was in conflict with the free movement of capital.

The United Kingdom government submitted that the legislation in question was objectively justified by the intention to promote the economy of the country by encouraging investment by individuals in companies which had their seat in the Netherlands.[149] The Court stated that "it need merely be pointed out" that it is settled case-law that aims of a purely economic nature cannot constitute an overriding reason in the general interest that justifies a restriction of a fundamental freedom guaranteed by the Treaty.[150]

---

147 In the joined cases C-519/99 to 524/99 and C-526 to 540/99 *Reisch and Others*, the ECJ stated regarding the rule-of-reason doctrine (para. 33): "Such restrictions may nevertheless be permitted if the national rules pursue, in a non-discriminatory way, an objective in the public interest and if they observe the principle of proportionality, that is if the same result could not be achieved by other less restrictive measures."

148 Case C-302/97 *Konle*, para. 40.

149 Case C-35/98 *Verkooijen*, para. 47.

150 Case C-35/98 *Verkooijen*, para. 48. In support of this view, the ECJ referred to case C-120/95, *Decker v. Caisse de Maladie des Employés Privés*, para. 39; and case C-158/96 *Kohll v. Union des Caisses de Maladie*, para. 41.

Furthermore, all the governments that had submitted observations on the case claimed that the Dutch legislation in question was required in order to preserve the coherence of the tax system of the Netherlands. The purpose of the tax exemption on such dividends was to mitigate the effects of economic double taxation.[151] Only those companies having their seat in the Netherlands would be taxed on their profits in that Member State. By restricting the tax exemption to dividends received from Dutch companies the coherence of the tax system was preserved as regards the objective of mitigating the effects of economic double taxation: if dividends from companies not having their seat in the Netherlands were also tax exempt there would be no double taxation to be compensated for because those companies would not be taxable in the Netherlands.[152]

The European Court of Justice confirmed that it had held that the need to ensure the coherence of a fiscal system *might* justify rules that restrict fundamental freedoms.[153] The present case was, however, considered different from the cases where the Court had applied fiscal coherence as a ground of justification. The Court underlined the following reasons for not applying the ground of fiscal coherence in the present case. In both case C-204/90 *Bachmann* and case C-300/90 *Commission v. Belgium* the Court declared that "… a direct tax link existed, in the case of one and the same taxpayer, between the grant of a tax advantage and the offsetting of that advantage by a fiscal levy, both of which related to the same tax".[154] In both *Bachmann* and *Commission v. Belgium* there was a link between the deductibility of contributions and the taxation of capital amounts paid by insurers according to old-age insurances and life assurance policies: the Court found that it was required to preserve that link in order to protect the coherence of the national fiscal system in question.

In the present case the reason was that there was no direct link between, on the one hand, the grant to shareholders resident in the Netherlands of income tax exemption regarding dividends received, and, on the other hand, the taxation of the profits of companies with their seat in another Member State. The Court concluded: "They are two separate taxes levied on different taxpayers."[155]

The European Court of Justice also discussed whether the Dutch legislation at issue could be justified by the objective of preventing loss of revenue for the Netherlands.

151 Case C-35/98 *Verkooijen*, para. 50.

152 Case C-35/98 *Verkooijen*, para. 51.

153 Case C-35/98 *Verkooijen*, para. 56. The ECJ referred to case C-204/90 *Bachmann* and case C-300/90 *Commission v. Belgium*.

154 Case C-35/98 *Verkooijen*, para. 57.

155 Case C-35/98 *Verkooijen*, para. 58.

The Court declared that "it need merely be pointed out" that such a ground *cannot* be regarded as an overriding reason in the public interest which could be relied on.[156]

Whether possible tax advantages for those Dutch residents who received taxable dividends from companies with their seat outside of the Netherlands could serve as a justification, was also considered by the European Court of Justice.[157] This ground could not be accepted by the Court as a ground of justification, and the Court related to extensive previous case-law.[158]

The Court accordingly found that the national legislation in question of the Netherlands was a restriction to Article 1 (1) of Directive 88/361/EEC, and the free movement of capital. I discuss the Court's view on Article 58 and the limitations and exceptions provided there, in section 6.5.3.

6.7.3 Case C-436/00 *X and Y* (21 November 2002)

Case C-436/00 *X and Y* has been dealt with in both Chapters 4 and 5, as well as previously in this chapter. The case is important because the Court made an analysis of the compatibility of the national measure with both the freedom of establishment and the free movement of capital. For the Swedish legislation at issue, see Chapter 4. In brief, the case dealt with Swedish legislation on corporate reorganisations, including foreign companies owned by Swedish individuals.

The Court found that the measure constituted a restriction on the freedom of establishment and considered several grounds of justification according to the rule-of-reason doctrine. The Court also considered the national measure to be in breach of the free movement of capital. The grounds of justification and the Court's considerations regarding them in relation to the freedom of establishment also applied in relation to the free movement of capital.

The European Court of Justice began by analysing whether the need to safeguard the fiscal system could justify the Swedish legislation at issue.[159] The Court reiterated the findings of the *Bachmann* and *Commission v. Belgium* cases: in those cases there was a direct link between the deductibility of contributions and the taxation of sums payable

[156] Case C-35/98 *Verkooijen*, para. 59. In support of this view the ECJ refers to case C-264/96 *ICI*.

[157] Case C-35/98 *Verkooijen*, para. 61.

[158] *Ibid.* The ECJ referred to, in relation to Article [43] of the EC Treaty, Case 270/83 *Avoir fiscal*, para. 21; case C-107/94 *Asscher*, para. 53; case C-307/97 *Saint-Gobain*, para. 54. In relation to Article [49] of the EC Treaty the ECJ referred to case C-294/97 *Eurowings*, para. 44.

[159] Case C-436/00 *X and Y*, para. 52-59.

by insurers under pension and life assurance contracts in question, and that link had to be preserved in order to guarantee the coherence of the fiscal system.

The present case was, however, different. The major difference was that there were tax treaties with other Member States, which altered the understanding of fiscal coherence when compared with the *Bachmann* and *Commission v. Belgium* cases. Because of the tax treaties there was considered to be no fiscal coherence in relation to any of the taxpayers when establishing whether there was a strict correlation between the deferral of capital gains tax and the final taxation of the gain.[160] Tax treaties moved the question of fiscal coherence to another level, according to the Court. That other level consisted of "the reciprocity of the rules applicable in the Contracting states in terms of the convention on the basis of connecting factors for the purposes of apportioning competence in tax matters".[161] The Court stated that the Member States were free to decide this form of fiscal coherence in the absence of Community measures.[162] The Court elaborated on this theme in the following way. Article 13 (4) of the Belgian-Swedish tax treaty, which is the same as the OECD Model Convention, provided that a contracting state taxed all gains on shares received by the transferors resident on its territory, but it did not tax gains made by transferors that were resident in the other contracting state, regardless of whether the transferor benefited from tax deferral at the time of the previous transfer or shares involved.

The risk that the transferor emigrated from Sweden in the case of type A share-transfers, which the national provision sought to prevent by denying tax deferral, was covered by Article 13 (4) of the Belgian-Swedish tax treaty on the basis of treaty reciprocity. The treaty article provided that only the contracting state to which the transferor had moved his residence for tax purposes could tax the capital gains in question. As an exception to this rule, Article 13 (5) of the Belgian-Swedish tax treaty specifically covered the alienation of shares in a company resident in one contracting state by individuals who were former residents. In that situation the contracting state would only lose its right to tax share transfers that took place more than five years after the definitive departure of the one time resident and transferor.

In addition, the European Court of Justice maintained that the refusal of tax deferral on type A and type B share-transfers "… is not necessary and proportionate to the objective it pursues".[163] The Court was somewhat contradictory here. On the one hand, it declared that the ground of fiscal coherence did not apply in the present case.

---

[160] Case C-436/00 *X and Y*, para. 53.

[161] *Ibid.*

[162] *Ibid.* In support of this view, the ECJ referred to case C-80/94 *Wielockx*, para. 24, and case C-307/97 *Saint-Gobain*, para. 57.

[163] Case C-436/00 *X and Y*, para. 57.

On the other hand it declared that the measure "in any event" was not necessary and proportionate. Such a statement necessarily opens up for a potential situation where a national measure in fact is justified by the need for maintaining fiscal coherence, but the provision seeking to achieve that purpose is not proportionate.

The Court specifically stressed that the situation in the cases of *Bachmann* and *Commission v. Belgium* were fundamentally different from the situation in the present case. In those cases it was likely that payments would evade taxation by the Member State which granted the tax benefit. In the present case, however, the avoidance of taxation was likely because the taxpayer, at a subsequent stage, was likely to emigrate. It was the view of the European Court of Justice that fiscal coherence could be achieved by measures which were "less restrictive or less prejudicial to freedom of establishment [free movement of capital]".[164] Here one could interpret the Court as if it admitted that the Swedish legislation at issue in fact preserved the coherence of the fiscal system but that the national measure was not proportionate, but this is somewhat uncertain.

The European Court of Justice considered that in the light of the objective of the national provision at issue, both the justification of tax evasion and of fiscal supervision overlap. The Court was critical to the reasoning put forward that the national legislation at issue fulfilled these two grounds of justification. The legislation at issue was not designed to exclude from tax benefits "purely artificial schemes designed to circumvent Swedish tax law".[165] The provision was instead found to cover any situation, for whatever reason, concerning the transfer at undervalue to a company established in another Member State or to a branch of such a company established in Sweden. According to the Court, tax evasion or tax fraud cannot be inferred generally from the fact that the transferee company, or its parent company, is established in another Member State and "cannot justify a fiscal measure which constitutes the exercise of a fundamental freedom guaranteed by the Treaty".[166]

6.7.4 Case C-242/03 *Weidert and Paulus* (15 July 2004)

Case C-242/03 *Weidert and Paulus* dealt with Luxembourg tax law granting relief from income taxation for individuals investing in Luxembourg companies. The case will be considered only in brief. The European Court of Justice considered this law to be in breach of the free movement of capital. Fiscal coherence as a ground of justification

---

[164] Case C-436/00 *X and Y*, para. 59. The ECJ applied the same reasoning on grounds of justification for both fundamental freedoms.

[165] Case C-436/00 *X and Y*, para. 61.

[166] Case C-436/00 *X and Y*, para. 62. In support of this view, the ECJ refers to case C-478/98 *Commission v. Belgium*, para. 45.

was considered by the Court. However, in view of the Court there was no direct link between the tax advantage in question and an offsetting fiscal levy.[167] The Court did not find that the fiscal coherence served as a ground of justification for the difference in treatment according to Luxembourg law.

6.7.5 Case C-319/02 *Manninen* (7 September 2004)

As previously mentioned, case C-319/02 *Manninen* dealt with the taxation of dividends in Finland. Finnish tax law contained a relief from economic double taxation of corporate profits (imputation system) at the shareholder level. A condition for this tax benefit was that the dividend distributing company was established in Finland. The European Court of Justice came to the conclusion that this system constituted a restriction on the free movement of capital.

The Court began its analysis by considering Article 58 (1)(a) of the EC Treaty. It declared that this provision must be interpreted strictly, and that it cannot be interpreted as meaning that any tax law making a distinction between taxpayers by reference to the place where they invest their capital is automatically compatible with the EC Treaty. The Court considered that the derogation in Article 58 (1)(a) is itself limited by Article 58 (3) prohibiting provisions constituting a means of arbitrary discrimination.[168] Hereafter, the Court interpreted these two provisions in the light of the rule-of-reason doctrine which it has developed in its case-law. The Court declared that to be compatible with the free movement of capital, the difference in treatment must concern situations which are not objectively comparable or are justified by an overriding reason in the general interest.[169] The Court also noted that even if those conditions pertain, the difference in treatment must not go beyond what is necessary in order to attain the objective of the legislation.[170]

Initially, the Court discussed whether the Finnish law conformed to the principle of fiscal territoriality, which was accepted by the Court in case C-250/95 *Futura Participations*. The Court began its analysis with the question whether the two situations – dividends received from a Finnish company on the one hand, and, on the other hand, dividends received from a foreign company – were objectively comparable or not.[171] The Court considered them to be objectively comparable. However, the Court did not consider that the Finnish law was an emanation from the principle of territoriality

[167] Case C-242/03 *Weidert and Paulus*, para. 22.

[168] Case C-319/02 *Manninen*, para. 28.

[169] Case C-319/02 *Manninen*, para. 29.

[170] *Ibid.*

[171] Case C-319/02 *Manninen*, para. 32.

– such a principle did not preclude the granting of a tax credit to a person subject to unlimited tax liability in Finland.[172]

Fiscal coherence is also discussed by the Court as a potential ground of justification. The Court repeats its findings of the *Bachmann* case, and adds that case C-9/02 *de Lasteyrie du Saillant* emphasised that fiscal coherence must be examined in the light of the objective pursued by the tax law at issue.[173] AG Kokott reasoned her opinion to the *Manninen* case quite thoroughly in terms of fiscal coherence. She noted the well-known findings of the Court in the *Bachmann* and *Commission v. Belgium* cases, that there must be a direct link between a tax advantage and a compensating levy. She also confirmed the fairly recent specifications by the Court in case C-168/01 *Bosal Holding* and case C-251/98 *Baars* that no such link would exist if one dealt with different taxes or different taxpayers (or both). She found that with a system intended to avoid (economic) double taxation it is not of relevance where the one-time tax burden is placed, provided that the tax rates are the same. The Finnish system implied that the company has paid and advance tax on behalf of the shareholder.

Moreover, in the view of AG Kokott, a single taxpayer is not always a precondition for the coherence ground to apply: two taxpayers could also meet the requirements. For that to apply two conditions must be met. First, even if the tax is not imposed on the same taxpayer, it is at least imposed on the same income or the same economic process. Secondly, the legal construction of the system guarantees that the tax advantage is received by one of the two taxpayers only when the disadvantage in effect hits the other taxpayer and to the same extent as the first one.[174]

AG Kokott found that the Finnish imputation system fulfilled this definition of fiscal coherence. However, if the imputation system works to the detriment of shareholders in foreign companies in cross-border situations, fiscal coherence would not be at issue. Consequently, the Finnish system was not justified by the need to preserve fiscal coherence. AG Kokott's opinion is still of general importance: in her view fiscal coherence could in principle be extended to two taxpayers and even to two different taxes, at least in special cases.

The Court found that the context of the present case was different from the one in the *Bachmann* case. The objective of the Finnish law at issue could also be achieved by extending the tax benefit to dividends distributed by Swedish companies and not only to dividends from Finnish companies.[175]

---

172 Case C-319/02 *Manninen*, para. 38.

173 Case C-319/02 *Manninen*, para. 43.

174 Cf. Mutén, *op. cit.*, at p. 1156.

175 Case C-319/02 *Manninen*, para. 48.

6.8 The Free Movement of Capital in Relation to Third Countries

6.8.1 Introduction

An important issue relating to the free movement of capital is whether this freedom also applies in relation to third countries. If one makes a literal interpretation of Article 56 of the EC Treaty, there is good reason to believe so: "… all restrictions on the movement of capital between Member States and between Member States and third countries shall be prohibited …". In this section it will be discussed to what extent such a literal interpretation is possible.

One introductory remark should be made here concerning the relationship between the freedom of establishment and the free movement of capital vis-à-vis third countries. The freedom of establishment covers activities within the Community,[176] whereas the free movement of capital, at least literally speaking, also applies in relation to third countries. As previously discussed, the free movement of capital is parallel to situations where the freedom of establishment applies. However, when an entrepreneurial activity takes place in a third country, the freedom of establishment does not apply, but the free movement of capital might apply.

6.8.2 Territorial Scope of the EC Treaty

The territorial scope of the free movement of capital is somewhat more difficult to determine. A starting point for the discussion is Article 299 of the EC Treaty, which defines the territorial scope of the Treaty itself. This provision is of course important when deciding both who is covered by the Treaty, i.e. national of a Member State, and what constitutes a third country. The territorial scope of the European Union is of course important when deciding what a "third country" is. Article 299 (1) stipulates that the Treaty shall apply to the (at present) 25 Member States of the Union. Article 299 (2) makes it clear that the provisions of the EC Treaty also apply to the French overseas departments, the Azores, Madeira and the Canary Islands. But as regards these territories, exceptions are accepted, according to the very same provision. Accordingly, the Council, acting by a qualified majority on a proposal from the Commission, may adopt specific measures on the application of the Treaty to those regions.[177] When adopting those measures the Council shall take into account areas such as customs and trade policies, fiscal policy, free zones and agriculture and fisheries policies.[178]

[176] Here, I am not considering the EEA agreement and the relationship with Switzerland.

[177] Article 299 (2)(2) of the EC Treaty.

[178] Article 299 (2)(3) of the EC Treaty.

Article 299 (3)(1) provides that the special arrangement for association set out in Part IV of the EC Treaty shall apply to the overseas countries and territories listed in Annex II of the EC Treaty.[179] The EC Treaty shall, however, not apply to those overseas countries and territories having special relations with the United Kingdom which are not included in the list contained in Annex II.[180]

Furthermore, the provisions of the EC Treaty shall apply to the European territories for whose external relations a Member State is responsible.[181] The provisions of the EC Treaty shall also apply to the Åland Islands in accordance with the provisions in Protocol No 2 to the Act on the conditions of the accession of Austria, Finland and Sweden.[182] Article 299 (6) stipulates that the EC Treaty shall not apply to either the Faeroe Islands or the Sovereign Base Areas of the United Kingdom in Cyprus. Finally, the EC Treaty shall apply to the Channel Islands and the Isle of Man only to the extent necessary to implement the arrangements for those islands set out in the Treaty concerning the accession of new Member States signed on 22 January 1972.[183]

6.8.3 Wording of Articles 56-59 of the EC Treaty

Article 56 (1) of the EC Treaty stipulates that all restrictions on the movement of capital between Member States and between Member States and third countries shall be prohibited. A strict literal interpretation of this provision unquestionably gives reason to assume that there is also a prohibition on restrictions on capital movements between Member States and third countries. There are, however, limits on the prohibition of such third-country restrictions already in the EC Treaty itself. Article 57 (1) permits national (or Community) measures that constitute third-country restrictions if they existed as of 31 December 1993.

Furthermore, Article 57 (2) provides that the endeavour to achieve the objective of the free movement of capital between Member States and third countries shall be pursued to "the greatest extent possible". The general rule is that the Council may, acting by a qualified majority on a proposal from the Commission, adopt measures

[179] Those territories are, according to Annex II of the EC Treaty, Greenland, New Caledonia and Dependencies, French Polynesia, French Southern and Antarctic Territories, Wallis and Futuna Islands, Mayotte, Saint Pierre and Miquelon, Aruba, Netherlands Antilles (Bonaire, Curacao, Saba, Sint Eustatius, Sint Maarten), Anguilla, Cayman Islands, Falkland Islands, South Georgia and the South Sandwich Islands, Montserrat, Pitcairn, Saint Helena and Dependencies, British Antarctic Territory, Turks and Caicos Islands, British Virgin Islands, and Bermuda.

[180] Article 299 (3)(2) of the EC Treaty.

[181] Article 299 (4) of the EC Treaty.

[182] Article 299 (5) of the EC Treaty.

[183] Article 299 (6) of the EC Treaty.

on the movement of capital to or from third countries, involving direct investment – including investment in real estate and establishment. However, Council unanimity is required for such measures that constitute a "step back" in Community law as regards the liberalisation of the movement of capital to or from third countries.[184]

Article 59 provides an escape clause as regards capital movements to or from third countries. On the condition that such movements, in exceptional circumstances, cause, or threaten to cause, serious difficulties for the operation of economic and monetary union, the Council may take action with a qualified majority on the proposal of the Commission and after consulting the European Central Bank, but only if it is "strictly necessary". There is a six-month time limit for such measures.

There are few cases from the European Court of Justice where the territorial extension of the free movement of capital has been subject to consideration. There is one important exception, which I will discuss in the following section, the joined cases C-163/94, C-165/95 and C-250/94 *Sanz de Lera and Others*.

6.8.4 Joined Cases C-163/94, C-165/95 and C-250/94 *Sanz de Lera and Others* (14 December 1995)

The territorial scope of the free movement of capital was subject to consideration in the joined cases C-163/94, C-165/95 and C-250/95 *Sanz de Lera*.[185] Case C-163/94 concerned Mr Sanz de Lera who was a Spanish national resident in Spain. He was apprehended in France while driving to Geneva, Switzerland, and in his car was found ESP 19,600,000 in banknotes. Case C-165/94 concerned Mr Diaz Jimenez who was a Spanish national resident in Great Britain. In a security check at an airport in Madrid, he was found carrying ESP 30,250,000 in banknotes. Mr Diaz Jimenez was intending to board a flight to Zürich, Switzerland, with a connecting flight to London. Case C-250/94 dealt with Mrs Kapanoglu, who was a Turkish national resident in Spain. She was arrested at a Madrid airport when boarding a flight for Istanbul, Turkey.

None of the individuals had sought authorisation from the Spanish authorities for the transfer of the capital. The European Court of Justice found that the need for prior authorisation was in conflict with the free movement of capital. In all cases the movement to third states outside of the territorial scope of the Treaty was at hand. Even so, there was a conflict with the free movement of capital because that freedom also applies in relation to third states.

[184] Article 57 (2) of the EC Treaty.

[185] Joined cases C-163/94, C-165/94 and C-250/94, *Sanz de Lera and Others*.

One should be careful not to draw any hasty conclusions from these cases. The reason is that the cases only dealt with the transfer of banknotes and similar means of payment even if they were legal tender.

Even if there are few cases from the European Court of Justice, there are at present cases on the national level on the issue of third-country relations and the free movement of capital. In a few years there will no doubt be a considerable case-law also from the Court on this issue. In the following section I will discuss two such national cases from the Swedish Revenue Law Commission.

6.8.5 Other Cases

Recently there have been two decisions from the Swedish Revenue Law Commission (*Skatterättsnämnden*) on the possible extension of the free movement of capital in relation to third countries.[186] Both decisions have been appealed to the Supreme Administrative Court (*Regeringsrätten*). It is likely that the Supreme Administrative Court will ask the European Court of Justice for preliminary rulings.

The first decision by the Revenue Law Commission dealt with the taxation of small and medium-sized companies. For such companies special rules applied on how much of the profits could be distributed as dividends to the owners. The reason for the special legislation was the considerably lower tax rate in Sweden for dividend income. The question was whether salaries paid to employees of a permanent establishment in a third country – the Russian Federation to be specific – would increase the profit amount, according to a special "formula", that could be distributed as dividends. The calculation was restricted to salaries paid in Sweden. From Swedish case-law it was clear that the inclusion of salaries paid within the European Union was accepted on the basis of the freedom of establishment.[187] The Revenue Law Commission concluded that the free movement of capital applied in this case and, consequently, the third country salaries could be added when making the calculation. The free movement of capital was interpreted as applicable also in relation to third countries such as the Russian Federation.

The second decision by the Revenue Law Commission dealt with a Swedish set of provisions called "*Lex Asea*", and more specifically with chapter 42, sections 16 and 16a of the Income Tax Act. That provision granted tax exemption on dividends paid in the form of shares in a subsidiary of the distributing company. The tax exemption was intended to facilitate corporate reorganisations. There was a tax deferral until the

[186] Both rulings of the Revenue Law Commission are dated 19 February 2003.

[187] RÅ 2001 ref. 47 I and II.

point in time when the received shares were alienated. There were specific conditions that had to be fulfilled for the tax exemption to apply. All of those conditions were at hand, except that the distributing company had to be a Swedish company. However, according to chapter 42, section 16a of the Income Tax Act, a foreign company would be treated as a Swedish company if it was resident in the European Economic Area or in a country with which Sweden had concluded a tax treaty providing for the exchange of information. The distributing company was resident in Switzerland, a country not part of the European Economic Area. The 1965 tax treaty between Sweden and Switzerland, with subsequent additions and amendments, did not contain a clause on the exchange of information. However, in a protocol of the tax treaty, there was a minor clause on the exchange of information for the application of the treaty, but that clause was not such an article as the ones referred to in the national Swedish provision at issue. The Revenue Law Commission considered that Article 56 of the EC Treaty applied for the transfer of such assets that were at issue. In support of this view the Revenue Law Commission referred to a case from the Supreme Administrative Court, RÅ 2001 ref. 40.[188]

Next the Revenue Law Commission considered whether the condition on the exchange of information could be justified according to Community law. In general such measures were acceptable, according to the Revenue Law Commission, but the condition at issue was not proportionate to the aims it was designed to achieve. Consequently, the dividends deriving from Switzerland were tax exempt in Sweden.

In conclusion, the Swedish Revenue Law Commission has given a wide interpretation of the territorial scope of the free movement of capital, when also applying it in relation to the Russian Federation and Switzerland. Evidently, the value of these two decisions by a preliminary judicial body in Sweden is limited. Both decisions have been appealed to the Supreme Administrative Court, and it is likely that the Supreme Administrative Court will ask the European Court of Justice for a preliminary ruling on the territorial scope of the free movement of capital.

[188] In that case the Swedish Supreme Administrative Court in turn referred to case C-35/98 *Verkooijen*.

7 General Conclusions

7.1 Introduction

The general objective of this study has been to analyse the case-law of the European Court of Justice in the field of direct taxation and fundamental freedoms. In particular, the freedom of establishment and the free movement of capital have been the focus of this study.

It is evident that comparatively little has been achieved by the European Union over the years in the field of direct taxation, at least regarding Community legislation. It is true that a few directives have been adopted, most recently in 2003 with the Tax Package on Harmful Tax Competition. Still, the requirement of unanimity in the Council regarding matters of direct taxation constitutes an obstacle to decisions in that specific area of law. The growing number of cases from the European Court of Justice bears evidence that there is a need for the Member States to adopt further measures on harmonising their systems for direct taxation.

7.2 The Meaning of Discrimination and Non-discriminatory Restrictions in Cases on Direct Taxation

Regarding the meaning of discrimination and non-discriminatory restrictions, the analysis of the case-law of the European Court of Justice indicates the following. In its early case-law, with cases such as Case 270/83 *Avoir fiscal* (1986), C-330/91 *Commerzbank* (1993), but also the fairly recent case C-311/97 *Royal Bank of Scotland* (1999), the Court made considerable efforts to define what form of discrimination the national legislation at issue constituted. The Court meticulously defined the situations which were compared in order to establish whether there was a case of discrimination, and, furthermore, whether there was a case of direct or indirect discrimination.

Case C-250/95 *Futura Participations* (1997) was in principle different from previous cases dealt with by the Court. In this case the Court made it clear that also national legislation on direct taxation may constitute a non-discriminatory restriction. The *Futura Participations* case is important from other aspects, in particular regarding the application of the principle of proportionality, the significance of the directive on mutual assistance in tax matters, and the fiscal principle of territoriality as a ground of justification.

In a large number of cases after the *Futura Participations* case, the Court has refrained from declaring a measure to be discriminatory, according to the definitions modelled in its early case-law. Instead, the Court has merely declared the national measure at issue to constitute a barrier – or a similar vaguely described impediment – to the fundamental freedom at issue. There may be several reasons for this approach by the Court. One important reason is related to one of the conditions of the rule-of-reason doctrine. One condition of the rule-of-reason doctrine is that the national measure, in order to be justified, has to be "non-discriminatory". This condition severely limits the scope of application of the rule-of-reason doctrine. If the national measure is discriminatory, be it either directly or indirectly, the rule-of-reason doctrine does not apply. That is at least the result of a literal interpretation of the doctrine as stipulated by the Court in case C-55/94 *Gebhard*.

I believe that the Court considers itself bound by the formulation of this condition, even if this restricts it from applying the rule-of-reason doctrine to measures that are discriminatory. Even so, the Court considers it a problem that it cannot apply the rule-of-reason doctrine to measures that are discriminatory. In order to circumvent that problem, the Court refrains from making a "discrimination analysis" in its recent case-law, or at least it refrains from making the conclusion that a specific national measure is discriminatory, even if it could very well have made such a conclusion. There are several such examples in the recent case-law, for example case C-436/00 *X and Y*, case C-324/00 *Lankhorst-Hohorst* and case C-9/02 *de Lasteyrie du Saillant*. However, in none of these cases did the Court actually find that the grounds of justification put forward were applicable. Still, that does not alter the general conclusion, that the Court has moved away from the discrimination analysis in order to be able to apply the rule-of-reason doctrine. If the Court had no desire to do that in the previously mentioned cases, it would only have had to declare that the national measure at issue constituted discrimination and consequently the rule-of-reason doctrine would not apply. But the Court does not do that, and that is the reason why at least some of the Judges probably are dissatisfied with the condition of "non-discriminatory" measures in the rule-of-reason doctrine. It would lead to much greater clarity if the Court expressly declared that the rule-of-reason doctrine also applies in relation to measures that in fact are discriminatory.

Moreover, the Court actually applied the rule-of-reason doctrine in the *Bachmann* case, which one could very well consider as a case of indirect discrimination.

Furthermore, there are reasons to be critical of the fact that the European Court of Justice defines direct and indirect discrimination in different ways regarding, on the one hand, companies and, on the other hand, individuals. It is the interaction between the definition of nationality according to the EC Treaty and residence for tax purposes according to national tax law that constitutes a problem. Regarding individuals it is rarely nationality that is the sole criterion that determines residence for tax purposes. It is more common for criteria such as where he is present during the taxable year, where he has a permanent home or where he has his centre of vital interests to determine an individual's residence for tax purposesa ccording to national law.

In contrast to individuals, the way in which the EC Treaty defines nationality for companies coincides with the way in which many states determine a company's residence for tax purposes. Article 48 of the EC Treaty stipulates that companies (or firms) formed in accordance with the law of a Member State and having their registered office, central administration or principal place of business in the Community shall be treated in the same way as "natural persons" who are nationals of Member States.

For the area of direct taxation this dichotomy between individuals and companies regarding, on the one hand, "nationality" and "corporate seat", and, on the other hand, residence for tax purposes has the following consequence.

An individual may be a "non-national" of a Member State, but he may at the same time very well be resident for tax purposes in that Member State. Suppose that the tax law of that Member State in some way constitutes a denial of one of the fundamental freedoms of the EC Treaty due to a difference in treatment between residents and non-residents. Such a difference in treatment is likely to constitute indirect discrimination. However, if the tax legislation of a Member State differentiates between resident and non-resident companies, it is very likely that resident companies also will be "nationals" – with their seat or similar in that state – and non-resident companies will not be "nationals" of that state. The difference in treatment is in this case likely to constitute direct discrimination.

This difference in treatment between companies and individuals may have repercussions on the application of the rule-of-reason doctrine. In case C-55/94 *Gebhard*, the Court stipulated as a condition for the rule-of-reason doctrine to apply that the national measure at issue was applied in a non-discriminatory manner. Thus the Court has extended the application of the rule-of-reason doctrine also to measures that constitute indirect discrimination, and case C-204/90 *Bachmann* is such an example in the area of direct taxation. This is a strong reason for the Court to extend the rule-of-reason doctrine also to measures constituting direct discrimination. If the Court did so, there would be no danger that "floodgates" of grounds of justification would open up. Even if there are some grounds of justification which the Court accept in principle, it follows from this study that the Court very rarely finds them applicable.

7.3 Grounds of Justification Considered in Cases on Direct Taxation

7.3.1 Introduction

In all cases examined here, the Court has considered a large variety of grounds of justification that have been put forward as part of the rule-of-reason doctrine. In conclusion there seem to be four grounds that the Court, in principle, has accepted: (i) prevention of tax abuse, (ii) preservation of fiscal coherence, (iii) effectiveness of fiscal supervision, and (iv) preservation of the fiscal principle of territoriality.

The rejected grounds of justification which have been identified and discussed in this study are (i) the lack of tax harmonisation, (ii) counterbalancing advantages, (iii) new form of establishment would mean equal treatment, (iv) lack of Community competence in the field of direct taxation and (v) reduction of tax revenue.

7.3.2 On Grounds of Justification Accepted in Principle

Of the four identified grounds of justification which the Court in fact has accepted, there is only one that has been applied for certain by the Court as a justification: the preservation of fiscal coherence. The preservation of fiscal coherence was applied in cases C-204/90 *Bachmann* (1992) and C-300/90 *Commission v. Belgium* (1992). Both cases dealt with the right to deduct contributions according certain sickness, pension and life assurance contracts. A Member State was entitled to deny the deduction of such contributions if the sums payable from such insurance contracts were not taxable in the same Member State.

The preservation of fiscal coherence has been advocated in a number of cases after these 1992 cases. In no case, however, has this ground been applied by the Court. Moreover, the conditions for applying fiscal coherence seem to have been narrowed by the Court. From the *Bachmann* case, the following conditions have been deduced by the Court. First, there has to be a direct link between, for example, the deduction of an insurance contribution and the taxation of the sums payable from that insurance. Secondly, the taxpayer at issue has to be the same: it has to be the same taxpayer that makes the deduction for an insurance contribution as receives the sums payable. In several cases, governments of Member States have invoked fiscal coherence – to no avail – regarding the taxation of parent companies and subsidiary companies, for example cases C-324/00 *Lankhorst-Hohorst*, C-168/01 *Bosal Holding* and C-35/98 *Verkooijen*. However, the European Court of Justice has, at least so far, maintained that a parent is a separate legal entity from its subsidiary, even if they together constitute a corporate group.

The existence of tax treaties has also affected the meaning of fiscal coherence. In the *Bachmann* case, fiscal coherence was secured at the level of national legislation of a

Member State (Belgium). However, in the view of the Court, the existence of a tax treaty transfers the question of whether fiscal coherence is preserved to the level of the bilateral tax treaty. One might interpret the Court as stating that the existence of a tax treaty, which has been negotiated and agreed upon by the two contracting states, is in itself an expression of fiscal coherence. The significance of tax treaties in this respect was first recognised by the Court in case C-80/94 *Wielockx*, and has been confirmed in case C-136/00 *Danner*.

The ground of effectiveness of fiscal supervision was also recognised and in principle approved by the Court in case C-250/95 *Futura Participations*. Luxembourg tax law that required branches of non-resident companies to hold "proper accounts" was in principle justified by the need to preserve the effectiveness of fiscal supervision. However, that requirement did not meet the test of proportionality because of the existence of Directive 77/799/EEC of 19 December 1977 on mutual assistance between the Member States' tax authorities ("competent authorities"). The information required by Luxembourg was considered to be accessible by means of the exchange of information according to the 1977 Directive. In the view of the Court, there was accordingly no need for a national provision stipulating that accounts should be held according to the law of that state.

The Court's reference to the 1977 Directive has been subject to criticism, largely because the actual use of the Directive is limited and it is not considered as an effective way of acquiring information from other Member States.

The prevention of tax abuse is also a ground of justification accepted in principle. However, this ground has not been considered to apply in any of the cases so far decided by the Court in the field of direct taxation. The Court has a narrow concept of what constitutes a law rule aimed at preventing (tax) abuse. For a national law rule to be aimed at preventing tax abuse it has to have the specific purpose of preventing wholly artificial arrangements, which are designed to circumvent taxation. Legislation with a general anti-avoidance objective seems to have little chance of qualifying as anti-abuse legislation according to the definition applied by the European Court of Justice. In case C-324/00 *Lankhorst-Hohorst* the Court ruled that German legislation against thin capitalisation did not qualify as an anti-abuse legislation. In other cases, legislation with the primary objective of preventing the tax base of a state has been examined and considered not to qualify as anti-abuse legislation according to the Court's standards, consider for example cases C-264/96 *ICI* and C-436/00 *X and Y*. Even if a provision would meet the Court's narrow definition of anti-abuse legislation, such a rule would, according to the rule-of-reason doctrine, in addition have to meet the proportionality test. That will not make it easier for such a rule to pass through the eye of the Court's needle. The Court has so far not considered whether CFC legislation is in conformity with the freedom of establishment and the free movement of capital. Most Member States have CFC legislation and it varies considerably between the different states. However, it is highly questionable whether any CFC legislation would be considered to be in conformity with the previously mentioned freedoms. The reason is that CFC legislation, just as thin capitalisation rules, is a mechanical way of taxing income of residents. The legislation is "mechanical" because it stipulates certain levels of ownership and acceptable rates of taxation of foreign base companies. There is a risk that such legislation will target the holding of foreign companies where the establisher has had no objective of circumventing the legislation of the state where he is a national (resident).

In my view, the fiscal principle of territoriality has in principle also been accepted by the European Court of Justice, which the Court declared in case C-250/95 *Futura Participations*. The Court was not explicit on the meaning of this principle. A loose description could in my view be that – according to the principle of territoriality – a state has the right under international law to tax income which is substantially connected with its territory, for example because the income is generated in that state or the income is earned by an individual or a legal person likewise connected with that territory. In the *Futura Participations* case the territoriality principle concerned a condition for the right to carry forward losses: the losses had to be economically linked to an income earned in that state. However, in case C-168/01 *Bosal Holding*, the Court seems to have abandoned the territoriality principle. The territoriality principle may have been put in the same category as the other grounds of justification discussed in this section: accepted in principle, but in effect subsequently never applied by the Court.

7.3.3 On Rejected Grounds of Justification

A wide range of grounds have been put forward in the cases dealt with in this study that the European Court of Justice has rejected as not valid. Even so, it is worth noting that such grounds may have been rejected quite early in the Court's case-law, but that has not refrained Member States from advancing them again and again. One may only speculate on why Member States continue to put forward grounds which the Court has rejected for so long. In my view, one reason could be that at least some Member States wish that the Court would make a change of position and accept the ground in question. The Court has made such fundamental changes before, for example in the *Keck and Mithourd* case (joined cases C-267/91 and C-268/91) on what constitutes discrimination regarding the free movement of goods.

The lack of harmonisation in the field of direct taxation was advanced in several early cases, for example C-270/83 *Avoir fiscal* and C-81/87 *Daily Mail*. In Chapter 2, I discussed the measures in the field of direct taxation which the European Union in fact has adopted. Admittedly, there has been relatively little compared to some other fields of law. However, that has not hindered the European Court of Justice from declaring legislation on direct taxation to be in breach of fundamental freedoms contained in the EC Treaty. This is in my view a correct approach: it is obvious that legislation on direct taxation affects, for example, cross-border investments, and had such measures not been covered by the scope of the fundamental freedoms, cross-border movements would have been severely hampered.

The existence of counterbalancing advantages has also been rejected by the Court as a valid ground of justification. Examples of such cases are Case 270/83 *Avoir fiscal*, C-330/91 *Commerzbank* and C-307/97 *Saint-Gobain*. In its case-law, the Court has made an isolated consideration of the tax measure at issue, thereby abstaining from taking the total tax situation of a person into account. Although it might seem natural to consider a person's aggregate tax situation, such an approach would lead to decisions that do not provide any general guidance on the interpretation of the fundamental freedom at issue. There is a risk that the decision would be complex and difficult to interpret for those not familiar with peculiarities of the national tax system at issue.

The ground that a new form of establishment would mean equal treatment has not been accepted by the Court, at least not in the situations so far presented to the European Court of Justice. I have found this reason put forward in Case 270/83 *Avoir fiscal*. In that case, if the foreign companies had established subsidiaries instead of branches in France, they would have been granted the tax benefit at issue. This rejected ground of justification is closely connected to the issue of neutrality between different forms of establishment, which was a matter discussed in Chapter 4 on what constitutes discrimination or non-discriminatory restrictions. From the Court's case-law one can draw the conclusion that as regards the host state, there seems to be a requirement according to the freedom of establishment that branches of foreign companies and resident companies are treated in the same way. Whether that requirement of equal treatment also applies regarding the home state is still uncertain. Maybe the Court's decision in the *Marks & Spencer* case will shed some light on that issue.

Lack of Community competence in the field of tax treaties has also been advanced as a ground of justification – see for example Case 270/83 *Avoir fiscal* and C-307/97 *Saint-Gobain*. It seems to have been rejected by the Court. Article 293 second indent of the EC Treaty stipulates that the Member States shall, so far as is necessary, enter into negotiations in order to secure the abolition of double taxation within the Community. Apparently, tax treaty law is an area of Community interest and the EC Treaty urges Member States to be active in this area. In the *Saint-Gobain* case the European Court of Justice has extended the rights conferred by German tax treaties to persons not resident in Germany for tax purposes, albeit present there through branches. This is not considered by the Court to be a breach of the treaty at issue. In my view this is a rather radical approach by the Court. When tax treaties were concluded by Member States of the European Union it is reasonable to assume that those states did not believe that the treaty benefits would be extended to residents of other Member States. Today, however, there could hardly be any Member State holding such a belief. Whether Community law also includes a most favoured nation requirement is, however, a different matter. It is questionable whether there is such a requirement, but it would still not come as a total surprise if the Court decided that there is.

7.4 Neutrality between Different Forms of Establishment

In Chapter 4 on the freedom of establishment, I discussed the issue of neutrality between different forms of establishment. More precisely, the discussion was on neutrality between the establishment of branches and subsidiaries. A further element of this discussion is whether there is any difference between the case where an establishment is made – from the perspective of the establisher – in the host state and in the home state.

In my view, it is clear that for several years the Court has sought to establish neutrality regarding the (direct) taxation of branches and subsidiaries in the host state. Examples of that are cases C-330/91 *Commerzbank*, C-311/97 *Royal Bank of Scotland* and C-307/97 *Saint-Gobain*. It follows from these cases that the freedom of establishment requires a high degree of neutrality in the host state between the establishment of branches and subsidiaries. However, the degree of neutrality the freedom of establishment requires regarding the home state is still uncertain. The decision in pending case C-446/03 *Marks & Spencer* may bring light upon this issue. The *Marks & Spencer* case highlights the question on how one should make the comparison leading to the question whether the national law is discriminatory or not. The Special Commissioners in the United Kingdom court of first instance target a weak point in the recent case-law of the European Court of Justice: seemingly the Court tries to circumvent the discrimination analysis and instead resorts to the vague "barrier" approach. The Special Commissioners make a comparison between the establishment of a branch and a subsidiary, and come to the conclusion that they are not comparable. If the European Court of Justice chooses to apply that comparison, it may come to the same conclusion. However, I find sympathy for Gutmann's[1] reasoning that the United Kingdom system for group relief has made the branch alternative comparable to the subsidiary alternative. Still, I believe that the Court will apply a comparison between the establishment of a subsidiary in the United Kingdom and a subsidiary in another Member State.[2] This was the comparison made in the *Bosal Holding* case, and I think the Court will use it also in the *Marks & Spencer* case.

1 Section 4.6.2.

2 I am here simplifying the alternatives of establishment somewhat, see section 4.6.

7.5 Convergence between the Freedom of Establishment and the Free Movement of Capital

The relationship between the freedom of establishment and the free movement of capital is a question of growing importance in the Court's cases on direct taxation. For some time it has been the Court's practice in such cases not to deal with the free movement of capital, if the conclusion is that the national measure at issue is in breach of the freedom of establishment. Even if the freedom of establishment and the free movement of capital target different cross-border transactions they do to a large extent cover the same scope of transactions.

The freedom of establishment typically covers the entrepreneur who establishes a business activity in another Member State. However, it is difficult to imagine such an establishment not also containing the cross-border transfer of capital, for example through the distribution of equity capital and the purchase of offices, factories and similar property, as well as the lending of capital from a parent company to a newly formed subsidiary company. The relationship between the two freedoms is dealt with in the EC Treaty, partly in Article 43 (2), partly in Article 58 (2). Both of these provisions indicate the strong relationship between the two freedoms. Suppose that both freedoms apply to a specific cross-border transaction, which freedom should apply? Largely from the Court's decision in case C-436/00 *X and Y* one might conclude the following policy. A national tax measure should be considered in relation to the freedom of establishment up to the point where the activity ceases to be an entrepreneurial business activity. From that point it should be considered in relation to the free movement of capital.

This close relation between the freedom of establishment and the free movement of capital raises the question to what extent the rule-of-reason doctrine applies in the same way regarding those freedoms. This question is emphasised by the inclusion of Article 58 of the EC Treaty in the 1992 Maastricht Treaty. Article 58 provides limitations and exceptions to the free movement of capital regarding national tax measures. It follows from the cases C-35/98 *Verkooijen* and C-478/98 *Commission v. Belgium* that, in the view of the Court, Article 58 seems to be a codification of what the Court had already upheld in its previous case-law.

7.6 The Free Movement of Capital in Relation to Third Countries

According to Article 56 of the EC Treaty the free movement of capital also applies in relation to third countries. There are limitations in the chapter on capital and payments in the EC Treaty, but they are considerably restricted, most notably Article 57 which accepts restrictions in relation to third countries regarding measures which existed on 31 December 1993. A literal interpretation of Article 56 can only lead to the result that restrictions on the free movement of capital in relation to third countries are prohibited. There is little case-law from the European Court of Justice confirming this result, notably, however, the joined cases C-163/94, 165/94 and 250/94 *Sanz de Lera* cases concerning the transfer of banknotes. Still, one has to ask whether this literal interpretation is acceptable from a policy perspective. The declaration in Article 56 is unilateral: there is no guarantee that the third countries will grant Member States of the European Union an equal right. In the case-law of the European Court of Justice, the material scope of the free movement of capital within the European Union has proved to have wide implications. Was it the policy objective of the EC Treaty that such rights also should be granted in relation to third countries?

Within a few years the European Court of Justice will deliver its interpretation. At present there are several cases before national courts on the third country issue. In view of the Court's generally progressive approach, one might expect that the Court will find the free movement of capital to apply also in relation to third countries in a way similar to its application between Member States.

Bibliography

1 Books and Articles

Arnull, Anthony, *The European Union and its Court of Justice*, Oxford University Press, Oxford, 1999.

Avery Jones, John F., "Carry on Discriminating", *European Taxation*, 1996, pp. 46-49.

Avery Jones, John F., "Flows of Capital between the EU and Third Countries and the Consequences of Disharmony in European International Tax Law", *EC Tax Review*, 1998, pp. 95-106.

Avery Jones, John F., "A Comment on 'AMID: The Wrong Bridge or a Bridge Too Far?'", *European Taxation*, 2001, p. 251.

von Bahr, Stig, "Något om EG-domstolens praxis på skatteområdet", in *Festskrift till Gustaf Lindencrona*, Arvidsson, Melz and Silfverberg (ed.), Norstedts Juridik, Stockholm, 2003, pp. 67-82.

Barnard, Catherine, "Fitting the Remaining Pieces into the Goods and Person Jigsaw?", *EL Rev.*, 2001, pp. 35-59.

Barnard, Catherine, *The Substantive Law of the EU. The Four Freedoms*, Oxford University Press, Oxford, 2004.

Bengoetxea, Joxerramon, Neil MacCormick and Leonor Moral Soriano, "Integration and Integrity in the Legal Reasoning of the European Court of Justice", in *The European Court of Justice*, de Búrca and Weiler (ed.), Oxford University Press, 2001, pp. 43-85.

Bergström, Sture and Anette Bruzelius, "Home-state Restrictions on the Freedom of Establishment in a Swedish Income Tax Perspective", *Intertax*, 2001, pp. 233-241.

Bernitz, Ulf, *Sverige och Europarätten*, Norstedts Juridik, Stockholm, 2002.

Bernitz, Ulf and Anders Kjellgren, *Europarättens grunder*, 2nd ed., Norstedts juridik, Stockholm, 2002.

Bernitz, Ulf, "EG-rättens likabehandlingsprincip som instrument för skatteharmonisering", in *Festskrift till Gustaf Lindencrona*, Arvidsson, Melz and Silfverberg (ed.), Norstedts Juridik, Stockholm, 2003, pp. 93-108.

Bolkestein, Frits, "EU Corporate Tax Refom: Progress and New Challenges, Opening Address at the European Commission Conference on Company Taxation", *EC Tax Review*, 2004, pp. 5-6.

de Broe, Luc, "Cases Filed by Belgian Courts: the AMID Case", in *Direct Taxation: Recent ECJ Developments*, M. Lang (ed.), Schriftenreihe zum Internationalen Steuerrecht, Band 25, Linde Verlag, Vienna, 2003, pp. 11-33.

Concise Oxford English Dictionary, 10th ed., Oxford University Press, Oxford, 2002.

Cordewener, Axel, *Europäische Grundfreiheiten und Nationales Steuerrecht, Rechtsordnung und Steuerwesen*, Band 29, Verlag Dr. Otto Schmidt, Cologne, 2002.

Cordewener, Axel, "Case-note on C-136/00 Danner", *CML Rev.*, 2003, pp. 965-981.

Cordewener, Axel, Mattias Dahlberg, Pasquale Pistone, Ekkehart Reimer and Carlo Romano, Carlo, "The Tax Treatment of Foreign Losses: Ritter, M & S, and the Way Ahead (Part One)", *European Taxation*, 2004, pp. 135-142.

Cordewener, "The Prohibitions of Discrimination and Restriction Have Both Been Intended to Achieve a Fully Integrated Internal Market in the European Union", Report to the 2004 EATLP Conference in Paris, unpublished manuscript, 19 pp.

Craig, Paul and Graínne de Búrca, *EU Law. Text, Cases and Materials*, 3rd ed., Oxford University Press, Oxford, 2003.

Distaso, Marcello and Raffaele Russo, "The EC Interest and Royalties Directive – A Comment", *European Taxation*, 2004, pp. 143-154.

Dörr, Ingmar, "A Step Forward in the Field of European Corporate Taxation and Cross-border Loss Relief: Some Comments on the Marks and Spencer Case", *Intertax*, 2004, pp. 180-186.

Dyrberg, Peter, "Full Free Movement of Companies in the European Community at Last?", *EL Rev.*, 2003, pp. 528-537.

Edwards, Vanessa, "Secondary Establishment of Companies – the Case Law of the Court of Justice", *Yearbook of European Law*, Oxford University Press, Oxford, 1998, pp. 221-257.

Ehlers, Dirk, "§ 7 Allgemeine Lehren", in *Europäische Grundrechte und Grundfreiheiten*, Ehlers (ed.), de Gruyters Recht, Berlin, 2003.

Eickher, Klaus, "EC Tax Scene", *Intertax*, 2002, p. 521.

Emiliou, Nicholas, *The Principle of Proportionality in European Law*, London 1996.

Farmer, Paul, "National Anti-abuse Clauses and Distortion of the Single Market: Comments on Prof. Rädler's Article", *European Taxation*, 1994, p. 314.

Farmer, Paul, "EC Law and Direct Taxation – Some Thoughts on Recent Issues", *EC Tax Journal*, 1995/96, pp. 91-108.

Farmer, Paul, "EC Law and National Rules on Direct Taxation: a Phoney War?", *EC Tax Review*, 1998, pp. 13-29.

Farmer, Paul, "The Court's Case Law on Taxation: a Castle Built on Shifting Sands?", *EC Tax Review*, 2003, pp. 75-81.

Flynn, Leo, "Coming of Age: Free Movement of Capital Case Law", *CML Rev.*, 2002, pp. 773-805.

Gammie, Malcolm, "The Role of the European Court of Justice in the Development of Direct Taxation in the European Union", *Bulletin*, 2003, pp. 86-98.

Gundel, Jörg, "Die Rechtfertigung von faktisch diskriminierenden Eingriffen in die Grundfreiheiten des EGV", *Jura*, 2001, pp. 79-85.

Gutmann, Daniel, "The Marks & Spencer Case: Proposals for an Alternative Way of Reasoning", *EC Tax Review*, 2003, pp. 154-158.

Gutmann, Daniel and Luc Hinnekens, "The Lankhorst-Hohorst Case. The ECJ finds German Thin Capitalization Rules Incompatible with the Freedom of Establishment", *EC Tax Review*, 2003, pp. 90-97.

Hakenberg, Waltraud, in Lenz and Borchardt (ed.), EU- und EG-Vertrag, *Art. 49/50*, 3rd ed., Bundesanzeiger Verlagsgesellschaft mbH, Cologne, 2003.

Hartley, T.C., *The Foundations of European Community Law. An Introduction to the Constitutional and Administrative Law of the European Community*, 5th ed., Oxford University Press, Oxford, 2003.

Helminen, Marjaana, *The Dividend Concept in International Law*, Series on International Taxation, Kluwer Law International, The Hague/London/Boston, 1999.

Hettne, Jörgen and Ulf Öberg, *Domstolarna i Europeiska unionens konstitution*, SIEPS, 2003:15, Stockholm, 2003.

Hinnekens, Luc, "AMID: The Wrong Bridge or a Bridge Too Far? An Analysis of a Recent Decision of the European Court of Justice", *European Taxation*, 2001, pp. 206-210.

Hinnekens, Luc, "The Search for the Framework Conditions of the Fundamental EC Treaty Principles as Applied by the European Court to Member States' Direct Taxation", *EC Tax Review*, 2002, 112-119.

Hinnekens, Luc, "European Court Challenges Flat Rate Withholding Taxation of Non-resident Artists: Comment on the Gerritse Decision", *EC Tax Review*, 2003, pp. 207-213.

Hinnekens, Luc, "Justifications – EC Perspectives for Justifications of Discriminatory and Restrictive Tax Measures of Member States", Report to the 2004 EATLP Conference in Paris, unpublished manuscript, 10 pp.

International Tax Glossary, IBFD, Larking (ed.), 4th ed., Amsterdam, 2001.

Jann, Peter, "Das Vorabentscheidungsverfahren: Grundfragen, Verfahrensablauf und aktuelle Entwicklungen", in *Das EuGH-Verfahren in Steuersachen*, Holoubek and Lang (ed.), Linde Verlag, Vienna, 2000, pp. 13-24.

Kapteyn, P.J.G. and P. VerLoren van Themaat, *Introduction to the Law of the European Communities*, 3rd ed., Kluwer Law International, London/The Hague/Boston, 1998.

Kemmeren, Eric, "The Termination of the 'Most Favoured Nation Clause' Dispute in Tax Treaty Law and the Necessity of a Euro Model Tax Convention", *EC Tax Review*, 1997, pp. 146-152.

Knobbe-Keuk, Brigitte, "Restrictions on the Fundamental Freedoms Enshrined in the EC Treaty by Discriminatory Tax Provisions – Ban and Justification", *EC Tax Review*, 1994, pp. 74-85.

Kostense, H.E., "The Saint-Gobain Case and the Application of Tax Treaties. Evolution or Revolution?", *EC Tax Review*, 2000, pp. 220-232.

Lang, Michael, "The Binding Effect of the EC Fundamental Freedoms on Tax Treaties", in *Tax Treaties and EC Law*, Gassner (ed.), Kluwer Law International, Series on International Taxation No 16, London/The Hague/Boston, 1997, pp. 17-31.

Lang, Michael, "Kapitalverkehrsfreiheit und Doppelbesteuerungsabkommen", in *Kapitalverkehrsfreihet und Steuerrecht*, Lechner, Staringer and Tumpel (ed.), Linde Verlag, Vienna, 2000, pp. 181-196.

Lang, Michael, "Die bedeutung des Vorabentscheidungsverfahrens für das Abgabenverfahren", in *Das EuGH-Verfahren in Steuersachen*, Holoubek and Lang (ed.), Linde Verlag, Vienna, 2000, pp. 99-118.

Lehner, Moris, "Limitation of the National Power of Taxation by the Fundamental Freedoms and Non-discrimination Clauses of the EC Treaty", *EC Tax Review*, 2000, pp. 5-15.

Lindencrona, Gustaf, *Skatter och kapitalflykt. Beskattningens inverkan på det finansiella kapitalets och dess ägares rörlighet över Sveriges gränser mot bakgrund av den pågående ekonomiska integrationen i Västeuropa*, Rätts- och samhällsvetenskapliga biblioteket 4, Jurist- och samhällsvetareförbundets Förlags AB, Stockholm, 1972.

Lodin, Sven-Olof and Malcolm Gammie, *Home State Taxation: Tax Treaty Aspects*, IBFD, Amsterdam, 2001.

Lodin, Sven-Olof, Gustaf Lindencrona, Peter Melz and Christer Silfverberg, *Inkomstskatt*, 9th ed., Studentlitteratur, Lund, 2003.

Lodin, Sven-Olof, "EU och inkomstbeskattningen – varför händer så litet?", in *Festskrift tillägnad Edward Andersson*, Sevón, Frände, Olsson, Ryynänen and Tikka (ed.), 2003, pp. 135-150.

de la Mare, Thomas, "Article 177 in Social and Political Context", in *The Evolution of EU Law*, Craig and de Búrca (ed.), Oxford University Press, Oxford, 1999, pp. 215-260.

Martín Jiménez, Adolfo J., *Towards Corporate Tax Harmonisation in the European Community. An Institutional and Procedural Analysis*, Series on International Taxation No 22, Kluwer Law International, London/The Hague/Boston, 1999.

Mattsson, Nils, "Does the European Court of Justice Understand the Policy behind Tax Benefits based on Personal and Family Circumstances", *European Taxation*, 2003, pp. 186-194.

Mattsson, Nils, "Är de svenska CFC-reglerna förenliga med EG-rätten?", *Skattenytt*, 2004, pp. 165-191.

Meussen, Gerard, "The Marks and Spencer Case: Reaching the Boundaries of the EC Treaty", *EC Tax Review*, 2003, pp. 144-148.

Moëll, Christina, *Proportionalitetsprincipen i skatterätten*, Acta Societatis Juridicae Lundensis, No 147, Juristförlaget i Lund, 2003.

Mohamed, Sideek, *European Community Law on the Free Movement of Capital and the EMU*, Stockholm Studies in Law, Kluwer Law International, The Hague/London/Boston, 1999.

Mohamed, Sideek, *European Financial Integration Law*, Skrifter utgivna av Juridiska fakulteten vid Stockholms universitet, No 68, Jure, Stockholm, 2001.

Mutén, Leif, "Skattesuveräniteten och det internationella samarbetet – några funderingar", in *Festskrift tillägnad Edward Andersson*, Sevón, Frände, Olsson, Ryynänen and Tikka (ed.), 2003, pp. 211-223.

Mutén, Leif, "ECJ Advocate General Issues Opinion on Finland's Imputation System", *Tax Notes International*, 29 March 2004, pp. 1154-1157.

Mutén, Leif, "EG-domstolen och exitskatten", *Skattenytt*, 2004, pp. 294-300.

Nelson, Maria, "Ursprungsstatens rätt bestämmer aktiebolags rätt till utlandsetablering", *Svensk Skattetidning*, 2003, pp. 138-153.

Nielsen, Ruth, *EU ret*, 2nd ed., Thomson/Gadjura, Copenhagen, 1999.

Offermanns, René and Carlo Romano, "Treaty Benefits for Permanent Establishments: the Saint-Gobain Case", *Bulletin*, 2000, pp. 180-189.

Peters, Cees, "Non-discrimination: The Freedom of Establishment and European Tax Law", in *Legal Protection against Discriminatory Tax Legislation*, Gribnau (ed.), Kluwer Law International, London/The Hague/New York, 2003, pp. 101-122.

Peters, Martine, "Capital Movements and Taxation in the EC", *EC Tax Review*, 1998, pp. 4-12.

Pinto, Carlo, *Tax Competition and EU Law*, Eucotax Series on European Taxation, Kluwer Law International, The Hague/London/New York, 2003.

Pistone, Pasquale, *The Impact of Community law on Tax Treaties. Issues and Solutions*, Eucotax Series on European Taxation, Kluwer Law International, The Hague/London/New York, 2002.

Prechal, Sacha, "Does Direct Effect Still Matter?", *CML Rev.*, 2000, pp. 1047-1069.

Prechal, Sacha, "Direct Effect Reconsidered, Redefined and Rejected", in *Direct Effect. Rethinking a Classic EC Legal Doctrine*, Prinssen and Schrauven (ed.), The Hogendorp Papers (3), Europa Law Publishing, Groningen, 2002, pp. 17-41.

von Quitzow, Carl Michael, "Exit Bachmann, bienvenue Danner? – Eller när en dom har blivit så urholkad att den nästan får anses vara 'overruled'", *Skattenytt*, 2003, pp. 89-92.

Rädler, Albert J., "Tax Treaties and the Internal Market", Annex 6 to the 1992 Ruding Report, pp. 371-379.

Rädler, Albert J., "Do National Anti-abuse Clauses Distort the Internal Market", *European Taxation*, 1994, pp. 311-313.

Rädler, Albert J., "Most-favoured-nation Clause in European Tax Law?", *EC Tax Review*, 1995, pp. 66-67.

Rasmussen, Ole, *On Law and Policy in the European Court of Justice: a Comparative Study in Judicial Policymaking*, Dordrecht, Nijhoff, 1986.

Reimer, Ekkehart, "Die Auswirkung der Grundfreiheiten auf das Ertragssteuerrecht der Bundesrepublik Deutschland – Eine Bestandsaufnahme", in *Grundfreiheiten im Steuerrecht der EU-Staaten*, Lehner (ed.), Münchener Schriften zum Internationalen Steuerrecht, Heft 23, pp. 39-101.

Ruding, Onno, "The Long Way to Removing Obstacles in Company Taxation in Europe", *European Taxation*, 2002, pp. 3-6.

Scheuer, Alexander, in *EU- und EG-Vertrag*, Artikel 43, Lenz and Borchardt (ed.), 3rd ed., Bundesanzeiger Verlagsgesellschaft mbH., Cologne, 2003.

Schön, Wolfgang, "Europäische Kapitalverkehrsfreiheit und nationales Steuerrecht", in *Gedächtnisschrift für Knobbe-Keuk*, Schön (ed.), Verlag Dr. Otto Schmidt, Cologne, 1997, pp. 743-777.

Schön, Wolfgang, *The Free Choice between the Right to Establish a Branch and to Set up a Subsidiary – a Principle of European Business Law*, EBOR, 2001, pp. 339-364.

Schön, Wolfgang, "The European Commission's Report on Company Taxation: a Magic Formula for European Taxation?", *European Taxation*, 2002, pp. 276-286.

Schuch, Josef, "Pending Cases Filed by Austrian Courts: the Lenz Case", in *Direct Taxation: Recent ECJ Developments*, M. Lang (ed.), Schriftenreihe zum Internationalen Steuerrecht, Band 25, Linde Verlag, Vienna, 2003, pp. 137-152.

Scoon, Iain, and Sasha Carter, "EU Savings Directive Saved at Last?", *Tax Notes International*, 23 June 2003, pp. 1179-1184.

Sedlaczeck, Michael, "The Prohibition of Discrimination and Restrictions", *European Taxation*, 2000, pp. 14-27.

Sevón, Leif, "Rättskällor och lagtolkning i EG-domstolen", in *Festskrift tillägnad Edward Andersson*, Sevón, Frände, Olsson, Ryynänen and Tikka (ed.), 2003, pp. 335-341.

Ståhl, Kristina, *Aktiebeskattning och fria kapitalrörelser. En studie av beskattningen av den löpande avkastningen av aktieinvesteringar på bolags- och ägarnivå mot bakgrund av EG:s fria kapitalrörelser*, SJFU No 51, Iustus förlag, Uppsala, 1996.

Ståhl, Kristina, "Beskattning av fria kapitalrörelser – inom EU och mot tredje land", in *Festskrift till Gustaf Lindencrona*, Arvidsson, Melz and Silfverberg (ed.), Norstedts Juridik, Stockholm, 2003, pp. 493-512.

Terra, Ben and Peter Wattel, *European Tax Law*, 3rd ed., Kluwer Law International, London/The Hague/New York, 2001.

Tridimas, Takis, *The General Principles of EC Law*, Oxford University Press, Oxford, 1999.

Tridimas, Takis, "Knocking on Heaven's Door: Fragmentation, Efficiency and Defiance in the Preliminary Reference Procedure", *CML Rev.*, 2003, pp. 9-50.

Usher, John, *The Law of the Money and Financial Services in the EC*, 2nd ed., Oxford University Press, 2000.

Van der Linde, Ruud, "Some Thoughts on Most-favoured-nation Treatment within the European Community Legal Order in Pursuance of the D case", *EC Tax Review*, 2004, pp. 10-17.

Van Raad, Kees, *Nondiscrimination in International Tax Law*, Kluwer, Deventer, 1986.

Van Raad, Kees, "The Impact of the EC Treaty's Fundamental Freedom Provisions on EU Member States' Taxation in Border-crossing Situations – Current State of Affairs", *EC Tax Review*, 1995, pp. 190-201.

Van Thiel, Servaas, *EU Case Law on Income Tax, Part 1*, IBFD, Amsterdam, 2001.

Van Thiel, Servaas, *Free Movement of Persons and Income Tax Law: the European Court of Justice in Search of Principles*, Volume 3, Doctoral Series, IBFD, Amsterdam, 2002.

Vanistendael, Frans, "The Role of the European Court of Justice as the Supreme Judge in Tax Cases", *EC Tax Review*, 1996, pp. 114-122.

Vanistendael, Frans, "No European Taxation without European Representation", *EC Tax Review*, 2000, pp. 142-143.

Vanistendael, Frans, "The Compatibility of the Basic Economic Freedoms with the Sovereign National Tax Systems of the Member States", *EC Tax Review*, 2003, pp. 136-143.

Vanistendael, Frans, "Bosal?!", *EC Tax Review*, 2003, pp. 192-193.

Wathelet, Melchior, "The Influence of Free Movement of Persons, Services and Capital on National Direct Taxation: Trends in the Case Law of the Court of Justice", *Yearbook of European Law*, Eeckhout and Tridimas (ed.), Volume 20, Oxford University Press, Oxford, 2001, pp. 1-33.

Wathelet, Melchior, "Direct Taxation and EU Law: Integration or Disintegration?", *EC Tax Review*, 2004, pp. 2-4.

Wattel, Peter, "Progressive Taxation of Non-residents and Intra-EC Allocation of Personal Allowances: Why Schumacker, Asscher, Gilly and Gschwind Do Not Suffice", *European Taxation*, 2000, pp. 210-223.

Weber, Dennis, "The Bosal Holding Case: Analysis and Critque", *EC Tax Review*, 2003, pp. 220-230.

Weber, Dennis, "Exit Taxes on the Transfer of Seat and the Applicability of the Freedom of Establishment after Überseering", *European Taxation*, 2003, pp. 350-354.

von Wilmowsky, Peter, "Freiheit des Kapital- und Zahlungsverkehr", in Ehlers (ed.), *Europäische Grundrechte und Grundfreiheiten*, de Gruyter Recht, Berlin, 2003, pp. 290-317.

Wiman, Bertil, "Pending Cases Filed by Swedish Courts: the X and Y Case and the Skandia and Ola Ramstedt Case", in *Direct Taxation: Recent ECJ Developments*, Schriftenreihe zum Internationalen Steuerrecht, Band 25, Lang (ed.), Linde Verlag, Vienna, 2003, pp. 191-206.

Winther-Sørensen, Niels, *Beskatning af international erhvervsindkomst*, Thomson/Gadjura, Copenhagen, 2000.

Wouters, Jan, "The European Court of Justice and Fiscal Barriers to Companies' Cross-border Establishments", in *Current Issues of Cross-Border Establishment of Companies in the European Union*, Wouters and Schneider (ed.), Maklu, Nomos, Juridik & Samhälle, Antwerpen, 1995, pp. 101-141.

Wouters, Jan, "The Principle of Non-discrimination in European Community Law", *EC Tax Review*, 1999, pp. 98-106.

Wymeersch, Eddy, "The Transfer of the Company's Seat in European Company Law", *CML Rev.*, 2003, pp. 661-695.

2 All Cited ECJ Cases

2.1 Numerical Order

Case 270/83, *Commission of the European Communities v. France ("Avoir fiscal")* [1986] ECR 273 159, 170, 267, 327

Case 182/83, *Fearon v. Irish Land Commission* [1984] ECR 3677 142

Case 18/84, *Commission v. France* [1985] ECR 1339 159

Case 302/84, *Ten Holder v. Nieuwe Algemen Bedrijfsvereniging* [1986] ECR 1821 246

Case 60/85, *Luijten v. Raad van Arbeid* [1986] ECR 2365 246

Case 79/85, *D.H.M. Segers v. Bestuur van de Bedrijfsvereniging voor Bank- en Verzekeringswezen, Groothandel en Vrije Beroepen* [1986] ECR 2375 134

Case 157/85, *Luigi Brugnoni and Roberto Ruffinengo v. Cassa di risparmio di Genova e Imperia* [1986] ECR 2013 313

Case 352/85, *Bond van Adverteerders and Others* [1988] ECR 2085 78, 95

Case 81/87, *The Queen v. H.M. Treasury and Commissioners of Inland Revenue, ex parte Daily Mail and General Trust plc* [1988] ECR 5483 183, 266, 332

Case 305/87, *Commission v. Greece* [1989] ECR 1461 67

Case C-175/88, *Klaus Biehl v. Administration des Contributions du Grand-Duché de Luxembourg* [1990] ECR I-1779 45

Case C-61/89, *Criminal proceedings against Marc Gaston Bouchoucha* [1990] ECR I-3551 90

Case C-221/89, *The Queen v. Secretary of State for Transport, ex parte Factortame Ltd and Others* [1991] ECR I-3905 240

Case C-288/89, *Stichting Collective Antennevoorziening Gouda and Others* [1991] ECR I-4007 81

Case C-61/89, *Bouchoucha* [1990] ECR I-3551 90

Case C-2/90, *Commission v. Belgium (Walloon Waste)* [1992] ECR I-4431 123

Case C-76/90, *Säger v. Dennermeyer & Co. Ltd* [1991] ECR I-4221 81

Case C-204/90, *Hanns-Martin Bachmann v. Belgian State* [1992] ECR I-249 96, 128, 242, 316, 329

Case C-300/90, *Commission v. Belgium* [1992] ECR I-305 128, 242, 316, 330

Case C-369/90, *Mario Vicente Micheletti and others v. Delegacion del Gobierno en Cantabria* [1992] ECR I-4239 139

Case C-111/91, *Commission v. Luxembourg* [1993] ECR I-817 94

Case C-112/91, *Hans Werner v. Finanzamt Aachen-Innenstadt* [1993] I-429 88, 140, 165

Case C-148/91, *Vereniging Veronica Omroep Organisatie v. Commissariaat voor de Media* [1993] I-487 313

Joined cases C-267/91 and C-268/91, *Criminal proceedings against Bernhard Keck and Daniel Mithourd* [1993] ECR I-6097 332

Case C-118/96, *Jessica Safir v. Skattemyndigheten i Dalarnas Län, formerly Skattemyndigheten i Kopparbergs Län* [1998] ECR I-1897 110, 292

Case C-158/96, *Kohll v. Union des Caisses de Maladie* [1998] ECR I-1931 315

Case C-264/96, *Imperial Chemical Industries plc (ICI) v. Kenneth Hall Kolmer (Her Majesty's Inspector of Taxes)* [1998] ECR I-4695 190, 235, 272

Case C-336/96, *Mr and Mrs Robert Gilly v. Directeur des services fiscaux du Bas-Rhin* [1998] I-2793 90

Case C-134/97, *Victoria Film A/S* [1998] ECR I-7023 18

Case C-212/97, *Centros Ltd v. Erhvervs- og Selskabsstyrelsen* [1999] ECR I-1459 133, 146

Case C-222/97, *Manfred Trummer and Peter Mayer* [1999] ECR I-1661 283

Case C-254/97, *Société Baxter and Others v. Premier Ministre and Others* [1999] ECR I-4809 175

Case C-294/97, *Eurowings Luftverkehrs AG v. Finanzamt Dortmund-Unna* [1999] ECR I-7447 122

Case C-302/97, *Klaus Konle v. Republik Österreich* [1999] ECR I-3099 284, 315

Case C-307/97, *Compagnie de Saint-Gobain* [1999] ECR I-6161 221, 267, 270, 334

Case C-311/97, *Royal Bank of Scotland plc v. Elliniko Dimosio (Greek State)* [1999] ECR I-2651 104, 167, 327

Case C-391/97, *Franz Gschwind v. Finanzamt Aachen-Aussenstadt* [1999] ECR I-5451 101

Case C-439/97, *Sandoz GmbH v. Finanzlandesdirektion für Wien, Niederösterreich und Burgenland* [1999] ECR I-7041 305

Case C-35/98, *Statssecretaris van Financiën v. B.G.M. Verkooijen* [2000] ECR I-4071 283, 295, 302, 315

Case C-55/98, *Skatteministeriet v. Bent Vestergaard* [1999] ECR I-7641 122

Case C-190/98, *Graf v. Filzmozer Maschinenbau GmbH* [2000] ECR I-493 79

Case C-200/98, *X AB and Y AB v. Riksskatteverket* [1999] ECR I-8261 192, 319

Case C-251/98, *C. Baars v. Inspecteur der Belastingdienst Particulieren/ Ondernemingen Gorinchem* [2000] ECR I-2787 150, 199, 246, 289

Case C-367/98, *Commission v. Portugal (Golden share)* [2002] ECR I-4731 300

Joined cases C-397/98 and C-410/98, *Metallgesellschaft Ltd and Others, Hoechst AG, Hoechst UK Ltd v. Commissioners of Inland Revenue, H.M. Attorney General* [2001] ECR I-1727 107, 172, 248

Case C-405/98, *Konsumentombudsmannen (KO) v. Gourmet International Products AB (GIP)* [2001] ECR I-1795 76

Case C-478/98, *Commission v. Belgium (Eurobond)* [2002] ECR I-7578 297, 335

2.2 Alphabetical Order

Case C-167/01, *Kamer van Koophandel en Fabrieken voor Amsterdam v. Inspire Art Ltd* [2003] ECR I-10155 148

Case C-175/88, *Klaus Biehl v. Administration des Contributions du Grand-Duché de Luxembourg* [1990] ECR I-1779 45

Case C-302/97, *Klaus Konle v. Republik Österreich* [1999] ECR I-3099 284, 315

Case 115/78, *Knoors v. Secretary of State for Economic Affairs* [1979] ECR 399 90

Case C-158/96, *Kohll v. Union des Caisses de Maladie* [1998] ECR I-1931 315

Case C-405/98, *Konsumentombudsmannen (KO) v. Gourmet International Products AB (GIP)* [2001] ECR I-1795 76

Case C-19/92, *Kraus v. Land Baden-Würtemberg* [1993] ECR I-1663 108, 213

Case C-324/00, *Lankhorst-Hohorst GmbH v. Finanzamt Steinfurt* [2002] ECR I-11779 175, 238, 330

Case C-28/95, *Leur-Bloem v. Inspecteur der directe Belastingen/Ondernemingen* [1997] ECR I-4161 119, 242

Case 157/85, *Luigi Brugnoni and Roberto Ruffinengo v. Cassa di risparmio di Genova e Imperia* [1986] ECR 2013 313

Case 60/85, *Luijten v. Raad van Arbeid* [1986] ECR 2365 246

Case C-222/97, *Manfred Trummer and Peter Mayer* [1999] ECR I-1661 283

Case C-369/90, *Mario Vicente Micheletti and others v. Delegacion del Gobierno en Cantabria* [1992] ECR I-4239 139

Case C-446/03, *Marks & Spencer* (pending) 205, 334

Joined cases C-397/98 and C-410/98, *Metallgesellschaft Ltd and Others, Hoechst AG, Hoechst UK Ltd v. Commissioners of Inland Revenue, H.M. Attorney General* [2001] ECR I-1727 107, 172, 248

Case C-242/03, *Ministre des Finance v. Jean-Claude Weidert and Élisabeth Paulus* [2004] n.y.r. 309, 319

Case C-336/96, *Mr and Mrs Robert Gilly v. Directeur des services fiscaux du Bas-Rhin* [1998] I-2793 90

Case C-237/94, *O'Flynn v. Adjudication Office* [1996] ECR I-2617 79

Case C-107/94, *P.H. Asscher v. Staatssecretaris van Financiën* [1996] ECR I-3089 89, 150, 180, 245

Case C-484/93, *Peter Svensson and Lena Gustavsson v. Ministre du Logement et de l'Urbanisme* [1995] ECR I-3955 285, 306

Case C-319/02, *Petri Manninen* [2004] n.y.r. 310, 320

Joined cases C-92/92 and C-326/92, *Phil Collins* [1993] ECR I-5145 66

Case 8/74, *Procureur du Roi v. Benoît and Gustave Dassonville* [1974] ECR 837 73

Case 7/78, *Regina v. Thompson and Others* [1978] ECR 2247 290

3 Table of Secondary Legislation

3.1 Directives

Council Directive 90/436/EEC of 28 June 1990. Convention on the elimination of double taxation in connection with the adjustment of profits of associated enterprises.

Council Directive 88/361/EEC for the implementation of Article 67 of the EEC Treaty.

Council Directive 90/434/EEC of 23 July 1990 on the common system of taxation applicable to mergers, divisions, transfers of assets and exchanges of shares concerning companies of different Member States.

Council Directive 90/435/EEC of 23 July 1990 on the common system of taxation applicable in the case of parent companies and subsidiaries of different Member States.

Council Directive 77/799/EEC of 19 December 1977 concerning mutual assistance by the competent authorities of the Member States in the field of direct taxation.

Council Directive 2003/48/EC of 3 June 2003 on taxation of savings income in the form of interest payments. (not yet in force).

Council Directive 2003/49/EC of 3 June 2003 on a common system of taxation applicable to interest and royalty payments made between associated companies of different Member States.

3.2 Proposed Directive

Proposal for a Council Directive concerning arrangements for the taking into account by enterprises of the losses of their permanent establishments and subsidiaries situated in other Member States. COM(90) 595 final of 6 December.

3.3 Communications

Tax policy in the European Union – Priorities for the years ahead. COM(2001) 260 final.

Company taxation in the internal market. Commission staff working paper. COM(2001) 582 final.

An Internal Market without company tax obstacles achievements, ongoing initiatives and remaining challenges. COM(2003) 726 final.

3.4 Official Reports

Report of the Code of Conduct group on business taxation as submitted to the ECOFIN Council on 29 November 1999 (referred to as "the Primarolo Report")

Report of the Committee of independent experts on company taxation. March 1992 (referred to as "the 1992 Ruding Report").

Company taxation in the Internal Market. SEC(2001) 1681 (referred to as "the 2001 Staff Report")

3.5 Other Materials

Conclusions of the ECOFIN Council meeting on 1 December 1997 concerning taxation policy. OJ C2 of 6 January 1998, p. 1. (including "Code of Conduct" for business taxation).

Draft treaty establishing a Constitution for Europe. Adopted by the European Convention on 13 June and 10 July 2003. Submitted to the President of the European Council in Rome. 18 July 2003. 2003/C 169/01.

Council Regulation (EEC) No 1408/71 of 14 June 1971 on the application of social security schemes to employed persons and their families moving within the Community (OJ English Special Edition 1971 (II), p. 416).

4 National Case-law and Public Material

4.1 Sweden

The Supreme Administrative Court (Regeringsrätten)

The Revenue Law Commission (Skatterättsnämnden)

Rulings of the 19 February 2003

Government Bills

Prop. 2003/04:10 Ändrade regler för CFC-beskattning.

4.2 The United Kingdom

Marks and Spencer plc v. Halsey (Inspector of Taxes), decided 17 December 2002, by UK Special Commissioners Dr John F Avery Jones CBE and Malcolom Gammie QC 205, 334

5 EFTA Court

Case E-1/00, *State Debt Management Agency v. Íslandsbanki-FBA hf* on the interpretation of Articles 4, 40, 42 and 61 of the EEA Agreement. Decided on 14 July 2000. 313

Index

EUCOTAX Series on European Taxation

(1) *The Compatibility of Anti-Abuse Provisions in Tax Treaties with EC Law,* Peter HJ Essers, Guido JME de Bont and Eric CCM Kemmeren (eds).
ISBN 90-411-9678-1

(2) *The Principle of Equality in European Taxation,* Gerard TK Meussen (ed.).
ISBN 90-411-9693-5

(3) *Tax Treaty Interpretation,* Michael Lang (ed.).
ISBN 90-411-9857-1

(4) *The Impact of Community Law on Tax Treaties: Issues and Solutions,* Pasquale Pistone.
ISBN 90-411-9860-1

(5) *The Entrepreneurship Concept in a European Comparative Tax Law Perspective,* René Offermanns.
ISBN 90-411-9887-3

(6) *Settlement of Disputes in Tax Treaty Law,* Michael Lang and Mario Züger.
ISBN 90-411-9904-7

(7) *Tax Competition and EU Law,* Carlo Pinto.
ISBN 90-411-9913-6

(8) *CFC Legislation, Tax Treaties and EC Law,* Michael Lang, Hans-Jörgen Aigner, Ulrich Scheuerle and Markus Stefaner.
ISBN 90-411-2284-2

(9) *Direct Taxation in Relation to the Freedom of Establishment and the Free Movement of Capital*, Mattias Dahlberg.
ISBN 90-411-2363-6